THE
MODERN
MAN'S
GUIDE TO
LIFE

THE
MODERN
MAN'S
GUIDE TO
LIFE

by
DENIS BOYLES,
ALAN ROSE,
ALAN WELLIKOFF
and a bunch of other guys

Harper & Row, Publishers, New York
Cambridge, Philadelphia, San Francisco, Washington
London, Mexico City, São Paulo, Singapore, Sydney

This book is dedicated to
our brothers:

David Boyles
Michael Rose
Michael Wellikoff

An excerpt originally appeared in *Playboy* magazine.

Library of Congress Cataloging-in-Publication Data
Boyles, Denis.
THE MODERN MAN'S GUIDE TO LIFE. Includes index.
   1. Men—Conduct of life. I. Rose, Alan. II. Wellikoff, Alan. III. Title.
BJ1601.B68 1987 640'.24041 87-45024
ISBN 0-06-055092-9   87 88 89 90 91 RRD 10 9 8 7 6 5 4 3 2 1
ISBN 0-06-096133-3 (pbk.)   89 90 91 RRD 10 9 8 7 6 5 4 3

CONTENTS

THE MODERN MAN: Introduction

Here's a true story: A couple of guys are out to buy tropical fish. It sounds unlikely, sure, but it happens. You wake up one morning, look around the house for an improvement project, and you realize that there's not a damn tropical fish in sight. So you call up a pal and say, "Hey, what do you know about tropical fish?"

The other guy says, "Not much, but I'm game to find out." Next thing, you're walking into Guppy World looking for plastic seaweed, a little castle, some green gravel and a few neon tetras. You don't know beans about tropical fish, and in the end it shows; you buy the wrong stuff and spend the next six months flushing fish down the toilet. What went wrong? You needed some advice but you didn't have the right friend to turn to.

Well, there's nothing in this book about tropical fish. Which simply goes to show you can't know everything and that a lot of what you do in your life is bound to end up down the john.

That we have nothing about tropical fish is a bit of a surprise, actually. A year or two ago, we sent out what amounted to a chain letter, asking for advice and common knowledge, suggesting a few hundred topics and hoping somebody would have something to say about tropical fish or anything else. Our hope was that we could raise a subject in a sort of extended barroom conversation, and get the best take on the topic from three or four guys sitting down there under the TV and next to the pretzels. We could say, "Hey, what you think of rats?" for example, and somebody would tell us probably a little more than we really needed to know about rats. And mice and other pests (q.v.).

MODERN MISGIVINGS

Instead we not only got the lowdown on rodent control, but we also got a basketful of notions of what advice guys have for each other to make life a little easier. Most important, we discovered something about figurative colorization.

Colorization is what they do to old black-and-white movies so they can make some more money off the re-release of the films. They take a movie that you've seen a dozen times and translate all those shades of gray into colors and sell it for prime-time TV broadcasting. It's easy, it's interesting and it's very progressive. Trouble is, it screws up some chap's film in the process.

Colorization of one kind or another is everywhere. All the stuff that is supposed to make our lives so much easier only makes it more complicated. The most trivial daily activities — getting dressed and going to work, for example — have become fraught with political, social and moral implications. To be a man in the late twentieth century is to be a confused oppressor who dresses funny. That's first.

Second, the old-fashioned New Man that we spent the better part of the '70s trying to make work just broke down completely. The guy wimps around and cries on cue and is very sensitive and all, but he's useless in the sack and a pain at work, and worst of all, it turns out that girls, who were supposed to be the market for the New-model Man, hate the sucker.

And, finally, in a world polarized between the morality mongers on the right and their self-righteous counterparts on the left, a decent Modern Man needs a bunker where he can duck the cross fire for a while. He needs to know that the slop served up on television and in the newsweeklies — familes are on the rise or on the decline, men are good or bad, women are mad or sad — isn't really *real*. That is, it's just somebody's passing notion of reality, the view of the world expressed by a bunch of hipsters one morning in a meeting last week. It's all colorization. The stuff that really counts is on the end of a fishing line or off at Brave New World Day School.

The Modern Man is an old-fashioned kind of guy, a reasonably thoughtful fellow who has listened with varying amounts of patience to all the new ideas so passionately advocated by well-intentioned people (sometimes including himself) over the last two decades and has discovered that while all of them may be new ideas, 90 percent of them are also *bad* ideas. It is all the result, we decided, of

THE MODERN CONCEIT

The Modern Conceit is the presupposition that whatever idea is the latest idea is the right idea.

That this is an absurd and often dangerous fallacy should be obvious. Yet the Modern Conceit is pervasive; it has informed popular views on everything from parenthood to ethics and religion, from design ideals to dating dilemmas.

That seemed bad enough. Then we discovered

RECTITUDE,

the new, clean fuel that propels the Modern Conceit. Because rectitude is a by-product of moral values, it is subject to change without notice.

It also feels great, since it allows for the quick and easy passage of moral judgments and prevents serious discussion of moral topics. The possessor of rectitude also owns the franchise on the moral bottom line.

Rectitude is not only flexible, it's fickle. At the moment, it's the province of the correct left, although it vacillates across the sociopolitical spectrum according to the climate of the times or what's on TV.

So what appears here is conventional wisdom. Much of it was conventional twenty-five years ago; much of it will be conventional for the foreseeable future. And that's all just as well.

What interests us most at this point, however, is what *doesn't* appear here. If you know something that might interest some other guys, please make a note of it and send it off to

Modern Man
P.O. Box 15565
Springfield, MA 01115.

(In the back of this book, just after the list of contributors, is a piece of paper you can use to submit your entry.) Thanks.

We don't know most of our contributors. Their names appear at the end of this book (unless they asked us not to print their names), and we don't know where they picked up their info. Our assumption is that it was just something they knew, and passed it along as something other men could use to make this passage a little easier; if any of this material is from a published source, and we knew about it, it has been credited under acknowledgments. (Some guys sent printed stuff; unless it was something from the government — which is credited as USG — we didn't use it.) If something appears here uncredited that appeared someplace else first, we didn't know, and we apologize.

We also have to make this disclaimer: We're not liable for any consequences whatsoever arising from the use of this information, and neither are our contributors. Advice is never a substitute for experience. (DB, AR, AW et al.)

A MODERN DISCLAIMER

This book costs a lot less than an hour of professional advice on almost any subject covered here. So it stands to reason that if you really want help solving some of life's more vexing problems, you ought to go out and get some expensive, professional assistance. You get what you pay for, as they say, and what you aren't going to get in this book is a substitute for the care and advice of people who are paid to dispense such care and advice. The contents of this book are for information only.

CHAPTER **1**

Outdoors

To most Modern Men, Mother Nature's just plain old Mom, and getting along at Mom's house is easy — sort of second nature.

The confusions of indoor life are most easily seen from the outside looking in: Men slink down the corridors of commerce, guilty lies burning bright between the lines of their résumés, and duck into offices where they die of terminal nonsense, while others, gifted in the art of subterfuge, imitate success. The modern wilderness areas are mostly indoors.

Living outdoors, on the other hand, imposes a neater set of priorities. Outside, the rules are not only quite clear (build a fire or freeze, pitch a tent or sleep wet), but they are the stripped-down, no-fooling rules we all have to live by, like it or not. Outside, incompetence won't get you promoted, it'll get you lost in the woods.

Don't feel bad if a logger's life isn't for you. Some Modern Men are less interested in camping than others. We know men whose favorite camp-grounds have double beds, color TVs and honor bars, and who dig latrines by snapping off the sanitized strip around the toilet bowl. They figure men have fought wars for tens of thousands of years to see who would have to sleep outside and who wouldn't, and they hate the idea of betraying history.

For them we say, **see also** *Golf.*

C O N T E N T S
Chapter One: *OUTDOORS*

LIVING OUTDOORS

This is where Modern Men are either made in the shade or

LOST IN THE WOODS

If you come to a stream, your chances of finding civilization are much greater if you travel downstream. (KGO)

See also *Orienting with Only a Compass* **and** *Finding Directions without a Compass* **in** *HIKING,* **below.**

HOW TO SHARPEN AN AXE

The blade of an axe should not just chew up the wood it strikes. Rather, it should be able to deliver a clean, even cut. Keeping an axe blade sharp, however, requires careful maintenance — and, especially, regular honing with a whetstone, coupled with occasional filings to remove nicks along the blade's edge.

To file an axe, lean it against a log with the edge of the head facing upward. Place the file along the edge and push down hard. File the entire bit with long, even strokes from toe to heel. Keep the file in light contact with the blade on the return strokes. After you have brightened the entire length of the bit, turn it over and do the other side. Always follow filing with honing. (BT)

To hone an axe blade, hold its head in such a way that the handle points up and slightly away from you (**see illustration**), and stroke the dry stone over the edge of the blade from the heel (or bottom) to the toe (or top). Then rotate the axe until the handle is turned down and hone the other side from toe to heel. A well-sharpened axe blade will never show up as a bright line when you look directly at it, so don't be discouraged by appearances.

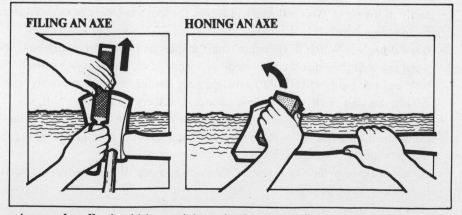

FILING AN AXE   **HONING AN AXE**

An axe handle should be straight-grained and well-finished. Never buy an axe or hatchet with a painted handle, as the paint has usually been applied to mask flaws. (BT)

Sight down an axe blade to make certain that it aligns with the center of the handle. The axe's handle should fit snugly into the head and show no cracks. (BT)

In cold weather, warm an axe or hatchet blade and handle before chopping. (MQ)

Other edged implements: Keep your knives sheathed or sunk into a log at a long angle; likewise, your axes. There's a hunch that green wood will draw the temper from steel, but nobody's proved it. Lay crosscut saws teeth-down between two logs, or flat on the ground with the teeth *under* the bottom curve of a log. Sheath the blades of small saws; use a rag or the sleeve of an old shirt if you don't have anything else. (MQ)

Texas was won back in '46, so we don't need those giant Bowie blades anymore. A six-inch blade is long enough for anything, including murder. A carbon-steel blade will discolor the moment it comes into contact with meat, but it'll keep its edge better than the pretty stainless jobs. Camp knives should have inflexible blades with a long, straight edge that curves into the tip; knives used for skinning should have a shorter edge and a longer curve. (MQ)

CAMP LIFE

For many Modern Men, the best campgrounds have names like Motel Six. But for those more inclined to continue the fight against Nature, here are a few battle plans.

TENTING TONIGHT

When selecting a campsite, consider the following (in order):
1. The likelihood of flooding (watch out for dried-up riverbeds)
2. The levelness of the site
3. The availability and proximity of water and firewood
4. The nearness of dangerous wild animals (WG)

Specifically, avoid any of the following:
* *Rockfall:* Don't hitch your tarp or tent to high, loose rocks which can dislodge easily in the night. Check slopes and ledges for loose boulders before making a camp at their base
* *Dead branches:* Watch it. Butternut, some maples and pines are really bad. The worst are dead trees that are still standing: a white birch can be rotten beneath the bark and can easily fall. (WAP) Low-hanging conifer branches probably won't fall off; use your axe to remove these hazards. Use them for kindling. (MQ)
* *Electrical storms:* A lightning storm makes a lone tree a high target, so don't camp under one. The safest place in an electrical storm is in your car, where the tires provide decent insulation.
* *Hornet, wasp or yellow jacket nests:* Yikes! Stay away! By the by, yellowjackets live underground, like ants.
* *Poison ivy, sumac and oak:* You're gonna need an ocean of calamine lotion; you can look, but you better not touch. (**See under** *FIRST FOLK AID REMEDIES* **in** *CHAPTER SIXTEEN: MODERN MISHAPS.*)

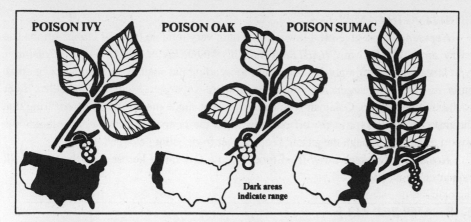

POISON IVY   POISON OAK   POISON SUMAC

Dark areas
indicate range

- *Flash floods:* If you're camping by a stream or brook, make sure you're not on the floodplain; look for the high-water mark, which should be indicated by a continuous line of debris left at the flood-level water's edge. Don't make camp in a dried-up riverbed in the American Southwest, or anywhere there might be an upstream farmer with a pond to drain. (MQ)

Camp layout: Pitch your tent so the morning sun will warm it and the afternoon shade will cool it. Look out for overhead threats (dead branches and the like).

Arrange the camp fire, or TV primeval, so it's downwind of the tent and at least ten feet away from anything flammable. That includes the woodpile, which should be sheltered and kept away from the fire. If a camp stove is used, make sure no laundry, towels, sleeping bags or whatever is likely to blow across it. Keep fires away from tents.

Keep reserves of kerosene and alcohol in the car. Keep a dry bundle of kindling with you in the tent. (GGMcD) **See also** *Lighting in Camp,* **below.**

Keep the camp icebox in a shaded area near the dining and cooking area. Keep other food in a stout wooden box or chest to spare it from being ravaged by raccoons or skunks. In bear country, even food stored in your car won't last any longer than a Blaupunkt in a Boston BMW, so spare yourself the trouble of replacing both the grub and the passenger window by placing the food in a sack suspended at least ten feet high off the ground. (**Or see** *Bear Alarm,* **below.**) (AW)

Keep water in the shade and near the icebox. Keep a bucket of water near the fire as an extinguisher.

Keep the axe and other tools together, preferably near the woodpile. Unsheathed axes and knives should be stuck in the wood.

Garbage should be buried downwind of camp, maybe someplace near the latrine. The latrine should be clearly marked so it's visible at night. Neither the garbage dump nor the latrine should be near or uphill from any source of water.

Place guy ropes and clotheslines where they will not be a hazard. Attach strips of white cloth to them to help strollers avoid tripping over them. (GGMcD)

LIGHTING IN CAMP

Kerosene lamps give off a low light, but are very reliable (**see** *Oil Lamps* **under the entry on** *LIGHTING* **in** *CHAPTER TWELVE: MODERN MANORS),* while *Coleman-type lanterns* give off a good, strong light for reading but require an abundance of spare parts in case of emergencies (you'll need spare vaporizers, vaporizer needles, fiber washers and mantles). Coleman-type lanterns can be made more reliable by ensuring that the on/off knob is kept in the off position when the lamp is not in use. This holds the vaporizer needle through the jet and keeps the jet from getting clogged. (WG)

Keep your kerosene away from food. Even a tiny bit of kerosene in the larder will ruin your chow. (WG)

THE CAMP BED RULE

Put as much under you as over you. (AW)

TENTS

What to look for: Tents should be made of fabric of uniform thickness with strongly sewn seams turned over on themselves to form a series of interlocking U-shaped stitches. On a good tent, the waterproofing will not rub off the fabric; on a lousy tent, it will, since cheaper tents use a sort of wax filler. The corners should be reinforced, with grommets set well back from the edge of the material. Zippers should be strong, rustproof and secure. Zippers sewn into the material are preferable to flap ties (except where very cold weather might lead to their freezing). Look for tents made by reputable firms.

Before taking the tent out, pitch it at home and water it down with a garden hose. After it dries check it for shrinkage. (GGMcD)

TENT TYPES

Pup tents: These have been in use since before somebody popped one off at Fort Sumter. Newer ones have screened doors, sewn-in floors, storm flaps and exterior aluminum frames. They're great for overnight camping. *Pros:* Functional, lightweight, easy to erect and strike. *Cons:* Unsuitable for foul weather; lack of interior room.

Mountain tents, or miner tents, are similar to pups. *Pros:* High-ended — some have up to six feet of headroom; back window for ventilation. *Cons:* Increased weight.

Wall tents are the traditional, cabinlike tents. *Pros:* Easy to erect; inexpensive, if you buy at army surplus; walls roll up for ventilation; nice and old-fashioned. *Cons:* Usually lack windows, floors or screened passageways; standing room only in the center; difficult to carry and pack; old-fashioned.

Lean-tos, a.k.a. Baker or Whelan tents. The Baker type has a large awning in front. *Pros:* A good forest tent, offering ample exposure to daytime scenery and nighttime camp fires; inexpensive; easy to erect and easy to strike; awning suitable for keeping wood and gear dry. *Cons:* Usually windowless, and dark in foul weather when the front is closed. Limited standing space.

Umbrella tents are the ones most commonly seen these days. *Pros:* Come in models with side rooms and with easy-to-use exterior frames; rugged; windows, flaps, screened passageways and sewn-in floors standard; walking space; some models with built-in fiberglass frames or aluminum tubing can be transported without disassembly. *Cons:* Models with interior frames are horrible to erect; heavy models can weigh as much as seventy-five or eighty pounds. The exterior frame type costs more, but is definitely worth it. (GGMcD)

Pitching an A-type (pup) tent: The easiest way to erect the easiest tent:

1. Close the flaps and stake down each corner.

2. Assemble the front and rear tent poles and stick tent stakes into the ground approximately two feet from the center of each end; these are for guy lines. Insert the poles into the tent and guy them to the stakes.

3. Put stakes into the ground for side haulers and affix the lines. Adjust lines to ensure that they are trim. (BT)

EMERGENCY SHELTERS

Although the idea here is to provide yourself with shelter in an emergency, many hikers and campers opt for ad hoc shelter. The *basic premise* is a simple one: You find a shelter that Mother Nature has started — a fallen tree, a group of boulders, a wind-cave — then finish it yourself.

Caves and overhanging ledges are great, but inspect them for snakes, skunks and other undesirable tenants by probing around with a long, long stick. Lean poles against the overhanging edge and use leafy branches for thatching.

Evergreen shelters are simply the lower branches of a large coniferous tree. These are nearly ready-made bivouac. If the perimeter formed by the ends of the lowest branches doesn't come right down to the ground, use stones or logs to hold the branch tips down. There should already be a lush carpet of needles for your use, so simply cut an entrance and move in.

Fallen trees make excellent shelter. Lean short branches against the lee side of the tree trunk, making sure you leave enough room underneath to sleep. Cover the short branches with leafy branches and sticks and secure them. Fill in the floor with pine needles or grass. A fallen tree that has raised a great bump of earth at its base provides the best insulation.

Boulders: Lay a pole from the top of the boulder to the ground and complete the roofing along the windward side with sticks. Lash these to the pole and thatch them with leafy boughs or branches. Carpet the floor with pine needles or grass.

Winter bivouac: Use any of the techniques described above, but add snow for good insulation. You can also dig out a delta-shaped trench, partially cover it with pine boughs and place a heavy carpet of pine needles on the floor. Then build a fire at the small end.

Emergency shelter camp fires: There is a strong psychological benefit in building a good fire before darkness falls, even if that means postponing the construction of an

TEMPORARY EMERGENCY SHELTERS

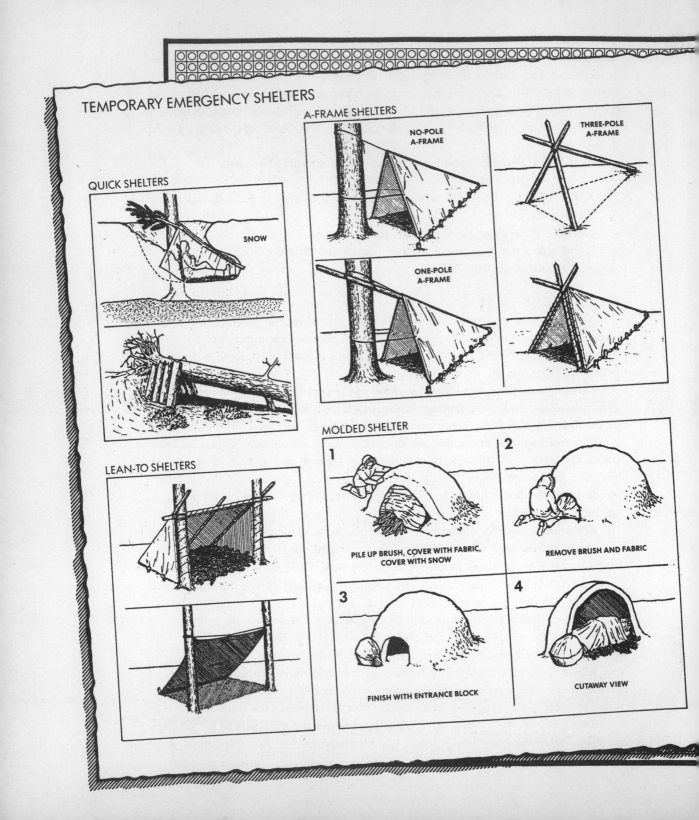

QUICK SHELTERS

SNOW

A-FRAME SHELTERS

NO-POLE A-FRAME

THREE-POLE A-FRAME

ONE-POLE A-FRAME

LEAN-TO SHELTERS

MOLDED SHELTER

1 PILE UP BRUSH, COVER WITH FABRIC, COVER WITH SNOW

2 REMOVE BRUSH AND FABRIC

3 FINISH WITH ENTRANCE BLOCK

4 CUTAWAY VIEW

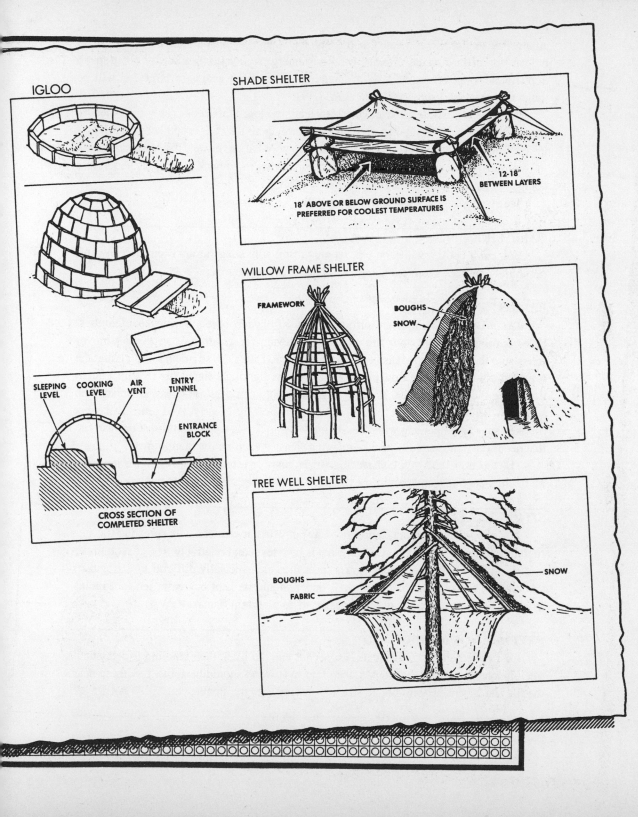

IGLOO

SLEEPING LEVEL · COOKING LEVEL · AIR VENT · ENTRY TUNNEL · ENTRANCE BLOCK

CROSS SECTION OF COMPLETED SHELTER

SHADE SHELTER

12-18" BETWEEN LAYERS

18' ABOVE OR BELOW GROUND SURFACE IS PREFERRED FOR COOLEST TEMPERATURES

WILLOW FRAME SHELTER

FRAMEWORK

BOUGHS · SNOW

TREE WELL SHELTER

BOUGHS · FABRIC · SNOW

emergency shelter. Keep it small, and if possible keep it against a boulder or a ledge on the lee side of your shelter. Remember, your emergency shelter is a sort of fire trap, so don't think about central heating or anything. A fire built against a large log will be tough to extinguish later. See *CAMP FIRES,* **below**.

If no fire is possible, lie with your back against a log. Stuff your coat with dry leaves in the front and back, zip it up and sleep in it. Turn up all the collars and keep your hands inside. Tuck your pants into your boots and keep your hat on, mister. If you shiver during the night and wake up, do some exercises before trying to go back to sleep. If you have a companion, share some feelings right up close. (MQ)

See also *Emergency Sleeping Bags,* **below.**

CAMP FIRES

You can't cook weenies on em, let alone sing silly songs around 'em, if you can't first build 'em, then keep 'em going. So all together now, campers . . .

BASICS

The principle is simple: A sufficient flow of oxygen is required to keep combustibles burning. So build your fire carefully, allowing for conditions, so that air moves freely into the fire. That means keeping the fire neat. Don't use so much kindling that the resultant ash obstructs the flow of air. Unless you're lighting a signal fire to attract attention, keep the flame modest. It's amazing how many campers are closet arsonists who somehow believe their camp fires should be held aloft by Liberty. And remember what Smokey says about playing with fire. A simple camp fire is a potential forest or bush fire that needs only one careless mistake to turn a pleasant evening into a nightmare.

The tepee method of woodstacking works best for most small fires, since it allows air to circulate freely and provides a shelter of sorts for the kindling (**see below**). (GWA)

SITING THE FIRE

It is important to build a camp fire on a spot where it cannot easily spread to the surrounding forest or brush. Choose a site that is both level and relatively free of such tinder as twigs, pine needles and mossy grass (peat fires are especially difficult to extinguish) and clean it down to the bare earth. All tinder should be kept beyond a ten-foot radius from the fire site; keep a pot of water nearby to douse errant flames. (GWA)

PREPARE YOUR FIREWOOD

First collect tinder (twigs, bark, dry weeds and the like), then kindling (dried, small tree branches or dry ground sticks), then fuel (wet wood should be split). Lay these near the fire site, arranged according to size and starting with the smallest bits. (GWA)

DOUBLE-STRIKE

Stretch your supply of matches by piercing each one with a sharp knife just below its head, then splitting the entire match lengthwise. (WG) This won't work so well if you split the match widthwise.

TYPES OF CAMP FIRES

Tepee: For quick, flaming fires suitable for boiling and frying, a tepee fire is probably the best. Start by placing a large mound of tinder on the ground, then encircling it with kindling sticks, the tips of which should come together in the manner of a tepee. When the kindling begins to burn, gradually increase the size of the wood.

Crisscross: A good crisscross fire will provide a healthy bed of coals for broiling or baking. Begin with a large pile of tinder flanked by kindling and smaller fuel pieces laid side by side. Then lay kindling sticks across the parallel pieces to form a square enclosure. Next, lay thin kindling sticks crosswise over the square and continue upward in this fashion, increasing the size of the wood as you go.

Three-point fireplace: This is a simple fire for a single pot or pan. The whole idea is to make a small fire in a shallow pit surrounded by three largish rocks.

Starfire: This is a Boy Scout favorite, an Indian-style camp fire that's easy to build and even easier to maintain. Start out as if to build a tepee fire, then place five logs in a radial position around the fire so that the ends of the logs are slightly elevated and meet over the fire. Push the logs into the fire as they burn.

Council fire: This is an upside-down crisscross fire, with the smallest tinder on top. Light the tinder and as the council or meeting or singsong or whatever progresses, the fire will descend to the largest pieces on the bottom. (GWA)

STARTING A FIRE WITHOUT MATCHES

First, forget that stuff about rubbing two sticks together. Diligent spinning of a small twig in a groove cut in a larger piece of wood will work, but only if you're willing to twirl the twig until the sun comes up. Instead, use what's around you. Flint against flint sparks nicely, of course, but so does metal against quartz or any other hard stone. The best tinder (upon which you should let the sparks fall) is straw or hay. If you manage to produce a faint glow in the tinder, fan it gently but steadily.

If hay isn't available, look for dried grass or dried cowshit shredded into fine chunks. If you're really desperate, tear off a piece of the shirt on your back (or find another piece of cotton), unravel it as best you can, and use that. (WG)

In a pinch, *a telephoto lens* will also work to start a fire. Open the lens to the maximum aperture and focus a tiny spot of sunlight on dry tinder by holding the lens at the optimum distance for the concentration of the light. Be patient; this method can take fifteen or twenty minutes. (AR)

WIND AND RAIN

Use a rock to block the exit of the wind from beneath the flame. This will allow the air to circulate and force the hot air up for use in cooking. If the wind is very strong,

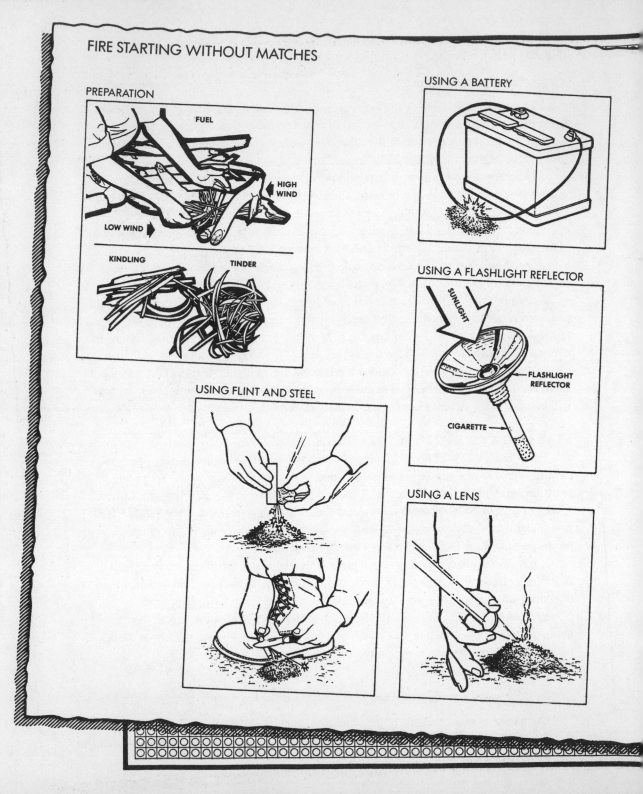

FIRE STARTING WITHOUT MATCHES

PREPARATION

FUEL

HIGH WIND

LOW WIND

KINDLING

TINDER

USING A BATTERY

USING A FLASHLIGHT REFLECTOR

SUNLIGHT

FLASHLIGHT REFLECTOR

CIGARETTE

USING FLINT AND STEEL

USING A LENS

FIRE CONSTRUCTION

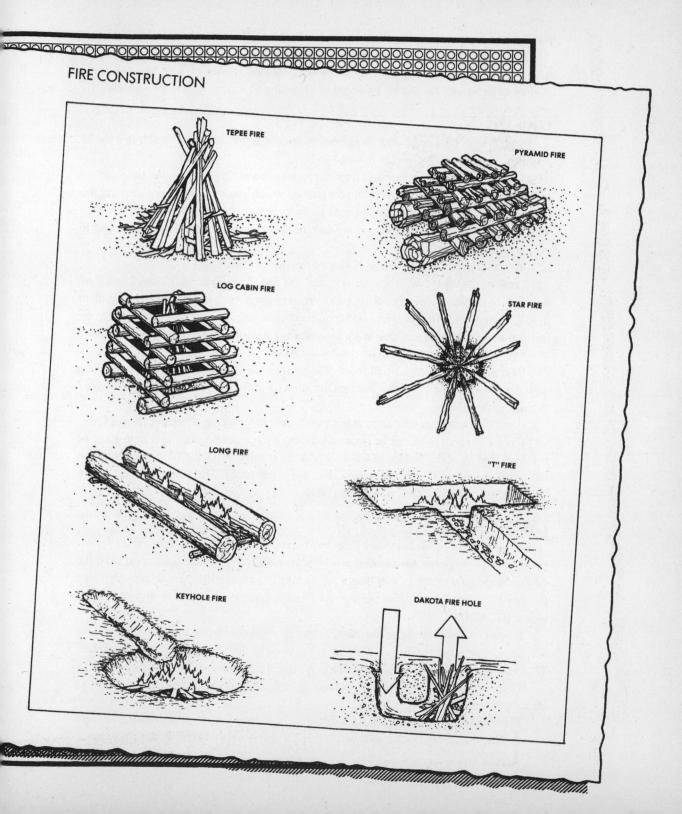

TEPEE FIRE

PYRAMID FIRE

LOG CABIN FIRE

STAR FIRE

LONG FIRE

"T" FIRE

KEYHOLE FIRE

DAKOTA FIRE HOLE

place the cooking utensil adjacent to and downwind from the fire.

If the ground is wet, build up the area where the fire is wanted with a foundation of stones and a grout made of mud, with a smooth, flat mud surface on top. Another group of stones can be used for storing firewood and kindling so it stays off the ground. (WG)

COOKING

A good rule is to *cook with flame,* rather than with hot ash, since building a useful pile of hot ashes is wasteful of both wood and time.

A makeshift grill can be made from very green wood. If you have the time and inclination, you can easily fashion a support pole on which you can hang a pot over the fire by pounding a stake into the ground next to the fire, then finding a stout, green branch with a fork. Attach the two ends of the fork to the stake and allow the stoutest end to protrude over the fire.

In a pinch, you can also use an X-shaped tire iron as a grill.

Cook food slowly, when appropriate, and use tinfoil as a baking device. There's no easier — or better — way of cooking ears of corn or potatoes than simply wrapping them in foil, along with whatever spices and condiments suit you. Several layers of very strong foil can be used to make a little oven in which a piece of meat or chicken is wrapped along with whatever vegetables come to hand. (WG)

Real grills: Perforate a small piece of sheet iron (say three feet by eighteen inches) with many small holes. Put the sheet on the stones and over the campfire to make your cooking easier. (WG)

Bring the rack from your oven at home. It'll ease the cooking chores in camp. (SAR)

Ovens: A camp oven can be improvised from a large pot by placing it atop a bed of hot coals that lie at the bottom of a hole dug in the ground. Place the food to be baked in the pot and cover it (if a lid is unavailable, use a flat rock). Then cover the lid with a layer of dirt and build a fire on top of it. (WG)

LOW-TECH CAMP TIPS

Waterproofing matches: Stick them head first into molten candle wax. (WG)

If you've forgotten the clothespins, loop the clothesline around a tree and twist the doubled rope around like pretzel dough as you take it across to its opposite support. Once the line is suspended, just slip the corners of each garment that you're drying into the twists. (GGMcD)

If you remembered the clothespins, use them with your tarp to make a wind- or sun-screen, to cover the food on a table in a storm or to attach rain curtains to porches. They're also great for resealing food wrappers, especially potato chips. (SAR)

Thar she crawls: Turn your binoculars around for close inspection of insects or to locate splinters or thorns. (MQ)

The Swiss Army pin: A box of safety pins is a handy and versatile thing to have about camp. Individual safety pins can be used to temporarily mend clothing and tents;

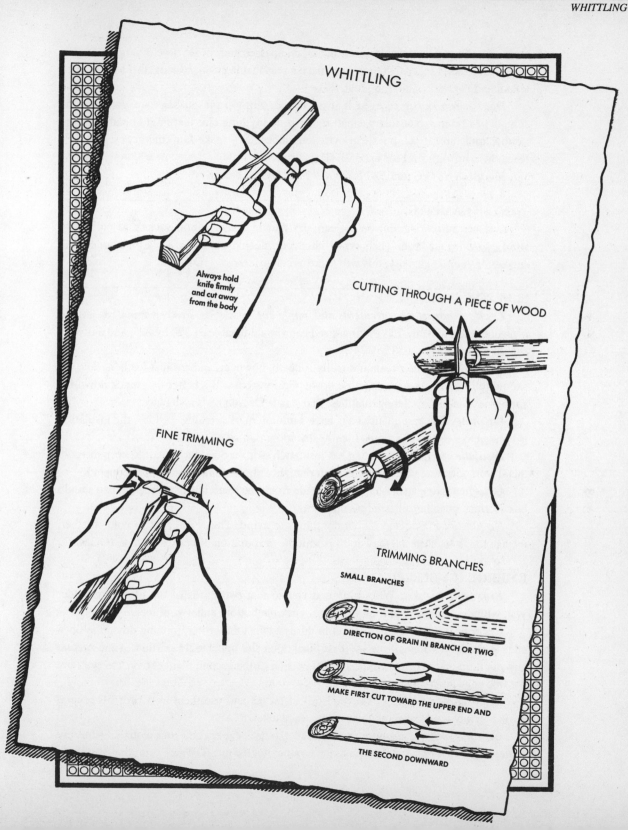

WHITTLING

Always hold
knife firmly
and cut away
from the body

CUTTING THROUGH A PIECE OF WOOD

FINE TRIMMING

TRIMMING BRANCHES

SMALL BRANCHES

DIRECTION OF GRAIN IN BRANCH OR TWIG

MAKE FIRST CUT TOWARD THE UPPER END AND

THE SECOND DOWNWARD

clean out clogged burners; secure watches, compasses and money to clothing; and make rude fish hooks. Linked together, they make a reasonable chain, so long as the stress isn't lateral and the length isn't too great. (SAR)

Don't wrap it, bag it, even if it isn't food. Zip-top plastic bags are great for the storage of cameras, binoculars, small firearms or anything else that might be affected by sand or moisture. If you put them over your shoes, they make fair emergency galoshes. Keep them up with a rubber band. (GGMcD)

See also *HIKING* and *EATING OFF THE LAND,* below.

WINTER CAMPING

Just before retiring, put on a clean, dry pair of heavy cotton socks and pull a dry wool cap on your head. Then crawl into your sleeping bag for a warm, comfortable snooze. If your feet are dry, this will make a real difference. (JO)

SLEEPING BAGS

Look for honest measurements and ample cut: A regular-sized sleeping bag should measure at least 33" by 75". A king-sized bag should be at least 39" by 82", and a double should measure at least 50" by 74".

Down is best: Make certain it really is down, however, and not just feathers. The tag should tell you if it's duck or goose down. Go for goose. It's better than duck down for springiness and its insulating qualities. Man-made Dacron 88 is also okay.

Stitching: The best quality bags have a minimum of stitching; instead, the insulation is bonded to the bag. The more stitching, the more thin spots.

Insulation strips: A good bag has insulation strips around the zipper to keep the cold metal from touching you and to keep out draughts. (Better bags have nylon zippers.)

Colorfast: No matter what they're made from, the materials in a sleeping bag should be colorfast, nonallergenic and porous.

No plastic: Plastic and rubber are things to avoid. They can crack in cold weather, they're tough to clean and they don't permit the evaporation of body moisture. (GGMcD)

EMERGENCY SLEEPING BAGS

From one blanket: Wrap it around you so that two-thirds of the blanket is under you, with the remaining portion over you. Tuck the bottom under your feet.

From two: Fold the first blanket in thirds against the center, pinning down the open edge (see illustration). Place the first blanket on the upper-right portion of the second and pin it up on the bottom. Fold the left portion of the second blanket over the first, pin the free edge and fold the bottom over.

From garbage bags: Fill several full of leaves and use them as a bed; fill several more halfway with leaves, and use them as a blanket. (TAE)

Ground cloths: Use anything — blankets, tarps, seat covers, your clothes — but use *something.* Most heat loss is through the ground, not the air. (GWA)

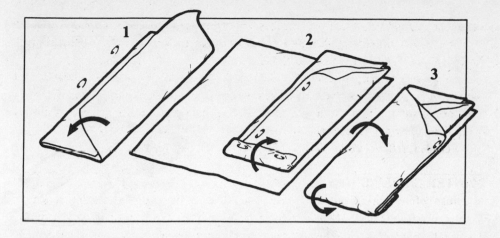

AIR MATTRESSES

Air mattresses come only in rubber or plastic. The plastic ones are cheaper, but easier to puncture and can go stiff in cold weather. The older rubber ones are sometimes heavier. There are new cellular mats that double as ground cloths; they're flat as a dime and work like a charm. They weigh nothing and there's no pumping. You just let them absorb air, then squeeze them out when you roll them up.

The old rubberized fabric models are great to sleep on, but they can be a bitch to inflate. Make sure the valve has a metal cap and not a plastic (or rubber) plug, and use a hand pump. (GGMcD)

CAMP SHOWER

A camp shower can be fashioned by fitting a shower hose into the bottom of a plastic bucket and hanging the assembly from the branch of a tree. Erect a tent under the bucket (with some floorboards, if you really want wilderness deluxe) and put some hot rocks fom the campfire into the bucket for a little heat. Be careful, though, since porous rocks will explode if subjected to variations in temperature. (WG)

BEAR ALARM

A bear can smell food that's still sealed in a tin can and will gladly invade your camp to get at it. Take the precaution of providing yourself with a bear alarm that will permit you to rest easier. Before retiring, place all your food beneath a stack of pots and pans so the bear will have to make a lot of racket to get the goods. This will have you awake and on your preselected route to safety before he can consider pawing at you. Bear alarms are best set up away from camp — ideally in a canoe or flatboat that's been tied fast to the shore.

Don't mess with a bear. *They* don't know they're cute and cuddly. One swipe from even a middlin' bear and you're a goner. (AW)

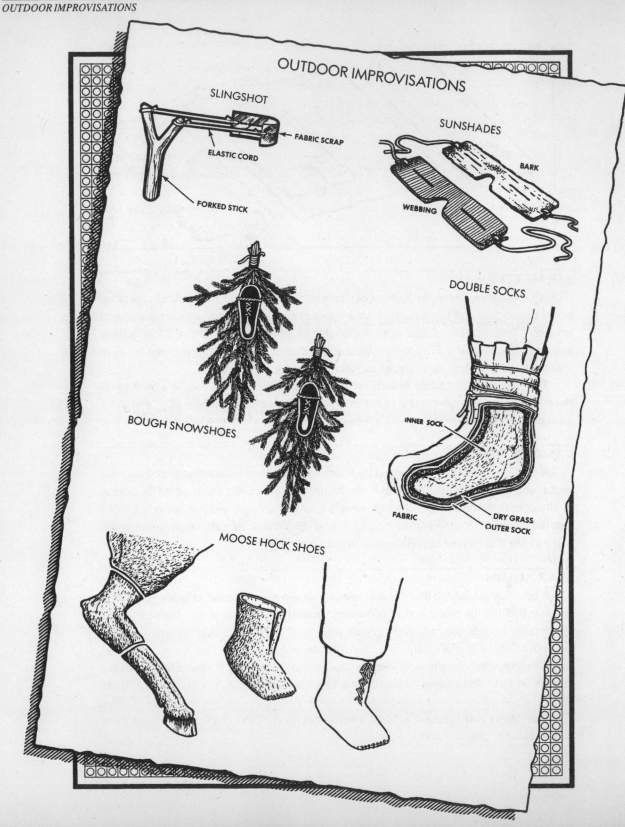

OUTDOOR IMPROVISATIONS

SLINGSHOT

FABRIC SCRAP

ELASTIC CORD

FORKED STICK

SUNSHADES

BARK

WEBBING

DOUBLE SOCKS

INNER SOCK

FABRIC

DRY GRASS
OUTER SOCK

BOUGH SNOWSHOES

MOOSE HOCK SHOES

YOU DON'T NEED A WEATHERMAN

The wind: If the wind is from the west, that usually means clear weather, except in Florida or California, where west winds are loaded with ocean moisture. East of the Rockies, an east wind will often bring rain; in the north, easterly winds will bring cold and clear weather and in the south, hot, humid weather and showers.

Both summer rains and winter snows arrive with northeast winds, while northwestern ones can break summer heat or end a winter cold snap. A southwestern wind is warm in winter and very hot in summer; a wind out of the southeast is the dampest of them all.

The clouds: Just as mackerels' scales and mares' tails make lofty ships carry low sails, so cloud formations can warn of all kinds of changes in the weather. Key types:

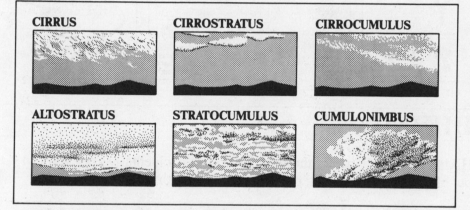

- *Cirrus* clouds are the loftiest and indicate calm weather.
- *Cirrostratus* clouds are a high, thin layer that also indicates calm weather.
- *Cirrocumulus* clouds (the mackerels' scales alluded to above) resemble a pattern of large, white flakes. Calm weather.
- *Altostratus* clouds indicate squalls, They are characterized by gray curtains of moisture through which the sun and moon are barely visible.
- *Stratocumulus* clouds are dark and twisted, but bring little rain.
- *Nimbus* clouds are black, low-lying rain-bearing formations.
- *Cumulonimbus* clouds are thunder clouds. They are black, sometimes anvil-shaped cousins of the fluffier, whiter cumulus formations. (BT)

GROUND-TO-AIR SIGNALS

These are universal signals for physical communication with searchplanes. They should appear as large as possible from the air by tramping them out in the snow or sand or outlining them with stones or logs (**see illustration**). In some situations, ground-to-air signals can be made using grass fires or overturned earth. (GWA)

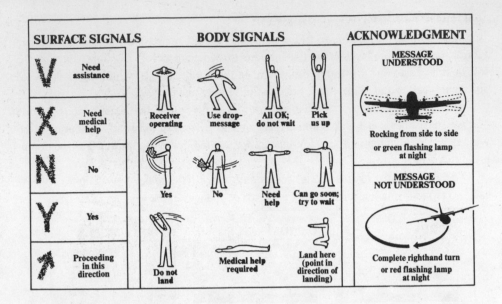

HIKING

Hiking is not only one of those things you do accidentally after you run out of gas, it's also honest, old-style transportation.

TOPOGRAPHICAL MAPS

The ideal scale for hikers is 1:24000, and the whole country is available. Ask for a map index and an order form when you write to

Branch of Distribution, U.S. Geological Survey
1200 South Eads Street
Arlington, VA 22202 (AW)

HOW TO READ A TOPOGRAPHICAL MAP

What they are: All topographical maps show distance and various elevations of an area in complete detail, designating rivers, lakes, villages, important buildings and other features of the landscape by means of symbols and the use of a variety of typefaces. Topo-maps also show the name of the area described and show where it is on the planet by means of latitude and longitude.

Inspection: You can orient your topographical map by inspection. That means you align it so that a feature shown on the map corresponds to one in front of you in real life. This will put you right in relation to the terrain through which you wish to hike.

By compass: To orient yourself by compass, set the compass at 360 (north) and place it on the margin of the map with one edge flush with the line indicating magnetic

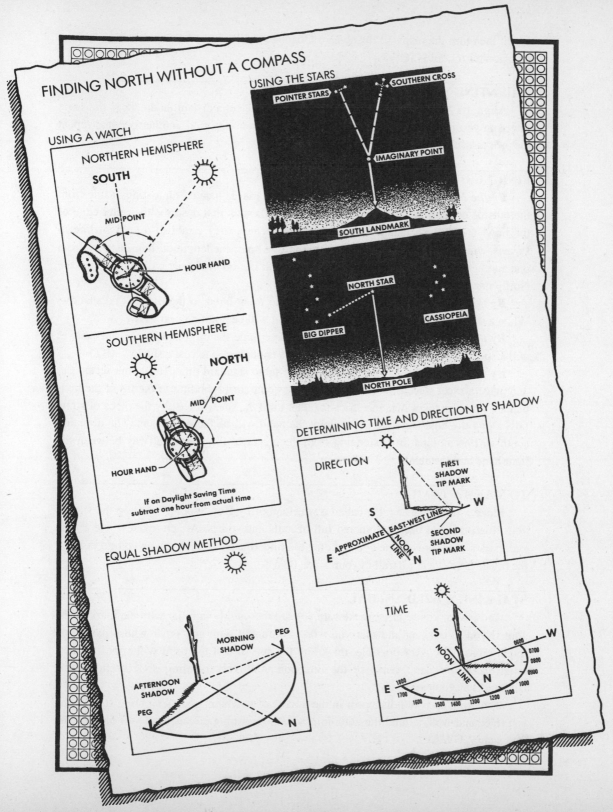

FINDING NORTH WITHOUT A COMPASS

USING A WATCH

NORTHERN HEMISPHERE

SOUTH

MID-POINT

HOUR HAND

SOUTHERN HEMISPHERE

NORTH

MID POINT

HOUR HAND

If on Daylight Saving Time subtract one hour from actual time

USING THE STARS

POINTER STARS

SOUTHERN CROSS

IMAGINARY POINT

SOUTH LANDMARK

NORTH STAR

BIG DIPPER

CASSIOPEIA

NORTH POLE

DETERMINING TIME AND DIRECTION BY SHADOW

DIRECTION

FIRST SHADOW TIP MARK

W

S

E   APPROXIMATE EAST-WEST LINE

NOON LINE

N

SECOND SHADOW TIP MARK

EQUAL SHADOW METHOD

MORNING SHADOW

PEG

AFTERNOON SHADOW

PEG

N

TIME

S

W

NOON LINE

0600

0700

0800

0900

1000

E   1800

1700

1600   1500   1400   1300   1200   1100

N

north; then turn the map and the compass together until the needle sits over the compass rose pointer for north. (GWA)

ORIENTING WITH ONLY A COMPASS

Align the compass needle with true north, then select a distant landmark in the same direction you're heading. When you arrive at the landmark, find another one and repeat the process. (BT)

FINDING DIRECTIONS WITHOUT A COMPASS

By the North Star: The North Star (a.k.a. Polaris) is located on a straight line from the outside edge of the Big Dipper's bowl; the two stars that describe the outer edge of the bowl are, in fact, called the pointer stars because they establish a straight line to Polaris, which shines brightly at a point about five times the length of their distance from one another. Meanwhile, back on Earth, true north lies on the horizon directly below the North Star. (BT)

By the sun: Stick a short, straight stick into the ground so that it casts no shadow. When a shadow emerges about six inches long; it will be pointing east. (BT)

By the moon: The same method used to determine the direction by the sun (above) will also work with moonlight, provided there's enough of it to cast a shadow. (BT)

By your watch: First, your watch must be set to standard time. Hold your watch flat and place a short piece of straw upright at the point corresponding to the tip of the hour hand. Then, turn the watch and straw together until the shadow cast by the piece of straw falls along the hour hand, at which point the hand will be facing the sun. The direction south will lie along a line extending from the center of the watch halfway between the hour hand and the number 12. (GWA)

TO MAKE A TRAIL

Make a tindermaker (also called a whiffelpoof by Boy Scouts) — a log the size of your thigh that has been hammered full of nails and spikes. Attach a screw eye at one end, pass a rope through the eye and drag the tindermaker behind you as you go through the brush. You'll leave a trail in your wake. (GWA)

STALKING A WILD ANIMAL

Know what you're after; make sure you are thoroughly familiar with the mark of the animal you're tracking and that you won't confuse it with any other whose paths you might cross. Whenever possible, track into the sun so that the print will appear in best relief; keep a general sense of the direction you'll be traveling and carefully note landmarks as you pass them.

If the trail seems to disappear in the middle of nowhere, plant a sighting stick at the last trace and walk around the stick in gradually widening circles until you pick up the trail again. (GWA)

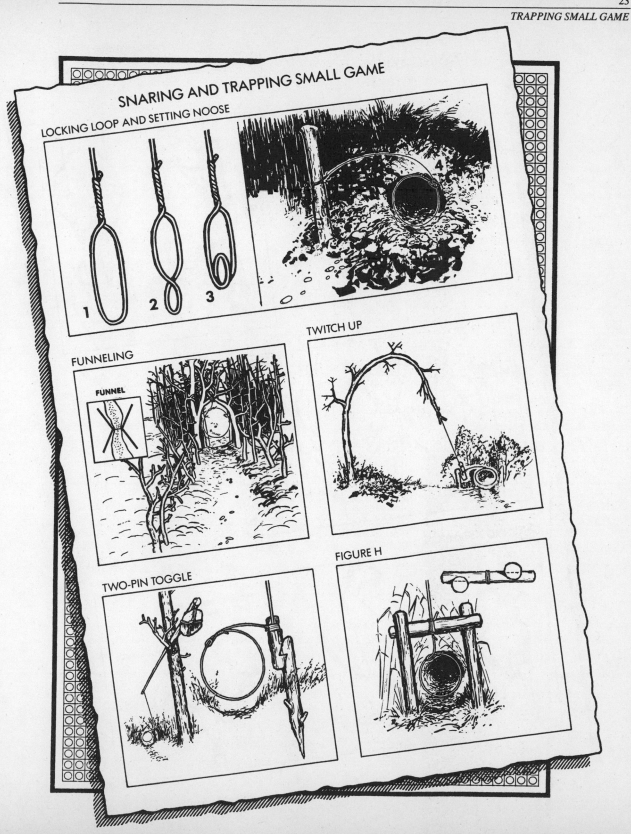

SNARING AND TRAPPING SMALL GAME

LOCKING LOOP AND SETTING NOOSE

1 2 3 4

FUNNELING

FUNNEL

TWITCH UP

TWO-PIN TOGGLE

FIGURE H

DRESSING AND SKINNING SMALL GAME

SMALL-ANIMAL SKINNING

CUT

GLOVE SKINNING

CUT

DRESSING A RABBIT WITHOUT A KNIFE

A

B

C

A:
GRASP TIGHT WITH BOTH HANDS AT RIB CAGE

B:
SQUEEZE TIGHTLY TOWARD THE STOMACH

C:
SQUEEZING TIGHTLY, FLING CARCASS BETWEEN YOUR LEGS

BACKPACKING

Place most of the weight you carry in a backpack on your hip belt by packing the heaviest objects high and close to your back. (GWA)

SLEETS DON'T HAIL ME NOW

Very few hiking boots are truly waterproof. You can however keep your feet dry by wrapping a couple of small plastic bags around your stocking feet before you put your boots on. Use a rubber band as a garter. (JO)

EATING OFF THE LAND

And probably someone else's land, at that. After all, if you're eyeballing real estate with a view to dinner, your investment portfolio's probably a bit thin. Eating off the land should be distinguished from living off the Land, a concern of the welfare state.

WILD EDIBLE PLANTS

There are two categories here: *sweet greens* and *bitter greens*. Sweet greens are dandy for salads and as condiments; bitter greens should be boiled twice and used in soups.

Sweet greens:	*Bitter greens:*
Watercress	Common milkweed
Sheep sorrel	Dandelion leaves
Chicory leaves	Stinging nettles
Lambs' quarters leaves	Lambs' quarters tops
Purslane sprigs	Black mustard leaves
Chickweed sprigs	Purslane stems and
Cattail sprouts (spring)	tops
Dandelion leaves (spring)	(BT)

BREADSTUFFS

No matter what you use, you'll have to mix it with flour to make it work. The best wild ingredients are ground and leached acorns and cattail pollen. But it's rarely worth the effort. (SAR)

ROOTS AND TUBERS

These should be boiled or roasted not only for the best flavor, but also to avoid

EDIBLE PLANTS

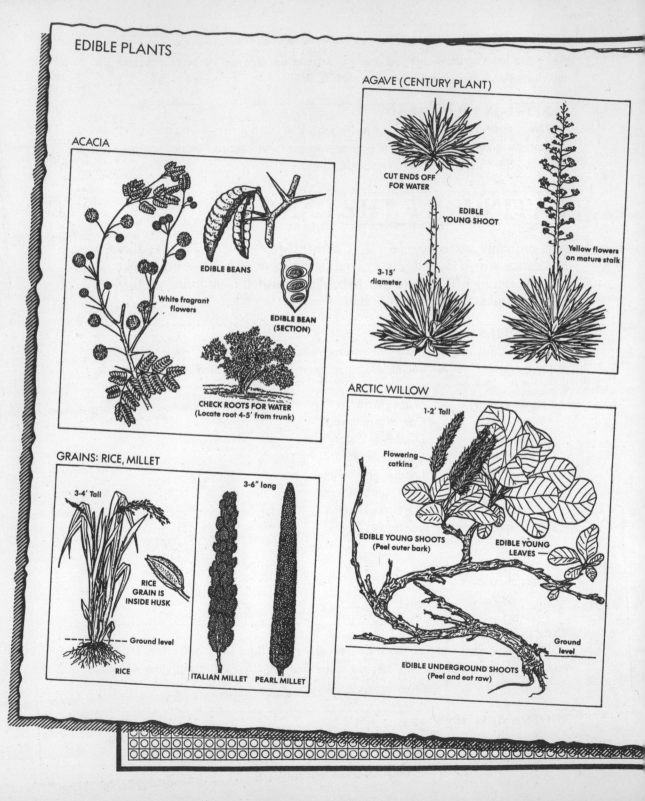

ACACIA

EDIBLE BEANS

EDIBLE BEAN
(SECTION)

White fragrant
flowers

CHECK ROOTS FOR WATER
(Locate root 4-5' from trunk)

AGAVE (CENTURY PLANT)

CUT ENDS OFF
FOR WATER

EDIBLE
YOUNG SHOOT

3-15'
diameter

Yellow flowers
on mature stalk

ARCTIC WILLOW

1-2' Tall

Flowering
catkins

EDIBLE YOUNG SHOOTS
(Peel outer bark)

EDIBLE YOUNG
LEAVES

Ground
level

EDIBLE UNDERGROUND SHOOTS
(Peel and eat raw)

GRAINS: RICE, MILLET

3-4' Tall

3-6" long

RICE
GRAIN IS
INSIDE HUSK

Ground level

RICE

ITALIAN MILLET   PEARL MILLET

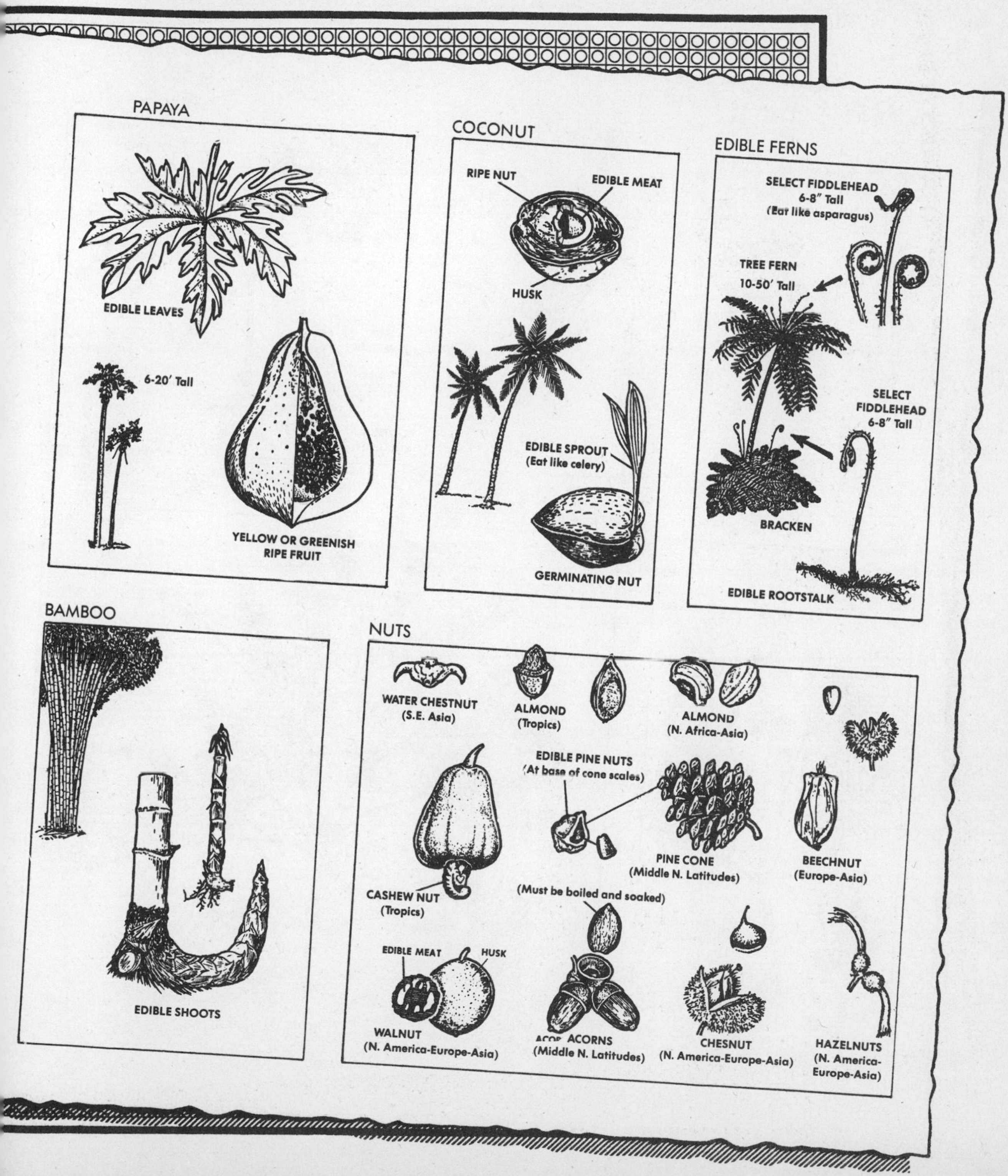

PAPAYA

EDIBLE LEAVES

6-20' Tall

YELLOW OR GREENISH
RIPE FRUIT

COCONUT

RIPE NUT

EDIBLE MEAT

HUSK

EDIBLE SPROUT
(Eat like celery)

GERMINATING NUT

EDIBLE FERNS

SELECT FIDDLEHEAD
6-8" Tall
(Eat like asparagus)

TREE FERN
10-50' Tall

SELECT
FIDDLEHEAD
6-8" Tall

BRACKEN

EDIBLE ROOTSTALK

BAMBOO

EDIBLE SHOOTS

NUTS

WATER CHESTNUT
(S.E. Asia)

ALMOND
(Tropics)

ALMOND
(N. Africa-Asia)

EDIBLE PINE NUTS
(At base of cone scales)

PINE CONE
(Middle N. Latitudes)

BEECHNUT
(Europe-Asia)

CASHEW NUT
(Tropics)

(Must be boiled and soaked)

EDIBLE MEAT   HUSK

WALNUT
(N. America-Europe-Asia)

ACOR ACORNS
(Middle N. Latitudes)

CHESNUT
(N. America-Europe-Asia)

HAZELNUTS
(N. America-
Europe-Asia)

POISONOUS PLANTS

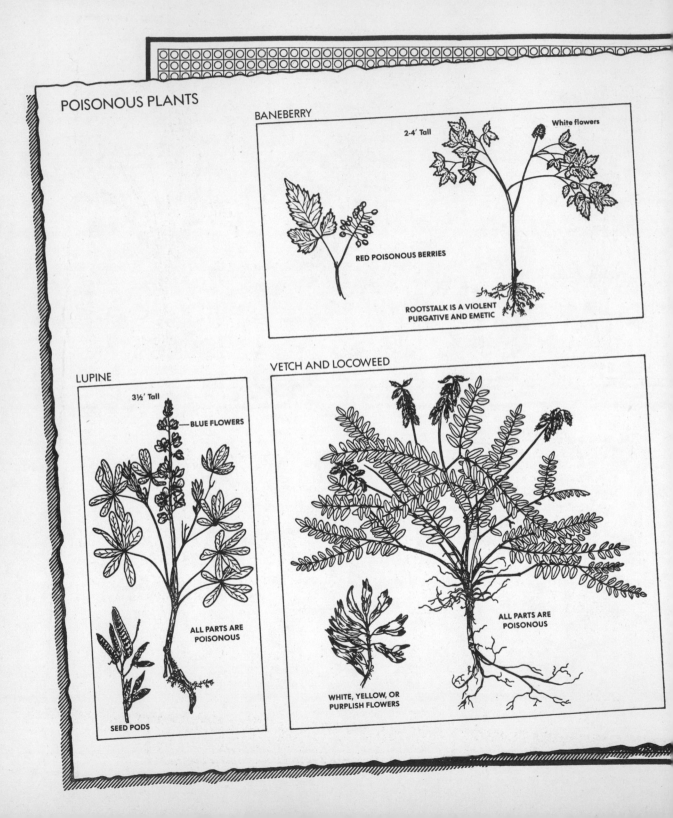

BANEBERRY

2-4′ Tall

White flowers

RED POISONOUS BERRIES

ROOTSTALK IS A VIOLENT
PURGATIVE AND EMETIC

LUPINE

3½′ Tall

— BLUE FLOWERS

ALL PARTS ARE
POISONOUS

SEED PODS

VETCH AND LOCOWEED

ALL PARTS ARE
POISONOUS

WHITE, YELLOW, OR
PURPLISH FLOWERS

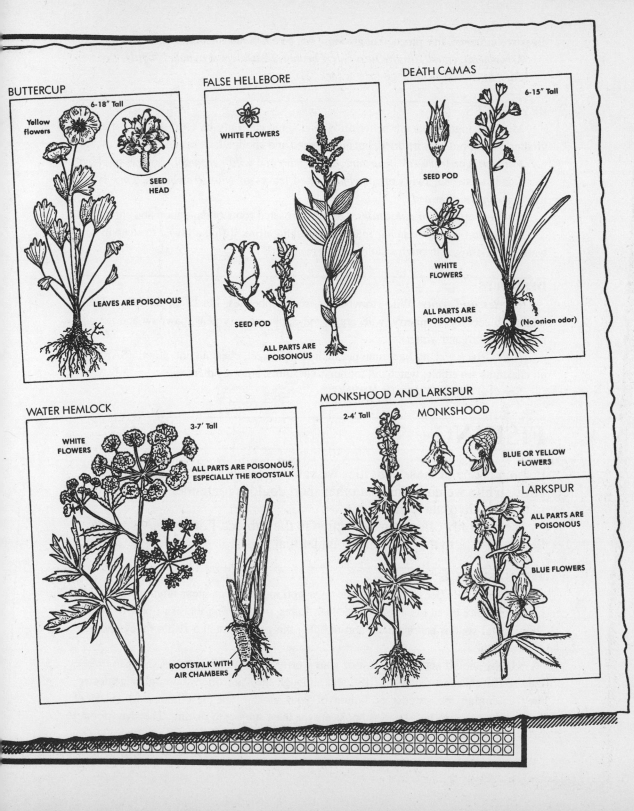

BUTTERCUP

Yellow flowers

6-18" Tall

SEED HEAD

LEAVES ARE POISONOUS

FALSE HELLEBORE

WHITE FLOWERS

SEED POD

ALL PARTS ARE POISONOUS

DEATH CAMAS

6-15" Tall

SEED POD

WHITE FLOWERS

ALL PARTS ARE POISONOUS

(No onion odor)

WATER HEMLOCK

3-7' Tall

WHITE FLOWERS

ALL PARTS ARE POISONOUS, ESPECIALLY THE ROOTSTALK

ROOTSTALK WITH AIR CHAMBERS

MONKSHOOD AND LARKSPUR

2-4' Tall

MONKSHOOD

BLUE OR YELLOW FLOWERS

LARKSPUR

ALL PARTS ARE POISONOUS

BLUE FLOWERS

digestive violence. In a pinch, though, these can be eaten raw. All must be dug in the fall:

Arrowhead, cattail, prairie turnip, hog peanut, Jerusalem artichoke, daylily.

For year-round rooting, go for *burdock.* (BT)

BEVERAGES

Most tea ingredients are better dried (and some can only be used dried); coffee ingredients must not only be dried, but also roasted and chopped.

For tea: The leaves of *spearmint, peppermint* and *wild bergamot;* flowers of *elderberry* and *basswood;* twigs of *spicebush;* dried leaves of *wild strawberry, black birch, wintergreen* and *fireweed.*

Coffee stretchers or substitutes: Dried and roasted roots of dandelion and chicory.

In addition, *staghorn sumac* makes a refreshing drink if first allowed to steep in cold water, then strained through a cloth and sweetened. (BT)

DESSERTS

Berries and fruits: Wild strawberries, red raspberries, blackcap, dewberry, huckleberry, blueberry, cranberry, wild grape, mayapple, prickly pear, pawpaw and persimmon (in the fall and winter).

Nuts: Black walnut, butternut, pecan, hickory, hazel, chestnut and piñon. (SAR) Not all chestnuts are edible; watch out for horse chestnuts, among others.

See also *OUTDOORS* **and** *HIKING.*

FISHING

Fishing is one of those activities we call a sport so we don't have to feel guilty while we do it. In what other sport could a contender read a novel in the middle of the action?

We can only offer an introduction to the subject. For more, visit your library or talk to that man sitting under that tree.

THE BASIC RIG

Bait or lures: Use whatever seems to be working. Bait can mean anything from little lumps of white bread to chunks of cheddar. Lures are anything that isn't bait — usually shiny metal spoons and spinners and the like, things that catch a fish's fancy and help you catch the fish.

Hooks should not be the least of your worries if you're a rookie fisherman. While they're the cheapest part of the rig, and although they are often thoroughly neglected, they determine the success or failure of your tackle. The best hooks are made of tempered steel wire, but stainless hooks are the least subject to rusting. The size (or bite) of a hook is determined by its bend.

Leader: The leader is the short piece of line (usually a foot or two in length) that links the hook to the main line. If you use a leader, make sure your knot is secure, since that will be the weakest point in the whole line.

Swivel: The swivel is positioned between the leader and the line; get one with a snap closure for ease in changing lines.

Sinker: Usually, sinkers are made of lead, and although they all have one self-described function, there are a number of different types. A *pyramid* is for beach casting, and will bury itself in the sand. An *egg* sinker will allow live bait to swim freely. The simplest type, though, is a *clincher* which is an easy-to-use, crimp-on sinker.

Line: Of the two basic types, *braided* and *monofilament,* braided is the more expensive, but also the longer lasting. Both are made of nylon and Dacron, but braided line will stretch a little and will spread more evenly on the reel while allowing fewer loops. Braided line, which will allow a fisherman a bit more latitude in sporting a stubborn fish, is responsible for the majority of record catches.

Rod: There are five types of fishing rods:

- *Bait casting:* Also used with spoons, spinners and plugs. Usually between five and six feet long.
- *Spinning:* Used with artificial lures. Six to seven feet in length.
- *Flycasting:* Long rods, seven to nine feet in length, but extremely light, some weighing as little as three ounces.
- *Heavy-duty:* Used for trolling and big game fish.
- *Spin-cast:* A multipurpose rod suitable for both spinning and bait casting.

Get a *reel* to match your rod. (JY)

BEWARE

of cheap, foreign-made tackle. Buy from long-established manufacturers and from shops that specialize in fishing equipment. You'll get the best advice there, too. (GP)

LICENSES

are available at most tackle shops. (GP)

EXCEPT EELS

Freshly caught fish can be grasped more easily during cleaning if you first cover your hands with salt. (RP)

NAILED

You can clean catfish and bullheads easier by nailing them through the head to a board. (WD)

NEVER GO

fishing without a landing net or you'll come home with stories instead of fish. (WS)

POISONOUS FISH

PUFFER FISH

OILFISH

TRIGGERFISH

FILEFISH

PARROT FISH

SURMULLET
or GOATFISH

PORCUPINE FISH

SURGEONFISH

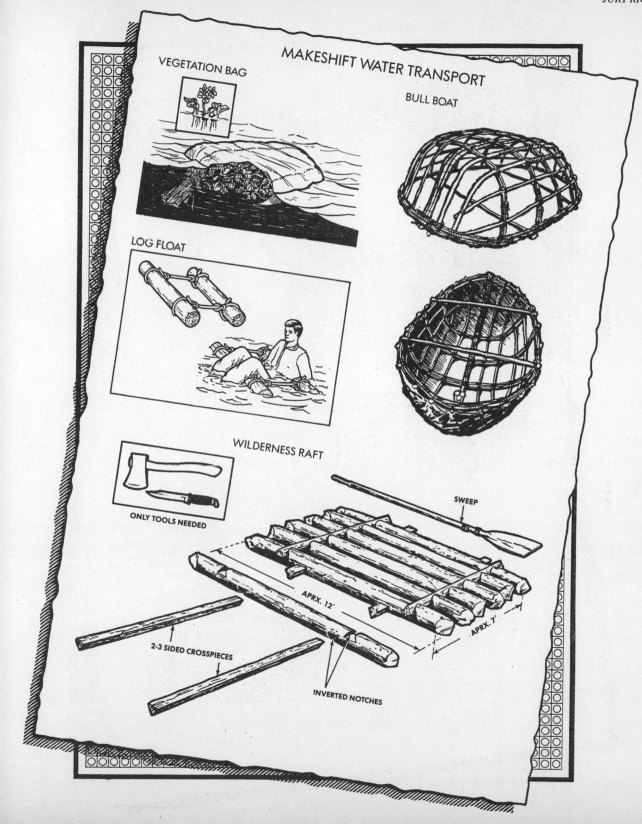

MAKESHIFT WATER TRANSPORT

VEGETATION BAG

BULL BOAT

LOG FLOAT

ONLY TOOLS NEEDED

WILDERNESS RAFT

SWEEP

APRX. 12'

APRX. 7'

2-3 SIDED CROSSPIECES

INVERTED NOTCHES

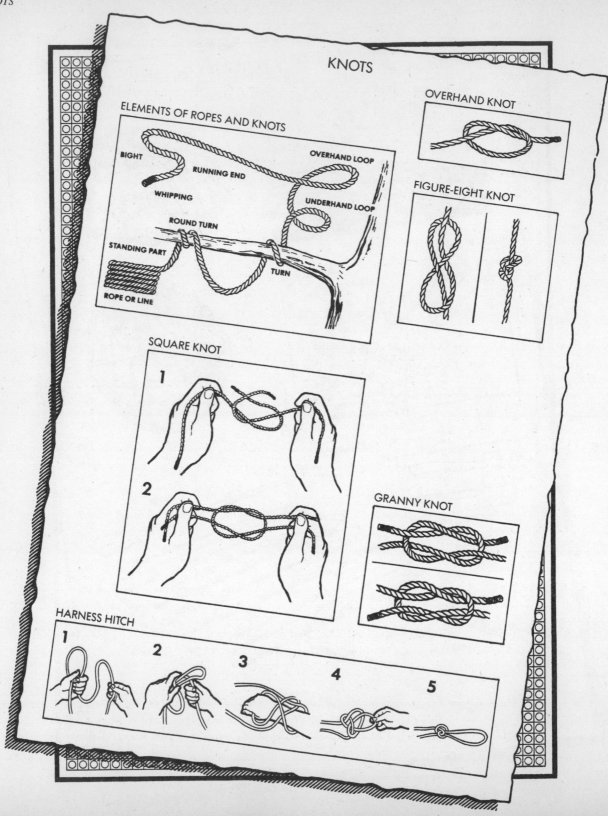

KNOTS

ELEMENTS OF ROPES AND KNOTS

BIGHT

RUNNING END

OVERHAND LOOP

WHIPPING

UNDERHAND LOOP

ROUND TURN

STANDING PART

TURN

ROPE OR LINE

OVERHAND KNOT

FIGURE-EIGHT KNOT

SQUARE KNOT

1

2

GRANNY KNOT

HARNESS HITCH

1 2 3 4 5

KNOTS

Give yourself enough rope and you can make it shorter by tying knots in it.

But if you only know one knot, it should be the *bowline*, truly the king of all knots. A proper bowline will tighten when cinched, will stay together until the rope breaks and be untied in a snap. If you don't know which knot to use, use a bowline.

Look at the illustration here. It's a picture of a bowline in the making. The mnemonic maxim used is this: "The rabbit comes out of the hole, goes 'round the tree and back down the hole." You can repeat this saying as you learn to tie a bowline — but repeat it to yourself. (AR)

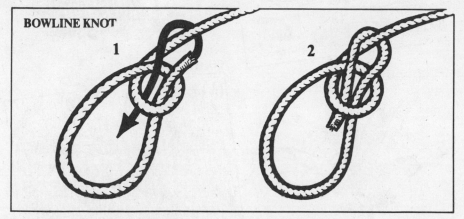

BOWLINE KNOT
1
2

A SERIES

of short lengths of line used to attach or bind something is superior to one long length that has been doubled and redoubled; a long length of cord or rope is much more prone to loosening — and if it comes off, there is no backup. (KD)

PURE WATER

Boil suspect water for at *least* ten minutes to kill harmful bacteria. If you intend to filter the water (through sand, or, better, through charcoal, which eliminates foul smells), do so before purifying.

Water can also be chlorinated by using bleach powder (two or three tablespoonsful per quart). Water with too much chlorine tastes terrible, so if you can't stand to drink it, you shouldn't. It should taste somewhat like overchlorinated swimming pool water. (DB)

PROCURING WATER

WATER FROM BAMBOO

BEACH WELL

DRY SAND

OCEAN

FIRST DUNE

DIG FOR WATER

SATURATED SAND

COLLECTING WATER

ABSORBENT CLOTH

WET GRASS

PIT RAIN COLLECTOR

WATER FROM A BANANA PLANT

CUT HERE

CUT OUT BOWL

WATER WILL FILL BOWL FROM ROOTS

NATURAL SEEPAGE

will partially purify water from a hole dug beside a flowing river or stream. *Do not use alum crystals* to purify water. They cause kidney stones. (WG)

INDIAN SWEAT HUT

First, some commonsense warnings: Don't do this more than once a day or for longer than thirty minutes. Don't burn yourself on the rocks — they should be extremely hot. Some types of rocks will explode if water is poured on them when they are very hot. Test a few in safety. Don't let your fire burn down the forest. If you have a heart or respiratory condition, the Indian Sweat Hut will be enough to kill you. Finally, any warnings we might have about frolicking in the woods naked would be too situational. Watch your ass.

The construction of an outdoor sauna will take all day, but if successfully completed and used, will place you securely next to godliness. The technique outlined here has been used by cleaner Indians for centuries:

First, a shopping list of essentials:

- A dozen rocks about the size of footballs
- A good supply of firewood
- A pile of old blankets, carpet remnants, old tents or similar coverings
- A shovel, an axe, a water container (a 5- or 10-gallon bucket will do) filled with fresh water, a knife and a candle and matches
- Proximity to a lake, stream, river, pond or snowbank
- A willing pal or two

Start by building a healthy, medium-sized fire. Add the rocks to the blaze and let them heat for several hours while you build the hut. (Be careful; certain kinds of rocks explode when subjected to high temperatures.)

Clear a ten-foot-wide circle for the structure, which, when completed, will be a hemisphere six or eight feet in diameter, and about four feet high.

First, dig a pit about two feet wide and a foot deep in the center of your site. Next, construct the frame by bending over green saplings in arcs. Fix the bottoms of the saplings to trees, other saplings, or by sticking them in the ground like tent stakes. Next, cover the frame with the blankets or carpets, making sure that the ends overlap so that no heat can escape from inside the hut. Remember to leave a flap for the entrance. Seal the edges around the bottom leaves and dirt, and weight the fabric with stones or logs.

When the hut is complete, use the shovel to take four or five of the stones from the fire and transfer them to the pit inside the hut. Take the bucket of water and a lit candle inside (careful, now). Leave all your clothing outside, and seal the flap.

It should be very dark in the hut, and soon it will also be very steamy and hot and the air will be difficult to breathe.

Take turns. One person tends the candle and the other tends the water. At intervals, spray the rocks with a drizzle of fresh water, and, if necessary, get a nonparticipant to bring more hot stones.

If you've done the job properly, you'll sweat as you've never sweated before. The intense heat in the thick air will be excruciating. Use the candle as an oxygen meter: if it goes out, you must allow air from outside into the hut — but just enough to replenish the oxygen supply. If you can relight the candle, you've got plenty.

Don't stay inside any longer than thirty minutes, and don't hesitate to leave early if you feel you should.

When your time is up, leap from the hut and plunge into the water or roll in the snow. You'll feel fantastic, honest. It's better than drugs. And about as dangerous. (AR)

Modern Man at Work

Women can do it all, really. A woman can graduate from UCLA, write a novel, enter med school, cure cancer and bear children — although admittedly she won't have a lot of free time left for bowling or anything.

So women are known by what they are as well as what they do. Men, on the other hand, are known *only* by what they do. As a result, most men have successfully persuaded themselves that there is meaning in a life of paper-pushing or spot welding. In fact, so authentically and convincingly has the façade of meaningful work been constructed that lots and lots of women also want to go to work so they can find meaning in their lives, too.

Hence, work, once a gentlemanly sort of place, is now thoroughly coed, and sharing the joint with women brings on weird problems only a savvy Modern Man can solve.

C O N T E N T S
Chapter Two: *MODERN MAN AT WORK*

**HIRING ON AND OFF: Help Wanted: Classified Nonsense
— The Interview — The Politics of Unemployment:**
Affirmative Action / Comparable Worth **— Asking for a Raise
— I'm Fired, You Quit: The Smooth Getaway — WORLD
OF WORK: Never Steal — Brain Power — Business Calls:**
Phone dodges / Honesty pays / Secretary wars **— Business
Letters — Daily Steps to Getting Organized — Office
Politics:** *Five qualities essential to survival / The virtue of
incompetence / Politics and skill / Mergers* **— Caution: Women
at Work — Unions — Five Things You Should Know about
Delegating Responsibility — Supervising — Firing People —
Scams — POWER: Having It and Using It — SPEECH:
When to Talk and When to Shut Up — Jaws: Know What
You're Going to Say before You Start — Making a Speech:**
*Dress / Greetings / Wit / Gestures / Making points / Voice
quality / Conciseness / Closing / Fielding questions* **— Making
a Toast — TITLES: The Value of a Title — Titles** *versus*
**Cash — THE ART OF THE MEMO: A Sample Memo — A
Dissent on the Worth of Memo — REVENGE: Make It Fast
— Get a Good Return — Clichés and Revenge — SMALL
BUSINESS AND SELF-EMPLOYMENT: Estimating —
Fixing a Fee — The Wrong Shopping List — The Right Stuff
— GLAMOR JOBS — TV NEWS CAREERS**

HIRING ON AND OFF

Work, if you must. Just don't take work seriously. Take *getting* work seriously.

HELP WANTED

Classified ads are a waste of time if you're looking for a skilled or professional position. If you don't know somebody who knows somebody, take your chances on cold-calling on the telephone or shotgunning résumés around town. Any decent job that appears in the classifieds has already been filled by the time the ad runs. Many employers have a policy of advertising every vacancy, even though the job was filled the instant it became available. (JKF)

Think of yourself as a marketable commodity. Realistically evaluate your worth to a potential employer. Don't allow yourself to think that you're worth anything because you're a nice guy. Companies run on profits. (PNW)

THE INTERVIEW

The obvious: Don't try to get an interview without an appointment. (AP)

Son of the obvious: Appearance counts. Proper dress and grooming makes a tremendous impression on some stranger who has the task of evaluating your worth.

Plenty of time for the sergeants: Secretaries and receptionists are the key people in any outfit, and making a favorable impression on a secretary is often almost as good as making a favorable impression on your interviewer, who probably walked out to ask the secretary what *she* thought the moment you left the office. So be charming while you wait. But if you can't be charming, be invisible. Secretaries can spot a phony a mile away; they work for one all day.

Cool heels: If you're kept waiting to the point where you jeopardize your next meeting, the best move is to leave a brief note of explanation for the assistant to give to the interviewer. The note should contain an apology for not allowing enough time and some mention of your intention to phone for a rescheduling.

When meeting the interviewer, do not offer your hand unless he first offers his. *Do not smoke.* Make yourself comfortable; remember, you've both been through this before.

Let the interviewer think that he's running the show. Don't ramble off into lengthy discourses on love and nature. Keep your answers very brief and to the point; the interviewer should see a sign floating over your head that says "Pithy R Us."

Don't interview the interviewer. You are interviewing for a job, not trying to get somebody to sell it to you. Forget the questions about overtime, sick pay and vacation allowances. The *only* things that should seem important to you are the possibilities of advancement and what the company expects of you. Your salary shouldn't be discussed until after you've been offered the job. You should appear to be motivated by opportunity, not money — although if the interviewer brings up the question of salary, don't look like a Peace Corps volunteer. If the subject is on the table, address it cautiously but without fear. You should assume that the company would not pay you less than you're worth — or less than the amount you were earning before.

If the salary is just sufficient, accept the position without becoming a martyr. If the salary is too low, simply say you can't afford to take the job, politely apologize, thank him and leave. (AP)

Good for you? Job interviews are like foreplay: If it's good, what's coming will be better. If it's a drag, the job (or boss or firm or whatever) won't be much better. (GLS)

THE POLITICS OF UNEMPLOYMENT

Let them eat tofu: You can't feed a family of four on special interests. (LP)

Affirmative action: While popular political ideals invariably carry a germ of grassroots wisdom, those seeking to elevate ideals to policy can become totalitarian in the extreme. Hence, there is institutionalized racism and sexism in most personnel offices, where under the guise of affirmative action it is assumed, as a matter of policy, that blacks and women are not capable of competing for jobs with white males. (AW) Recent legal action regarding affirmative action, such as the March 1987 Supreme Court decision to allow the promotion of women over better qualified men in order to move women up the business ladder is unjust and destructive of the social fabric. Among other things, it undermines the equal justice provision of the Constitution and flies in the face of the very laws which, after a great deal of struggle, were enacted to eliminate sexist hiring practices. This obvious example of interpreting the law to allow the ends to justify the means is a dangerous precedent. Beyond that, it is social engineering at the cost of equality and justice — and competence.

Comparable worth: If the principle of equal worth is worth implementing, it must be more than just another sexist issue. To achieve validity, it must be a true labor issue. Hence, if secretaries should make more than gardeners, then poets, painters and sculptors should make more than union leaders, federal judges and politicians, and school teachers should be paid more than basketball players. (AP)

Sitting ducks: Watch out for governmental interference in the workplace, where any fashionable policy (say, a rule against smoking, or a mandatory union dues assessment) can be put into effect and made a compulsory part of an employment agreement. If these policies were made a compulsory part of *citizenship,* we'd call it tyranny. *(Anon.)*

See also *Caution: Women at Work* **in** *WORLD OF WORK,* **below.**

ASKING FOR A RAISE

There's only one big rule in a salary negotiation: Be prepared to take it or leave it. You may in fact get the raise you're seeking but you must also face the possibility that your bluff will be called in which case you swallow your pride and devalue your worth to your employer, or quit.

If you aren't prepared to quit if your request is refused, don't ask at all. And if you ask and are turned down, don't get pissed off. It's an employer's job to make an objective decision about wages, and it's your job to get as much as you can for the work you do. If the two jobs are incompatible, don't get angry about it. Don't burn bridges behind you.

The best time to ask for a raise is when a routine raise is imminent and you're afraid it won't be enough. If you're *certain* that your increased performance rates a raise, then go ahead. Remember, your increased value to the company is your *only* leverage. Be confident but pleasant; don't be aggressive or apologetic. Seek advice on how to better serve the company or ask for more money for your whole department. Make it clear you're not in a great hurry for an answer. And above all, *make no threats.* (AP)

I'M FIRED! YOU QUIT!

Aside from dying at your desk, the only way to get out of a job is to get fired or to quit. So don't make a big deal out of either one. These things happen.

If you leave a job with bitterness, conceal your feelings from your co-workers and your boss. Always, *always* keep your tail covered. If you explode and storm out, you'll just be leaving a group of people behind you who will happily gossip about you and call you a jerk behind your back. Go with grace and dignity; if anyone asks, give them a "too bad it couldn't work out" speech.

Organize your affairs. Even if the parting is full of anger, rise above it and go out like a professional. Leave no loose ends, even if it means working overtime. (AP)

See also *FAILURE* in *CHAPTER SEVENTEEN: THE DEPORTMENT DEPART-MENT.*

WORLD OF WORK

The office is where you live the most meaningless hours of your life. To admit this, however, would be to wear a Gillette bracelet, so go to work and get serious. Acquire wealth and power. Exploit markets and labor. Win. Win so hard it hurts good.

NEVER STEAL

anything from your employer with a market value of less than one year's salary. This includes stamps and pencils. (DT)

BRAIN POWER

No matter how many hours you spend working, your brain won't give you more than six hours a day. You'll notice that if you work longer, you become more distracted and require more rest intervals. You can think about this as long as you like, but after six hours, you'll be on overtime and running on empty. (MR)

BUSINESS CALLS

Get to the point: Assume everyone is as busy as you are. (JGF)

Phone dodges: There are a million different ways to get out of talking to someone on the telephone. So just choose one. But choose one that works.

Gotta go: The best way to duck out of a long-winded telephone conversation is to be straightforward and honest. Say, "I'm sorry, but I'm too busy to stay on the phone right now. Can we continue this later?" Try to accurately suggest how busy you are; unless you say so, your caller has no idea what's going on in your office.

Honesty is the best policy, but there are less honest alternatives: you'd like to continue the conversation face to face, you'll have to schedule an appointment; your secretary just slipped you a note saying you're late for an urgent meeting; you've got to call Europe before noon or three or five. (FHG)

Get back to you: You can save yourself a lot of unwanted incoming calls by being honest and informative. If somebody's calling to get information or a decision from you and you aren't ready to talk to them, either get on the line and say so (as briefly as you wish) or have your secretary say so. Offer an approximate call-back day and time, then try to stick to it. After all, when somebody is calling you for information or a decision, they are only asking you to do your job. (SB)

Never *not* return a phone call. Someday the guy trying to reach you may be trying to dodge you. You must be certain that you never, *ever* want to speak to somebody whose calls you aren't returning. (JGF)

Wrong line: If your secretary or receptionist has had a squabble with a caller, try not to get involved. The chances are, it was a misunderstanding between the two of them and the consequent embarrassment you could cause sorting it out would inevitably outweigh any benefit (provided, of course, the caller did not violate the bounds of decency or that your secretary didn't just lose your firm its biggest customer). Sometimes, callers are jerks who just like getting annoyed at secretaries, but if this happens with more than three different callers over the span of a year, it's probably your secretary's fault. (HH)

See also *Telephone Etiquette* **in** *CHAPTER SEVENTEEN: THE DEPORTMENT DEPARTMENT* **and** *Phone Contact* **under** *DATE DESIGN* **in** *CHAPTER SEVEN: MODERN MATING.*

BUSINESS LETTERS

should be as *brief* as possible. The point of the letter should be indicated in the first paragraph, and unless the subject is a rather complex one, the letter should not occupy more than a single page. (JE)

Learn to dictate on a dictation machine, thereby saving yourself and your secretary time. Remember, if she's a good secretary, she could be doing more important work than listening to you figure out your next sentence (and if she's *really* good, chances are she'll edit and rewrite the whole thing anyway). (GWa)

(**See also** *Five Things To Do Every Day to Help You Get Organized,* **below.**)

Officially unofficial: Company letterheads should be used for company correspondence only. (HK)

Dear Confused: If you aren't sure whether or not to use someone's first or last name in a letter's greeting, use both: i.e., "Dear Bob Smith." This is also the best practice if you aren't sure of a person's gender. (JG) If there's no personal name indicated on a piece of correspondence, it is acceptable to use "Dear Sir/Madam" if you aren't sure who your reader is. (RBr)

Your mstake: More than half the women in the country do not like Ms. as an honorific. Therefore, use the traditional Mrs. or Miss unless otherwise requested. (LKP) (This claim is unverified; **see also** *Feminine Honorifics* **under** *Introductions* in *CHAPTER SEVENTEEN: THE DEPORTMENT DEPARTMENT.*)

FIVE THINGS TO DO EVERY DAY TO HELP YOU GET ORGANIZED

If possible, do this stuff the night before; you'll sleep better.

1. Set your priorities by making a careful and thoughtful list. This is such an obvious aid that most people just skip it. Don't. Take the time to make a list every day.

2. Do the items you want to do least the first thing in the morning and get them out of the way.

3. Get all correspondence out of the way immediately, and if possible early in the day. (See also **Business Letters,** above.)

4. Meet with your staff frequently and make sure channels of communication are wide open. Make sure you always allow time to be available to discuss the staff's various projects and problems.

5. Commit one hour at the end of the day for reading. Go through all those newspapers and magazines that you'll lug around for weeks because you think there might be something useful in them. (GWa)

OFFICE POLITICS

Five qualities you must have in order to survive office politics (in order of importance):

1. Deceit. Learn to lie and deny with conviction. You must kiss ass without bending your knees.

2. Inscrutability. You must be able to smile sincerely at a guy whose back will carry your knife by quitting time.

3. Selective visibility. There are times when you must be seen to be believed. Other times, you want to be invisible.

4. Manipulativity. You must be able to convince some people to go with you while at the same time undermining the credibility of your competitors.

5. Talent. If you have more than you need, hide it. (RBr)

The virtue of incompetence: Awareness of one's own incompetence can be helpful since it teaches you to keep your head down and your ass covered. (KUG)

How much of corporate success is due to political agility and not talent: A canvas shows

- 65 percent (JGu)
- 75 percent (JGF)
- 85 percent (LKP)
- 65 to 90 percent, depending on the stakes. The higher the position, the safer the assumption of incompetence coupled with political skill. (RBr)

Mergers: Companies in the throes of a merger produce the most dangerous political situations. Be careful you don't choose the wrong side when two managers collide, as they inevitably will. If you do, you're out, along with the loser. (RBr)

The best survival tactic for office politics is to avoid them as much as possible. Scheming office politicos, back-stabbers and shortcut artists inevitably get their comeuppance — and often their pink slips. Forget about pleasing anyone but your immediate superior (and the more power he has the better). His loyalty will sustain you through any political housecleanings — provided he survives them himself. (RC)

CAUTION: WOMEN AT WORK

Harassment: Sexual harassment is the manifest power of sleaze. Men (and women) who use a position of professional superiority to intimidate a worker deserve all the hard knocks they will inevitably get.

Tell a friend: If you see a friend and colleague using power as a basis for intimidation, set him straight about the rules of decent behavior. Sexual harassment is the epitome of rudeness, since it provides the basis for actions that are extremely offensive. Don't presume to understand why a woman has elected to enter the workforce or why she has chosen to take a particular job. On a personal and nonideological basis, it doesn't matter, it's none of your business. Everyone should get an equal shot.

On the other hand, don't rush to convict every man accused of harassment. Everyone should get an equal break, too.

Don't forget, sexual harassment is a two-way street, and women in positions of power have also used sexual harassment as a workplace ploy. (LP, DB)

Don't mess around at work. It's never, ever worth it. One false step and you're looking at misery as a career perk. (SGH)

See also COURTLY MANNERS **and** CARDINAL RULES **in** CHAPTER SEVENTEEN: THE DEPORTMENT DEPARTMENT **and** *The Politics of Unemployment* **in** *HIRING ON,* **above.**

Never remain alone in a room with any female co-worker, unless you know her and trust her completely. (DF) Oh, *sure.*

Do not assume that your female co-workers have the same sense of humor your male colleagues have. The slightest off-color joke can mean the end of your job. (*Anon.*)

When your boss is a woman, and she starts crying, do *not* offer her any comfort. It may enrage her and it may spell the end of your career. (PTK)

Forget the rules you have learned as a man if a woman is your boss or colleague. Women tend to approach professional questions in a much more intuitive manner. Because this approach makes justification somewhat difficult, you must be cautious in attempting to impose a logical framework. I was demoted when I asked for clarification of a new policy developed by a woman recruited fresh from college. She was subsequently transferred when it was found to be an unworkable policy, but it took me a year to recover my position. So be careful. (*Anon.*)

UNIONS

The power of labor unions is directly correlated to lack of production and inability to compete in an open market. Unions of course were once necessary; now, however, unjustified exploitation of labor is generally subject to better redress by civil courts. (ER)

Most unions have successfully conveyed the impression that they're run by gangsters interested in cheating working men out of their money. They only remain in business because most companies have successfully conveyed the impression to working men that management is incompetent and insensitive. (*Anon.*)

FIVE THINGS YOU SHOULD KNOW ABOUT DELEGATING RESPONSIBILITY

1. Choose wisely: Carefully match the person and the task.

2. Follow up: Be realistic, but allow the person to whom you've delegated a task free rein to accomplish his work.

3. Critique and encourage: Give the task a value by taking the time to examine the way in which it was done. Encouragement is especially vital. (**See** *Supervising,* **below.**)

4. Up the ante: Demonstrate your confidence by making the next task a more demanding one.

5. Delegate almost everything: Save your time for the really important five percent of all tasks. (GWa)

SUPERVISING

Never underestimate the importance of supervisory encouragement. Pay is important, but assuming the salary is right, proper encouragement is crucial to your employees' continued high self-esteem, morale and performance. The better they look, the sweeter you smell. (RBr)

FIRING PEOPLE

Firing people is the downside of all the other upsides you enjoy as an employer or supervisor.

Start your conversation by reinforcing yourself as the employer. You're going to be more nervous, most likely, than the employee who doesn't know what's coming and it's not such a bad thing to show it. If possible, have someone else in the room (preferably someone to whom you report), as the employee will be less likely to get out of hand and misbehave if there are two people present.

Build your case over a period of time — and make sure it's in writing. Lawyers are everywhere.

Always fire them first thing in the morning. It will be easier on your psyche and cut down on the *angst*. Try never to do it on a Friday. (You don't want him to have a whole weekend to think about it and then have to attend his funeral on Monday morning.) In fact, Monday is the ideal day for an axing because he can go directly from his former office to the unemployment office and the employment agencies: giving him an immediate opportunity to do something about his new state of unemployment will help give him a sense of control over his situation.

Be positive. Talk about his good or strong points and encourage his worth. Don't overdo this or he won't understand why you're doing it and you might forget and the whole thing will get so confused that he might end up with your job. (GWa)

SCAMS

We all know a few people who spend their lives working very hard at trying to get rich without working. (PJO)

POWER

For secular success, this is the big one, the only one that counts.

WHO HAS IT

Almost nobody has real power. Look around you. Divide your working world into two groups; let the first group represent those who have the power to say "yes" or "no" and let the second group represent those who have only the power to say "no."

Your first list will have very few names on it: The President, maybe the Chairman of the Board. Almost everybody will be on the second list: receptionists, secretaries, administrative assistants, vice-presidents. Anyone can say "no."

The trouble is, nobody wants to appear powerless. Therefore, those who have the power to say "no" exercise their franchise with wild abandon, since admitting they will have to ask a superior for the power to say "yes" is crippling to their self-esteem. (PJO)

SPEECH

The power of speech is the ultimate double-edged sword. A well-timed, cutting word aims at your adversary's jugular. If your timing's off, however, it'll wrap around your wrist.

WHEN TO SPEAK

At meetings: Never to fill empty air. Think of every opportunity to speak as a scoring opportunity in basketball. Don't waste your shots. Watch the play progress, keep your eye on the ball.

During an argument: Think of words as ammo. Let your partner use up all of his before you even load. Until then, you should speak only so much as is necessary to keep the argument on rational lines. An argument usually has only one or two key points. Address yourself to these points only. (RD)

WHEN NOT TO SPEAK

Never utter a word when you're not certain of its effect. It goes without saying that you should never speak when you don't know what you're talking about. (RD)

Idiot Savant: If you don't know, say so. Saying "I don't know" removes the pressure from everyone else in the room who would feel compelled to answer with a lie a question to which they have no answer. (GLS)

JAWS

Unless you are perfectly sure of your ground and equally sure that the person or people you are with want to hear what you have to say, remain silent. That way, you'll keep your feet and other foolish things out of your mouth. (GC)

MAKING A SPEECH

Making a speech is *almost* a no-win proposition. If you do a bad job or a fair job or an average job, it's all one to the audience, most of whom will think you're catfood. But if your speech is absolutely *brilliant* — the best public utterance since Quintilian — you've won. So loosen up. Relax. You're dead meat.

Focus on the content of your speech, rather than on the impression you think you'll make. If you're confident of the subject matter, the speech can be written in outline form.

If you try this, you should also try to *rehearse* the speech once or twice in front of your family, or in front of your family dog. If you're successful in using brief notes or an outline, it will give your speech an improvised quality that will spotlight your command of the subject. The other way open to you is to write the speech out in full; this will help your confidence, but unless you also memorize big chunks of the speech, it'll put your audience to sleep watching you read out loud.

Dress in a dark business suit with a conservative tie, unless the occasion clearly calls for something different. You should try to convey an attitude of confidence and credibility. Don't chew on your necktie.

Thanking whoever introduced you is one way of warming up and getting used to the sound of your own voice. If you really want to go Oscar-style, you can thank the guy who introduced you, then the presiding officer of the meeting or the director of the sponsoring organization, then the organization, and finally the ladies and gentlemen present. Don't thank your wife for having faith in you unless you really are accepting an Oscar.

If you're sure it's funny and somehow appropriate, you can start your speech with an observation or anecdote.

Gestures help, but make sure they're natural. Don't wave your hands around like a chicken would, but don't jam them in your pockets, either. If you can't help it and you just *have* to put your hands in your pockets, make sure you don't have any keys or change that will make a racket.

Don't make any important points during the first minute or so; your audience also needs a little time to warm up.

The quality of your voice is very important. It should be low in pitch, but projected well enough to reach the back of the room. Avoid monotony and slow down — the speech should unroll at the rate of a hundred words a minute (that's a little less than one-half of a double-spaced, typed page).

Be concise and to the point: If you start to ramble, the audience will start to snore. Keep it simple; avoid pretentious language.

Close without fading away: Wrap it up with some wit. Say thank you and get out.

Yes? No, you in the pink leisure suit. If there is a question period, conduct yourself with breathtaking honesty, so that when somebody asks something you don't know, you can say, "I don't know," instead of trying to fake something. If somebody gets the floor and threatens to make a speech even longer and more boring than your own, cut him off by interrupting and asking him, What is your question? (GT)

MAKING A TOAST

Brevity should increase with sentimentality ("To my beloved wife, Annie") but may be inversely proportional to the quality of wit. Make an attempt to keep the toast appropriate to the occasion. (GT)

French toast: For drinking in the presence of foreigners, a list:

British	*Cheers*	French	*A votre santé*
German	*Prosit*	Irish	*Sláinte*
Italian	*Salute*	Polish	*Na zdrowie*
Russian	*Na zdorovye*	Spanish	*Salud*
Swedish	*Skoäl*	Hebrew	*L'Chayim*

TITLES

Up to age thirty-five or so, titles count more than cash. After age thirty-five, the money and the moniker should go hand-in-hand; generally, a company that gives you a better title without a concurrent raise is asking you to shop around. To figure the dollar value of your title in such circumstances, here's how:

Take the amount of your present salary and subtract it from the amount you would be earning if you were making a salary commensurate with your title. Next, add the amount that you would be willing to sacrifice in order to get out of your present job. This is a fixed number for people aged thirty-six, thirty-seven, thirty-eight and thirty-nine. Once you turn forty, you have to multiply this figure by 1.5 for each year up to age fifty; people aged fifty and over should multiply by a factor of 1.75 per year. (TPD)

BE WARY

of the method of determining a title's value by its ability to impress others. There is inevitably the risk that sooner or later someone will discover exactly what it is you *really* do, and if that happens, after the laughter dies down they'll call you a snob and stop inviting you to play golf. (This method is useful, however, when lining up one-night stands in foreign cities.) (JO)

NO PAYOFF

Taking the title instead of the raise rarely pays off. If you're counting on the title to take you up in a lateral move, forget it. A title almost never takes you that far. (RBr)

MEMO, THE ART OF THE

A truly great memo is worth approximately 2.75 truly great meetings. A great memo lives longer than a great man; once circulated, it is filed under "P" for plagiarism, and will reappear on an almost daily basis throughout the history of the company. So make sure your name's on it where it says "From" and make sure your present boss (and any potential future boss) has his name where it says "To."

MEMORANDUM

Day, month, year
To: Did you read the paragraph above?
From: Did you?
Re: A Subject That Seems to Puzzle Everyone But You

As you know, the first sentence of your memo should make clear the subject of the document in terms that are nonthreatening to your superior, perhaps by framing the statement as an obvious observation that you both share. The second sentence should be much more straightforward.
1. The First Subhead:
    The first subhead should be followed by several sentences that establish the limits of

the argument to which this memo will address itself. One sentence should outline several crucial factors: It should do this briskly and with confidence; it should not shirk from pinpointing uncomfortable fallacies; it should summarize, not catalog. At the same time, however, there are other perhaps contradictory factors that must also be considered, factors that must weigh in the decision you are going to help your superior make by the time this memo is complete.

2. The Second Subhead:

This is the middle of the memo, and in this section, every sentence should tell a story. Each story must build on the one that precedes it. And each must move the argument a little further along the lines you wish it to follow. So these sentences are important. Together, they must bear the scrutiny this central section invites. They must have a structural integrity sufficient to support the architecture of your argument.

Then the truth can come out in a single, simple sentence.

3. The Third Subhead:

This is the dénouement; everybody reading this memo already knows your point of view. All that's left is for you to try to show why the idea that you and your superior have shared together in this intimate document is a brilliant one not only for the common good of everyone else, but especially for you two. So make this section short — maybe three or four sentences. (TD)

ANOTHER, SOMEWHAT DISSENTING, VIEW

Memo writing remains one of the last bastions of original and creative expression in the corporate world. It is crucial to remember, however, that the results of good memo writing are delayed in time. No one will read your memo contemporaneously. It will be thrown away on the spot by everyone without being read; it will survive in an obscure file which will be used against you in the future, probably when you're up for a promotion after your current assignment falls to pieces.

The secret to successful memo writing falls into three categories. First, say as little as possible. *The ideal memo says nothing at all.* Keeping in mind that every memo will be received poorly by at least one person in a more powerful position than yours, you must develop the flexibility to assign several meanings to everything you write. Once you put a complete thought in print, you lose the ability to deny having said anything. Think of memo writing as playing out a bad hand at poker: you need to show worthless cards in such a way that you present a message without having revealed what you're really holding.

Second, sound informed. It is not necessary that you know what you're talking about, so long as you sound like you do. Copious use of graphs and charts and devoting a major portion of the memo to restatements of the obvious are superior means of achieving this. Appeals to authority must be avoided: Quoting someone in a position superior to yours may seem to be an attractive idea, but it's not. While quoting the CEO will no doubt make you sound well-informed, when it comes time for the CEO to change his mind, somebody has to be made a liar. Guess who?

Third, always be prepared to blame someone else, preferably someone with a lower position than yours (superiors have been successfully blamed, but it's very risky) for an unexpected failure. There are some standard phrases used to accomplish this — "based on discussions with our planning department" or "in accordance with our sales manager's new policy" — but care must be taken to prepare a strong defense in case the person blamed decides to fight back. Then the underlying premise is that the person with the most documentation wins. So doctor your telephone diary and set up your secretary so she can confirm that you actually were on the phone. Anything goes, so use your imagination and have a little fun. (JO)

REVENGE

Revenge must be seen as a risky investment in which you will either gain a great deal or lose much more than you can afford. Therefore, we don't recommend it. If, however, you just can't help yourself

MAKE IT FAST

Don't mess around. Don't stew over it. The romantic notion that you will wait a lifetime to avenge some slight is bullshit. The chances are, the longer you wait, the more your determination to seek revenge will cool. (GeY)

THE RETURN

Be sure the screwing you give is worth the one you'll get. (TRF)

CLICHÉS

Every cliché I've ever heard about revenge is true, especially the one about success being the sweetest variety. If you really want to get even with a cheating girlfriend or wife, get along better without her than you did with her. (*Anon*)

SMALL BUSINESS AND SELF-EMPLOYMENT

Self-employment is the natural state of servitude, the preferred circumstance of employment. The beauty bit is you can't get fired unless you go out of business; the bad bit is you've got nobody to blame when you're fired.

Starting a small business, on the other hand, is like volunteering for reptile duty.

ESTIMATING WORK

Figure your time and materials, then double them. (JJF)

FIXING A FEE

For people working free-lance, an hourly rate is best. You'll receive fair compensation for your services, and you're not as likely to be abused by doing a lot of extraneous work under a fixed price. The client is happier, too, because he can bail out at any time, or restrict your employment to those areas in which you possess some expertise and delegate the rest of the job to other experts.

If you charge a high hourly fee, you'd better justify it by producing at a high rate, or you'll price yourself out of the market. (JJF)

THE WRONG SHOPPING LIST FOR THE NOVICE ENTREPRENEUR

There's a world of things out there you think you ought to own when you open your own shop. Here are some of the most seductive (and most useless):

- A postage meter
- An answering service
- A receptionist's area
- A set of personalized pens and mugs
- Four-color brochures
- Radio and TV spots
- A complicated telephone system
- A computer bigger than the one your kids have at home
- A company car
- A company credit card   (DSF)

THE RIGHT STUFF

The whole idea is to keep overhead low so that when your business grows, you're playing with house money, not your own.

- Stamps
- A cheap answering machine
- Simple business cards, envelopes and letterhead
- A Western Electric desk phone with Touch-Tone dialing (two lines, maximum)
- An Apple computer, Macintosh is good. Get something that everybody can learn to use quickly. Unless you're involved in technology, the kinds of computers that are beloved by scientists are an office burden. In an office, a computer should be as simple to operate as a standard typewriter or a photocopier.
- One decent, steady client whose monthly invoices will cover your nut. (DSF)

See also *DECISION-MAKING, PROTECTING AND SELLING AN IDEA* **and** *AC-COUNTANTS* **in** *CHAPTER THREE: MODERN MONEY* **and** *STATIONERY* **in** *CHAPTER NINETEEN: A MODERN MISCELLANY.*

RETIREMENT ACCOUNTS
   See under *SAVING MONEY* **in** *CHAPTER THREE: MODERN MONEY.*

GLAMOR JOBS

For some men, the most glamorous jobs are the ones that make strange women act like fawning jerks when you tell them what you do. Modern Men, of course, know that there is no such thing as a glamorous job.

For women, however, the *most* glamorous jobs are in the TV broadcasting biz, while other jobs become glamorous if women do them instead of men. Women working as welders, priests and firefighters thereby accrue vocational glamor as part of their paycheck. (JHe)

Anyone who has what many consider to be a glamorous job knows it is in reality much closer to a job than it is to glamor. (EDM)

TV NEWS CAREERS

   First, read the entry *GLAMOR JOBS,* **above.**

In the TV news business, almost all jobs are jobs that might be considered glamorous by many postadolescent girls and some preadult boys. Many youthful people, for example, consider a TV journalist's job to be the most glamorous job in the world.

Tawny Little did. Tawny Little was a nice girl from Westchester who won a beauty contest. As a result, she became a well-tanned news reader on the ABC outlet in Los Angeles, and later she married a guy who played a fast-driving hillbilly on a TV show that got canceled.

Maria Shriver, one of the Kennedy children (better yet, one of the Kennedy children without a police record), thought it would be glamorous to get up before dawn and go to CBS's 57th Street building and interview people as rich and famous as her relatives. So she did, and later she married a weightlifter from Austria.

When Diane Sawyer was a secretary in the civil service, who would ever guess that she would eventually get a job on *60 Minutes* where she could lord it over other glamorous types, like Geraldo Rivera, whose real name is Jerry Rivers. Happily, her secretarial slot was at Nixon's White House, so her wish came true. Alas, *People* magazine recently pointed out that she was an "old maid," and might, therefore, never get married to somebody as glamorous as she is. But she probably dates a lot.

It should be clear by now that glamorous jobs lead to glamorous lives. (*Anon.*)

WHAT IT TAKES

If you want to be a TV news personality, here's what it takes:

1. *You should be female,* preferably a female member of a minority group. You must, however, try as hard as possible to sound like a white male. Listen to women who work in radio and TV news. Do you think they talk like that around the house?

If you're something other than female, you should have close family members in the dentistry and hair-care fields.

2. *You should be a college graduate* who majored in something called Communications. A network news personnel director — an old hand at the business — pointed out with some sadness that the networks are no longer interested in hiring print journalists, the traditional background of correspondents and anchormen. "The people we're hiring can't write complete sentences," he said.

3. *You must be able to project what one network vice-president called "believability."* You can cheat on your wife and cheat on your taxes, but if you can look straight into a camera and pretend you understand what you're saying, you can get on TV no sweat.

4. *Although you don't necessarily need to be able to write* the language you speak on the air, it helps enormously if you can read it. Generally, as a TV newsman you read what other, more literate people write. Devices like TelePrompTers exist so that TV news personalities will have something to say that can be understood by a majority of people. Sometimes, though, you have to come up with something yourself. In that case, do what countless radio and TV journalists do every day: read the morning paper and plagiarize like crazy. In England, where truth in packaging counts, anchorpersons are called news readers.

5. *Be pretty.* Winning a beauty pageant qualifies you to cover the news. But if you can't pass muster on the beauty front, be cute. Jane Pauley's cute, and she gets a lot of money to say cute things on NBC every morning. Sometimes, the cute things she says even make sense. It depends on what kind of night you had.

6. *If you have a normal attention span, shorten it.* Ditto, your vocabulary.

7. *Make certain that your view of every story you cover conforms to conventional wisdom.* If you work in TV, you probably won't have much of an independent point of view anyway, so talk to a lot of people around the office and see what they think of the world. If you get seriously divergent opinions on an issue, ask for a show of hands. Get someone to help you count. (*Anon.*)

See also under *How to Sharpen an Axe* **in** *CHAPTER ONE: OUTDOORS.*

Modern Money

If you compare money with something more inherently compelling — like, say, sex, or maybe vice — you can see that something's right with the priorities of Modern Men. Not only did we draw more contributions from guys on the other two subjects, the stuff we got was a lot more fun to read.

    Money is what you make when you run out of jokes. That's why everybody takes it so seriously. But Modern Men know that while money pays the bills, sex and vice is what it buys.

C O N T E N T S
Chapter Three: *MODERN MONEY*

DECISION-MAKING

Ever since the days of boar hunting for groceries, the choice of the right alternative has been a make or break situation.

No choice: When confronted by two complex alternatives (say, a big promotion you've been offered will involve your being away from your family for weeks at a time), try to discern any possible benefit or liability on either side that is so compelling as to decide the matter for you — in effect, leaving you no choice to make.

If no such factor emerges, you will have at least streamlined the situation to the point where you can rank the benefits, decide which alternative is the best one and (most important) which one you ought to forget. (AW)

PROTECTING AND SELLING AN IDEA

The frustrating thing about great ideas — all those better mousetraps — is that it's far more difficult and certainly more expensive to protect and sell a better mousetrap than it is to dream up the mousetrap in the first place. In fact, a tremendous amount of time and money is required to make your idea into a financially rewarding reality.

Start with a good patent attorney; if he's competent, he'll evaluate your idea for you and try to discourage you if he feels the idea isn't potentially profitable. If he encourages you to proceed, however, here's a rough timetable of key events with approximate costs:

- The patent search. Cost: $500. Time: Six weeks
- Filing the patent application. Cost: $1,000. Time: 30 days
- Negotiation and petition. Cost: $700. Time: Three years
- Federal patent fee. Cost: $200. Time: Varies

So you're looking at a substantial investment. By the time everything is settled, you may have spent as much as $3,000. (SR)

APPROACHING A COMPANY

To start with, do some homework. A company that specializes in soap isn't going to be particularly interested in your new computer peripheral. Write or call the company you wish to approach and request a submission form. Discuss the form with your attorney, if you like, then sign and return it, along with your proposal.

The proposal can be as humble or as elegant as you like. It's a straightforward marketing decision on your part to determine whether or not it's appropriate for your product. If you decide to go for the glitz, contact one of the many businesses that are prepared to do this kind of work. It will have art directors, copywriters, photographers and creative directors that will charge you a lot and deliver a slam-bang presentation. (But watch them. You're better off if you know what you want before you go to them.)

Once you've made your pitch, you've done all you can do for the moment. If the company accepts your idea, get your attorney to join in the negotiations for royalties. If it says no, then shop around for another customer and try again.

The companies that you approach with your idea will be far more inclined to take it seriously if you have the patent process underway.

If you exhaust your possibilities without success, you must confront an even larger commitment than the patent process: You must decide whether or not you should manufacture your invention yourself. If you reach this point, and you don't have very deep pockets and a lot of free time, hang it up. (SR)

BEWARE

Watch out for companies that run ads claiming to be able to successfully market your invention — especially if they contact you. They can become very expensive and the work they do can be nearly worthless. Most of them — in fact, all of them that we know of — have a zero success rate in selling anybody's idea. (SR)

PARANOIA STRIKES DEEP

And often not without cause. But please bear in mind that although it has happened, a very small number of ideas are actually stolen by companies and individuals from inventors. As a rule, watch out for toy manufacturers; publishers, at the other extreme, tend to be surprisingly ethical. (If you want to see the sad side of product paranoia, watch a poet go to the trouble of filing a copyright on his work. Incredible.) (SR)

SAVING MONEY

Unless you are fortunate enough to have developed a mature sense of responsibility rather early in life, saving money isn't something you think much about during the first years of your bachelorhood. For many of us, the notion of saving money is pleasant but somehow remote until we find ourselves faced with those obligations that inform the Modern Man: providing for the needs of a family and ensuring the comfort of our wives and ourselves in old age.

KEOGHS AND INDIVIDUAL RETIREMENT ACCOUNTS

If you're hearing it here first, you're already in trouble: if you're under the age of forty or so, you will never see a cent of all that money the Social Security Administration has been borrowing from you all these years. Never. No matter what they say. That gives even more importance to IRAs and Keogh accounts. They are a wonderful financial invention; strict adherence to an IRA plan will keep you safe in your dotage. And even if you have to borrow from the bank to feed your fund, you're still coming out ahead. (*Anon.*) *Note:* Recent tax law changes may have had an effect on IRAs and Keoghs.

POCKET CHANGE

One way of accumulating a healthy five hundred dollars or so every year is to save all your change. And we mean *all* your change. This forced savings program means you often have to be a pill with cashiers, because the rule is to never, ever, spend change. You must always break bills, no matter how small your purchase. Every evening, separate your coins into containers. Once a year, roll the coins and take them to the bank for deposit into your IRA or to augment a holiday budget. The inevitable acceptance of the dollar coin (which will, we predict, never be of the quarter-sized Susan B. Anthony variety) will result in significantly increased savings. You should bear in mind that this sort of savings plan is rather expensive, since tin cans full of coins pay no interest during the time you take to accumulate them. Pennies are simply not worth the bother (it would take twenty years to save $1000 worth of the things), but should instead be used to round off odd-cents purchases. (AR)

NUMBER ONE

The old chestnut "pay yourself first" is one of the most important parts of a personal savings plan. If you get a regular paycheck, sign up for a payroll deduction plan. Let someone else put some of your money aside before you get a chance to misspend it. (TV)

MONEY MEMORY

Once you put money into a savings account, forget it. It never existed. Don't even think about it. Leave it alone. (DA)

See also *FINANCIAL PLANNING* **and** *INVESTMENTS,* **below.**

FINANCIAL PLANNING

Once the sole province of the confused rich, these days financial consultants often find themselves working on behalf of the confused middle-income client.

Financial consultants are certified by the IAFP Registry of Financial Planners in Washington, D.C., or by the Denver College of Financial Planners. Try to get a statement of the consultant's financial resources and situation.

Planners work on either a commission basis or a fee basis and are usually affiliated with a financial institution (bank, brokerage house, insurance company and the like). Don't be shy about asking for references and how long your planner has been in business. It's a new field, so five years is about average.

Exposing your monetary situation and your financial aspirations to a stranger can resemble a visit to a psychiatrist's office. The main thing to remember is to trust your instincts. If it just doesn't feel right, or if you start having serious misgivings, get out. (LO)

A dissent: Financial planners are part of a huge nonservice industry that has grown up around the pretensions of the middle class; they encourage perfectly normal people to behave like paranoid creeps.

You don't need a financial planner until your income reaches the level of a major corporation. An angry God has already visited accountants and lawyers on us and there is little benefit in inviting another helping of wrath. (MNR)

See also *SAVING MONEY* **and** *INVESTMENTS* **in this chapter.**

INVESTMENTS

The guy editing this once invested in a small business and he's still paying the bills for his mistake. So, with that understood, take what advice you like from here, but since the purpose of investing is to make more money from money, you have to reckon there's a variable chance of also making a lot less money from money.

Here're some elementary rules:
- Keep your debts under control
- Set aside enough money for maintenance of your home and car and to take care of inevitable emergencies
- Any spare money should be diversified. You'll want some funds to be liquid (in bank accounts, for example), some for inflation protection (property, say, or precious metals), and some as a boom hedge (stocks and bonds).

You can, if you wish, take every cent you own and, based on what you read here, invest it all in some wild and weird widget venture. We won't be responsible for the outcome if you lose it all; we will expect a 20 percent commission, however, if you clean up. If there were absolute rules governing surefire investment winners, we'd be buying and selling paper and not printing low-cost advice on the stuff. After all, even hot insider tips like these don't come with any guarantee.

COMMON SENSE

Don't invest in things you don't understand. If you don't know how the restaurant business works, for example, how can you possibly make an informed decision about whether or not you should invest your savings in a new diner? Or if you want to specu-

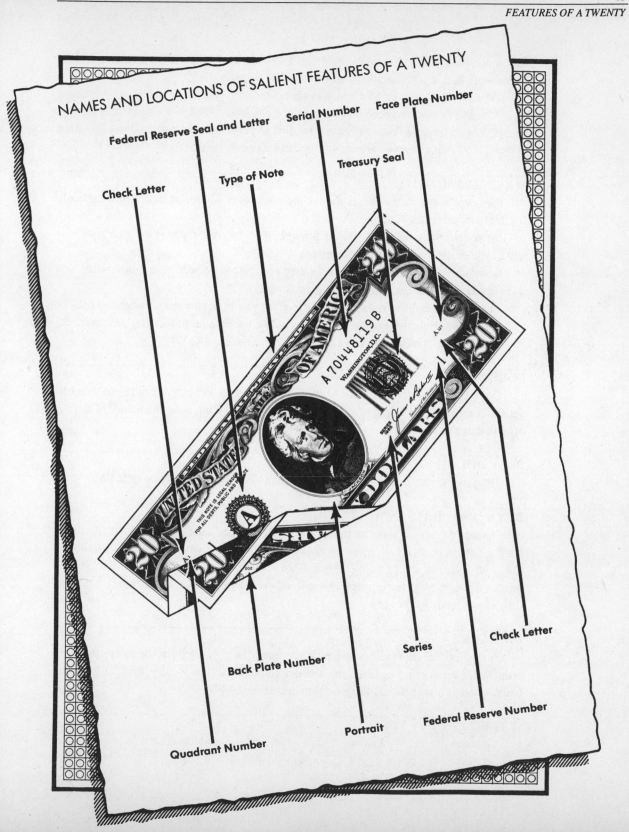

NAMES AND LOCATIONS OF SALIENT FEATURES OF A TWENTY

Federal Reserve Seal and Letter

Serial Number

Face Plate Number

Check Letter

Type of Note

Treasury Seal

Check Letter

Series

Back Plate Number

Portrait

Federal Reserve Number

Quadrant Number

late in computers, fine. But make sure you know as much as possible about how computers work before you throw your money into the industry. (AR)

A dissent: Follow your best hunch or the best advice you can get from an investment counselor and don't try to become an expert in the field in which you've put your money. Few people understand semiconductors, but lots of people have made a killing investing in them. How many people understand a savings account, for that matter? (*Anon.*)

MAXIMUM MAXIMS

Buy cheap, sell dear. This is the bedrock maxim of all commerce, and it certainly applies to investments.

Do your homework, think things through, then buy what you think everyone else will buy after they've done *their* homework. (JKL)

Remember, it's better to buy an investment than to be sold one; figure what you want in advance, then go find it before it finds you.

Avoid investing in anything that is offered to you by a stranger through the mail or over the phone. He's not making you a great offer because he thinks you're a beautiful guy who deserves a break. He's just hoping you're a sucker. (RSW)

FORGET IT

Do as old ladies do. Buy some blue chip stocks when you can afford them, then forget about them and let them grow. Pretend like the whole thing never happened. The payoff will come in your old age. (WR)

PLAY DOUGH

"Playing" the market is tricky, uncertain, and very rarely makes one rich. (WR)

BUY STRAW HATS IN WINTER

Owning fashionable stocks might bring you lots of flattery on the cocktail circuit, but the patient purchase of unfashionable ones will pay off when it counts. Although it seems obvious that stocks riding high in April are doomed by economic inevitabilities to be shot down in May, most people are still inclined to buy into a winner ready to plunge than a loser ready to rise. (*Anon.*)

C-CHANGE

A market that's episodic or going nowhere may be signaling that the forces that have propelled it are starting to falter and a major commodity shift — say, from utilities and banks to drugs and chemical firms — is in the offing. (AW)

IF IT FIZZES, BUY IT

To some degree, stocks rise and fall generically. A sudden upturn in one beverage firm, for instance, might signal a sympathetic rise in the stock of its competitor, as investors, anxious to capitalize on what they perceive to be a growing beverage market, turn to it in an effort to get in on the action. (*Anon.*)

GO-GO BROKERS

While there are no risk-free investments (outside the banks), the conservative — or vanilla — mutual funds give a good, steady long-term performance for those with only a few thousand a year to invest. Somewhat riskier, but not really dangerous, are the "go-go" mutual funds available through your broker. (AW)

THAT AIN'T WORKIN'

Stock options: Any man with a relatively small amount of money to invest and who is nonetheless looking for some interesting market action should consider the options market.

In the options market, a buyer pays a premium — the price of the option — for the right to buy or sell a specific stock at a set (or "striking") price within a predetermined period of time. This gives the investor who believes that a certain stock is about to move dramatically up or down the opportunity to make a substantial profit while limiting his risk. Here's an example of how it works:

Say you believe that the stock for a firm called — what? — Shoes for Industry, now selling for fifty bucks a share, will double in value over the next three months. If you wanted to go out and buy a hundred shares of SFI you know that you'd be risking five grand for the acquisition. Rather than take this risk, you decide to go the options route and ask your broker to buy you a "call" option, which is an option to *buy* shares (options to *sell* shares are called "put" options), for a hundred shares of SFI with a set price of fifty dollars and an expiration date three months down the road. The options tables in your local paper (or at your broker's office) tell you that SFI call options for that set price (fifty dollars) over that length of time (three months) is three and a half, meaning that your option purchase price for the stock is $3.50 per share, or $350 for the hundred shares you want. (I got the basics for this example from Sylvia Porter's *Money Book,* but I learned about it through firsthand experience.)

Here's what can happen to your investment over the course of the three months:

• *Shoes for Industry climbs* to about ninety-five bucks a share — almost what you'd predicted. Exercising your option, you now purchase the hundred shares for fifty dollars each, then turn right around and sell them on the market for ninety-five dollars each, netting you about $4000 profit ($9500 for the sale of the stock, less $350 for the call option, less $5000 for the purchase of the stock at fifty dollars each, less about $150 in broker's fees). That's more than a 1000 percent return on investment.

• *Shoes for Industry walks off a cliff* and lands somewhere around thirty bucks a share. Your loss, however, is limited to the $350 (plus about twenty-five dollars in brokerage fees) that went toward the purchase of your option. You comfort yourself by figuring how much you'd be out if you'd bought SFI at fifty dollars three months earlier.

There are many other methods of investing with options. Additional information can be obtained for free from:

The Chicago Board of Options Exchange

141 Jackson Boulevard

Chicago, IL 60604. (*Anon.*)

Stock index options: Recently, the Chicago Board of Options Exchange (CBOE), the underwriters of all option purchases, introduced a new type of option called a stock index option, which enables an investor to speculate on the *overall* performance of the market.

This reduces half your decision-making. With a stock option, you not only have to be right on the stock, but also on your market timing. With a stock index option, you only have to be right on the timing — you don't have to worry about one single stock, since you own them all.

How do they work? They're based on any one of the three market indicators — the Standard & Poor's 100, the Standard & Poor's 500 and the Value Line Index.

Let's say we want to use the S&P 100 for our option. As I write, the S&P 100 is at 182. You purchase an option on this index (just as you would on an individual stock); let's say you choose a three-month expiration at 180. The cost will be approximately five hundred dollars. If the market moves your direction between now and when the option expires, you make your money. You couldn't care less about any individual company's performance; remember, all you care about is overall performance. (JDeN)

WHAT CAN YOU EXPECT FROM A BROKER?

Here's a list of things you should expect from a good broker:
- *Accessibility.* Can he meet your request for information?
- *An understanding* of your investment goals
- *The ability* to hold your hand when you're losing

And here's what you should *never* accept from a broker:
- *Advice.* Be your own man. If you haven't the time to research and choose your own investments, then you should avoid the stock market. (JDeN)

See also SAVING MONEY **and** FINANCIAL PLANNING **in this chapter.**

ACCOUNTANTS

Only a doctor can deliver worse news than an accountant. But while doctors are regarded as mystics and sages, accountants have been burdened with an undeserved reputation for being dim and boring number-crunchers. In fact, if you were as smart as your accountant, you'd be as rich as your accountant, which you probably aren't. And as for imagination, the federal pens are chock full of imaginative accountants.

THE TRINITY

Accountants — unlike some other white-collar pros — are actually necessary to bring significant improvements to the quality of the practical side of your life. They are the grown-ups in a world made messy by adolescent fiscal tantrums. (DB) Accountants come in three varieties:

Bookkeepers are the junior partners of the accounting industry. They keep records of expenses and credits, balance the checkbook and sometimes even write the checks. Bookkeepers are essential to small-businessmen and the disorganized self-employed.

Corporate accountants, to use one of the more descriptive terms for noncertified accountants, keep track of the financial interests of the companies and firms by which they are employed.

Certified public accountants: These are the ones we're interested in here. CPAs are the pros, the heavy cruisers of the columnar books who handle complicated company and individual accounts. The CPA also supervises and reviews the work of the other two varieties of accountants. When it seems to you that you need an accountant, you need a CPA. Certified public accountants are tested and licensed by each state; national CPAs are federally accredited. (RW)

IF YOU HAD TO SAVE UP TO BUY THIS BOOK

you don't need a CPA for your taxes — you just need a stamp and a 1040 short form. If you're a slightly confused W-2 kind of guy and you hate arithmetic, go see H&R Block or some other such tax preparer. But if you have a fair amount of interest income from investments like real estate, stocks or mutual funds, or if your tax forms start including schedules C, F or E and information about partnerships and all that, then go to a CPA. Self-employed types can also benefit from the services of a CPA. (RW)

PLAY IT STRAIGHT

CPAs can lose their state licenses if they betray their own stringent code of ethics. So don't ask a CPA to lie for you, cheat for you or otherwise misbehave on your behalf. They aren't going to turn you in to the IRS police or anything, but they also aren't going to do anything dishonest for you, so don't even ask. Also, they can't work from the bottom line up. CPAs charge hourly rates or assess fees on a retainer basis; they don't accept a commission on what they save you on taxes. And finally, CPAs are quite useless if you give them useless or false information.

In filing your taxes, a CPA is responsible for any math or filing error, but his responsibility ends with the information you have provided him. If you alter your income or expenses, it's your ass on the line, not his. (RW)

AN ACCOUNTANT IS NOT AN INVESTMENT COUNSELOR

or a money manager or a financial planner. A CPA can advise you on the tax consequences of a given investment, but it's not his job to determine the direct worth of an investment. Occasionally, however, he may hear of a good investment that would suit your financial structure or suggest investments that will specifically help your taxes. (RW)

KEEP IN TOUCH

with your CPA. You'll avoid a lot of surprises that way; if you only talk to your accountant in April, don't be shocked if he tells you that you owe ten grand by the end of the week. Keep your accountant periodically informed of your financial situation — at least once a quarter. A CPA only knows what you tell him; if he isn't kept current, don't expect him to provide you with instant answers and solutions to your financial problems.

You can get as financially intertwined with your accountant as you wish (or as much as you can afford to). The requirements for a close relationship vary from person to person and circumstance to circumstance; some require a CPA for only a few hours annually, while others need an accountant on a daily basis. (RW)

FINDING A CPA

is best done by word of mouth. Get references from friends and colleagues. (RW)

BRIBERY, THE ART OF

Bribery almost never happens. "Almost" is the operative word, however, since a bribe is never spoken of nor alluded to. Instead, it is something that simply passes by, like a spring shower.

Present the cash to the person you're trying to bribe by letting him see it while making it apparent that the offering might be simply an oversight. For example, if you're trying to bribe a cop for a traffic offense, hand over your wallet with a bill pulled partway out. If he takes the money and returns your wallet, say absolutely *nothing* about the money. If, on the other hand, he asks if you're trying to bribe him, answer that you're not, and if he asks about the exposed bill, simply say that you must be more careful with your money. The principle of presenting money accidentally on purpose is the same with all bribes. The amount should never be less than twenty dollars, and a fifty- or one-hundred-dollar bill may be required in some circumstances.

The method of bribing politicians, magistrates, corporate executives and military buyers is considerably different, involving much greater sums of money. (*Anon.*)

See also *How to Bribe a New York City Housing Inspector under CHAPTER FOURTEEN: MODERN MAINTENANCE* **and** *Fixing a Ticket* **in** *CHAPTER SIXTEEN: MODERN MISHAPS*.

Modern Motors

Does just the thought of leaving the warmth and comfort of your home to go out and purchase a motorcar smack of gross self-abuse?

Modern Men assume an element of disposability in the use and maintenance of cars; after all, you could drive yourself nuts trying to figure out how much you don't know about automobiles. So while showing up at an automobile dealer's showroom might seem like volunteering to do dentistry for sharks, there is in fact a right way to go about buying a car.

C O N T E N T S
Chapter Four: *MODERN MOTORS*

NEW CAR BUYING: New Car Salesmen — Homework: Make a Checklist — Shopping — Test Drive — Bottom Line: *The Final Deal / Options / Financing — Leasing: Open and Closed Agreements — Beware the Banks* — USED CARS: Types — Prices — When to Shop — When to Sell — Ready for Repairs? — Where to Shop: New and Used Car Dealers / Rental Agencies / Auctions / Classified Ads — Those Who Ignore History Buy Lemons — Rebuilt Blues — Wreck-mechs: Trainee Grease-Monkeys — How to Inspect a Used Car — Cheap Two-Tone Trash: Best Rolling Wrecks — The Modern Man High-Mileage, Ultra-Reliable Used Car Hall of Fame — CAR CARE: Periodic Maintenance — Fluids and Filters Change Schedule — Tune-ups — Ignition System **— Exterior — Interior — Buying Tires — Spare Parts — Keeping a Junker Rolling — The Last Straw: When to Wreck a Wreck — Car Problems You Can Fix Yourself — The Modern Man Grand Unified Theory of Automobile Troubleshooting — Auto Troubleshooting Chart — CAR EMERGENCY KIT: What You Shouldn't Leave Home Without — The Carburetor**

NEW CAR BUYING

There are basically two kinds of cars you can buy: cars with new problems and cars with old problems. We'll start with new ones:

NEW CAR SALESMEN

Car salesmen do not occupy a separate zoölogical territory from the rest of us. In fact, most of them aren't all that bad. They're just people trying to make a living selling cars. A true professional will even look out for your interests — as well as his own, of course — because he's aware of the importance of word-of-mouth advertising and because he'd like to have you back as a repeat customer. (GW)

HOMEWORK

The first thing you should do is decide what type of car you want — a small convertible or a large van. This may seem elementary, but eliminating impulse decisions from car shopping is important, and you'd be surprised how many people walk into a showroom thinking about a sports car and drive out in a station wagon.

Make a checklist of features, options and specifications that are important to you: five-speed or automatic transmission; premium stereo or knob-tuned AM radio; power steering; trunk capacity; anchors for child-safety seats and the rest. Be sure to leave room to note whether each feature is standard or an extra. List the price of each extra, then rate them in order of priority.

Do a little research and determine the value of your old car. Trading in a car amounts to selling it to a dealer at wholesale, a move that could cost you several hundred dollars, for the sake of the convenience of not having to sell it yourself. (If a dealer offers you more for your old car than it's worth, he's probably charging you more for the new car you're buying.)

Think about everything and don't forget details, like financing. (GW)

OFF TO MARKET

Start by leaving your checkbook at home; you don't want to make an impulse buy.

The first dealer visits should be for information only. Sit in each car. Try the seatbelts for comfort. Try the accessories and controls. Ask questions, gather brochures and prices, use your checklist. If the salesman won't talk price without some high-pressure hassle, copy them from window stickers. Make it clear to the salesman that you're a serious buyer, but that you aren't interested in buying today. (GW)

HOMEWORK II

Now go home and look over all your information. Reevaluate your checklist, modify your priorities. (GW)

TEST DRIVE

On the second visit, test drive the models in which you're most interested. A test drive is so crucial that you must insist on it; if a salesman says, "Sorry, no demo," you must say, "Sorry, no sale."

In the test, drive the model closest to the one you want. Don't test drive the automatic V6 if the car you want is the four-banger with the five-speed. Drive the car on hills, through parking lots, on freeways, in stop-and-go traffic; drive it the way you normally use your car, not just around the block. (GW)

BOTTOM LINE

To save money, take the time to shop — not just for the best deal on the car, but also for insurance and financing. Don't settle for the first package that comes along if it doesn't suit you.

The deal: A dealer finances his inventory and pays interest every month, so he's usually willing to deal to get rid of a car he already has on hand. (But watch for extras, high dealer prep charges and something called ADP — Additional Dealer Profit.) Keep in mind that the manufacturer's "Suggested Retail Price" on the window sticker is just what it says — a *suggested* price. If the car is a slow seller, it'll cost less; if it's a popular model, it'll carry a little extra ADP. If you must have the car that everyone's standing in line to buy, at least shop the price; find one that isn't overly loaded and try to buy it at the best time — near the end of the month, or when there's a sales incentive in effect.

Options: If, on the other hand, you choose a car that isn't in stock, you can pick and choose your options, and thereby keep the price down. Remember, the salesman works on commission, and the more you spend, the more he makes. Don't get talked into options you don't want or need. It does, however, pay to remember that the car has to have an attractive resale value when it's time to sell it. Popular options like air conditioning, power steering and automatic transmission usually make the car easier to resell and make the car worth more later. Watch for option packages (sometimes called "comfort and convenience groups") that put together complementary option packages that will cost you less than ordering each option separately and will also increase the resale value of the car.

Financing: Long-term financing keeps the payments down but costs much more in interest. You can save money by going for the lowest rate at the shortest term. (GW)

LEASING

New-car leasing has grown in popularity, but there are significant pros and cons.

The biggest advantage is the small cash down-payment — usually one month's payment plus a security deposit. The biggest disadvantage is that leasing a car is like renting a house: at the end of the contract, you have nothing to show for your money. And the total cost of the lease is probably more, unless you can write off the use of the car as a business expense.

A *closed-end* lease lets you walk away after a fixed number of payments.

An *open-end* lease costs you more but gives you the option to buy the car at the end of the contract.

Both are based on the difference between the selling price and the estimated used value; you're responsible for insurance, service and repairs.

Another type of lease offers payments based on assumed depreciation and a large "balloon" payment at the end. The monthly payments are kept low, and you can sell the car or refinance it when the balloon is due. (GW)

AGREEMENTS

Get everything in writing. While many dealers are honest, there are plenty of opportunities for misunderstandings. To fully protect yourself, make sure the contract spells out every detail. *No verbal promise is reliable enough.* Be sure the deal, when it's finally struck, is not subject to later change, and that it's signed by the sales manager or somebody else with a valid and binding signature. (GW)

BEWARE THE BANKS

Banks, working through dealers, often try to sell no-money-down financing packages that are seductive because they allow you to drive away with a brand-new car for nothing. But you'll pay and pay and pay. Not only will your monthly payments be astronomical, but you'll always be "upside down" with the car; that is, you'll *always* owe more than the car is worth. (FE)

USED CARS

This is where the manufacturing sector gets its bad name. You must remember there are only three reasons why used cars exist: first, because somebody couldn't afford them as new cars and the bank came one day and took the car back; second, because the previous owner decided it was time to get a brand-new car, even though there was absolutely *nothing* wrong with the old one; and third, because it was a piece of junk and the previous owner was ashamed or afraid to drive it anymore.

A used car dealer or a selling owner will not be able to distinguish among these three; to them, their used cars represent a fourth category: a perfect machine at a bargain price. Watch your step. (FE)

TURN JAPANESE

Pick any kind of used car you like, so long as it's Japanese; their cars have, by far, the most consistent record for dependable, long-term performance. (PNe)

DETERMINE THE FAIR PRICE

of the car you want. The NADA (National Automobile Dealers Association) Blue Book will give you the official market value of any given kind of car, but the *real* market prices will be found in the classified ads. Once you've determined how much you should expect to pay, you'll be in a better position to determine which offers are bargains. (RES)

WHEN TO SHOP

Traditionally, the period following Christmas is the bargain season. Another benefit to winter shopping is that cars are at their worst at this time of year. Winter is hard on cars, and a good-looking, sweet-running car bought in January will look like a shining beauty in April. (CWS)

WHEN TO SELL

When any single repair is greater than the car's replacement cost, dump it. (RF)

GET READY

You should count on spending at least four hundred dollars in repairs immediately following the purchase of your used car. It's going to need something right away. You can also figure on spending another four hundred or so in maintenance and service during the first year of ownership. Something will come up — exhaust, tires, *something* — you can bet on it. (FE)

WHERE TO SHOP

New car dealers sell their best used cars on their own lots, while the more marginal vehicles they receive are offered to wholesalers who, in turn, sell them to used car dealers. (It is therefore safe to assume that every used car on a used car dealer's lot will have had at least three previous owners.) At a new car dealer's lot, the cars will probably be quite good, but bargains will be few and far between (after all, by selling good used cars, they are competing with themselves). You may be able to get a limited warranty on a used car from a new car dealer.

While *used car dealers* will have a wider selection than new car dealers, and the prices will be lower, the risk will be much, much higher. Often, cars on a used car dealer's lot will have been subjected to significant but temporary cosmetic improvements; mechanical and other defects will have been carefully hidden. Some used car dealers are honest, but many are notorious; even where warranties are offered, you'd be wiser avoiding used car dealers altogether unless you're absolutely certain of the lot's trading reputation.

Rental agencies often sell their old stock, and while rental cars will have seen a good many miles, they will also have been very well maintained. Rental companies can usually produce good records of a car's maintenance history.

Police and bank auctions are often good places to line up a bargain — if you know something about cars. Go to the viewing and inspect the car in which you're interested as carefully as possible. A good idea of a fair market price is indispensable information.

Right now, you're probably within ten feet of some sort of *classified ad* for a car. You can get badly stung in the classified marketplace, but you can also do well, if you're careful. Just as at an auction, mechanical savvy is important, and so is a good horse-trading instinct. (FE)

See also *AUCTIONS* **in** *CHAPTER NINE: CONSUMPTION.*

THOSE WHO IGNORE HISTORY ARE DOOMED TO BUY LEMONS

One of the hardest things about researching a used car is trying to get a notion of how well it was maintained and how astute the previous driver was.

Buying a car from the original owner gives you an enormous advantage here. If you can figure out what kind of guy he is, you'll be a long way toward figuring out what kind of driver he was and how well he treated his car. Watch out for guys carrying raw meat in their pockets.

See if you can get the previous owner to show you the car's maintenance records, including any oil changes and tune-ups. Whether you buy the car from the first owner or from some subsequent owner, try to get as many clues as possible regarding the vehicle's use, servicing, major repairs and former owners. (DJ)

REBUILT BLUES

A six-year-old car advertised as having a new or rebuilt motor is not always a great bargain. The engine is but one component in a very complex contraption, and a fresh engine on a car that only has six or seven years on it signals something wrong — probably a lot of abuse and neglect. There are plenty of other things that can go wrong on a car that's been thrashed about. (FE)

WRECK-MECHS

Incompetent mechanics can often cause more harm than anyone else. If parts have been improperly maintained or replaced or rebuilt, you're bound to have additional woes. Not only will the bad parts be affected, but so will the other components in that part of the car's system. (MJF)

INSPECTING A USED CAR

If you're not a mechanic or someone who knows a lot about the way cars work, your best bet is to figure out a way to get the car and the mechanic together at the same time in the same place.

Never inspect a car at night or in the rain. You'd be better off buying gemstones blindfolded. Even an experienced mechanic will miss giant flaws if the inspection is done under poor conditions. (CDr)

What to look for: First, look the car over *before* starting it.

- *Look underneath* for leaking fluids and rust. (SDr) Body rust you can deal with, but if the car you've chosen has frame rust, choose another car. (RJF
- *Look at the tires and wheels.* Check for even tire wear; if the wear is uneven in the front, the suspension components or wheel alignment may be suspect. Grab each tire near the top and yank it back and forth; if you can feel or hear something, you'll be feeling and hearing lots more of it later, and none of it will feel or sound good. (FE) If regular tire wear is the only problem, don't shy away. Tires, exhaust system and tune-up parts are relatively cheap, and you can live with a torn-up interior. Concentrate on drive train and body integrity. (RJF)
- *Look at the shocks* and test the suspension by pushing down firmly on each corner of the car; it should spring back at once. If it bounces a few times, the car will need new shocks soon. (FE)
- *Look at the exterior* where paint overspray may be detected on rubber window molding or around chrome details. If you see evidence that the car has been repainted, check closely for body repairs. Tap along repainted areas and listen for a change in tone that reveals some putty patchwork, which in turn might indicate a major front-end accident. (FE)
- *Look inside the wheel wells* for hidden rust or holes. Look out for patches. (FE)
- *Look at the interior,* where wear will suggest the car's previous care. Look for worn pedal covers and damaged seatcovers. Check the odometer; if the wear and tear doesn't correspond to the number of miles on the car, something's definitely fishy. (EFS)
- *Look under the hood.* Check for correct fluid levels. Look for chewed up or rounded nuts or bolt heads, indications of incompetent repair efforts. Check the spark plugs and the other ignition components to see if they are newer than the rest of the engine; it's a good sign if they are, since it generally indicates that the car has been periodically tuned. (FE)
- *Look down the carburetor throat* with the butterfly valve open. Clean carbs are best; brown stains are okay; black stains show a lot of engine wear. (AWG)

Finally, ***test drive the car.*** Arrange your visit so the car will be cold when you take it out. When you start the car, listen carefully to the sound of the engine. A cold car will tell you a lot more than a warm one will; anything that's wrong will be much more obvious in a car that hasn't been warmed up. (FE)

Before you move the car — but with the engine running — conduct these ***two preliminary tests.*** First, listen carefully while depressing and letting out the clutch pedal. If there is any noise difference, it may be a sign of a faulty clutch bearing. Second, depress the brake pedal fully and keep it down for at least a full minute. If the pedal travels farther and farther, there's a leak in the brake system. (SDr)

Drive the car around as if you were going about your daily business; get out on the expressway, then take a detour through city streets. Don't be shy about insisting on a complete test drive. (SDr)

Check the transmission: An automatic transmission should not make any loud clunking sounds or have a balky feel. Any hesitation in the gear changes should be carefully noted; it may be a problem with the transmission or with the rear end. The gear selector should operate smoothly. A manual transmission should operate smoothly. Test for a worn clutch by going slowly uphill in a higher-than-normal gear; if the clutch is good, the engine will lug, struggle shakily and nearly stall. If the engine revs but the car doesn't go any faster, then the clutch is bad. (FE)

The 90-weight oil from the gearbox in a standard transmission will have metal filings in it if the gears are going. Another clue to worn gears is if the car pops out of gear as you drive. Ask a mechanic for his opinion. (RJF)

If the automatic transmission fluid smells burnt and has a dark color, there may be trouble ahead. Get an Aamco check-up. (RJF)

Check the brakes: On a road with no traffic, accelerate to between 40 and 50 MPH (65 to 80 KPH). Brake hard while you lightly touch the steering wheel. The car should stop without pulling to either side and without making any scraping noises. (FE)

Check the gauges: At 60 MPH, the ammeter, water temperature and oil pressure gauges should read at the halfway mark. Also, at 60, the wheel should not shimmy. (FE)

Listen for rattles and noises. Loud clunks from below, especially ones that can be slightly felt in the steering, are symptoms of ailments that are usually expensive to fix. A bumpy road will make a good test course for this sort of thing. (FE)

Check the controls, wipers, lights, heater, radio and air conditioner. The air conditioner should engage smoothly, without a noticeable drop in engine performance. Don't forget to check directional lights from the outside. (FE)

Check the health of the engine with the assistance of a friend. Drive at highway speed, lift off the throttle completely for a couple of seconds, then floor it. If a cloud of blue smoke appears, think twice about the car. (FE)

Listen to the car idle. A good engine will have a smooth idle at low RPM. If the engine won't idle, there are problems. Sometimes, a tune-up will cure what ails it, but if not, don't buy the car. There are plenty of little-old-lady cars out there that idle. (RJF)

CHEAP TWO-TONE TRASH

Don't spend more than one hundred to three hundred dollars for the heap. Wherever you live, look in the classified ads and you'll see lots of cars worth no more than a couple hundred bucks or so. Don't forget that you're buying somebody else's fully depreciated piece of equipment.

Buy American, and preferably from the '60s. Look for any Chrysler product with a slant-six engine, a GM with a small-block V8 or an aluminum V6, or a large-body gas-guzzler like a Ford with a 350-cubic-inch V8 for trips around town. American cars aren't bad, even though the auto workers who made the heap have all since been early-retired. At least by buying American, you'll be supporting the schmuck in Cleveland who rebuilds the water pumps. And if I don't miss my guess, he'll do you proud.

Avoid cars from the '70s. All that pollution control, bad design and production inefficiencies make these cars dogs and generally undesirable.

Cars from the '50s have a great deal of style, but some prices may be inflated and some parts may be difficult to find. If you pick up some thirty-five-year-old beauty, be prepared to restore it — and any time you mention restoration, the vehicle becomes a "project" and something outside the realm of cheap transportation. (RJF)

Any GM car with a 283-cubic-inch engine that's in reasonable shape is likely to run longer than any other car with any other comparable engine. (AM)

Never buy a car to keep. Assume every car is as disposable as an empty Bic. Buy 'em cheap and trash 'em quick. (DB)

See also *Keeping a Junker Rolling,* **below, and** *DRIVING* **in** *CHAPTER FIVE: MODERN MOBILITY.*

THE MODERN MAN HIGH-MILEAGE ULTRA-RELIABLE USED CAR HALL OF FAME

- 1960–1974 Volkswagen Beetle
- 1964–1968 Ford Mustang
- 1965–1969 Full-size Chevy (any model)
- 1968–1972 Ford Pinto
- 1969–1974 Dodge Dart
- 1972–present Toyota (any model)
- 1977–present Japanese car (any, doesn't matter)

CAR CARE

Look at it this way: There are plenty of people out there who will sell their honor, their self-esteem, their very *souls* for a lot less money than the price of a midrange family sedan. Since most automobiles are therefore worth more than many people, car care is an important alternative to most humanitarian concerns.

Unless you're a hobbyist, the trick is not trying to get them to last forever, anyway. The trick is trying to get them to last until the next tax refund.

PERIODIC MAINTENANCE

will help keep your car in good condition. It's hard to concentrate on routine mechanical attention, since the rewards are not immediate. Nevertheless, greasing the chassis, changing the oil and the oil filter and rotating the tires, not dramatically beneficial, should be as carefully seen to as more obvious improvements, like tune-ups. (FE)

PLENTY OF FLUIDS

It's important to see that all the car's juices are kept up to snuff:

The oil and the oil filter should be changed simultaneously. Not replacing the filter will cause the new oil to be quickly contaminated. An old filter can become so clogged that a by-pass valve will open and the oil will not be filtered at all. (LC)

Antifreeze should be changed periodically. Rust inhibitors and lubricants added to antifreeze can, in time, break down, allowing rust to gum up the cooling system. (FE)

Hydraulic brake fluid slowly accumulates water from the atmosphere; after a time, the water will rust the inside of the brake assemblies.

Automatic transmissions rely on a special oil to operate. Although ATF is not subject to the heat and other influences that engine oil must endure, it too will become dirty in time and will lose its viscosity. The filter should be changed when the fluid is replaced.

Manual transmissions and differential oils receive the least punishment of all the car's fluids, but they too must be changed on a scheduled basis. (FE)

FLUID CHANGE SCHEDULE

Duty	Intervals		
	Fanatic	*Methodist*	*Teenager with Dad's Car*
Engine Oil and Filter	2000 mi	4000	6000, skip the filter
Antifreeze	Yearly	Biennially	Once
Automatic Transmission Oil	10,000 mi	20-30,000	Once
Manual Transmission Oil	30,000 mi	50,000	Never
Differential Fluid	30,000 mi	50,000	Never
Brake Fluid	Two years	Four years	Occasional top-ups (FE)

TUNE-UPS

Although tune-ups are expensive, they do wonders for your car — and your ego. You drive your old crank in on a wheeze and a prayer and drive out sideways with your tires going up in smoke.

A comprehensive tune-up should include

- New spark plugs
- New ignition points
- New rotor
- New distributor cap
- New condenser (if applicable)
- New air filter
- New fuel filter
- New PVC valve
- Point adjustment
- Carburetor adjustment
- Timing adjustment
- Smog control adjustment

A tune-up should be done at least once a year. (FE)

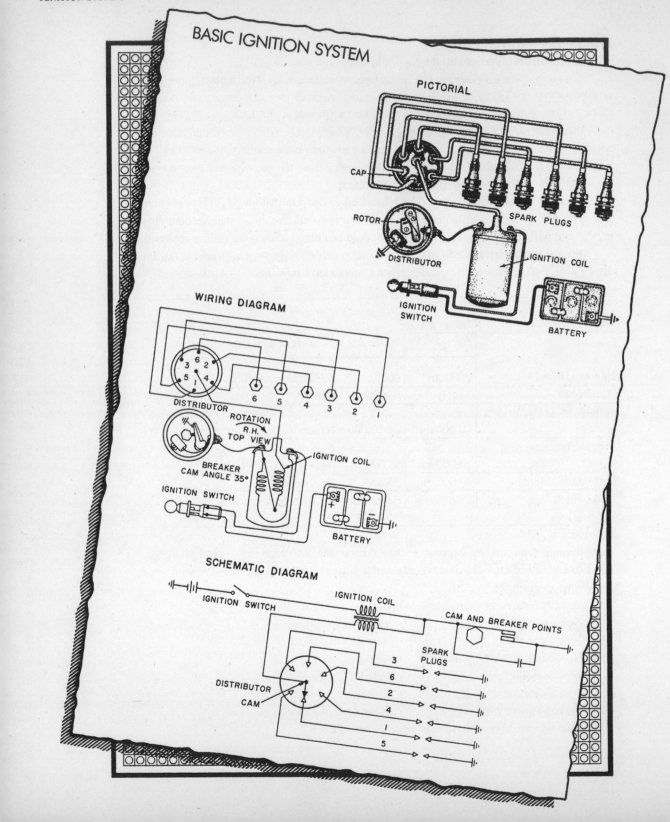

BASIC IGNITION SYSTEM

PICTORIAL

CAP

SPARK PLUGS

ROTOR

DISTRIBUTOR

IGNITION COIL

IGNITION SWITCH

BATTERY

WIRING DIAGRAM

3 6 2
5 1 4

DISTRIBUTOR

6 5 4 3 2 1

ROTATION R.H. TOP VIEW

BREAKER CAM ANGLE 35°

IGNITION COIL

IGNITION SWITCH

BATTERY

SCHEMATIC DIAGRAM

IGNITION SWITCH

IGNITION COIL

CAM AND BREAKER POINTS

SPARK PLUGS

3
6
2
4
1
5

DISTRIBUTOR CAM

EXTERIOR

maintenance is important, too. When you wash your car, wash the underside, too. That's where the important parts of a car are; the part you can see from a street corner is the least important part. (LC)

A body treatment of a poly-coating, followed by annual renewals, can free you from waxing for life. They really work. (GDr)

Like washing, *waxing* the parts you can't see is important. Rocker panels, wheel wells and body seams should get special attention. Use a good wax at least twice a year for satisfactory protection (although the more often, the better). Avoid the hot spray wax stuff at car washes. (LC)

INTERIOR

maintenance is important, especially if you are under the age of eighteen and live within five hundred miles of a drive-in. *Rubber, vinyl and plastic treatments* like Armorall are great for the non-fabric areas of a car's interior. Seats and dashboard tops exposed to the sun often crack or wrinkle; a good treatment will cure this. Rubber and vinyl take especially well to a good treatment with Armorall or something similar. Apply the stuff, let it sit overnight, then wipe it off. That's all. This will make exterior rubber look great, too, but only for a while; rain will rinse Armorall off. (LC)

BUYING TIRES

If you need four new radial tires for your car, no matter what the ads say, no matter what kind of special sale is on, no matter what kind of a deal you cut, by the time you get done, you'll have spent two hundred dollars. (MR)

RARE SPARES

Egge Machine Company will supply a comprehensive list of newly machined parts for pre-war (and early post-war) cars on receipt of $1.50. The address:

Egge Machine Company
8403 Allport Avenue
Santa Fe Springs, CA 90607
Telephone 213/945-3419 (AHSC)

The English should be prohibited by international law from designing, engineering or manufacturing automobile parts. Their carburetors are particularly loathsome. (RJF)

KEEPING A JUNKER ROLLING

As soon as you get the thing on the road, go to the ten-minute oil change place and get all the necessary fluids and filters checked and probably changed.

Slap a tune on it. Do it yourself if you have the tools and the inclination. Let somebody else do it if you don't.

Get decent tires. Radials are good because they hold the road better, even cheap ones will take you a long way, and in a pinch you can use them as snow tires. *Never match radials with nonradials.* (RJF)

Don't mix tire sizes on the rear-end. Different-size tires on the rear constitute an opposing rolling ratio and will eat your differential in quick order. (MR).

THE LAST STRAW

Here's how to recognize when your investment for a cheap car has reached the point of diminishing returns:

- *When the transmission goes,* since most tranny repairs will be more than the value of the car.
- *When the engine blows.* Just one loud *clunk* is enough to call the junkyard — maybe they'll let you keep the tires.
- *When you hit a tree* or any other seriously immovable object and sustain front-end damage, since the repair will cost more than the car is worth. (RJF)

CAR PROBLEMS EVEN *YOU* CAN FIX

Even in front of your girlfriend. No sweat, you say, I'll just adjust this muffler bearing sprocket, and . . .

Overheating: The most common fault (unless it's a hot day and you're driving through the desert) is a loose or broken fanbelt. To tighten a belt, get a wrench and loosen the bolt that attaches the alternator to the engine, and the alternator adjusting bolt. Use a stick as a lever to force the alternator away from the engine, thereby tightening the belt. If the belt is broken, replace it by loosening the alternator, putting on the new belt, and tightening the alternator as described above.

When the battery is not charging, you can figure both the problem and the solution are often the same as for overheating.

Starter cranking poorly: Bad contact at battery cables is the first likely cause (assuming the battery isn't low or dead). To fix it, loosen the cable clamps on the battery bolts, wiggle them around a bit to clean them, then retighten them.

Won't start even after you've tried real hard to get it to go: It's flooded, as your girlfriend has probably already told you. In most modern cars, press the accelerator to the floor and keep it there as you continue cranking the starter.

Stalls after running for a while. Maybe the fuel filter is fouled. Nothing to do but replace it. Loosen the two fuel lines, pull out the old filter and put in the new one. (LC)

In reality, of course, there are thousands of reasons why an engine might fail. The sketches above and the guide below show only the general principles and concepts.

THE MODERN MAN GRAND UNIFIED THEORY OF AUTOMOBILE TROUBLESHOOTING

As a rule, cars stop running for one of two reasons: Either they aren't getting gas or they aren't getting spark.

Troubleshooting involves determining which of these two things is going wrong, then working back along the system until you isolate the fault. Always start at the end of the line: check the spark by removing a plug, reattaching the ignition wire, then grounding the plug on something metal (preferably iron or steel) while somebody cranks the engine. *Don't hold the spark plug in your hands or you'll light up like Vegas.* If you get a small blue or white arc at the base of the plug, then you're getting spark. This means the problem's probably in the fuel system. To check this, take off the air cleaner cover, open the choke butterfly valve and look down inside the carburetor throat; you may need a flashlight (please don't use a match). Have someone pump the throttle; you should be able to see and smell the fine mist of petrol in the carburetor cavity. If so, you've got gas.

If you're getting spark and gas at these, the last points in the chain, the car should run. If one of the two systems isn't doing its part, trace that system backward checking at every point for a fault. For example, if you've eliminated spark as a problem, then check the carburetor (as described above). Then check the carburetor, follow the fuel line to the fuel pump; then trace the line to the fuel filter; check that, and if it's okay, follow the line on down to the gas tank. You should spot a blockage or a leak. (LC)

AUTO TROUBLESHOOTING

Trouble is always in season for auto owners. The information that follows is only a basic guide, something to get you headed in the right direction. If you want to get real serious, get a shop manual.

All these lists show faults and should therefore be checked in sequence.

Starter doesn't turn
1. Dead battery. Test: Try the lights
2. Loose battery connections
3. Faulty ignition override switch
4. Faulty ignition switch
5. Starter gear jammed
6. Faulty starter

Starter turns slowly
1. Low battery
2. Loose or dirty electrical
    connections
3. Faulty starter
    A. Worn commutator
    B. Worn brushes
    C. Dirty or worn starter switch
4. Internal engine damage

Engine does not fire,
or fires intermittently

1. Electrical problems:
    A. Check spark at plugs
    B. Faulty coil
    C. Worn or incorrectly set points
    D. Faulty ignition wires
2. Fuel problems:
    A. No gas
    B. Filter blocked
    C. Fuel line broken
    D. Faulty fuel pump
    E. Clogged air filter
    F. Throttle or choke closed
    G. Flooded

Engine runs poorly
1. Runs rough at low speeds or stalls:
    A. Low battery
    B. Clogged air filter
    C. Worn, dirty or improperly

set plugs
D. Faulty points or damp or faulty
distributor cap
E. Stuck choke
F. Incorrectly set carburetor
G. Valve clearance too small

2. Runs rough at high speeds:
A. Faulty ignition wires
B. Faulty points
C. Worn or dirty spark plugs
D. Clogged fuel filters
E. Clogged air filter
F. Leak in the vacuum line
G. Incorrect valve clearance

3. The engine backfires:
A. Clogged fuel filters
B. Faulty fuel pump
C. Worn or dirty plugs
D. Faulty points
E. Worn, damp or dirty
distributor cap
F. Incorrect engine timing
G. Leaking manifold
H. Valve clearances too small

4. Lack of power:
A. Clogged air cleaner
B. Incorrect ignition timing
C. Worn or dirty spark plugs
D. Faulty points
E. Worn or dirty distributor cap
F. Faulty ignition wires
G. Faulty coil
H. Clogged fuel filter
I. Faulty carburetor
J. Blocked exhaust
K. Broken valve spring
L. No compression in cylinder(s)

5. The engine overheats:
A. No water in the radiator
B. Leaking hoses
C. Loose or broken fan belt

D. Stuck thermostat
E. Clogged radiator
F. Incorrect ignition timing
G. Incorrect mixture setting on
carburetor

Engine noises

1. Squealing sounds:
A. Loose fan belt
B. Worn water pump bearings
C. Worn alternator

2. Loud knocks:
A. Worn connecting rod or main
bearings
B. Very worn piston

3. Light clicking or tapping:
A. Worn ignition wires
(spark jumping)
B. Incorrectly set valves
C. Broken valve springs
D. Worn piston

4. Irregular pings or knocks:
Worn spark plugs (preignition)

5. Light pinging:
Incorrectly set ignition (too
advanced)

6. Hissing:
Leak in vacuum line

7. Other strange engine rackets:
A. Loose fastening nuts or bolts
B. Worn rubber mountings
C. Loose or broken springs
D. Loose mounting brackets
E. Worn or dry bearings:
i. In the water pump
ii. In the alternator
iii. In the distributor

Electrical problems

Most nonengine-related electrical systems fail for one of the following three reasons:

1. No current

2. A broken electrical component
3. An ungrounded circuit

Check the following:
1. Dead bulb (if applicable)
2. Blown fuse
3. Dirty or loose connection
4. Broken component or switch
5. Worn wire insulation (possibly causing a short)

Clutch problems
1. The clutch chatters or shudders:
    A. Damaged linkage
    B. Loose engine mounts
    C. Grease on the driven plate
    D. Loose driven plate hub
    E. Clutch plate wear
    F. Misalignment of transmission to bell housing
2. The clutch slips:
    A. Lack of free movement of pedal
    B. Linkage needs lubrication
    C. Weak or broken pressure plate springs
    D. Worn clutch plates
3. The clutch drags:
    A. Too much free movement of the pedal
    B. Incorrect release lever adjustment
    C. Damaged pressure plate
    D. Warped or damaged driven plate

Manual transmission problems
1. Noise in all gears:
    A. No transmission oil or the wrong oil
    B. Worn bearings
    C. Damaged or worn gears
2. Noise in one gear only:
    A. Worn constant mesh gears

B. Worn synchronizer or bearing
3. Gears difficult to change:
    A. The clutch is dragging
    B. The linkage needs lubrication
4. The gears disengage:
    A. Worn pilot bearing in the engine crankshaft
    B. Bent transmission shaft
    C. Bent shifter fork
    D. Worn gears or bearings

Automatic transmission problems
1. Low fluid level
2. Incorrectly adjusted linkage
3. Linkage needs lubrication
4. Clogged filters
5. Loose mounts
6. Loose bolts

Steering problems
1. Hard steering:
    A. Low front tire pressure
    B. Loose pump belt
    C. Low fluid level
    D. Incorrect wheel alignment
    E. Faulty pump
    F. Air in the hydraulic lines
    G. Damaged hydraulic lines
2. Vague steering, or steering that pulls to one side:
    A. Incorrect front tire pressure
    B. Incorrect wheel alignment
    C. Incorrect brake adjustment
    D. Damaged springs
    E. Damaged shocks
    F. Worn wheel bearings
    G. Faulty pitman arm
3. Wheels wobble:
    A. Low tire pressure
    B. Worn wheel bearings
    C. Incorrect wheel balance
    D. Incorrect wheel alignment

E. Worn front end parts

Problems with disc brakes

1. Groaning:
   A. There isn't a problem. They groan, that's all
2. Scraping:
   A. Loose wheel bearings
   B. Faulty splash shield
   C. Worn pads
3. Grabbing or pulling to one side or fluctuating:
   A. Low fluid in the master cylinder
   B. Air in the hydraulic lines
   C. Grease on the rotors
   D. Incorrect tire pressure
   E. Incorrect wheel alignment
   F. Bent or pinched brake line
   G. Loose caliper
   H. Incorrect caliper alignment
   I. Faulty caliper piston
4. The pedal is depressed, but nothing happens:
   A. Reservoir fluid low
   B. A leak in the master cylinder
   C. A leak in the hydraulic lines
   D. The bleed cock is open
5. It's hard to press down the pedal:
   A. Oil or grease on the rotor
   B. Bent or pinched brake line
   C. Faulty master cylinder
   D. Faulty caliper pistons
   E. Stuck metering valve
6. Pedal travel increases with pressure:
   A. Reservoir fluid low
   B. Broken or leaking hydraulic line
   C. Air in the system
   D. Weak hoses

Problems with drum brakes

1. Squeaking noises:
   A. Worn or glazed linings
   B. Fluid on the linings
   C. Excessive dust in the drum
   D. Worn or broken springs
   E. Scored drum
2. Grabbing or dragging:
   A. Fluid on the brake linings
   B. Leak in the system
   C. Improper adjustment (including the parking brake)
   D. Worn or broken return spring
   E. Shoe pivot pins need lubrication
   F. Contaminated fluid
   G. Faulty master cylinder
   H. Faulty wheel cylinder
3. Pulling to one side:
   A. Incorrect front end alignment
   B. Improper brake adjustment
   C. Brake shoes distorted
   D. Fluid on the brake linings
   E. Worn brake linings
   F. Worn or broken brake springs
   G. Bent or pinched brake line
   H. Excessive dust in the brake drum
   I. Broken automatic adjusters
4. Pedal pulsates:
   The drum is no longer round
5. You depress the pedal, but nothing happens:
   A. Reservoir fluid low
   B. Air in the system
   C. Leak in the system
   D. Damaged brake line
   E. Incorrect brake adjustment
   F. Faulty wheel cylinder
   G. Faulty master cylinder

6. It's hard to press down the brake pedal:
    A. Pinched or bent brake line
    B. Pedal linkage bent or needs adjustment or lubrication
    C. Faulty wheel cylinder

Rear axle problems

Noise in the rear axle is caused by one of the following:
    1. Insufficient or incorrect gear oil
    2. Incorrect adjustment of gears
    3. Worn gears

Drive shaft problems

Vibration or clunking is caused by:
    1. Loose bolts at attachment points to the transmission or rear axle
    2. Worn universal joint

Ride problems

Clunking noises can be caused by:
    1. Worn spring shackles
    2. Broken springs
    3. Worn or broken suspension joint bushing
    4. Worn or damaged shock mount
    5. Worn or damaged rubber suspension bushing

An undulating ride is caused by:
    1. Worn shock absorbers
    2. Worn or damaged shock mounts
    3. Tired springs
    4. A broken spring

CAR EMERGENCY KIT

As some other less Modern Men once said, "Be prepared." This Modern Man emergency kit takes up just a little bit of room, but it's worth about nine cubic yards of foresight.

Parts:
- Top and bottom radiator hoses
- Fan belt (or a set of them if your car's engine uses more than one)
- Extra fuses
- An inflated spare tire and a jack
- Battery jumper cable

Tools:
- Lug wrench
- Plain screwdriver
- Phillips screwdriver
- Locking pliers (Vise Grips)
- Adjustable wrench
- Penknife
- The following most commonly used wrenches (either open-end, sockets or both):

American size	*Metric size*
three-eighths inch	10 millimeter
one-half inch	12 millimeter
nine-sixteenths inch	14 millimeter
five-eighths inch	17 millimeter

- A spark-plug wrench
- Miscellaneous, including duct tape, electrical tape, a few rags, a blanket, a candle, a lighter, flashlight, epoxy glue, flares and the owner's manual. (AR)

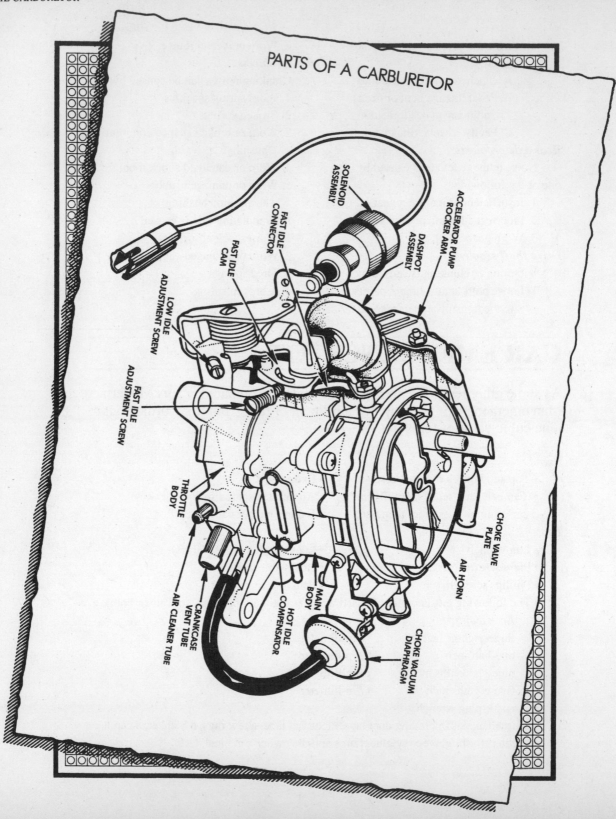

PARTS OF A CARBURETOR

Modern Mobility

Destination: Earth.

Back in the '50s, the future of travel looked so rosy that it seemed that getting there would be a lot more than half the fun. We were going to have individual jet-packs strapped to our backs for space-age commuting; the modern mom was going to be able to drop the kids off at school in her new aeronautical automobile; and best of all, we were going to be able to go to Mars during summer vacation.

No dice. Not only has travel become much more inconvenient in the last thirty years, it's also become a lot less friendly. A Modern Man may know that when you've got to go, you've got to go. But he doesn't have to like it.

C O N T E N T S

Chapter Five: *MODERN MOBILITY*

DRIVING

Driving a car is not interesting unless you're driving a car while breaking the law. The intrinsic boredom associated with automobile travel cannot be relieved by assimilating the facts below. Read them anyway. We got a lot of them in the mail (many so commonplace we aren't using them), so somebody must be interested, and besides, they're mostly concerned with easing the bone- and mind-crushing aspects of one of life's more cheerless activities.

In fact, driving around in a car is so dreadful it might be better to invest most of your automotive budget in a truly fine stereo and spend whatever's left on a car in which the stereo can be fitted. Then you won't have to spend your time driving, really. You can spend your time listening to David Byrne, Philip Glass and Ry Cooder. Life on the other side of the safety glass will become a docudrama, like on PBS, and you can think about the plight of modern society and get real morbid and depressed. (ND)

PICK A SPOT

When choosing a position within a lane, favor the left side. Drive as though you're riding on the divider line and you'll be two or three feet away from it. Drifting a litle toward the center will give you a slight advantage in case someone quickly opens the driver-side door of a parked car, a pedestrian darts into the road or a car pulls suddenly away from the curb and into traffic. (FM)

FOLLOW AN OLD RULE

about following and you'll find that in heavy traffic you have to allow a distance of ten feet for every ten MPH of speed between you and the car in front of you. (SBO)

IN CITY TRAFFIC

If you can read the number plate on the car in front of you, you're too close. (FGC)

KNOW WHERE EVERYONE IS

on the highway around you. Make sure you always have one instant-escape route open in case the car in front of you explodes or something. Check those mirrors. (*Anon.*)

EXPECT NOTHING SENSIBLE

from other drivers, especially if the situation turns dicey. On an expressway or in town, you should assume most drivers don't know what they're doing and will probably do the wrong thing. Drive defensively. (LGP)

A dissent: Control the situation around you; take charge of a lane of traffic and drive aggressively. You'll find that other drivers will behave with more common sense if

there's someone around who exhibits some sense of control. (CP)

DON'T TOUCH YOUR BRAKES

if you have a flat tire. In the case of a flat, simply let the car slow to a crawl, then gently apply your brakes. (CP)

ON ICE

or any other slippery surface, your car is likely to go into an unexpected skid in which the rear end of your car will want to come up front and see what's going on. In this case, always turn into the spin. It's good practice — and a lot of fun — to run through your antiskid technique in an empty, icy parking lot.

Use the highest gear possible in ice or snow. Don't lug the engine too much, but a higher gear will give you better traction. Second is helpful, especially in starting. (FMcA)

KEEP A CONSTANT SPEED

on long-distance trips. Not only is the endless changing of cruise speeds inconsiderate to other drivers, it also increases your fuel consumption, causes your engine unnecessary distress and will probably slow down your progress. Truckers, bus drivers and other long-haul experts follow a steady-speed formula. So should you. (JGP)

MOTORCYCLE MADNESS

A motorcycle is one of the most dangerous conveyances ever designed by man. Before the turn of the century, guys strapped on wings and attempted flight by jumping off buildings in homemade bird suits. They got smarter; now they ride motorcycles.

A motorcycle is a grossly overpowered, two-wheeled road machine that has a perilously high center of gravity, very little contact with the ground and no protection whatsoever for a rider who is left nearly invisible (literally and psychologically) to automobile drivers. When standing still, a motorcycle will fall over. On wet, sandy or oily surfaces, they are nearly beyond control. (TN)

WELCOME ABOARD

Although sensibly designed, the controls of a motorcycle are hopelessly confusing to first-time riders once they get the machine rolling for the first time. You can spend hours teaching them all about the controls, but as soon as they start moving, they develop amnesia — every single time. Beginners should have *plenty of open space* in which to practice, since most of them end up flat on their backs, piled against a tree or in a ditch. (GS)

Learn to handle a motorcycle adroitly at *very slow speeds* before learning to go fast. It's very difficult to control a motorcycle at a slow speed — especially in dirt. Many

motorcycle riders develop bad habits early on, then carry them over to high-speed driving, where they become more dangerous. (MR)

STOPPING

Stopping is important. It's the front brake on a motorcycle that does most of the work; learn to use it without locking up the front wheel.

Lock-up is imminent when you feel in the handlebars that the tire has begun to "squirm."

Apply the rear brake first, then apply the front and rear brakes simultaneously until the machine stops. Practice this until it becomes second nature. Applying the rear brake first sets the motorcycle.

If the road surface is exceptionally slick, stay off the front brake; a motorcycle with a locked front brake will go over, no question about it.

If you go into a turn too fast, don't apply your brakes in the middle of the curve; you'll likely crash. Brake before entering the turn and apply the throttle on exiting.

In fact, any sudden movement on a motorcycle can result in disaster. Concentrate on making your movements — braking, accelerating, shifting — smooth, fluid ones. (TN)

GOING

In traffic: Assume you are invisible to automobile drivers. It's not that they're evil or anything, it's just that they really *don't* see you. (TN)

On the highway: The most dangerous time to be on a motorcycle is the *first hour of a rainstorm* — particularly after a long dry spell. Rain on a dry road brings all the oils left by passing vehicles to the surface. This is more obvious on hills than on level stretches. (HGS)

Metal grates on bridges can be extremely dangerous; even the most experienced motorcycle rider has learned to approach them with justifiable fear. Motorcycles have very little road contact to begin with and riding over bridge gratings reduces that contact to almost nothing. The motorcycle's steering will become slushy and vague and both wheels will exhibit a tendency to drift sideways. There's not much you can do except use care. Resist the temptation to drag your feet; permit the motorcycle to wander slightly. A moving motorcycle is like a gyroscope and will seek to find its own equilibrium. (TN)

At traffic lights, always shift into neutral and release the clutch. Not only will this save wear and tear on the clutch plate, cable and bearing, it will also save you from calamity if the clutch cable snaps. It also reduces the natural inclination to rapidly accelerate through an intersection as soon as the light changes (after all, quick getaways are one of the attractions of motorcycles); the foolishness of this practice is obvious to any motorist who has ever raced through an intersection trying to catch the last nanosecond of the yellow light. (TN)

FIVE THINGS YOU WANT TO DO ON A MOTORCYCLE BUT SHOULDN'T
1. Ride without a helmet
2. Ride without shirt or shoes
3. Ride with your feet on the passenger pegs
4. Ride in the center lane
5. Pass on the right in cities or towns   (KD)

TEN TRICKS TO OFF-ROAD RIDING

While there are some substantial differences between highway biking and off-road riding, other elements are quite similar. Here are a few of the main things:

1. Unless you're stopped, keep your feet firmly planted on the foot pegs.

2. Standing on the footrests is tiring, but it will give you more comfort and control.

3. Don't force the motorcycle to follow your chosen course. Relax and maintain a light touch on the handlebars. In a sense, the motorcycle will steer itself. Its inherent stability will keep it on the straight and narrow, although this is very difficult for beginners to believe.

4. Greater speed will help you get through some of the rougher patches of an off-road course. Speed enhances a motorcycle's self-steering aspects.

5. Don't look at the obstruction you want to avoid. If you do, you'll probably smack into it. Instead, concentrate on the path to avoid it.

6. Slide back on the seat to obtain more traction. This is really helpful at the beginning of a climb and in sand or mud.

7. Crouch and lean forward while standing on the pegs to achieve more stability while climbing a steep hill. The added weight on the front wheel will help your control, and the forward center of gravity will help keep you from flipping over backward.

8. Leave the clutch alone. Uphill, downhill, around obstacles — it doesn't matter. Leave your bike in gear. You'll always need the traction — and sometimes an extra burst of power, too.

9. When going uphill, never stop. In fact, do *anything* other than stopping. Zigzag if you have to, or go back downhill and turn around and try again. But don't stop. You may never get going again.

10. Use the front brake or use compression braking when going downhill. Compression braking is riding with the ignition off and relying on the motorcycle's compression to slow the bike. (TD)

See *Auto Accidents* **in** *CHAPTER SIXTEEN: MODERN MISHAPS.*

BAD ROADS

On roadbeds where the corrugation occurs in a regular pattern perpendicular to the direction of travel (as is most often the case), a vehicle with decent suspension should be driven at speeds in excess of thirty-five miles per hour.

The slower you go, the rougher it gets. If driving a four-wheel drive vehicle, try using the two-wheel mode for better control. Quick stops can often lead to out-of-control skids which will follow the pattern of the corrugation. Obviously, you shouldn't drive so fast that your ability to keep the car under control is sacrificed. The best speed is the slowest speed that eliminates the jolts of the roadbed. (DB)

DWI: DRIVING WHILE INTOXICATED

DWI: Three little letters that stand for three little words that mean *there's a jerk*. There is no emergency so grave, no explanation so just that can ever excuse the transgression committed by a sentient human being who drinks too much, then decides to drive a car.

SIX TESTS FOR DRUNKS

Actually, if you're in sufficient doubt about your sobriety that you need to consider testing it, you can figure you're too drunk to drive. But just for the hell of it:

1. Peripheral vision: Booze does a pretty good job of wrecking your peripheral vision. To test for tunnel vision, stand with your arms extended away from your sides to shoulder level. Stare straight ahead and wiggle your fingertips. Then slowly bring your arms forward. If your arms travel more than five degrees, you're drunk.

2. Nose touch: Stand with your arms outstretched (as in the exercise above). With the index finger on your right hand extended, stare straight ahead as you bring your arm forward until your index finger touches the tip of your nose. Repeat with the left hand. The motion of the arm should be smooth and without hesitation.

3. Stand on one leg while you hold your other knee. Count slowly to 20 without losing your balance.

4. Play catch: Have a friend toss you three unbreakable objects (empty beer cans, maybe) from a distance of fifteen or twenty feet. If you miss any or even fumble them, don't chance driving.

5. Depth perception: Have a friend set three identical objects (soup cans, beer bottles, billiard balls, whatever) on an otherwise empty table. You sit in a chair at least twenty feet away with an unobstructed, eye-level view of the table. Avert your eyes while your friend arranges the three objects in such a way that their position is staggered by an inch or so. When your friend tells you to look, you should be able to determine the relative positions without hesitation.

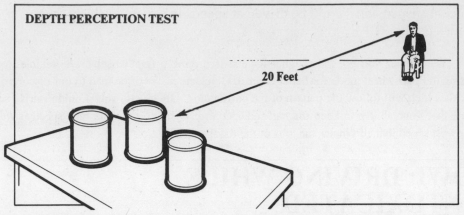

DEPTH PERCEPTION TEST

20 Feet

6. Straight line: Walking a straight line is the best (and oldest) sobriety test. That's why the cops use it. The line should be at least ten feet in length; walk toe to heel, then turn and walk back. If you sway, have trouble at the turns or just can't do it, you're too drunk to drive. (BV)

ONE PER HOUR

To avoid a drunk-driving bust, never drive if you've had more than one drink per hour of any alcoholic beverage. (VP)

See also *TROUBLE* **in** *CHAPTER SIXTEEN: MODERN MISHAPS.*

PACKING TO GO

The next time she tells you to get out:

SUCK A SULFUR TABLET

when traveling through regions where bacterial disease is prevalent. In malarial districts, *quinine* and its derivatives are still the only prophylaxes that work — and some strains are developing a solid resistance to them. (GH)

SUITCASES

Look at it symbolically: Suitcases are our portable follies, the measure of our vanity, the weight of our self-importance, the bulk of our insecurity. They are the traveling man's burden.

HARD CASES AND SOFT

Soft suitcases are light but offer little protection; hard suitcases offer protection, but are far too heavy and inflexible.

For most Modern Men, *the standard two- or three-suiter* is the ideal suitcase. It functions both as suitcase and closet and is the current version of the steamer trunk.

Because it's a soft bag, it can be overpacked if necessary; if it's underpacked, it can be folded into a minimum amount of space.

Best of all, it can be carried aboard most aircraft. (SAF)

OTHER TYPES

Unless you're under age eighteen or a soldier on maneuvers, don't carry a **backpack**. The serious damage done to your shoulders and neck is nothing compared to the incidental havoc you wreak as you pass. (DFO) But see *Backpacking* under *HIKING*.

Metal cases are great for photographers or for those carrying delicate equipment. For anyone else, it's too heavy and makes you into a target for thieves. (TFG)

PACKING CHECK LISTS

You're probably forgetting something and taking too much of something else. Start here before you pack to go there.

SKIING	TROPICS/BEACH	WILDERNESS
Skis, boots and poles	Thin, short-sleeved shirts	3 pair socks
Nonski winter boots	Baby oil	1 pair woolen trousers
Sock liners	Suntan lotion	2-3 pair khaki trousers
Heavy socks	Sun screen	2 sets long underwear
Long underwear	Hat	Turtleneck sweater
Ski pants	Antiseptic	Woolen shirt
Parka	Rain gear (tropics)	Rain gear
Sweater	Insecticide (tropics)	Boots
Ski mittens	Repellent (tropics)	Sneakers
Ski hat	Quinine (tropics)	Flashlight
Sunglasses	Heavy, cotton shirts	Knife
Lip balm	and trousers (tropics)	Tin cup
Suntan lotion	Boots/ heavy shoes (tropics)	Towel
Camera	Camera	Soap

See also *CHAPTER ONE: OUTDOORS* **and** *Packing a Suitcase,* **below.**

PACKING A SUITCASE

Knowing how to pack a suitcase is often the secret to a successful trip.

The Main Thing: Travel light. Figure the minimum you'll need, then cut it in half and you'll be right. (SC)

Essentials: Here's what you need for a ten-day trip to Europe:

1 pair jeans or corduroy trousers	3 pair underwear	3 pair socks
2 shirts (one blue, one white) and a tie	1 knit shirt	1 bottle of Woolite and
1 suit (washable, if it's summertime)	1 sweater	minimal toiletries

Carry your raincoat with you, and wear a blazer on the flight. If you're traveling on business, you can afford to use the hotel's laundry service — same day in almost all —

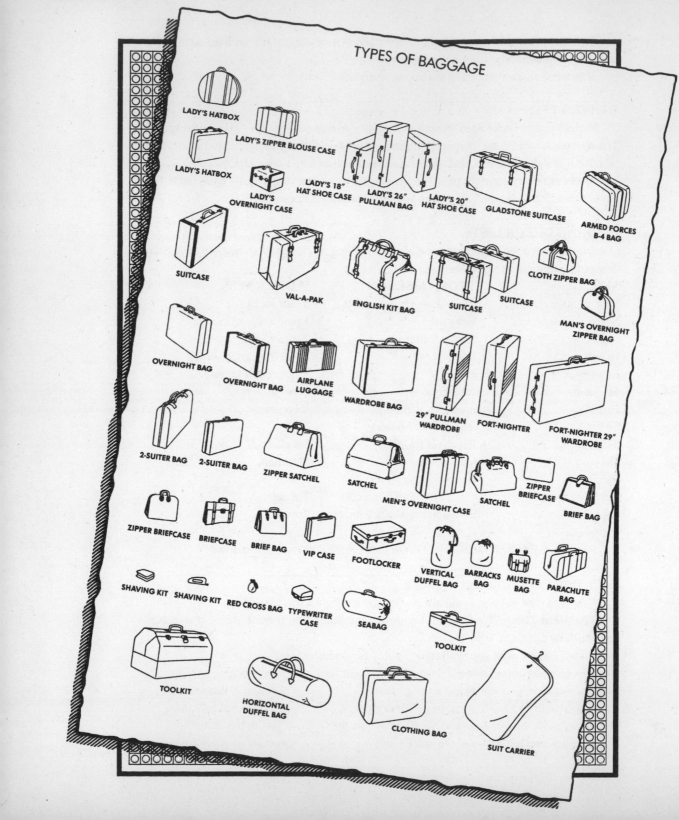

TYPES OF BAGGAGE

LADY'S HATBOX

LADY'S ZIPPER BLOUSE CASE

LADY'S HATBOX

LADY'S OVERNIGHT CASE

LADY'S 18" HAT SHOE CASE

LADY'S 26" PULLMAN BAG

LADY'S 20" HAT SHOE CASE

GLADSTONE SUITCASE

ARMED FORCES B-4 BAG

SUITCASE

VAL-A-PAK

ENGLISH KIT BAG

SUITCASE

SUITCASE

CLOTH ZIPPER BAG

MAN'S OVERNIGHT ZIPPER BAG

OVERNIGHT BAG

OVERNIGHT BAG

AIRPLANE LUGGAGE

WARDROBE BAG

29" PULLMAN WARDROBE

FORT-NIGHTER

FORT-NIGHTER 29" WARDROBE

2-SUITER BAG

2-SUITER BAG

ZIPPER SATCHEL

SATCHEL

MEN'S OVERNIGHT CASE

SATCHEL

ZIPPER BRIEFCASE

BRIEF BAG

ZIPPER BRIEFCASE

BRIEFCASE

BRIEF BAG

VIP CASE

FOOTLOCKER

VERTICAL DUFFEL BAG

BARRACKS BAG

MUSETTE BAG

PARACHUTE BAG

SHAVING KIT

SHAVING KIT

RED CROSS BAG

TYPEWRITER CASE

SEABAG

TOOLKIT

TOOLKIT

HORIZONTAL DUFFEL BAG

CLOTHING BAG

SUIT CARRIER

and you can scrap the Woolite. If you're on your own nickel, use the hotel room sink. The essentials will fit in a suitcase that can be carried aboard most aircraft. (DSH)

Packing sequence: From bottom to top: Folded pants on the bottom (although trousers that crease easily can be protected by folding them around the contents of the bag); then ties; then shirts, alternating collar to base; then rolled sweaters; then jackets. Underwear and socks should fit into nooks and crannies. A toilet kit should be near the top for easy access. Folded clothes take up the least room. (DSH)

How to fold a shirt: Start by buttoning the top two buttons, then every other one, so that the bottom button is also closed. **(See illustration.)** Place the shirt face down on a flat surface, and pull the shirt tight across the shoulders and across the bottom of the tail. Fold each side from the shoulder in towards the middle, then fold the sleeves back along the sides. Fold up the tail once, then again so that the shirt is only one-third its original length. Jackets can be folded the same way, although many travelers prefer their jackets folded inside out to minimize wrinkles and to preserve the collar. (AR)

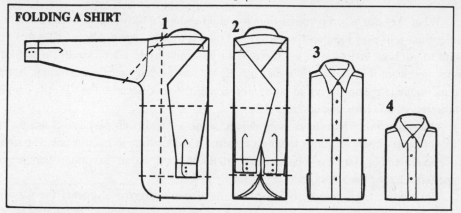

FOLDING A SHIRT

Toilet kit: The essential toilet kit:

Razor	Toothbrush
Toothpaste	Nail clippers
Aspirin	Pocketknife
Shampoo	Travel clock
Deodorant	Cologne or after-shave
Shaving brush (if needed)	(DSH)

Flexibility: Pack only your most versatile clothes; try to think of garments that can be mixed and matched. Remember how they used to try to sell suits in which every item was reversible, giving you an incredible 105-piece wardrobe for $69.95? That's the idea here. Gray, for example, is a color that can agree with any other color, so gray trousers might be a good choice. A navy blazer is another good choice (**see under** *Suits and Sport Jackets*). Items like your belt and shoes should be appropriate to your whole wardrobe; dark brown is the commonsense color for both. (EWS)

Bagging souvenirs can be a problem, unless you plan ahead. Pack a lightweight, collapsible bag inside your suitcase; you'll probably fill it up with souvenirs and new clothing if your trip is for pleasure and not business. (FB)

Line your case with plastic garbage bags. They weigh almost nothing and will prevent dampness from creeping in during a long ride in an unpressurized luggage compartment. They also come in handy during emergencies. (DSP)

Case-mates: If you're traveling with a companion, consider dividing up the wardrobes into two bags. That way when one bag gets lost, you'll still be covered. (JG)

TRAVEL AGENTS

Travel agents, properly employed in your service, can make your professional life a lot easier. Best of all, travel agents, while they're working for you, are paid by somebody else.

What they do: When it comes time to get up and go, a travel agent does all the horrible grunt jobs that you don't want to do. You tell a travel agent where and when you want to go, how you want to get there, what you want to do after you arrive and how much you want it all to cost. On your behalf, the travel agent spends frustrating, boring hours on the telephone trying to put it all together for you. Because the agent is paid by commission, this costs you nothing. (JO)

Choosing one: These days, with deregulation, anybody can play travel agent. But there are two important things to consider when it comes time to choose one. First, you have to remember that travel agents work strictly on commission. Second, if they are inexperienced, they know less about travel than you do.

There is an organization, IATA, that sort of works for travel agents the way the AMA does for doctors, and professional, well-trained travel agents belong to it. An IATA agent will respect your budgetary considerations more than his commission requirements. And because they have been properly trained, they will have access to a network of contacts that can provide solutions to fairly arcane problems. IATA agents frequently visit key destinations on familiarization junkets, so they can often recommend a hotel or restaurant they themselves have patronized. (FC)

EN ROUTE

Rich girl, she drive a big Cadillac;
Poor girl, she do much the same.
But my gal, she drives an old hay wagon,
Yeah, you know she's gettin' there just the same.
—Traditional.

TRAVEL WITH KIDS

On trains, take snacks, more snacks, books, maps, trash bags and a separate bag with kiddie bedtime clothes. This sort of tiny-tot travel tote will save you opening your larger suitcases a million times. (FJN)

On planes, children seem much better able to relax and amuse themselves. Nobody knows why, but perhaps it's the thinness of the air. (HDF)

SURFACE TRANSPORTATION

Cars: In most parts of North America and Europe, a car is a necessity. In large cities, though, like New York or Paris, owning a car is really silly. If you live in New York, and you need a car, rent one. (TRD)

Don't drive your dick: Motor vehicles have no hormones. (RDo)

Money for nothing: A car is a utilitarian purchase. It should be comfortable to sit in, economical to operate, safe to drive and clean. Spending $40,000 for a car is simply neurotic. (RD)

Airport buses: It's cruel and unusual punishment to ask your wife to take you to the airport when common sense tells you that the easiest way to get to and from an airport is in public transportation. From a driver's point of view, airports are always a horror show. This is one case where pretentiousness can really backfire. (WAR)

See also *Etiquette in Motion* **in** *CHAPTER SEVENTEEN: THE DEPORTMENT DEPARTMENT.*

TAKING A TRAIN

If you're traveling *coach class,* prepare or purchase an elegant meal (with wine or other beverage) for dining en route. Note that the cars at the front of the train are less jostled than the cars at the rear. Sit on the side of the car opposite the sun; it'll make watching the passing scenery much easier.

Taking a train in style: On day trains, first class means free meals, bigger seats, window curtains and an attendant. That's all very well.

But first class really takes on new meaning in a private room on a *sleeper.* For one person, a roomette is adequate, but if you're going to go to this much expense and trouble, take along a sleeping partner and reserve a bedroom; as a rule, you'll get two beds in an over-under configuration and an adjoining WC with a sink (some new cars even have a shower). Try to book your bedroom in the middle of the car — the ride is smoother, and it makes sleeping a little easier to not be directly over the trucks and wheels. Although meals are included, your own picnic will be much tastier.

Reserve early; sleepers are much in demand. Sometimes, however, if you're traveling coach and you get fed up with the hoi polloi, you can try to upgrade to first class en route; if there's been a last-minute cancellation, the conductor will collect the difference in fare and escort you to your room.

For primo-neato first-class travel, you can reserve a deluxe bedroom (in the

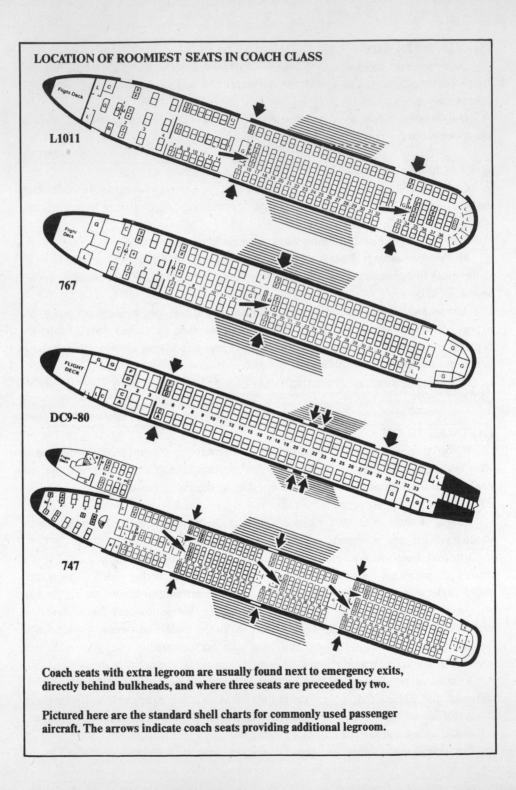

LOCATION OF ROOMIEST SEATS IN COACH CLASS

Coach seats with extra legroom are usually found next to emergency exits, directly behind bulkheads, and where three seats are preceeded by two.

Pictured here are the standard shell charts for commonly used passenger aircraft. The arrows indicate coach seats providing additional legroom.

American West), in which passengers are provided with a large sofa and recliner, two berths and a shower. (In the East, Amtrak's best is two adjoining bedrooms.)

The *ne plus ultra,* however, comes when you hire your own private car. Old, restored carriages with kitchens, baths with showers, and a traveling staff can all be obtained from members of AAPRCO, the American Association of Private Railroad Car Owners (244 Orr Drive, Somerville, NJ 08876). The Association will send a charter referral guide with a list of owners whose price negotiations are all done on an individual basis. Most members will handle everything; your car is attached to the back of the train and away you go. Ballpark rates should average at one thousand to two thousand dollars per day; many cars sleep ten. (SS)

FLIGHT PLANS

Fastest, easiest, most likely to make you feel like a Guernsey.

Where to sit on an airplane: For safety, the best bet is in the tail, as far back as you can get. The empennage on most aircraft is a sturdy structure, and if the airplane breaks up in midair, you've got a chance of "gyroscoping" down to earth, helicopter-style. But don't count on it. Often the tail breaks off of the fuselage during accidents that take place on the ground, and the occupants are delivered from the fire and smoke that can consume the main passenger compartment. (PJY)

For comfort, however, the section ahead of the fuselage is the quietest, the most comfortable and the most convenient. That's also where they stick first-class passengers.

Pressure drop: There are two tested and true ways of ameliorating the changes in pressure most air travelers encounter: One requires the constant *chewing of gum* on takeoff and landing. Candy is an okay substitute. The continual swallowing equalizes pressure on the middle ear. The other is to hold your nose, close your mouth and force air against the middle ear. Repeat as necessary. (WRu) But be careful; too much pressure can damage your ear.

Flying with a cold can have extremely painful consequences, since colds can block the Eustachian tube inside the ear, thus preventing pressure equalization between the inner and outer ear chambers. Altitude changes can exacerbate this problem and cause something doctors call a baro-trauma, resulting in excruciating pain.

The best preventive measure would be to wait until you've recovered before you take a flyer. If that's not possible, self-administer nose drops or spray ten minutes before takeoff (Neo-Synephrin will work, Dristan won't). As an alternative — or as an extra precaution — take a decongestant or cold tablet just before takeoff and landing. (WRu)

Coffee, tea, milk, water — in fact, anything will do. Just make sure you drink plenty of (nonalcoholic) fluids, since the air in a passenger plane is extremely dehydrating. If you insist on making trouble for yourself by drinking booze, which is itself dehydrating, try to drink two or three glasses of water for every drink. (JLH)

See also *Etiquette in Motion* **in** *CHAPTER SEVENTEEN: THE DEPORTMENT DEPARTMENT.*

RIDING THE RAILS

Although as an accepted mode of transportation freight-hopping has several drawbacks — it's illegal, the clientele is a bit downmarket, the hours are inconvenient — riding the rails is still possible.

Start by choosing a destination and a day to travel. On the morning of the selected day, call the local rail office and ask for the traffic manager. Tell him your truck, loaded with five-ton ratio bars, has busted an axle and you want to get a boxcar load on the next train headed toward your destination. Ask all the polite questions about rates, loading, handling and the rest. But also ask about departure and arrival times and train and track numbers. (You can press your luck a little and ask if there are any trains going out direct express.)

Next, *scope out the shipping yard* — from the vantage point of an embankment or overpass, if possible. Note for future reference the bull run (a gravel road flanking the tracks); the operations compound (a cluster of buildings opposite the bull run); and the traffic tower, which is where the office you called is located.

On entering the yard, *look for your train's number,* which will be posted over the locomotive's windshield. A yardman might help you out here if he's asked in a friendly and casual manner, but most of these guys are cool and aloof to outsiders.

The person you most want to avoid, obviously, is the bull, or yard dick. He's usually an old railroad worker and pretty aware of most tall tales you might tell. Bulls are, however, notoriously susceptible to hard-luck stories — although it's good to remember that they have the authority to detain you until the police arrive.

Once you've found the right train, *look for the cars going toward your destination.* You'll find this information in the form of scribbled abbreviations ("MNTL" or "MTL" for Montreal, e.g.) on cards wired to the doors of the car or chalked on the car's side.

A boxcar is obviously the carriage of choice, unless it's filled with bulk items — choking sawdust, grain or fertilizer — or if it has only one door open. (A sheared pin could result in your being locked in the car, so if you have no other choice, push a plank into the door frame for insurance.) The trouble with other cars — flatcars and gondolas and the like — is that while they're fine in warm weather, they don't provide any hiding place. Trailer-loaded piggybacks are windy and often checked by bulls, since they usually carry mail. Stay away from gondolas with loose coal — the dust will choke you to death — and be careful of easily shifted loads. Unless the engineer offers you a ride in the cab, the best place to be in cold weather is in one of the little cubby holes located at either end of a jumbo bulk loader. These are accessible through a 2.5-foot hole in the car's faceplate.

If your train stops at a siding, be sure to take your roll with you if you get out to stretch your legs. If you're waiting in the open for a train and want to catch some sleep, place an old spike across the rail; the spike will begin to dance as the freighter approaches, setting off a ringing like an alarm clock that'll wake you in plenty of time.

Never try to jump on a moving train, unless you are running *much* faster than the train before you jump. A moving train is death in action. If you're not running fast enough and you try to grab the train to gain some speed, you'll get pulled down. If you are able to hop, make sure you go for a car with catch rails, and grab for the front one or risk landing between the cars.

Pack warm clothing even in midsummer, and bring along plenty of reading material, since the delays are both inevitable and lengthy.

Keep your money in your shoe. (VBC)

WHAT TO DO IF THE PILOT DIES

So you're stuck 5000 feet above everything you hold dear, and there's a problem — say the pilot dies or something. Here's the word to remember:

MAYDAY

Unless Mother Earth is blocking the view out of the cockpit window, forget about flying the airplane for the moment. Airplanes are inherently stable, and if the guy has croaked in midflight, he's already adjusted the airplane to keep on the straight and narrow. Tune the radio marked "Comm" to the universal emergency frequency, 121.5. Pick up the mike, push the button and say, "Mayday." Stay calm. Repeat your message several times. Remember to release the button on the mike, or you won't be able to hear the air traffic controller who will start talking to you. Listen to what he says. Listen as if your life depended on it. Because if you're in this situation, it does. (DB)

HOW TO LAND A SMALL AIRPLANE

In a small, single-engine, fixed-pitch prop Cessna, Piper or Beechcraft:

Fly straight ahead, unless there's a mountain in the way. Unless you're on final approach or in a spin, you'll have time to experiment a little.

The rule to remember is that the throttle controls altitude; the stick or wheel controls air speed. Look at the instrument panel; there are only a few of these gauges you need to worry about. One of them says "Turn" or "Turn Coordinator" on it and bears the outline of an airplane. That's the one that shows whether or not the plane is in a turn. Try to keep the wings level by turning the wheel or control stick. *Use gentle control movements — do not yank at the control stick or wheel.* On the floor are a couple of pedals that control the rudder. By gently turning the wheel and pushing on one pedal or another, you should be able to balance the little ball in the turn coordinator in the middle. To fly straight ahead, keep the wings on the airplane level and keep the ball in the middle of the turn coordinator.

Next, locate the instrument that says "Climb" on it. On the left-hand side of this gauge is a little area that shows whether the airplane is going up or down. By very gently pressing forward on the stick or wheel, you can make the airplane go down and faster; by pulling gently toward you, you can make the airplane go up and slower. The "Climb" gauge will need a few moments to respond to your movements, so make these adjustments very gradually.

Now find the throttle. Giving the airplane more power will make it climb. Giving it less power will make it descend. If the airplane begins to descend too quickly, you must gently pull the wheel toward you. But if you hold the wheel back and try to make the airplane climb without giving it enough power to do so, the engine will stall, and you will need to push the wheel away from you to gain enough airspeed to make it run again. Conversely, if you hold the wheel away from you without reducing the amount of power, you'll quickly exceed the speed limitations of the airplane. *If you want the airplane to climb, you must give it power* while you gently pull the wheel toward your chest. *If you want the airplane to descend, you must reduce power* while gently pushing the wheel away from you.

You will almost certainly have enough fuel to accomplish your landing. You can double-check by glancing at the fuel gauge; unless you're really in the middle of nowhere, almost any measurable amount of fuel will be sufficient.

Find out where you are: Assuming you've been able to raise somebody on the radio, get them to help you find your way to an airport. They will tell you to turn right or left so many degrees. You will find the degrees marked on a compass on the panel (don't try to use the one that floats above the panel). The compass may have an outline of an airplane on it; the nose of the airplane will point in the direction you are traveling. When you turn the airplane, remember to balance the little ball on the turn gauge.

If you haven't been able to raise any assistance on the radio, look below you. First look near the horizon to see if you can spot a runway. If it's night, you'll see an alternating green and white beacon. If it's daytime, the runway will look like a tiny stretch of freeway. If you see nothing resembling a runway, look for a clear, flat stretch of land. Be careful of power lines — they usually run alongside highways and railroads.

When you have the landing area in sight: Circle, if necessary, until you have gradually reduced your altitude to 1000 feet or so. When you begin to descend, pull out the knob marked "Carb Heat" and if the engine begins to run rough, tinker with the knob marked "Mixture"; the lower you go, the leaner the mixture should be. *Remember, you can reduce your altitude by reducing the amount of power.*

When you seem to be at the right altitude and you are facing the runway, reduce the power substantially. Look at the speed indicator; to make the airplane go slower, pull the wheel toward you. When the speed has dropped below 100 knots or so, slowly activate the lever marked "Flaps." Start with ten degrees of flaps and gradually increase this to thirty degrees. Keep the airplane nearly level as it descends, allowing the nose to drop to keep the airspeed at approximately 70 knots. Try to line up the airplane with the center-

AIRCRAFT INSTRUMENT PANEL

VERTICAL ACCELERATION

GYRO HEADING INDICATOR

ALTIMETER

TURN AND SLIP INDICATOR

COMPASS

ATTITUDE INDICATOR

CLOCK

FULL PANEL INSTRUMENT GROUPING.

AIRSPEED INDICATOR

line of the runway or with an imaginary line drawn down the center of your selected landing spot. When you are over the edge of the runway, your air speed should be around 65 knots.

You can tell if you're on a proper approach if the runway shape remains constant. If the runway appears to shorten, you'll hit the deck short of the runway; if the runway seems to grow in length, you're likely to overshoot the strip. Attempt to aim the airplane at the point at which you'd like to touch down.

When the airplane is nearly on the ground: Try to keep the airspeed below 70 knots and try to cross the threshold of the landing area or runway while you are twenty-five feet or so above the ground. If you are too high or too fast, push in the throttle and the carb heat knob, reduce the flaps and pull up to circle and try again.

If it seems to be going okay, kill the power and let the airplane settle until it is just a few feet above the surface. Pull firmly but smoothly back on the wheel, and let the aircraft touch down with the nose slightly elevated. The object of the game is to make the airplane stop flying at the precise moment the machine meets the Earth. When the wheels touch the ground, let the nose fall slowly. The rudder pedals can now be used to steer the airplane; the control wheel, which acts only on the wing surfaces, is useless for determining direction. Keep backward pressure on the wheel or stick. If you press the tops of the pedals, you will apply brakes. *Do this gently, using both pedals at the same time.*

If the airplane bounces on touchdown, assuming there's enough runway, apply power and pull the wheel gently toward you; when the airplane stabilizes, try again to let it settle. If you have trouble or seem to be running out of room, apply full throttle power, reduce the flaps, push in the carb heat knob and climb to go around and try again.

Halfway: If the airplane has not touched down by the time you're halfway down the runway, apply power and climb to go around and try again.

To kill the engine, pull the mixture knob to the leanest setting. (DB)

The Vanities

Don't be a modern mess. Cleanliness is next to godliness and right behind good behavior in the Modern Man batting order.

C O N T E N T S

Chapter Six: *THE VANITIES*

HAIR CARE

Not just care, really. For those of us who have sacrificed follicles on the follies of youth, the hair that remains loyally on the top of our heads assumes a transcendent character. Not just hair care, then; hair-love, hair-regret, hair-horror.

SWEET PARTING

Traditionalists may favor the left for locating the standard part, but a man looks his best if he parts his hair along the same side that features his better profile. The part should begin at a point directly above the arch of the eyebrow, extend back to the crown, then stop and go no farther.

Parting departing hair: This is where consistency often goes down the drain. Generally, a man plagued with male pattern baldness should retain his natural part until it appears that he's developing a second one on the other side. Incipient chrome-domes may then want to go to a central or diagonal part (which connects the crown and the temple). Fully developed baldies should dispense with a part altogether to avoid slipping into a lowrider.

The Lowrider: This part is made very low on the head in a transparent effort to disguise a gleaming pate. Regarded with ridicule by both women and hirsute men — and by balding men with an admixture of sympathy and horror — men sporting lowriders are desperate enough to derive comfort from a cover-up that's pathetically unconvincing.

As a rule of thumb, resort to either hair transplants or a top-quality wig before a side-parted lowrider. Kill yourself before parting your hair in the rear and combing it forward.

COPING WITH BALDNESS

Men who have an overload of the male hormone testosterone get balder rather than badder. This occurs when the stuff (along with its precursor hormone, DHA) swamps the hair follicles, progressively shortening their growth phase. It seems odd that contemporary culture, which so disparages most of the effects of male hormonal activity, has found no cure for this one.

A flowing male mane has for so long symbolized virility that going bald is one of the most severe tests of a Modern Man's poise. And for those who just can't take it, here — in order of preference — are your choices:

1. Minoxidil-based solutions: Although these offer the unparalleled advantage of actually *growing* hair in a "natural" fashion, they work satisfactorily in only a small percentage of cases. Any effects can only be maintained by means of repeated applications of the stuff — at a cost estimated at something near a grand per year. Not only that, but the solutions work better the younger you are, so the thick-thatched thugs that prowl the streets today may be the first generation of hair-for-life males. Upjohn's Rogaine is the first in the market and is the leader. As we go to press, the substance has yet to be approved by the FDA, but is legally available in Canada and Belgium. Physicians can easily replicate the stuff, however. (Another drug, diazoxide, is used widely in hair treatments sold in Europe and Asia; the stuff acts as a sort of superconditioner, but has no effect whatsoever on hair growth.)

2. Hair transplantation. The surgical transfer of hair plugs from lush to barren parts of the scalp provides the balding with the nearest thing to real regrowth. Hair transplants aren't cheap — a good one will cost you a new Camaro — but unlike Minoxidil, there is a limit. "Micro" hair transplants, which help avoid the uneven, clustered effect of conventional transplants. are now available.

3. Toupées. The third choice — but only if you're willing to buy the best. Otherwise, forget it.

4. Snake oils and potions. There is anecdotal (and often even disputed clinical) evidence that some of these, such as polysorbate 60 and 80, have a prophylactic effect on hair loss. You must assume, however, that investing in these is a waste of time and money.

5. Tissue-expansion method. This, the latest baldness cure to be announced, adapts to the gleaming pate methods previously used by plastic surgeons to repair scars from burns and other accidents. With this method, two balloons are inserted into a pocket created in each side of the scalp near the dome. As the balloon is gradually inflated with weekly saline injections, the skin and underlying tissue slowly stretch. After about two months of this — by which time you will have developed an appearance so hideous and frightening that no amount of hair will ever be able to restore you to full self-esteem — the surgeon will remove both the balloons, along with the bald part of your scalp, which will then be covered by the hairy portions, pulled together and sewn at the top.

6. Hair extension. This process allows for the attachment of hairs one at a time to slow-growth real ones . Eventually, of course, they'll all fall out together. (HFD)

SCALP MASSAGE

After showering, use a towel and your fingertips to vigorously rub your scalp for at least a minute. Your scalp will be invigorated, healthy and nearly dry. (AY)

A dissent: Massaging your scalp increases the flow of the blood to the surface of the skin and to the area surrounding the hair follicles. Unless you have an unusually healthy and resilient head of hair, however, use a towel on your scalp but sparingly, mostly just to pat dry your hair. Rubbing a towel on your head pulls out hair by the handful, and for most of us, that's more hair than we can stand to lose. Use just your fingertips to massage your scalp. (BD)

SHAMPOOS

They're all the same. A recent test allowed participants to distinguish between different types of shampoos in unmarked bottles. They couldn't. You couldn't, either.

Incidentally, for good measure, several brands of dish soap were included. They all rated highly, and couldn't be distinguished from the shampoos. (AR)

CONDITIONERS
Don't use a conditioner every time you shower. Once or twice a week is plenty. (HJ)

BARBER SHOPS
must not be confused with hair styling salons.

In the first place, barbers in many states must complete a more stringent licensing procedure than stylists. In the second place, an older barber will have a wider range of experience (including a knowledge of head contours) than most stylists.

But most important, a barber shop comes as close as the law will allow to a men-only club. The scents and sounds of a barber shop are unchanging. The air reeks of Vitalis, and blue bottles of Barbicide are everywhere. A row of barbers with good scissors sounds like a castanet combo; the average barber opens and closes his scissors at an average rate of 150 to 200 times per minute, whether he's actually cutting hair or not. And best of all, unless you're into looking like some TV anchorman or something, the haircut you'll get in a barber shop will be heads above the one you'll get from some hair stylist — and at a fraction of the cost.

Conversation in a barber shop is open to all. If the guy two chairs down says something about the local team in a voice loud enough for you to hear, feel assured that you've been invited to join the discussion.

Choose a good barber shop and stick to it. Look for a shop with at least one barber older than sixty; he'll have been in business since the boys came back from WWII and will have seen it all. Besides, you owe the guy, since you probably helped starve his family in the late '60s when you were trying to look like Jesus. (*Anon.*)

Once a week: Visit your local barber for a shave once a week. It's an extremely therapeutic treat. (HJ)

BARBER SHOP TALK
A good barber will do whatever you say. So make sure you say it right.

Never ask for a trim when what you want is a thorough if light-all-over job. A trim, in the parlance of barbers, refers to the bottom of the back of the head only. If you want an all-over with a light touch, ask for a back and sides. (ABe)

THE BEST HAIRCUT
is one in which the barber uses the scissors only. Scissors alone can cut hair short without exposing the scalp. (FC)

MUG SHOTS
Once you get the haircut you want — when you really think it looks swell — get a

friend to take some Polaroids of it. Next time you need a haircut, bring the photos to the barber. If it can be done right once, it can be done right twice. (GLS)

SHAVING

It must always be remembered that this is a voluntary act.

WATER

Water is the ingredient most essential to a good shave. Your beard should be soaked with water for at least three minutes, but the longer the better. Soap or shaving cream is basically a lubricant; cream traps the moisture on your face and keeps the beard wet through the shave. If your beard has been thoroughly soaked, however, a little soap from a bar will suffice. (RF)

TOUGH BEARDS

If you do it right, removing even a tough, wiry beard can be made as easy as skimming profits from a pop stand.

First, you have to have a sharp, hollow-ground razor and a good shaving mug and brush; the best brushes are made of badger fur. And most of all, you need lots and lots of very hot water. Every good shave requires a successful interplay between your beard's wetness, your razor's keenness and your blade's angle of attack.

Adjusting for the ideal blade angle as you shave requires that you plug into the cosmos and become the kind of Zen bastard who can handle a razor blade the way Neal Cassidy did a '48 Hudson; it's where you must lose it in order to *really* find it.

To do this, first feel the direction of your beard's growth with your fingers; then, picturing in your mind the subcutaneous point on your whiskers' shafts where you want the blade to make its mark, pull your skin taut and draw your razor along in the *same* direction as your beard's growth. You may begin with light and tentative strokes to test your beard's resistance and your skin's sensitivity, but you should strive to shave yourself with the cold, brilliant boldness of a samurai by imaging yourself making long, clean and sure sweeps with your razor.

Now feel for rough spots; sense the tricky contours, the fantastic topography of your secular self. Then lightly relather and shave your face again, this time against the direction of your beard's growth. (AW)

FILL THE BASIN

with hot water rather than running the faucet. This is socially responsible behavior and necessary for the comfortable equanimity that a good shave requires. (AW)

Warm up the shaving cream by soaking the can for a minute in the hot water. (GLS)

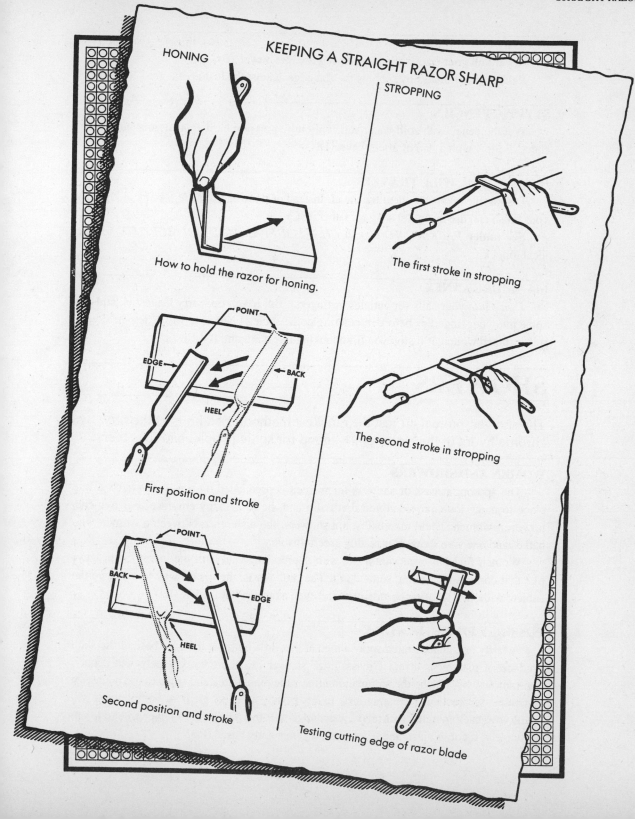

KEEPING A STRAIGHT RAZOR SHARP

HONING

How to hold the razor for honing.

STROPPING

The first stroke in stropping

POINT
EDGE
BACK
HEEL

First position and stroke

The second stroke in stropping

POINT
BACK
EDGE
HEEL

Second position and stroke

Testing cutting edge of razor blade

DULL EDGE

Never dull your razor's blade by drying it with a towel. (RC)

Rehone razor blades by rubbing the flat edge against the inside of a glass. (JKG)

STYPTIC PENCILS

Wet the pencil with cold water and apply it by pressing hard against your puffed-out cheek. Follow with a slap of after-shave. (DN)

HAVE BLADE, WILL TRAVEL

Disposable razors are ideal for travel. Instead of packing your mug, bring along only your brush and use the motel soap for lather. (SC)

See under *PACKING TO GO* **in** *CHAPTER FIVE: MODERN MOBILITY* for the ideal toilet kit.

MANICURE ANNEX

Don't bite your nails (or cuticles or fingers). But if you do, carry Chapstick and rub some into your fingertips before re-entering polite society. Not only will it help heal your self-inflicted wound, it'll stop you from looking like a mutant. (GLS)

SHOWERS

The shower, more than just the quickest method of bathing, is the tiny, chrome hydra of the bathroom — good for some people, bad for others.

WOMEN AND SHOWERS

The appropriateness of showers for women is predicated on use. A shower's a fine place to make love, provided you don't slip and die in a soapy embrace. For hygiene, however, women should take baths, not showers; the difference between a woman who bathes and one who showers is readily ascertainable.

Women find this observation rife with oppression. That isn't the intent. Some guys like that composting aroma, some don't. The problem is, there's no way to bring up the subject without a lot of embarrassment and even anger on both sides. (JH)

POSSIBLY PINEAL ECSTASY

A fairly hot, concentrated spray aimed at that little bump at the very base of the skull produces a marvelous effect ("massaging" shower heads work extremely well), but I don't know why. Maybe the stimulation affects the pineal area and triggers the release of histamine, serotonin and other amines. In any case, you'll feel great — your sinuses will open, your back muscles will relax, your lungs will feel like you've never smoked. Unfortunately, it doesn't last, and its effects vary on a daily basis. (RSB)

QUICKIES

When the chips are really down, when you've just got to, got to, *got to* shower in a hurry — in and out, dry and ready in less than five minutes — here's a tip: Jump in, put a good lather in your hair, and rub your hands over your body while you rinse. Whatever gets clean, gets clean. Unfortunately, nothing gets very clean, except your hair. Nevertheless, in a pinch, this will do. (RJF)

A CLOGGED SHOWER HEAD

can be fixed by simply tying a plastic sack filled with vinegar to the nozzle so that the shower head is immersed in the liquid. Leave it for half a day, and the ports in the nozzle will be clean. (EA) Remember, you always get more out of a shower than you put into it.

WASHCLOTHS

A dedicated-use product if there ever was one. Two views:

The washcloth as a laundry complication: Washcloths? Abandon them. You can clean yourself very well using your hands, just like God intended. Washcloths are hard on your skin, and unless laundered after *every* use, they are simply damp havens for bacteria and dirt. Streamline your laundry by taking your washcloths out of circulation. Use them for car rags, or something else. (RBS)

The washcloth as a hygienic aid: Using a washcloth for your face, arms, legs, chest, whatever, is silly. Use your hands, instead. The proper use of a washcloth can be found in using it to clean behind your genitals. (JMcD)

HOMEMADE DEODORANT

Good as store-bought. Smells fresh, costs less and keeps you nice to be close to all day long, as they say.

Mix equal parts of cornstarch and baking soda. That's it.

If you want some antiperspirant action, get some powdered aluminum chlorhydrate from your local druggist and add a little to your mix. (NW)

Aluminum chlorhydrate is a common ingredient in most commercial deodorants. Prolonged use of the stuff can have nasty effects — aluminum chlorhydrate works by simply plugging up your pores. Newest research points to possible cancer risks (what's new?) and a vague connection to Alzheimer's-like symptoms. (RBr)

NATUREMADE DEODORANT

Powerful natural deodorants are eucalyptus oil, turpentine, chlorine water, hydrogen peroxide, charcoal, dry earth, sawdust and potassium permanganate. (WG)

SCENTS

If you're in doubt about whether or not to use an after-shave lotion or cologne, don't. Using a fragrance is like choosing a necktie, and if your taste is bad, many people will find you affected. If you do use a scent, use it modestly. On men, a fragrance should be subtle.

TYPES OF SCENTS

There are three principal categories of men's fragrances: light citrus, medium woody and Oriental (or musk). European products are more subtle than American ones. (RT)

MIXING SCENTS

If you use one scent as a deodorant and another as a cologne, use both sparingly. Otherwise, the fragrance will resemble neither, and will be overpowering. (SWi)

TIME TO DRY

When using an after-shave or cologne, allow at least twenty minutes for the scent to dry and mingle with your own skin odors. (RT)

OLD SPICE

Old Spice is an Oriental scent that seems to be the most universally appealing fragrance to women. Maybe it reminds them of their fathers. In any case, it is the least pretentious of the most widely available scents. (GH)

AFTER-SHAVE

Women often seem to like the aroma of expensive colognes, but a good man and true will stick to either witch hazel or bay rum as an after-shave lotion. (AW)

Use minute applications of cologne in the evening if you have to, but don't fall for any of those pheromone cologne scams. (OH)

If your first after-shave was Old Spice, never change. If your first after-shave was anything other than Old Spice, you'll be changing scents annually until, in desperation, you try Old Spice. (ES)

Use patchouli oil only as a tasteless gag. (*Anon.*)

Broke and stinky? Pass the men's scent counter at your local department store on your way to a social or business meeting and test one of the samples. When you find one that works, you'll have done your research without an investment. (JFr)

CHAPTER 7

Modern Mating

Lies, distortions, half-truths and critical omissions are the qualities that bind salesmanship to courtship. Courtship, after all, is where life most resembles death, where love meets war and where anything goes. There is no bottom to the barrels many men scrape in order to woo and win.

Modern Men see it differently. Courtship is the peculiar social phenomenon that occurs almost immediately after two single people of the opposite sex are introduced to each other, and Modern Men know that while first impressions (q.v.) count, lasting impressions count more.

C O N T E N T S

Chapter Seven: *MODERN MATING*

FIRST IMPRESSIONS

Everyone has a theory about how to approach a woman with whom you are unacquainted. Humor is the best musk, so, as a rule, we advocate a courteous but funny opener — although if humor isn't one of your strengths, don't even try.

FUNNY FIRST LINES

If you try to say something truly funny when you first meet a girl, and it's not, you'll sound like a dork. If you think what you have to say is truly funny and it's not, you *are* a dork (your friends can help you here). If, on the other hand, what you have to say really is funny and she doesn't get it, *she's* a dork. A funny opener is the best opener, but it's also the riskiest. (*Anon.*)

If you can't be funny, be sincere. Sincerity can be a bit of a nod, but if you're consistent with it, it just might work. Try not to let it become sappy, though. (RBr)

Be natural and say whatever crosses your mind. Just don't be rude. (*Anon.*)

Some women, however, respond to gentle manners with a snore, and for them, we have a well-deserved but dissenting view.

A dissent: Getting a woman's attention when you first approach her can be a nasty business, as any man who has left an initial encounter reeling with rude rejection can tell you. A guy who can command a woman's love with his money and good looks has the luxury of going the hearts-and-flowers route. But for the vast majority of men who look and act just sort of nice, actually *being* nice means that you won't get the girl. When Leo Durocher said that nice guys finish last, he wasn't talking about the batting order.

Try intentionally hitting a raw nerve. Getting a woman peeved in this way works because women tend to confuse their strong emotions. At first, a woman will react to a rough remark much as a man does, but after a while all that she remembers is that something about you got her blood up. It follows, then, that hot blood must mean love, and, *voilà!* the two of you are down at the local catalog showroom checking out bedroom sets.

The rough introduction will never work unless conducted in a manly (even gentlemanly) fashion. If you come across like a sadistic cad given to peppering women with random cruelties and direct personal insults, you'll probably receive the contempt you deserve in return. Maintain, rather, the forceful and dynamic aura of a man who won't pander to a woman's opinions or need her approval to pursue the relationship. Feel free, in other words, to sideswipe her politics, administer a small puncture to her values or look askance at her life-style, and she'll thank you for it later. Otherwise, you can just be *nice* and risk winding up on the receiving end of all her complaints about the SOB she *really* loves. (AW)

THE METAMECHANICS OF THE OPENING LINE

In approaching a woman in a bar or other public place, remember that you'll almost never get back more than you give. A good opening line should always do two things: First, it should invite a response (other than a simple yes or no); and second, it should reveal something positive about you. Also note: while first lines are important, fifth and sixth and even seventy-fifth lines are crucial. If you don't have anything to say after she says hello, don't even start a conversation. Silent and passive rejection is preferable to active failure. (LM)

The less threatening the environment, the more aggressive you can become. In the produce section of a supermarket, you can use almost any opening line that comes to mind. (In the New York subway, nothing you say short of absolute brilliance will work.)

Tramps like us: A good opener will imply that something special separates the two of you from the rest of the crowd in the room, and beyond — i.e., What are two good-looking people with legs like ours doing in a dive like this? (JG)

DATE DESIGN

Don't be lazy when designing an evening out. Think it through.

STRUCTURAL THEORY

Every date should adhere to the principle of Aristotelian unity. There should be a beginning, a middle and an end; the sum of these three parts should not be greater than the whole. (It's not useful to view the end of every date as a sexual encounter.) (RES)

APPLICATION

This structure applies to every date. Here are two examples:

1. The TV date: You're going to spend the evening watching television at her place. The beginning, in this case, might be in the presentation of food: you have carefully considered the best ingredients for a TV picnic; you've assembled them with some sense of ceremony; and you have contrived to add at least one unexpected embellishment (3-D glasses and a carrot nose for the pâté, maybe). The middle part of the evening takes the most time, but it's also the most predictable: the TV's on presumably because you're watching it — if not the networks, maybe a rental video or old 8mm conversions of your family's film archives. For a finale, keep it calm. Since this has been designed as a stay-at-home date, don't jump up and suggest a drive through the suburbs. Instead, take her out on the porch and tell her a good story about something that happened at least a hundred years before she was born.

2. The first dinner date: This is the easiest of all dates to organize because it has such a well-defined function. The idea here is to get to know one another and among humans that's done through conversation. The beginning of the date should therefore be constructed around the principle of the conversational safe harbor, the one place in which either of you can find refuge if the talk grows thin. This can be manifested in a small gift you've brought or a story you can tell as you travel to dinner. But ideally, this beginning should involve her directly, so the best gambit is one that magnifies one of the few facts you knew about her before you asked her to dinner. That way, if she ever feels at a loss for words, she will feel comfortable talking about herself. And during dinner, that's what you want. Don't be a dope and play your whole tape. Just for once, keep quiet and listen carefully. You'll hear all sorts of things. For a finale, don't get corny and don't get weird. Wrestling a girl to a pin or trying to get her to declare unlimited love is not the best way to conclude a first date. Instead, just relax, show her that you're comfortable with her, that you consider her to be one of your friends. That's enough. (RES)

PHONE CONTACT

- Warn the girl that you will be calling her
- Identify yourself and get to the point of your call
- If you're inviting her somewhere, be specific

Asking her vague questions, like, What are you doing Saturday night, only creates an awkward situation for both of you. If you want to ask her out Saturday, say so, and tell her where you want to go. Then let her decide if that's what she has in mind for her Saturday evening. (*Anon.*)

FIRST DATE MISDEMEANOR

Ladies love outlaws sure enough, but just watch the opening scene of *Bonnie and Clyde* to see the effect of bringing women in on some spontaneous larceny. This doesn't mean that to win her heart you've got to risk an ambush by *federales*. But if robbing a bank on the first date got Clyde wrestled to the floor of his '29 Essex by an admiring Bonnie, then breaking into the zoo by moonlight or some similar misadventure ought to at least win you a smooch. (AW)

MYSTERY TOUR

As long as you're going to take her away for a long weekend anyhow, why not enhance the excitement by keeping your destination a secret? Just tell her what she'll need to bring. Trade favors for hints while you lay over at Yucatan International Airport. (AW)

THE LATE DATE

Status is conferred on you by the late date, in which you suggest a rendezvous after another of her appointments. This gives you a decided advantage over whomever she was with earlier, and can be an effective weapon in love-and-war skirmishes. On the other hand, if she says she'll meet you, then either doesn't show or calls to say she won't be able to make it, break out the white flags. (AW)

A dissent: Any woman who would accept a second date on the same evening should not be taken seriously. Assuming her first date is with a man who cares for her, the emotional violence (q.v., **below**) she is wreaking is not worth the massage she may be giving your ego. A woman who would willingly ditch one date to take on a second is not only emotionally irresponsible, she's also emotionally unstable. If you accept a late date with her one night, you'll be an early date another night. That's a promise. (DB)

SCEPTRE'D AISLES

The best seats in any section of a theater are in the third row. (AR)

STANDING ADVICE FOR THE FOURTH DATE AND AFTER

Apologize twice, then apologize again. It doesn't matter. Just say you're sorry. Act of God? So what. Say you're sorry. Say it again. Say it like you mean it. It's your fault. Apologize. (GAD)

CHEAP DATES

Every date has the same built-in problems and opportunities.

Honesty pays: The most important thing to remember about a 25¢ date is that you have to be up front about it right from the get-go. If your budget is small, say so. (VW)

Fun counts: Participating in any mutually enjoyable activity — from canasta to sunbathing to window shopping to gallery hopping — makes a perfectly enjoyable date, no matter how little you spend. (JO)

A *drinking girl* is never a cheap date, but she's usually worth it. (*Anon.*)

THE EXPENSIVE DATE

A relative term if ever there was one. Sometimes, though, it's fun to plan a deliberate budget-blast. One must still observe the principles of social entertainment, however.

The Six-Hour Indulgence: To plan a six-hour demonstration of fiscal irresponsibility, avoid movie houses and other ticketed, time-consuming venues and events. Instead, stay out on the streets and nightclub your credit cards into receivership. (*Anon.*)

Take her to dinner on another continent. (VW)

DOUBLE DATES

can be double trouble unless you're willing to pay as much attention to the dynamics of the group as you would ordinarily pay to your date if you were on your own. A double date as a first date is not a bad idea, but it must be a well-planned evening, with a decided emphasis on distraction. (*Anon.*)

Never devote more than half the time to activities or discussions involving the other couple with whom you're double-dating. Remember to devote some of the time to your companion — as if you were alone. (VW)

WHY WOMEN GO TO THE TOILET IN GROUPS

One of the great mysteries of dating rituals is found in the group migration of women to the toilet. There are ten good reasons why this happens:

1. To gossip about their dates or to decide who's going to end up with whom.
2. To check out the other guys in the bar or restaurant.
3. To do drugs.
4. Because only one of them has really good make-up.
5. Because they're bored.
6. To come up with a way to ditch their dates.
7. One (or both) of them is going to be sick.
8. Only one of them is carrying tampons.
9. Only one of them knows where the restroom is.
10. The real reason: Because both of them have to go. (MKa)

See also *RESTAURANTS* **in** *CHAPTER EIGHTEEN: MISBEHAVIOR* **and** *Six Examples of Gender Burden, What to Do with Your Eyes, Conversational Etiquette, At the Table, Theater Protocol, Smoking Etiquette* **and** *When to send flowers,* **all in** *CHAPTER SEVENTEEN: THE DEPORTMENT DEPARTMENT.*

RULES OF COURTSHIP

Just goes to show, there are rules for *everything*.

THE ULTRA-RULE

There is no such thing as an innocent lie.

Every lie you tell during courtship will come back and haunt you. A teeny, little white one about something completely inconsequential ruins your credibility forever. If you're found out in a fib about being late at work, you can forget ever being believed again; your flattery will go unwelcomed and your sincerity will sound like false flattery.

Modern Men — and most women — find that there is no charm in a lie, no endearing foible that justifies taking any liberties with the truth. (BC)

CHEATING

Never cheat on a woman about whom you care a great deal and expect to get away with it because she'll *always* find out. (PN)

NEATNESS COUNTS

Keep your emotions tidy. Tossing off meaningless emotional demands and tantrums is extremely irresponsible. (SD)

Know what you want. Don't make emotional submission a part of your sexual conquest menu. Making her jump through ego-hoops is not only dishonest, it's cruel. (PEC)

SYMBOLICALLY SPEAKING,

if you gave her a rose once a week while you were courting her, you must give her a rose once a week after you've won her. (*Anon.*)

See also *SCREENING A MATE* **in** *CHAPTER EIGHT: MODERN MATRIMONY.*

SEX AND SEDUCTION

Here's how it works:

FOOD FOR THE MOOD

Playfully feeding your date a morsel of food by hand is reputed to have a seductive effect. (JEM)

Then:

LOOK OUT FOR No. 1

The key to great sex is selfishness, not hypersensitivity. The best seductions begin with bold and unapologetically smoldering gazes and lead to a kind of foreplay in which your thoughts and moves subtly impart the message that you're going after what *you* want, no matter what. Then forget all you've ever heard or read about technique. In fact, forget about everything in the world, except for that part of it which is before you. No amount of tender (or timid) consideration will please her as much. Never ask if it was good and be sure to return to being a gentleman when the lights go back on. (AW)

That's how it works. Sometimes.

A dissent: Sex is the only thing that gets better when you stop thinking of yourself first. (GLS)

HOW TO RECOGNIZE A COME-ON

Body lingo: You can tell a girl is coming on to you by watching her body language. If she turns directly toward you and fluffs up her hair or arches her back, she's interested. (KHG) . . . if she's sitting on the other side of the room talking to somebody else, but her legs and body are turned toward you. (CFD)

The eyes have it: Dilated pupils and prolonged eye contact. . . (GY)

Rapt session: . . . if she seems to hang on your every word. (JOP) She'll either initiate conversation or eagerly follow up on any lame subject you broach. If you falter, she'll help you out, encouraging you to discuss yourself and laughing like a ninny at your dumb jokes. (AR) . . . if she keeps trying to get you to talk about yourself, despite your professed reservations. (DE)

Angles of attack: Her right-angle gaze at you is observable through the corner of the eye only. It appears during conversation with somebody else and imparts her desire to be where you are instead of where she is. (AW) . . . when she stands at a right-angle to you, thrusting out her breasts while ostensibly showing you another sight, like her cheap Wyeth print or the view from her balcony. (JGF)

Presenting behavior: She engages you in conversation at your desk, on top of which she has rested her elbows and placed her head in her hands. Don't be distracted by her derrière as it weaves figure-eights in midair. (JV) . . . if during the conversation she continually touches her mouth. (JGF)

HOW *ESQUIRE* AND PHIL DONAHUE FOOLED YOU

Women *hate* so-called "new age" men, despite the media's protestations to the contary. The idea of a man sitting down and weeping about his difficulties on the job or shedding tears of joy at the thought of a Saturday night dinner date is enough to make most sensible women puke. (*Anon.*)

WHEN YOU CARE ENOUGH

to show her that you had an especially good time, have something sent over to her the next day. Flowers (red for romance) are always a good bet, but a better one will prove to her that you were listening when she mentioned how well she likes Fairfield Porter paintings (send her a print) or grilled cheese and tomato sandwiches on wheat. (DF)

See also *Gifts* **and** *When to send flowers* **in** *CHAPTER SEVENTEEN: THE DEPORTMENT DEPARTMENT.*

VOCAL SEX

If you're one of those guys who takes a transistor along to the football game so you won't miss the play-by-play, you're also probably into vocal (not to be confused with oral) sex.

Pregame warm-up: Keep it vague. All pregame chatter is the same: I'm just looking forward to getting out there and giving it a hundred percent. There are a million ways of saying this. Choose one.

Color commentary: This provides interesting background analysis to the nonscoring actions that are occurring and the ones that will follow. Every good color man, however, knows not to express his analysis in terms of promises. They should be specific enough to excite interest, no more.

Play by play: This is a tough job, since all the action has to be explained as forcefully as possible just nanoseconds before it actually happens. In a spirited encounter, good play calls will be met by loud and insistent demands for a breakthrough scoring run.

Postgame analysis: Skip it. It's all bullshit; if you don't know how good it was for her, then for God's sake, *don't ask.* (MNB)

AN ENGLISH LANGUAGE/GIRL-TALK DIRTY WORD GLOSSARY

It's very fashionable for even very young girls to be remarkably foul-mouthed. But only in public. In private, intimate moments, when blunt words might be expected, women suddenly turn coy and revert to a language of chaste propriety. Below is a brief list of translations:

English	Girl-Talk
Cock	It
Balls	Those
Tits	These
Cunt	There
Shit	Freshen up
Fuck	Dinner and a movie (PJO)

TALK DIRTY AND LOWDOWN

Use the lower range of your voice as a weapon in the arsenal of seduction. Women respond to a number of sensations — sound is one. (GE)

THE BEST SEX MANUAL

is Alex Comfort's *The Joy of Sex*. If you're looking for technical information, look there. **Or see under** *KNOTS* **in** *CHAPTER ONE: OUTDOORS*.

PERFECT FOREPLAY

lasts forever. Don't hurry anything; make foreplay an end in itself. Play it like a board game, like multiple Monopoly. (*Anon.*)

PUBLIC DISPLAYS OF AFFECTION

Not just holding hands, either. Try lovemaking in a public or semipublic place some-time. Just the *fear* of getting caught heightens the experience enormously. (*Anon.*)

POLITICS AS FASHION FOR GIRLS

Grin and bear it when your new date begins lecturing you on radical Marxist-feminist orthodoxy. If you get truly bored, pick one subject of her monolog and pursue it in a disinterested fashion. *Do not get angry.* Politics-as-fashion exists primarily as a defensive element, something designed to keep you at arm's length. Go along with it. It's far and away the safest distance. (TDY)

When a date becomes political theater, and her anger (and behavior) clearly have little to do with you specifically, offer to take her home. When she refuses, leave. Do not lose your temper. If she doesn't call later to apologize, forget her. (*Anon.*)

THE ENDURANCE RUN

You can improve your endurance by extending foreplay as long as possible, then letting her get on top before making the big rollover. If you play this right, you can drag it out for an extra thirty minutes or so. (*Anon.*) (**See also** *PC Workout* **under** *FITNESS* **in** *CHAPTER SIXTEEN: MODERN MISHAPS.*)

EMOTIONAL VIOLENCE

Women routinely use emotional violence as a means of conducting their relationships. (*Anon.*)

A comment: This is the most succinct version we received of this particular observation. The sense seems to be that women have a fairly cavalier attitude about mens' feelings and that a confused woman who commits gratuitous emotional violence on a man is inflicting significantly more pain than if she'd belted him in the chops or hit him over the head with a board.

PHYSICAL VIOLENCE AGAINST WOMEN

The gender deal works like this: You stand there and you take it like a man. And if what you're taking is coming from a woman, you don't hit back. Never. *No matter what.* No matter what horrible, crazy, terrible thing she's done. You've heard it since you were two years old, and it's true: Don't hit girls. Violence — of *any* type — against women or children is the most unmanly behavior imaginable. If slugging girls and kids is something you're doing and you can't stop, something's wrong and you'd better get it fixed.

We could devote much more space to this, since it's an important premise of this book. But in the end, we'd be saying the same thing a dozen different ways: *No matter what, do not hit a woman.*

CONDOMS OR PROPHYLACTICS

That's a rubber to you. Because of the public concern over AIDS and because many of the contraceptives used by women have occasionally undesirable side effects, condoms are enjoying a substantial sales growth. Once available only from druggists, condoms are now sold on large racks in grocery stores and other consumer centers.

Two types: Latex and lambskin. The wide variety of "ticklers" and so forth are not real marketing strengths, since most people buy a condom for hygiene or birth-control.

Lambskin condoms are made from lamb's intestines. They offer a more natural feel, but the supply is somewhat limited. Perhaps the best condom on the market is sold under the name Naturalamb. (*Note:* At the time this book went to press, the efficacy of lambskin condoms in preventing the spread of the AIDS virus had not yet been proven. **See below.**)

Latex condoms are the only ones that have been tested for AIDS prevention. Preliminary tests conducted at the University of California show that the AIDS virus cannot pass through latex. Latex condoms are available with nipple ends and with lubricants.

Men tend to buy condoms for disease prevention; women, who are buying more condoms than ever, are turning to them for the contraceptive value. A condom is 98 percent effective, and although a latex condom may break if exposed to heat, the only people who think that they break are those who don't use them.

One size fits all: All condoms are manufactured to a standard seven-inch size (although a smaller size is manufactured in the Orient).

And keep your powder dry: The Australian military recently used condoms to keep their rifle barrels free from moisture. (MK)

See also *Condoms* **under** *CLAP, etc.,* **in** *CHAPTER SIXTEEN: MODERN MISHAPS.*

BIRTH CONTROL AND ABORTION

Ask: Don't assume anything. Ask your partner if she practices contraception. And ask her *before* you make love.

Responsibility: To view sex in purely *recreational* terms is to do violence to the prefix. Sex was not invented to make you feel swell about yourself.

Sex is a dangerous, truly life-altering experience, since no contraceptive device is absolutely foolproof, and pregnancy — which, after all, is what the whole exercise is about — is almost always a possibility.

The welter of contraceptives and the relative ease of obtaining abortions contrive to create a sense of lessened responsibility. Don't be fooled and think of contraception and abortion in purely personal terms. You are not a solo actor here. Others are involved.

Know where you stand: Abortion is wretched or worse, depending on your point of view. If you don't know how you feel about abortion, figure it out. And make your conviction clear to your lover. Abortion is an issue that's been monopolized by extremists; your own determination about abortion should be made in calmer, more reflective waters.

Parents: Abortion as a moral issue is not an exclusive province of women. Pregnancy is about parenthood, and your own feeling about abortions — whether surgically induced or, as with the new post-conception pills, chemically induced — must be factored into your decision about lovemaking.

If you can't accept the responsibility for an unintentional pregnancy, you have no business screwing around.

GIRLFRIENDS OF FRIENDS

(or why your best friend's girl is much uglier than you think)

Many women often have an extremely situational view of friendship, so it stands to reason that friendship between men is a strange (and threatening) concept to most girls. One of the first orders of business for women moving into a relationship is to pass judgments on most of the friends of her new consort. Often, she won't like any of them. If she finds one she does like, there's always a chance that she'll go for him.

DEFINITE BEAUTY

If your best friend has a truly beautiful girl — and you feel yourself being drawn into a compromising situation — pay special attention to her least desirable attributes. Still having a problem? Here's a foolproof way to make any girl ugly: When you talk to her, look directly into her nostrils and concentrate. (JF)

You can also look for the most obvious faults in other contexts. For example, how good-looking is a girl who would break the heart of your best pal? And what would stop her from breaking yours?

Your view of your best friend's girl should be tempered by two important factors. First, if your best friend is involved with a new girl and is still your best friend, it's because he's had to fight to keep your friendship intact in the face of strong domestic opposition. Second, and most important, your best friend will be your friend forever, but your best friend's girl won't be your's forever, and will *never* be your best friend. (RCP)

(**See also** *WIVES OF FRIENDS* **in** *CHAPTER EIGHT: MODERN MATRIMONY*.)

GIRLFRIENDS OF GIRLFRIENDS

As when they come from the girlfriend of your best pal, sidelong glances from the girlfriend of your best gal might be the result of something other than your irresistibility. So before walking into this particular minefield consider what kind of feminine intramurals might already be playing out on it — it'll help you do the right thing. (JF)

IMPOTENCE AND PERFORMANCE ANXIETY

The ugly twins of the bedroom.

NO LAST LAUGHS

Impotence is only funny if it's somebody else's problem. If it's your dick that's limp, it's a tragedy. (*Anon.*)

CHECK IT OUT

If you're lucky, you think to yourself, the problem's a medical one. It probably isn't, but body docs are cheaper than head docs, which is where you're headed next. That's the trouble with this stuff, it's either all in your head, or it's not at all.

Medical causes of impotence include diabetes, damage to the nervous or circulatory system or drug and alcohol abuse. If you have a history of any of these and are suffering with impotence, check with your doctor for treatment.

Bloodless: Ultimately, the only medical cause for impotence is that not enough blood flows to the penis to make it stiffen. (*Anon.*)

THERAPY

Through a variety of techniques, a therapist is going to make you do what you've been avoiding all along — you're going to have to talk about it.

Once that's done, the therapist is going to give you a series of exercises designed to reduce the tension between you and your partner — lots of fun and feely stuff.

Eventually, you'll figure it out, and it'll probably have something to do with fatigue or stress or suppressed anger or self-effacement or a combination of these. (DS)

THREE TYPES OF TREATMENT

I put together the following info on impotence treatments from articles I read in my wife's magazines and thought you'd like to have it:

1. Penile prosthesis: One of a variety of semirigid prostheses (including one with a hydraulic system that pumps the tissue full of fluid) is implanted into the sheath of the penis, enabling an impotent patient to perform sexually. The cost varies from $2000 to $4000, depending on the type of system preferred.

2. Injection: The NYU Medical Center is working on this method, in which a solution of papavirine hydrochloride and phentolamine mesylate is injected into the base of the penis to enhance blood flow. Although the success rate is high, the technique requires self-injection prior to sex.

3. Electrical stimulation: This technique, under study by Jefferson Medical College in Philadelphia, is highly experimental. The idea is that electrical stimulation of the nervous system through the anus will cause blood to flow through the pelvis and into the penis. A small device is inserted in the anus before sex and is triggered with a small, handheld switch. (*Anon.*)

DO-IT-YOURSELF

Think about it. What else is going wrong in your life? Has your impotence become your favorite obsession? Do you enjoy the anger it's producing in your partner? Think about it some more. Then you can call a doctor. (DS)

AFTER YOU

Men obsessed with premature ejaculation should consider the possibility that their condition is at least partly a function of what might be termed delayed orgasm. (AW)

ANOTHER NIGHT

Once, when the Orioles lost a crucial game on an error in the ninth, Rick Dempsey, the catcher, shrugged and said, "There's another game tomorrow." The baseball season is 162 games long. The sexual season is longer. (KE)

LOOK AROUND

Maybe your impotence is your body's way of telling you that you have the wrong bed partner. If you can't talk about it with her, then she's definitely the wrong one, and that's probably the source of your problem. (GLS)

BREAKING UP

There's only one rule here, but as much gloss as you like:

THE RULE

When it's over, it's over. (PG)

THE GLOSS

Your desperate attempts to patch things up — especially if you've been the one dumped — will make you look even more pathetic to your estranged honey, and to everyone else.

The more effort you put into trying to unbreak a breakup, the more unlikely is the possibility for an eventual reunion. (TRD)

If you do manage to get back together, you'll find the relationship has been fatally wounded by the whole experience, and before too long you'll break up again. (HF)

If you do convince her to give it another shot, she'll hate you for convincing her to do something she didn't want to do. (*Anon.*)

THE COMFORT

The chances are about 50–50 that if you let it go, she'll call you sometime within five years, and you'll discover you don't want the relationship anymore. (EFO)

Three months after you've split, you'll find yourself thinking you want her back. You're wrong. (GLS)

See also *MARRIAGE* **and** *DIVORCE* **in** *CHAPTER EIGHT: MODERN MATRIMONY*.

FANTASYLAND

You're traveling through another dimension — a dimension not only of sight and sound, but of mind, a journey into a wondrous land whose boundaries are that of imagination. There's a signpost up ahead. It reads . . .

ORGIES

Orgies? Right, sure. Here's a prediction: Your next orgy will take place in the smallest room in your house, with the door locked. You'll be alone. Nevertheless:

Never plan: The thing about orgies is that if they're planned, they turn out terrible. If they simply occur, they're fantastic. (LK)

Stranded: The primary ingredient for a successful orgy is a bunch of libertine houseguests that have nowhere else to go. Make sure everyone gets enough liquor and drugs, including yourself. Move every mattress in the house into one room so that everyone must either sleep together or not at all. Once it's under way, the main rule is to try to let go and do a whole bunch of stuff that you'd normally never even think of doing. These events are often more depressing than you can imagine. (*Anon.*)

You come here often? Never have swing sessions or orgies with friends. Invite only acquaintances. (*Anon.*)

Hold it, everybody: In this age of AIDS and other diseases, you might want to think about the *types* of people willing to indulge in group sex. Under no circumstances should you decide to have a conversation that requires language, let alone brain power — you'll be disappointed. And skip breakfast. (*Anon.*)

MUSIC OF THE SPHERES

Boobs make sounds. This is perhaps more of a poetic thing that one develops as time goes on. I don't even know if it's a real sound; it's more of a metaphysical sound, I suppose. Different tits, the way they move, they make these different sounds that are just totally exotic. Maybe it's a total fantasy, but I swear I hear it. Some days, I have to use a Sony Walkman out there, it gets so bad. Especially in the springtime. (RRa)

Modern Matrimony

Modern marriage is coated in oil; you slip and slide right through it, wash up and pretend it never happened.

For Modern Men, however, marriage offers no easy escapes, since it's part of an institutional component kit that also includes a bonus family module.

And if it does come apart, if the wires start to fry and the tubes start to pop, there's always modern divorce. But you come out of that covered with slime, and that doesn't wash off.

C O N T E N T S
Chapter Eight: *MODERN MATRIMONY*

SCREENING A MATE

You're never going to get one with a guarantee, so use common sense and one of these useful vetting devices:

TRAVELS WELL?

Go on a trip together. Travel has become one of the most stressful aspects of modern life. If you can't stand your nominee after four or five days of a journey, reconsider. (JO)

TRIPLE FEATURE

Take a nominated date to a triple feature. If she sits uncomplainingly through all three, it figures that she likes you enough to put up with your eccentricities. (APS)

VALENS VOWS

Suggest a Richie Valens wedding, with "La Bamba" as a processional, "Oh, Donna," as an anthem, and "Come Little Darlin'" as a recessional. Volunteer to have the music arranged in a baroque style, but make no other concession. If she goes for it, she's worth keeping. (FBD)

CHECK OUT MOM

and get a preview of things to come. Mothers are often quite generous in passing on their shortcomings to their daughters. (*Anon.*)

See also *Wife-for-Life* in *CHAPTER EIGHTEEN: MODERN MISBEHAVIOR.*

MARRIAGE

See also *DIVORCE,* below.

DON'T FORCE IT

After all, most men are biologically predisposed *against* marriage. Men are far more reluctant to surrender their adolescence than women are. Boys will be boys, and men want to be boys, too.

Men regard marriage as a pivotal step, a transition into late adulthood. Adult responsibilities, or the idea of them, frighten most men. Of course, the fear is worse than the reality, but men keep forgetting this. They see late hours at work, saving for the kids' education and a nightmare vacation, pouring money into insurance premiums, car payments, food, clothing and shelter. They have seen their friends rather suddenly become obsessed with a compulsion to make good, then make better. The daunting obligations of marriage make most men fear that the boy is gone forever. This feeling doesn't mean that he wants to ditch his wife and kids, but it makes him act screwy sometimes.

Generally, women regard marriage as a destination. To many of them, it may even become a universal affirmation of their own legitimacy. Women know a lot more than men do about obligations; they're usually the ones with the expertise on familial, social and even filial duties. At the risk of sounding unkind, women sometimes even confuse duty with affection, kindness, compassion or a feeling much closer to self-fulfillment. Men, on the other hand, tend to feel as though the ideals of duty are administered from the highest authority. For them, duty is not questioned; it is simply done. A man regards his duties as serious, neverending responsibilities. It's the weight of that conviction that makes men shy away from marriage.

The burden of marriage is usually less than most men anticipate. Ideally, there's a wife around who's willing to share some of the marital responsibilities. More important, a wife is also a boon companion — not the same as a man's buddies, but in some ways even better. (*Anon.*).

Besides, it must be okay. A lot of guys do it.

IT'S, LIKE, YOU KNOW, A *PROMISE* OR SOMETHING

The whole point of a marriage ceremony is for the exchange of *vows*. And a Modern Man is a Modern Man of his word. (*Anon.*)

THE LIST

Before you do anything rash, make a list of all your potential wife's assets and liabilities — and we're not talking finances here. Put her crooked nose and horse laugh on one side and her magnificent, mile-long legs on the other. Try to figure whether or not the good's worth the bad. If you think it is, keep the list so you can remind yourself of what the good side was while you're enduring the bad side. (RD)

SEX?

Sex is what got you to thinking about marriage in the first place. But ask any married person how important sex is in the long haul and if they tell you the truth they'll surprise you. Don't make looks and sex appeal your primary motivations for marriage. Women go from golden to Golda in the course of about eighteen crucial months. A basketful of song lyrics will provide ample evidence for this observation. (DB)

See also *SEX AND SEDUCTION* **in** *CHAPTER SEVEN: MODERN MATING*.

THE BEST MAN

The best man is the ringmaster for the groom's circus. If a man disagrees with his friend's proposed match, he should decline this honor.

In advance of the wedding: The best man should help plan the rehearsals and act to coordinate the participants' schedules. He should make himself available to the family of the bride, although it's not likely they'll have much need for his services.

Arrange the bachelor party, if there is one. These things can range from a simple, tasteful dinner party to something far more complex and tasteless.

On the day when his friend descends into utter helplessness, the best man should:

- *Make sure the groom gets to the church* at least a half-hour before the ceremony.
- *Arrange all the logistics.* Take charge of the car the bride and groom will use to leave the church or reception. It should be fueled and the baggage packed.
- *See that the groom's clothing* and accessories are available for the ceremony.
- *Make sure the groom has the marriage license and the ring.*
- *Get the parson's fee* from the groom and present it in a plain envelope to the clergyman following the service.
- *Keep the ring* in his waistcoat pocket so it's ready to be handed to the groom at the proper part of the ceremony.
- *Offer the first toast* to the bride and groom at the reception and at the bridal dinner, where the best man acts as a sort of compere. The toast should be simple and witty, but not too sentimental. Sincerity's okay, though.
- *Send a telegram* in the groom's name to the bride's parents thanking them for both the wedding and their daughter. (JD)

See also *Formal Wear* **and** *The Traditional Wedding Party Get-up* **in** *CHAPTER ELEVEN: CLOSETS* **and** *Table Manners* **in** *CHAPTER SEVENTEEN: THE DEPORT-MENT DEPARTMENT.*

NO ALTERATIONS

Once married, do not expect to remake your wife into someone she wasn't before you married her. By the time they're twenty-five or thirty most people are the person they're going to be until the grisly end.

Women undergo a massive personality change sometime in their twenties, and if you want to know what your fiancée is really going to be like, wait until after this crucial post-pubescent mutation. After that, what you see is what you get. (GFr)

MARRYING MONEY

Don't. That's all. Just don't do it. If you do, you'll regret it and suffer consequences far worse than everyday poverty. Clichés exist because they contain truth, and the appropriate cliché here is absolutely true: "The person who marries for money earns it."

Having married for any of the valid, traditional reasons (for family or for love or for companionship), you may find that your wife, incidentally, has money. If this is true, don't sacrifice your honor by sponging off her, unless that's all your honor is worth. Try your hardest to live off your income, saving hers for the education of children or the care of elderly parents. And never, under any circumstances, touch her principal. (TM)

PRENUPTIAL AGREEMENTS

These documents are now in fashion, and if signing one is going to make everyone happier, go ahead. (LCu)

A dissenting view: Prenuptial agreements presuppose the invalidity of a sacred promise. If you don't believe the word of the person you're thinking of marrying, don't marry her. (DB)

DIVORCE PREVENTION

Handy hints from all over:

Hard work: Don't be afraid to try to *force* your marriage to work. Your marriage should be a priority, taking precedence over anything else in your life. Complacency will kill a marriage faster than anything else. (MR)

Nurture dependency: Being Mr. I-Can-Take-Care-of-Myself may convince your wife that you should. (FTo)

Lung-stretchers: Don't be afraid to occasionally yell and scream. Not on a daily basis or anything, but exercise your vocal cords from time to time. It's good for you and won't hurt the marriage. Don't get vicious, just loud. (RDa)

Share common interests or develop a knack for freely exchanging information. Don't exclude each other from important parts of your lives. (JD)

See also *DIVORCE,* **below.**

MONEY TALKS

When both partners in a marriage contribute to mutual expenses, monetary conflicts can be reduced if each has a personal bank account and a joint account is maintained for household expenses. Compute a budget for shared expenditures and feed the joint account equally to cover these costs. Each partner's personal account provides the freedom to which a worker is entitled. Same rule applies to credit cards. (WCG)

A dissent: Money should never be the source of a quarrel in a marriage. Pool it and let the most practical partner manage it. (HC)

MULTI-MAN

To keep your wife happy and contented, these are the eight guys you have to be:

1. A good provider: Work hard, pay those bills.

2. A good date: The perfect dinner and dancing partner, a hearty party escort.

3. A great psychoanalyst: Discuss, scrutinize, analyze, figure it out. Sort out her moods, help her find meaning in life. Help her find a new meaning in life. Help her find a better meaning in life.

4. A good lover: Buck up like a raging stallion. But only when she whistles.

5. A good creative artist: Create imaginative testimonials to her beauty and worth.

6. A good suitor: And a perpetually unsuccessful one at that.

7. A good pal: A brother, a free shoulder, somebody who's always *there.*

8. A good dad: Nurse her along, give her confidence, fix it, mend it, make it better.

Do all of these, all the time. Easy, right? (DRe)

MAIL CALL

Never open your spouse's mail, unless you have specific or blanket permission. Aside from being a basic courtesy, you'll also avoid the risk of stumbling across information you'd rather not know. (JHe)

OPEN GRIPES

If you've got a gripe with your partner, talk about it. You can talk about it with everybody in town, but unless you talk about it with her, nothing's going to happen. Even petty stuff — toothpaste-tube quality disputes — have to be discussed or they'll turn into horrible, painful battles. (AL)

A SIX PACK OF ADVICE

Although filled with differences and disputes and adjustments, a marriage hinges on how well each partner seeks to do the following:
1. Be considerate.
2. Communicate.
3. Maintain a sense of humor.
4. Be flexible.
5. Share interests.
6. Value the marriage enough to work at it. (NC)

MARRIAGE AND MANNERS

If you've exhibited your best manners in a courtship, it would be an unpardonable gaffe to abandon them once you're married. Ill-mannered behavior is wrong anywhere, but especially when it's directed at your wife. (AR)

SORT IT OUT

Don't rush at your spouse with a basketful of woes. Try to sort out the petty ones yourself; try to figure out which are important and discuss only those. (*Anon.*)

MOUTH OFF

Learn this simple three-step figurative formula: One, hold your tongue; two, close your mouth; three, smile. (ALo) This is also called biting your nails. Ouch.

LABOR

Define the division of labor in the house. (FF)

BABIES AND CHILDREN

Fundamentally speaking, families are the only excuse Modern Men have for loitering around the planet; as males, we are the truly superfluous end of the species, useful only for a split second of ecstatic compulsion. We can try to hide this fundamental fact by doting over and providing for the families we help make. In fact, the disguise is the reality — men are what they do, nothing more. Women have us beat hands-down in the meaning-of-life sweepstakes.

The Modern Conceit (**see the** *Introduction* **to this book**) suggests to women that the elaborate rituals invented by men to disguise the meaninglessness of their days have some intrinsic appeal, that wasting twenty or forty years driving a desk is somehow more fulfilling than nurturing children and maintaining domestic sense. Women who opt for the Wonderful World of Work deserve all the career success they get.

Fathers who try to become mothers succeed mostly in making themselves and the rest of the family crazy. Fathers, alas, have an abundance of paternal instinct, which is not the same as maternal instinct.

This essential biological difference is not the result of early exposure to Little League. It is rather the result of an inescapable biological fact. Nobody is completely happy with this arrangement; it results in what women see as drudgery and what men see as emptiness. Unhappily, there seems to be no alternative. Despite a favorite tenet advanced as part of the Modern Conceit, there is a difference between human behavior and human nature: You can condition people to believe that it's "natural" or modern to wear their underpants on their heads, but you can't convince anyone to piss out of their ears.

As Modern Men, we have to view marriage as an option. Sometimes, that option might be predicated on the rearing of children; after all, it's difficult to find a woman with whom one might want to live for life just for the sheer pleasure of her company.

BABIES

are the only decent human beings. Until the age of puberty, they are the best things on the face of the earth. At age fifteen or so, they undergo the Universal Jerk Conversion Process and become intolerable, often for the duration. (DB)

HOW TO DELIVER A BABY

Tear up the sheets! Boil some water!

While this is not recommended as a do-it-yourself project, sometimes a delivery must take place before the mother can be taken to a hospital. If such a thing happens, it's important to remember two things: First, stay cool. Second, if a baby shows up unexpectedly, the chances are overwhelming that the birth will be very conventional. Difficult births almost always create circumstances that make an early trip to a hospital inevitable.

1. Call a doctor or an ambulance or an emergency paramedic. In a pinch, call the cops or the fire department.

2. Make the mother comfortable. She should be lying down in an area that is both clean and spacious enough to provide for your assistance. Stay calm and help her to stay calm, too. Gently reassure her that you will do your best to ensure her and the baby's safety. Reassurance and compassion are crucial ingredients in reducing her natural level of fear, and hence lowering the general level of trauma. Try to remember anything you might have read, seen or heard about coaching and natural childbirth, because childbirth out of a hospital doesn't get much more natural.

Make yourself comfortable, too. Don't panic and don't get caught up in the exquisite drama of it all. There's going to be a lot of yelling and screaming and bloody goo, so grit your teeth and do your job.

3. Wash your hands.

4. Do not touch the area surrounding the vaginal entrance.

5. Place a clean towel or folded sheet under the mother's hips for the baby.

6. Don't rush things. Let the baby come naturally. Don't tug and pull.

7. If the water has not broken, and the baby is still inside the sac, puncture the sac with a pin or the tip of a pair of scissors. Use a clean cloth to wipe the sac and fluid away from the baby's head and face. Paper towels won't do.

8. Wipe the baby's mouth and nose with a clean cloth *immediately* after the birth.

9. Move the baby to a clean spot between the mother's legs; make sure his head is elevated slightly and that any fluids or secretions are away from his mouth and nose. *Be careful not to stretch the umbilical cord.* Give the guy a little slack.

10. If medical care is on the way, don't mess with the umbilical cord. Cover the baby with a towel or blanket to prevent him from getting a chill, and leave him in the spot between his mother's legs. Leave his head uncovered so he can breathe. After a short time, you may wish to move the baby to his mother's breast, where it's warm and soft.

11. If medical care is **not** *on the way,* or it appears that nobody's going to show up within an hour or so, you must tie the umbilical cord. Find a couple of pieces of strong tape or twine and tie the cord in *two* places about two inches apart. The tie nearest the baby should be about six inches from his navel. Cut the cord between the two ties with a clean pair of scissors. When you have finished, *do not pull the cord to make it come out.* Simply wrap the baby back in his blanket or towel, leaving his head uncovered, and let him rest on his side in a warm place.

12. Let the afterbirth come out by itself. Save the afterbirth, with the cord, in a basin or on a newspaper for later medical examination.

13. Place your hands over the mother's uterus — a firm lump just below her navel — as soon as the afterbirth has emerged. Cup your hands around the uterus and massage it several times to keep it firm; if it doesn't stay firm, hold your hands on it until it does.

14. Clean the mother's upper thighs and buttocks, but do not touch the area around the vaginal entrance.

15. Monitor the baby's breathing while you see to the mother's comfort. Make sure the baby stays warm. The mother may drink coffee or tea or water, if she wishes.

16. Stay with the mother and child until medical help arrives. (USG)

THE CRYING BABY

Two schools of thought here: One requires *soothing* the infant either by timing your breathing to coincide with his or by softly "cooing" (any word with a long vowel will do; try "no") in time with his wails. (VT)

The other school advocates *shocking* the infant to silence: Make one loud bang — whack a book on the floor, for example — and surprise the kid. By the time the child has contemplated this new development, he may have forgotten what the first problem was. (PV) This sounds like last resort stuff, though.

Why they cry: There are only five reasons why infants (under the age of eighteen months) cry: They are wet, hungry, tired, frightened or in pain. Children do not cry over cosmic issues like boredom or depression. (NMO) If the pain is in the stomach, the cry is more of a wail and there are signs of ill temper. If the pain is a headache, the cry is more of a shriek and the baby will usually frown severely. (WG)

BABY BLUES

Anything can go wrong with babies until they reach the age of seventy-five or eighty, so there's no use worrying any more than you want to. Here's a short list of congenital normalities:

What to expect of a new kid: Not much. When humans are new on the scene, they can be outwitted by parakeets. Brand-new babies are strong on primal charm, however, and that's enough to forgive them for doing all the stupid things we've never done.

When the child is *a week old* or so, he should be in constant motion, opening and closing his fingers and pumping his legs up and down, frowning and pouting, rocking and rolling. *After about three months,* the kid ought to be able to concentrate for a short time on a shiny, moving object. For many parents, this astounding feat becomes a parlor trick; avoid this. At around six months, he'll grow teeth (although a serious delay in teething may indicate rickets). By the time he's been around a year or so, he should be up and semimobile. (DB)

Ten normal things you think are all wrong in normal babies: These are the things that will keep you awake nights for no good reason.

1. Jaundice: Most babies are a little yellow for the first ten days or so.

2. Stools: Baby doo looks horrible, all jungle green and thick, at first. That's the way it's supposed to look. It doesn't look any *better* later, but it does come in different colors.

3. Genitalia: The baby's sex organs may at first appear alarmingly swollen.

4. Breathing: Early breathing is often rapid and irregular. That's okay, as long as he keeps breathing. Babies aren't supposed to hold their breath.

5. Fontanelles: These are the gaps in the skull bones; the biggest one is in the top of the skull, where a pulse can often be felt. When the baby cries, this area will bulge out and scare the baby's Mom ("God! He's growing a *horn!*"). This part of the baby's head should not *permanently* bulge, though, nor should it be deeply hollowed.

6. Skin: The small pink blotches and marks on baby are part of the manufacturing process and will disappear just after the eighteen-month service warranty expires.

7. Tongue: Parents sometimes worry because their baby has no tongue range. It's okay. Babies are not supposed to be able to stick out their tongues like a reptile. The ability to poke out your tongue beyond the mesentery connected to the bottom of the tongue is something that comes slowly but surely, especially to twelve-year-old girls in history class.

8. Temperature: Temperature is not a very good indication of illness in babies because their thermostats aren't yet adjusted; exhaustion during illness is suggested by a deep hollowing of the eyes.

9. Bedwetting: This can only be considered abnormal if it persists beyond the fifth year or so. The best corrective is gentle psychology.

10. Convulsions: These are common in newborns. They shouldn't be ignored, though, and you should ask a doctor for advice. (WG).

Remember that talking to a doctor about baby ailments is an exercise not designed to make the baby better (he's just fine, thanks) but to make *you* feel better. (DB)

Instincts: Follow your instincts. You're the best judge of how your child feels. (RBr)

Mother knows best: If in doubt, trust a mother's instincts before a father's. (*Anon.*)

The facial expression on a baby is important. Brain diseases produce expressions quite foreign to childhood, such as deep worry lines. The head may also be drawn back and arched. The fontanelle should have closed over by the end of the second year (premature closure may be associated with mental deficiency; late closure is another indication of rickets). (WG)

HOW TO CHANGE A DIAPER

The easiest way is to roll the kid off the old diaper and onto the new diaper so he ends up looking at the ceiling. That gives you a chance to finish the job without covering yourself in excrement. Then do the usual: bring the bottom up between his legs and fasten it on either side.

Never change a boy's diaper without standing to one side. About 20 percent of the time, he's going to let fly with a piss. (KP)

THE SITUATION COMEDY AT HOME

should be *Father Knows Best,* not *The Life of Riley,* for a weak, vacillating and oafish dad will destroy his family as surely as a despotic one will. Still, "someone must be in charge," as the Duchess of York refreshingly stated in reference to her life with her prince prior to her marriage. And, as unpleasant as it may be for some, unless dad is in charge, the entire household will be thrown into unhappiness. The same will result if the father exercises such power without accepting his responsibility for being a good and righteous man — that is, one who will behave rationally and consistently while providing for his family as best he can, and not only with treasure, but also with love, kindness, patience and understanding. (AW)

MONEY MONEY MONEY

Moms get rich: Paternal authority brings with it massive responsibilities, the most pressing of which is the need to provide materially for your children. Any masculine pride that compromises a family's welfare by insisting that the man be the sole breadwinner is reprehensible, as seeing to children's needs is the most important role of family income. While recognizing the benefits of a mother's presence in the home, the talents and ambitions of both parents have a role to play if required to sustain their children's wellbeing. (CSA)

A dissent: Single mothers who *must* work to support their children are victims of sociological excesses. A truly benevolent welfare system would ensure that mothers could stay with their children for at least the first two or three years of the kids' lives.

This isn't the first time we've had an army of moms at work, and, presupposing it will one day cease, it'll probably happen again. The last big migration of women away from home didn't stop until labor laws protecting women and children were enacted. The effects on society of large numbers of women and children invading the labor market were devastating.

The need for two incomes *must* be seen in terms of a family emergency. Mothers at work these days means somebody else is playing mom with the kids. We are happily sending a generation of children off to *de facto* foster homes for the sake of a second income or to avoid boredom (or, worse, to avoid responsibility), sacrificing the welfare of our own children for the sake of extra cash and some weird, self-absorbed notion of ambition. Someday we'll pay the price for that sort of mindless greed. (*Anon.*)

CORRECT, CORRECT?

A father's duty is to *correct* wrongdoing in his children, not to play the bad cop in a two-cop precinct. Specifically, a father should never attribute a child's misbehavior to a flaw in the child's character — particularly as any such flaw is as likely to exist in your own character. (BDa)

FOREVER

and ever. Until you die. That's how long you're a parent. That's how long you must assume responsibility for your progeny. (NF)

MANNERS

The younger a child is taught good manners, the better. American children, in particular, are given tacit encouragement to interrupt their elders. (TCF)

THE NATURALS

Children should be encouraged along the lines of their natural inclinations, even if this requires both parents to restrain their egos somewhat. (*Anon.*)

OUT LOUD, THAT IS

Read profusely to your infants and children, choosing stories for the way they inspire the imagination rather than how they instruct. A father reading aloud to his family in the evening is an old and beautifully comforting tradition. Family book evenings can be arranged, too, with books passing from family member to family member, each reading a chapter. (AW)

GOO GOO

Never use baby talk beyond the natural cooing of infancy. To a child or any sensible adult, baby talk implies a lack of respect, not only for the child but also for the person doing the funny talking. It also debases the language. (*Anon.*)

FOUR WAYS FOR PARENTS TO KEEP TRACK OF THEIR KIDS

1. Cars: Teach your kids not to get into anybody's car or go into a house without your permission.

2. Don't leave your child alone in a public place — *not even for a moment.*

3. ID: Teach your kids your address and telephone number (including area code).

4. Listen to what your kids say about adults with whom they come into contact. Pay special attention if they tell you they don't want to be with someone. They may have a good reason. (NCM)

FOUR WAYS FOR KIDS TO KEEP TRACK OF THEIR PARENTS

1. In sight: Keep your parents in sight in a public place. If you get separated from them, ask somebody in charge to help you find them.

2. Never go anywhere without your parents' permission.

3. Telephone: Don't give any information about you or your parents or your house to people on the telephone.

4. Always walk with friends. Don't go to school or to the store or out to play by yourself. Always stay with your friends. (NCM)

ADVICE

Here's some advice: Ask your child from time to time his advice on various matters, especially those things that most directly affect him. (KH)

WIVES OF FRIENDS

Two things can happen when a pal gets married: One, his wife will think you're swell — in which case you haven't lost a friend, you've doubled your money. Two, his wife will hate you like no hate you've ever known — a deceitful, cutthroat hate.

PATIENCE

Either way, it'll all work out. If your buddy's wife thinks you're shit, don't fight it. In fact, *don't do anything*, except be polite, and after a few years she'll have cost him a lot of other friends, as well as a job or two and probably a handful of hair. Then he'll pack her off to bitter-woman heaven. And you've still got a friend. (GRo)

NOTHING'S A GREATER THREAT

to the wife of a friend than his friend. (FWi)

ONE RULE

will do when it comes to dealing with the wives of friends: Keep your hands to yourself. Otherwise, you'll be dealing with the wives of ex-friends. Or, worse, ex-wives of ex-friends. (JO)

DON'T DO IT

Just don't. The relationship between a man and his wife is, or at least ought to be, a sacred thing. No matter *what* the reasons, you boff the wife of your friend, you're shit. You deserve everything that happens to you after that, all the way to the grave. (DB)

See also *GIRLFRIENDS OF FRIENDS* **and** *Girlfriends of Girlfriends* **in** *CHAPTER SEVEN: MODERN MATING*.

FAMILY FEUDS

The devils you know:

SIBLINGS

Childhood sibling rivalries and jealousies re-emerge in adulthood as more sophisticated versions of kids' beastly beahavior. (AW)

Nothing is quite so surprising (and undeserved) as your brother's affection. (*Anon.*)

DEFENSIVE

Establish limits beyond which you will not allow your siblings to go in their aggressive behavior toward you. This will encourage them to leave you alone. (BS)

NONCONTROLLING

Try to establish improved relationships with individual family members while ignoring the dynamic effects on the group that may result. Don't look upon other relationships between family members either jealously or in Ally-Axis terms. (MS)

DIVORCE

If you're looking here for some good-buddy commiseration about hard-hearted women and the pain of alimony, forget it. Divorce is an admission of failure at one of the most important things in life, and if you were half to blame, you get no pity here, pal. And pay your child support; it's your duty. On the other hand, if you busted your hump and tried your best while she sort of lost interest or something, then here's a shoulder. **See also** *MARRIAGE,* **above,** but it's probably too late for that stuff now.

THE VERY FIRST THING

As a father, your responsibility for your children transcends any marital arrangement you might find yourself in. Don't use your divorce as an excuse to bum around. Your children are important, and it's important that *you* support them, not your ex-wife, no matter what the political-sexual climate of the times is. (NS)

See also *BABIES AND FAMILIES,* **above.**

SILENT RUNNING

Divorce is never having to say, "Hi, hon, I'm home" at one thirty A.M. (*Anon.*)

THE EX-FACTOR

The best ex-wife is one you never see or hear from again, since every time you're in contact with her it turns into either a guilt trip or a pitch for money. So forget the current ideal of "staying friends," as it rarely works. If you don't have children, then avoid, deny and ignore your ex with all possible vigor. Change your phone number and your address, and if she must call you, make sure she calls at the office, where you'll have plenty of opportunity for getting her off the line. If you have to pay her, do it by postal order and use your office (or a P.O. box) as a return address. After a while, the hassles of getting in touch with you will be more of a burden than harassing you is a pleasure.

If you have children, the plan changes radically, since in order to maintain contact with your children, you have to maintain contact with her. Remember that your kids didn't get divorced, *you* did — so don't blame them if you have to see your ex from time to time. In this case, the best you can do is find a balance that allows as much contact with the kids while involving as little contact with your ex as possible. A well-organized routine for picking up and dropping off the kids will help here.

Do not try to rush any new woman into knowing your kids. That only creates a situation that's unfair to everyone concerned. Let any relationship between a new woman and your children develop slowly and naturally, with a reasonable expectation that such a relationship may never develop at all.

Always remember that nothing can kill a new relationship faster than having an ex-wife reenter the picture — and, given half a chance, she will. (JO)

Don't find excuses to visit your ex and discourage her from doing the same. You'll accomplish absolutely nothing, and you will undoubtedly regret it. Keep all exchanges brief and businesslike. (JO)

FIND THE VILLAIN

In any situation involving failure, the first order of business is to find the villain. To your children, however, the villain is almost never you or your ex-wife. In fact, children themselves are most anxious to become the guilty party to any divorce. So grit your teeth and defend to the best of your ability your ex-wife's role as mother, even in the face of incursions by a new girlfriend. (*Anon.*)

DON'T WHINE

If your divorce is imminent or underway, don't whine too much. Your real friends understand all about it and your acquaintances don't give a shit. It's very unmanly to be a broken record on the subject. Just get on with it. (CR)

ONE BENEFIT

of divorce is that you rediscover your friends. (MR)

NO MATTER WHAT YOU SAY,

the divorce is half your fault. You married her. (VS)

ABSOLUTELY NEVER EVER

badmouth your ex-wife to your children. (TW) This should be repeated.

WHO, ME?

No-fault divorce is your best out — assuming you're still somewhat friendly. Laws vary from state to state, but if there's no big property, cash or kid problem, this is the most inexpensive form of divorce. (HF)

ANNOUNCEMENTS OF DIVORCE

are announcements of really vulgar taste. Unbelievably, this *déclassé* gesture has gained some currency, mostly by those with more money than common sense. (*Anon.*)

Consumption

If you're not the saving type, money is a hot potato: You get it, you get rid of it and the faster the better.

This is irresponsible behavior, of course, and leads only to depression. You feel lousy, life has no meaning, so you go out and buy something — anything — and it makes you feel swell. For about an hour. Then you feel lousy again. But at least you have a good reason.

The lesson is that you have to be careful. Modern Men know that you can die of consumption.

C O N T E N T S
Chapter Nine: *CONSUMPTION*

SHOPPING

There's a sea of sharks out there. Watch it.

IMPULSE SHOPPING

Avoid making a major purchase on impulse. A car, a new roof, an expensive insurance package are all things that should be carefully researched before you commit. Do comparison shopping — you'll always be surprised — and remember to figure terms and financing charges as part of the purchase price. (ACT)

ECONOMIZING

Economizing is always laudable; it's difficult to admire waste. Still, watch for the point of diminishing returns. Always remember that your time is worth money, too. Figure the amount of time you spend trying to find something at a better price is worth approximately three-quarters your hourly wage. (DFR)

Here's some news: You can economize by simply spending less than you earn. Live like people in the income bracket *below* yours. They do it; so can you. And if you're successful, you'll have found the only sure footing on a very slippery slope. (ARa)

See also *SAVING MONEY* **in** *CHAPTER THREE: MODERN MONEY*.

THE BULK MALE

Watch for sales on heavily used daily items, then buy in bulk, as much as they'll let you carry away. (JH)

CLIP-N-SAVE

Don't use coupons in food stores if they force you to purchase something you would otherwise never buy. (WAR)

THE WELL-FED SHOPPER

Never shop for food when you're hungry, or without a list. Look for the best buys on the top and bottom shelves of a supermarket. (RY)

A dissent: Shop only when you're starved. You'll come home with much more interesting items. (PJO)

RECIPES FOR SUCCESS

Pick up any product with a recipe on the container. Use the recipe as your shopping list. (AW)

PAY TO SAVE

What does it cost to economize? There are hidden surprises everywhere. For example, if inflation is running at 10 percent and the bank is paying 9 percent, can you honestly say that the rigors of economizing are worth the amount you're paying yourself? Would your life be, say, 12.5 percent happier if you spent everything? If so, then saving is a false economy indeed.

For most middle-class savers, ruthless economizing is a little like volunteering for poverty so that you can live in diminished circumstances at some later, possibly postnuclear, date. (DB)

SURPRISE SHOPPING

To save yourself time in the supermarket while you introduce an element of surprise into your daily menus, scout the aisles for a no-nonsense mom or a sensible grandmotherly type pushing a full cart. When her back is turned, make off with her selection of groceries. Chances are, you'll benefit from her experience and find yourself with a basketful of bargain-priced, wholesome stuff. (GSt)

CREDIT CARDS

You know, you really do have to pay the bills you run up on these things, so the safest way to use them is as if they were cash. If you figure you absolutely, positively *must* pay the full balance due at the end of the month, credit cards are handy. But if you figure you can put all your purchases on time, credit cards will eventually ruin your credit.

Remember, credit cards were invented to make sure you pay more for the things you buy than you need to. Essentially, they're for suckers.

NO-RISK MONEY

Would you like to earn approximately 20 percent on your money with no risk whatsoever? Pay off your credit card balances. If you're paying interest on a topped-out credit account, your life is 20 percent more expensive than everyone else's. (AR)

EXPENSE ACCOUNTS

Credit cards are excellent ways to keep an accurate expense record. Use cards only to pay for those items which you are certain will be reimbursed to you. Most important, use the reimbursement you receive to pay off the card balance in full. If you're going to cheat on your expense account, for crying out loud, don't cheat yourself. (JGR)

PRESTIGE CARDS

If you're so insecure that you're willing to pay extra for a fancy puce-colored credit card, you're a chump. The most prestigious credit card is the cheapest one. Most national credit cards (American Express, Visa and the rest) now offer premium cards that carry with them a few completely useless services and an extra-high yearly fee. If you're going

to get a platinum card, wear it on your lapel. On the other hand, if you know someone with one of these things, go to dinner with them as often as possible, since they'll be quite anxious to use it for the bill. Pretend to be impressed. It's worth a free meal. (RET)

COLLECTING STUFF

Everybody collects something. In the museum of your mind, you're the curator in charge and no matter how obscure the collection, there's a certain charm in comprehensiveness and maybe even an expectation of marginal profit.

See also *ANTIQUE, JUNK AND THRIFT SHOPS* **and** *AUCTIONS*.

AS AN INVESTMENT

collecting, while not among the chanciest ventures, has its share of risk. Rare collectibles appreciate in good times and depreciate during stable or bust periods. The value of antiques, for example, generally will follow the precious metal market (although after a sometimes considerable delay). Keep your eye on gold and silver rates if you really want to have a jump on the antique market. (TRD)

QUALITY, SCARCITY AND CONDITION

Those are the three factors that best establish the value of any collectible. (SAW)

KEEP CALM

You're browsing through a catalog for antique widgets one day and you see a 1937 MagnoWidget — exactly like one you have in your own collection — with a $5000 price tag next to it. What do you do? Jump for joy and start spending the money? No. Unhappily, you'll never get anything like five grand for your widget. Dealers, like the one who published the catalog, buy at wholesale rates, while galleries and auction houses charge a substantial commission. The fact is, you have to find the one person out there who loves old widgets as much as you do — in fact, he has to love them *more* than you do, because he has to be willing to pay big bucks to acquire something you already own.

Meanwhile, the profits from the sale of an item from your collection will probably be subject to capital gains tax; the IRS classifies some (but not all) collectibles as investments. Consider the tax effects of losses and gains when selling off your collection. (AR)

GET SMART

To avoid fakes and to be able to acquire the best stuff at the best price, you must become an expert in the area of your collection. You probably began collecting as a hobby anyway, so you probably won't look at gaining knowledge in a field that interests you as much of a chore. Still, after a certain point, a collection of even marginally valuable ar-

tifacts becomes a semiprofessional obligation — a job, if you like — and keeping up with changes in your field can become time-consuming. (SAW)

BIBLIOMANIA
Rare books appreciated better than 20 percent annually during the 1970s. (HGK)

ANTIQUE, JUNK AND THRIFT STORES

Antique and junk dealers constitute one of the few retail industries in the country that operate on a negotiable price basis. If an antique or junk furniture dealer won't negotiate with you, you can safely assume either that the price you suggested was ridiculous or that the shop sells exclusively to interior decorators and others who spend other people's money on a commissionable basis.

BARGAINING
To bargain successfully, you must convince first yourself, then the shop owner that you do not necessarily *need* the item you have chosen. Be humble; praise the piece, but be fully prepared to let it go if the price is out of line. Remember that your budget and the value of the item are not always the same. Don't waste your time and the shopkeeper's by haggling over an item that doesn't come close to your budgeted price. Some old pieces really are worth more than you would ever have imagined.

The shopkeeper is playing the negotiating game in reverse. He has his price, too, and is going to be watching you to see how far up he can move you from your starting point.

If you wish to negotiate in good faith, have some knowledge about the item you want to buy. A little homework will also help you spot good bargains when you come across them.

Friendliness and sensitivity to the expertise of the dealer will expand your dollar's buying power. (AR)

See also *COLLECTING STUFF,* **above.**

THRIFT SHOPPING
Goodwill, the Salvation Army and a number of other organizations operate thrift stores. They're listed in the Yellow Pages.

Unlike antique and junk shops, thrift stores tag most items, and bargaining is pretty much out of the question.

You can look for furniture and other collectible items in a thrift shop, of course, but the chances are that most of the local dealers will have beat you to the best stuff. Settle instead for those items that you know will always be on hand: You can equip a kitchen

for pennies at a well-stocked thrift store, and you can put together a reasonable wardrobe, if you don't mind sorting through a thousand paisley shirts to find one that an actual person might wear.

If you're looking for collectible items at a thrift shop and you don't have much luck the first time you visit, try again. Eventually, something will turn up, and when it does you'll be able to buy it at a great price.

Thrift shops are great places to buy anything in an economic emergency. (CD)

RECOUPING

Buying antique furniture and Oriental carpets and the like will allow you to recoup at least some of your investment in home furnishings — although unless you're very clever or very patient, you probably won't come out ahead since you will normally buy at retail and sell at wholesale. (Finding the right buyer who will pay top dollar for your fantastic Newport mahogany drop-leaf Pembroke table will take a lot of time.) You can, however, take comfort in the knowledge that you will be able to recover much more of your investment than if you'd bought new stuff. (LT)

THE RULE OF THREE

Never buy anything — furniture, old shoes, anything — from an antique or junk shop if there are three or more things wrong with it. (CD)

OLD AND ANTIQUE

Traditionally, for interior furnishings, an antique is a piece that is at least a century old. Unfortunately, many uninteresting pieces achieve antique status because of a happy life in an attic someplace. Other pieces do not adhere strictly to the century rule. Furniture that was influential in design or created by a celebrated architect or famous artisan can be seen to escalate in value despite a relatively recent date of manufacture.

Regardless of age, however, the most desirable furniture is that which embodies elements of design widely acknowledged to be significantly influential. Quality adds value to any piece of furniture.

If you're new at this, rely on close study and consultation. It's a tricky field. (AR)

See also *DECORATING WITH ANTIQUES* **in** *CHAPTER TWELVE: MODERN MANORS.*

AUCTIONS

George Leinwall, a noted bibliophile and the smartest man in the world, provided the most useful rule for those attending auctions: "Keep your hands in your pockets, and your mouth shut."

Here's some more help:

CAVEAT EMPTOR

Always examine an object at auction before bidding on it. Go to the preview session or the viewing session immediately preceding the auction and carefully inspect the items for which you wish to place a bid. Otherwise, the experience could be only marginally less expensive than a blind date.

Before you attend the auction itself, fix a ceiling price and never exceed it. Remember, an auction is not a competitive sport: any fool can pay more for something than it is worth.

Note the conditions of sale, especially if you plan on spending a lot (see below). Most auctions expect payment in cash — and in full. (HGU)

HOW AUCTIONS WORK

Most auctions are advertised in the newspaper or are conducted on a regular basis at an auction house. There are a number of different types of auctions — estate sales, sheriff's sales, bankruptcy sales, unclaimed freight sales, post office sales — in which a wide variety of items will be made available. Each will have its own characteristics: a police impound car sale will have an unusually high concentration of automobile brokers, for instance, few of whom will be able to bid more than the low wholesale value for any car. Everything from houses and heavy machinery to thimbles and stamps are sold at auction.

The auctioneer is a broker working on behalf of one or more clients. His job is to ensure that every item up for bid goes at the highest possible price. He receives a healthy commission for his work, and it is not in his interest to assist you in obtaining a bargain.

Many items at auction have a floor value, and the auctioneer will not sell the item for less than that price. Floor values are usually set by the client in consultation with the auctioneer's appraisers.

Most auctions require registration, in which each bidder is assigned a number. At some auctions, a fee or deposit is required; it is applied against any purchase.

Pay close attention to the course of the bidding if you are trying for an object. If you are one of a number of bidders, remember that many of the rules of poker apply at auctions. Every bidder is trying to get the others out before the ceiling price is reached.

If you bid successfully for an item, be prepared to pay for it immediately in full — and in cash, unless there are other arrangements. At most auctions, you will be expected to remove the item at the time of sale. (HGU)

KNOCK-DOWN AUCTION HINTS

Wait the longest to open your bidding. (JDS)

Bid on items you don't want — and make sure you don't end up with them — just to develop a rapport with the auctioneer, who will recognize you as a player. (MR)

Never get carried away: Never violate your preset limit, not even by a dollar. (MR)

See also *Foreclosure Auctions* **and** *Tax Auctions* **under** *HOUSE-BUYING,* **below.**

GEMS AND PRECIOUS METALS

Perhaps it's symbolic that a girl's best friend will cut glass, while all a man's best friend can do is get your cheek wet.

How you get your hands on the rocks is your business (**see** *CHAPTER THREE: MODERN MONEY* for a start), but once you do, you ought to be able to take care of them — or at least spot the swine in the pearls.

AMBER

lives alone. Don't get it near water — or perfume.

To test for authenticity, amber will float in a brine solution (pickle juice will do). If you touch it with a hot needle, it will smell like pine. (LR)

DIAMONDS

really will cut glass. But don't mess with them. If you think they're real, take them to a jeweler for an appraisal. (JJ)

EMERALDS

will crack if exposed to heat. Folklore says that water is bad for emeralds; in fact, it's not the water, it's the temperature of the water. (LR)

GOLD

items can be examined by filing a small nick and looking for base metal. The marks on gold vary: carat weights indicated as "10K" or more (although marks in excess of 18K are rare) indicate the purity of American gold; European marks for purity ("7.50" and "9.90," for example) are different. (PA)

IVORY

should have a grained surface, like a very hard wood. (GBP)

JADE

should be handled as much as possible; the natural oils from your skin will enhance the stone's luster. It can be washed in soap and warm water; if the water's too hot, it will cause the jade to crack. To test for genuineness, apply a few drops of water to the stone. If it doesn't run off, it's the real thing. (LR)

OPALS

should be kept oiled with an occasional drop of honey or by rubbing them against the nose. Water can cause them harm. (LR)

PEARLS

can be tested for authenticity by rubbing them on the edge of your front teeth; if they feel gritty, they're likely to be real (unless, of course, your teeth aren't). (LR)

You can clean them by using soap and lukewarm water. (JJ)

PLATINUM

is heavier than other metals. The only way to distinguish it from, say, gold, is to weigh it. Platinum is marked "I.R.I.D." (LR)

SILVER

has a distinct smell, a surefire giveaway. American silver is marked "sterling." British silver bears a wide variety of hallmarks. (LR)

TOPAZ

To test for genuineness, try this: Rubbing topaz or exposing it to a gentle heat electrifies it and causes it to attract small bits of paper or strands of hair. (JJ)

TURQUOISE

The good stuff is difficult to distinguish from the plastic composite phony stuff. Apply a hot needle; if it smells like plastic, it smells fishy. (LR)

HARDNESS

All gemstones are given a number on a hardness rating scale that runs from one (the softest) to ten (the hardest). Each stone can be scratched by a stone with a higher number.

Diamond	10	*Turquoise*	6	*Jet*	4
Ruby	9	*Moonstone*	6	*Coral*	3
Sapphire	9	*Jade*	6	*Amber*	2
Emerald	8	*Lapis*	6	*Ivory*	2
Amethyst	7	*Opal*	6		
Garnet	7	*Malachite*	5		(JJ)

SYNTHETICS

Most high-quality synthetic gems have coloring much too vivid to be natural and have virtually no imperfections. (LR)

CLEAN JEWELRY

by dipping it in ammonia, then brushing with an old toothbrush. Rinse thoroughly and buff with a paper towel. (EA)

HOUSE-BUYING

A house is probably the most serious investment many of us will ever make. It pays, therefore, to do it right, having thoroughly acquainted yourself first with the basic principles of real estate.

AS AN INVESTMENT

Buying a house is a good way to save money. Mortgage payments are a top priority item; they should be faithfully paid, even at the risk of all others. If you buy at or below market value, owning a house is like eating your cake and having it, too. You get to live in the place, and, as the property appreciates in value, you also build equity for securing other loans. It's like an enforced savings plan. (EN)

See *SAVING MONEY* **in** *CHAPTER THREE: MODERN MONEY* **and** *No-Money-Down Real Estate,* **below.**

MARKET VALUE

Always remember, from an investment standpoint, it's always better to buy the worst house in the best neighborhood, not the best house in the worst neighborhood. (TTW)

BUYING A HOUSE AT A FORECLOSURE AUCTION

First notice of a private sale auction — usually one forced by a mortgage default — will appear in local newspapers three to five days in advance of the sale.

Cash up front: The advertisements for the auction will contain some important information in addition to the stuff about time and place. Look for the *minimum deposit* figure, which should be about 10 percent of the estimated auction sale price. You *must* have that amount with you at the auction in either a cashier's check or a certified check.

Cash in 21 days: Also specified in the ad are the *terms* of the mortgage. *If you are the successful bidder, you must satisfy these terms in full within 21 days of sale.* The seller will not finance you; if you don't come up with the money, you lose.

Arrange financing first: It should be obvious by now that this is a rich man's game. *Don't even bother going to a mortgage auction unless you go with a banker behind you.*

Do your homework: It's your responsibility to discover any outstanding liens (such as tax encumbrances, second mortgages and the like) held against the property. No one will tell you about these. You can generally assume there's a clear title, *but check to be sure.* The information is a matter of public record.

Ask the bank: Call the bank holding the primary mortgage on the property and ask them the current amount of the mortgage, whether or not there are any liens or encumbrances on the property and whether or not there's another financial institution holding paper on the property. Add the sum of all encumbrances and liens and consider that the *minimum* bid. Try to get prearranged financing through the bank that holds the primary mortgage, since they will be able to turn over the papers on the property fastest. But remember: *That bank will probably be your major competitor at the auction.*

This is a great way to find a bargain house provided you have the resources.. (MR)

BUYING A HOUSE AT A TAX AUCTION

This is where you'll find some good bargains. Compared to the requirements for a foreclosure auction, a tax auction seems tailor-made for the guy with a normal budget.

Terms vary from state to state, but they are usually spelled out in the notice of sale which as a rule appears in the local paper. The ad will also contain a telephone number to be called for additional information, the amount required for a deposit and the method of payment — usually a cashier's or certified check. *Different laws will complicate matters in different states, and it's essential that you be aware of the differences before you bid or buy.* For example, in Connecticut the person who owes the taxes on the property in question can repay you within a year (with interest) the amount you paid for the property and thereby reclaim it. If you've made improvements on the property, that's tough.

If you're the successful bidder, the balance of the bid must be paid within thirty days, so have your financing in order before you go to the auction.

The competition will generally fall into two camps: The first-time house-buyers trying to get a dream house for a song, and some very sharp, predatory real estate sharks.

Attend a few tax auctions to get a feel for how they work. (FFe)

AVOID REAL ESTATE AGENTS

and save yourself 10 percent, the amount they'd take as commission.

Real estate agents aren't bankers; they don't always negotiate in your best interest because they need to make a quick turnaround for a quick commission. (DG)

REAL ESTATE TITLE INSURANCE

Title insurance provides exactly the protection its name implies: It is an insurance policy that covers you against problems with the title to your property that are discovered after you own the land.

Two types: One type of title insurance protects the holder of a mortgage up to the amount of the mortgage. The other protects the owner of the property up to the purchase price. Many banks require you to get the mortgagee's policy and make it payable to the bank, so you may not have much of a choice on that one.

Lawyers and searches: You shouldn't get the owner's policy for yourself, because title insurance will cover problems that the lawyer's title certification will not. The lawyer is only required to check on things which appear in the public record when they do a title search. If a problem pops up that was not in the public record, the lawyer is off the hook — but you may not be.

For example, Mr. Smith has a child, Abel. When Mrs. Smith dies, Mr. Smith moves across the country, and Abel moves to Bangkok. Mr. Smith remarries, but never tells the

SIGNS OF STRUCTURAL DAMAGE IN HOUSES

Uneven foundation settlement: A, may result in a house badly out of square. Evidences may include B, eaveline distortion; C, sagging roof ridge; or D, loose-fitting frames or even binding windows.

Badly sagging horizontal member, A, has resulted in: B, uneven floor; C, cracked plaster; and D, poorly fitting door. (Defects accentuated to illustrate the problems.)

Check wood for decay at points of contact with concrete, such as: A, floor joists supported on concrete walls; B, framing supported in a pocket in a concrete wall; and C, wood post supported on a concrete floor.

Watch for sag at A, ridge; B, rafters; or C, sheathing. Rafters are frequently tied, as at ceiling joist, D, to prevent them from spreading outward. Flashing, E, is used at intersections of two roofs or between roof and vertical planes.

new Mrs. Smith he had a child from his previous marriage. Mr. Smith and his new wife then have two other children, named Baker and Charlie. Unfortunately, Mr. and Mrs. Smith die in a traffic accident, and in their will, they leave their house to Baker and Charlie, never mentioning Abel. Baker and Charlie decide to sell the house and you decide to buy it. Two years later, Abel shows up and wants a third of the house you now own.

The lawyer had done a title search and everything looked okay; Abel, after all, was never mentioned in the public record. So you can't go after the lawyer. Title insurance, however, would cover this situation. It may all seem a bit far-fetched, but it does happen from time to time; the cost of the insurance is negligible, and considering the amount you've invested in a house, very well worth it. (JO)

NO-MONEY-DOWN REAL ESTATE

You can buy anything with no money down, so long as you offer enough for it.

Here's an example: Let's say a seller has a house for sale at $100,000. His first mortgage is $65,000. You, go in and offer to buy his house for $105,000. The seller is ecstatic; you're offering him five thousand more than he asked for. You then tell him there's one small catch — you don't have any money. But you also tell him not to worry: All he needs to do is refinance his house for $80,000. He then pockets $15,000 (that is, the difference between his original first mortgage and the new one). Your seller then agrees to carry back a note for $25,000. Having done this, the deal can be consummated.

Look at it this way: The seller has received $15,000 in cash and he's carrying a second note at whatever interest rate you've negotiated. As long as the payments on the second don't start for, say, six months, he should be happy.

And what about the buyer? He's bought a $100,000 home with no money down for $105,000, he has a first mortgage of $80,000 — the payments on which start immediately — and a second note of $25,000, the payments on which start in six months. Your seller has gotten a great price and all you've done is create paper.

Now you have two options: One, you can find a greater fool who will purchase your new property at a profit, or, two, you can find an equity-sharing partner — called an ESP.

What's an ESP? Here's an example: A young couple who, even though they are both working, don't have a sufficient combined income for a home purchase by conventional means. You offer them a 50 percent equity in this home if they'll agree to carry the outstanding mortgages. You also agree that after five years, they either buy out your half of the house at fair market value or you sell the house and split the equity. The worst that can happen is that you will wait five years for your reward. If you can't find an ESP? Walk away from the deal. The seller gets his house back and you won't have spent a cent.

People say you can make a living doing this. If so, it would have to be a full-time job — one requiring lots of work with no guarantees. (JDeN)

See also *INVESTMENTS* in *CHAPTER THREE: MODERN MONEY.*

Techs/Mechs

Both figuratively and literally, there are already too many gadgets in our lives. Modern Men know that the future is now, but it's switched to auto-rewind.

C O N T E N T S
Chapter Ten: *TECHS/MECHS*

AUDIOMANIA: Record Storage — Record Care — Piracy — Digital Playback — Amplifiers and Receivers — Antennae — Room Acoustics — Speaker Placement — Wiring Speakers — VIDEOMANIA: Choice of Format — Stereo HiFi — CHOOSING A COMPUTER: Internal Memory — Software — Obsolescence — Information Services — Small Business Computers — PHOTOGRAPHY: Practice — Skin Shots: Measuring Light — Bracketing — Film Types — Lenses — Camera Shake — Filters — Fancy Equipment — Motor Drives — Negative Storage

AUDIOMANIA

You have to draw the line someplace, so don't get carried away listening for something you can't hear. We say if you have a dog's ears, spend your money on a plastic surgeon.

RECORD STORAGE

The ideal containers for record storage are plastic milk crates — although not all sizes will work, and neither will all shapes (square ones are better than rectangular ones). The crates are stackable, but to preserve the records, set the boxes on their sides.

Never store records stacked one atop the other. Records must be stored in a vertical position, side by side. (AD)

RECORD CARE

Never use an *automatic multiplay turntable.* The records are severely damaged when they drop down on top of each other. (JHP)

Clean your records before each play. An antistatic cleaner is best. (*Anon.*)

Dust destroys the grooves on a record; the needle presses them into the vinyl and the result is distorted sound. One way to keep disks dustfree is to store them the way you bought them — with the inner sleeve inside the jacket with the opening side up. (WLD)

Be sure to throw away the shrink-wrap in which your new album is packaged. Variations in temperature can cause the shrink-wrap to shrink some more. The result may be a warped record. (KLB)

HAR, JIM LAD

It's a pretty lame copy of piracy, maybe, but smart money plays a disk once and records it at the same time. Cassettes are much hardier than records. The notion that this is an abridgment of copyright is nuts — unless, of course, you start selling your taped copies. (WLD)

Perfect tape dupes can be made using a compact-disk player connected to a hi-fi video tape recorder. (KT)

PLAYBACK

It seems likely that the recent advances in consumer digital recording and playback equipment will soon render conventional turntables and tape decks obsolctc (except for archival purposes). Digital technology is the most significant departure in sound reproduction since the introduction of Edison's analog invention.

While conventional records and tapes rely on a magnetic "image" of the sound they reproduce, digital recording assigns every sound a binary code which is scanned by a laser and translated back to the original sound. Every digital record and tape is a first-generation recording. The result is a significant enhancement of playback quality, one that is virtually free of extraneous noise and distortion and sounds startlingly realistic.

Because there is no physical contact between the medium and the decoding device, old problems of surface wear and damage no longer apply. (SKL)

The introduction of radically new digital equipment (including a digital cassette unit) precludes any realistic coverage of conventional playback components here.

AMPLIFIERS AND RECEIVERS

are available in a wide range of configurations with varying power capabilities. Something in the neighborhood of 15 watts per channel is sufficient power to drive the majority of home speakers in most average-sized rooms. While more powerful amps can help fill very large rooms with sound or reduce bass distortion, the increase in available wattage is almost never worth the increase in price. Fifteen or 20 watts of power and a pair of good, efficient speakers will do most humans just fine. (PNe)

ANTENNÆ

for most FM receivers are an often overlooked accessory. Cable systems in some parts of Europe and, more rarely, in North America, provide a separate wall jack for a link to a powerful community antenna. For most of us, though, we are happy to place the blame for poor stereo reception on our tuners when the problem could be easily fixed by simply attaching a more suitable FM antenna. A good antenna will help pull in FM stations thirty to sixty miles away with greater clarity and fidelity; a directional antenna has the added advantage of being able to help combat sound "blurriness" (technically referred to as multipath distortion).

The best FM antennæ are the sort that look like TV antennæ and are designed to sit on your rooftop. Even indoor directional antennæ, as a second choice, are far better than a simple wire — or nothing at all. (SKL)

ROOM ACOUSTICS

There is a lot of controversy surrounding the optimum room configuration for the best sound reproduction. Wall dimensions, ceiling height and reflective properties of the room surfaces are often discussed at length by amateur acoustic engineers. But, simply put, if a room *feels* warm and congenial, the chances are very good that it is acoustically congenial, too. And while that maxim may rely overmuch on psychology, it also has some basis in fact, since large glass surfaces, smooth floors and unadorned walls — indicative of cold, modern decor — are reflectors of sound, and music in such a room can sound shrill because of echoing. A more inviting room — one with area rugs, light curtains, comfortable furniture, shelves of books and architectural details — provides not only a good room in which to listen to music, but also allows for a good mix of sound reflecting, absorbing and diffusing qualities. (MP)

SPEAKER PLACEMENT

A lot of lip service is paid to speaker location in a room, but the only way to really figure out the right speaker configuration is through trial and error. Here are some options: Speakers can be placed in corners, laid on their backs to reflect sound off the ceiling, angled toward walls, stuck on walls and on shelves, or hung on the ceiling. (SKL)

Basics: A maxim: Small room, small speakers; large room, large speakers. (REP)

Keep them apart: A pair of speakers should not be placed closer together than six feet. Generally, a separation of eight to twelve feet is optimum for most rooms. (SKL)

Front row, center: If you want to approximate a center orchestra seat, arrange your speakers and your favorite chair in an equilateral triangle. The speakers should be just slightly below eye level. (PCV)

A fuller depth of omnidirectional sound can be achieved by aiming the speakers at an angle toward the walls. The sound bounces off the walls, increasing the sensation of acoustic spaciousness. Reflecting the sound off a near wall will greatly reduce the importance of listener position, but also sacrifices some separation. (SKL)

Top treble: If you're positioning your speakers, be sure to place them so that the treble speaker is atop the bass. (PCV)

Use the walls: Putting small speakers near the corners of a room can help compensate for their lower bass response by using the walls to extend the bass end. Corner placement can also boost high frequency coverage. (PCV)

Floor it: Although there is not universal agreement on this, it seems to be generally acknowledged that placing a large speaker enclosure directly on the floor will not only anger the downstairs neighbors, but will also result in bass distortion. Raising the speakers four to six inches can reduce the boom of a speaker on the floor. (SKL)

Put your speakers on blocks made of wood, or, even better, Styrofoam packing pieces, rather than directly on the floor. (PCV)

Place your speakers before completing the wiring. (PCV)

WIRED

Speakers should be wired so they work in "phase" — that is, both speakers should perform the same function in tandem or flex in and out simultaneously. The wires from the positive and negative terminals on the amplifier should be joined to the corresponding terminals on the speaker enclosures.

Beyond that, *both speakers must be wired the same.* Speaker cables are color coded (as a rule one is silver and one is copper-colored), which makes it easy to determine which is which. (If you use lamp cord, the coding is trickier. One cord on the lamp wire has a raised ridge on it; one doesn't.) (SKL)

Keep your leads consistent. The wires that link the amp to the other components must be joined according to the color-coding for channel separation and polarity. Turntables and other components often have a thin ground line that should be attached to an appropriate post on the back of the amp. (SKL)

Use good quality wire for speaker connections. Stereo and electronic stores sell thick, good-quality cable (Monster and Powerline are two of the brand names), but a good alternative is 14- or 16-gauge lamp cord. It should be the kind with fine strands of wire inside the insulation. Lamp cord is less than one-fifth the price of special speaker cable. (MP)

Shopping tip: High-end stereo retailers often provide a trade-in service for their best customers — the dedicated audiophiles who routinely replace their components with whatever is new on the market. And while dealers quite naturally prefer to sell new equipment, they also have to liquidate their trade-ins somehow. (Some retailers will keep a card file of their customers who are looking to divest themselves of certain pieces of equipment.)

This secondhand stock is often kept in an obscure corner of the shop, so you'll probably have to ask to see it. (MP)

VIDEOMANIA

The great thing about VCRs is that they allow you to watch mindless idiocy on one network, while recording the inanity on another. Now *that's* progress.

FORMAT

Go for selection. The choice is VHS or Beta, and if you are at all interested in watching rental videos of current films, you'll have a much better chance of finding the movie you want on VHS, simply because it's the overwhelmingly favorite format. New formats are rolling out all the time, but with the enormous catalog of VHS films already on hand, the format seems likely to remain the home format of choice. The new 8mm formats are still too new to evaluate. (FS)

STEREOOOO

and then some. The new hi-fi-capable VCRs deliver an enormously improved audio playback through your home stereo system.

New television peripherals are coming on to the market that emphasize using the TV set as the central monitor in a much more elaborate entertainment package that can also include some information services. That means that when you buy a new VCR, go for the best quality you can get for the money. Think of it as buying a cassette deck for your stereo, because in a way that's what it is. (FS)

Sound playback quality is important. (FS)

Programmability isn't. So you can program twenty different shows over a seven-year period. So what? All VCRs have some programmable recording feature. Don't get more than you really think you'll need. (JO)

Four-head units produce crisp images, even when viewed in slo-mo or in freeze-frame. (FS)

CHOOSING A COMPUTER

Actually, the first question you need to answer is what do you want with a computer? Be honest, now. If you want a computer to play games, that's okay. Want to preserve precise paranormal permutations of otherwise perfectly prosaic phenomena? That's jake, too. But don't try to hoodwink your bank manager into thinking you need a computer to balance your checkbook.

PSYCHO KILOBYTES

The internal memory of a computer is only important if the software is memory based. If the software is disk-based, storage is more important than memory. (FD)

SOFTWARE FIRST

First, figure out what you want the computer to do. Then find the software that best suits your needs. Then buy the computer that runs the software you've selected. (MFH)

STICK THIS IN YOUR RESIDENT MEMORY

By the time this book is in print, the computers available will have changed, rendering any recommendation obsolete. The best place to keep up with new products is at your local computer store. A good computer shop staffed by intelligent people is an important resource. Use it. (MFH)

INFO, PLEASE

If your system has a communications device called a modem, you'll be able to subscribe to one of the national information services, such as CompuServe or the Source. You can research obscure topics, flash stock quotations, book airplane seats and exchange electronic mail — but if you really want to show off, make sure you acquaint yourself with the instructions in private, or you'll look like a bozo. (MFH)

SMALL BUSINESS COMPUTERS

Don't make the mistake of buying more computer than you need. For most small businesses, a reasonable database program, along with a spreadsheet and an accounting package will suffice. If you spend more than six thousand dollars including the price of the printer you will have spent too much.

The other problem small businesses make for themselves when it comes to buying a computer is that they invariably buy a three-letter computer that requires extensive training before it can even say hello. Buy a computer that everyone in the office can use without spending useless hours taking courses in computers that will be obsolete by the time the course is over. If you can't make the computer useful within six hours of plugging it in, get another one. Same goes for software. (NEW)

PHOTOGRAPHY

Rule number one: Take off the lens cap.

PRACTICE PRACTICE PRACTICE

makes perfect. Take pictures until your shutter shudders. Don't stop. Reload. Wind. Click. You get the idea. Many pros shoot yards of film to get a single good shot; so should you. Film's cheap; processing, relatively so. So take pictures till you drop. Eventually, you'll get good at it. (AR)

SKIN SHOTS

The skin color on your hand is an excellent neutral tone for light readings. Hold your hand up so it receives the same amount of light as the object you want to photograph. Take a "reading" off the light reflected by your hand, set your camera and shoot. (BSA)

BRACKETING

Most professional photographers ensure the quality of their color shots by "bracketing" important exposures. Bracketing is shooting the same picture first at what is considered to be the correct exposure, then again at one stop underexposed, then at two under, then at one stop overexposed, and finally at two over. You should end up with five shots of the same thing; one will be a perfecto. Obviously, this works better with a stationary subject than with a moving one. (BSA)

LOYALTY

to one type of black-and-white and one type of color film pays off in the long run. You'll get to know all the idiosyncrasies of the stock, and exactly how to expose the film for a particularly tricky shot. (FS)

TYPES OF FILM

Pros regard color transparency (slide) film as the most universal film. They know it can translate into any medium — publication printers get the best results from separations made from slides; a good color print can be made from one; an adequate black-and-white print or slide can be made, too. No other film type can make those claims, as they say, and besides, slides provide a positive image for proofing and editing, and they're more easily stored and retrieved. (PNe)

UNIVERSAL FILM AND PROCESSING

If you're ever in doubt about which brand of film to buy or where to get it processed, go for Kodak. They've maintained a consistently high standard of quality and their labs are everywhere. (BSA)

LENSES

The three most often used lenses for the 35mm format are the 35mm wide-angle lens, the 50mm "normal" lens and the 90mm telephoto. These focal lengths cover 90 percent of the photo situations you may encounter. For some reason, the weighty 135mm telephoto is almost never used. A zoom lens will do nicely, even though there will be a very slight sacrifice in optical quality and maximum aperture. (BSA)

CCAMERA SSHAKE

is quite clearly the enemy of sharpness, and although many are ready to blame their lenses (or dogs or children or earthquakes) for fuzzy pictures, the answer is in their own hands. Telephoto lenses are the biggest problem. A good rule of thumb is that the lowest handheld shutter speed should be no lower than the focal length of the lens (i.e., no slower than one-fiftieth of a second for a 50mm lens, one-ninetieth of a second for a 90mm lens, and so on). An even safer rule is to not handhold the camera at a speed lower than *twice* the length of the lens (one one-hundredth of a second for a 50mm lens). If in doubt, use a tripod; a good one is almost certainly the first accessory you'll want to add to your kit. (BSA)

FILTERS AND SHADES

When you buy a new lens, spend the extra money and get a skylight filter and lens shade for it. The filter will protect the lens and the shade will keep out extraneous light from entering a lens from side angles, causing flare. Pros add these two items to any lens as a matter of course. (BSA)

DON'T SHOOT FROM THE WALLET

Don't fall prey to the notion that fancy equipment will make you a better photographer. Expensive rigs *might* help you control certain situations, but good pictures come primarily from a good working partnership between the brain and the eye. Going out and buying a brace of Leicas with a trunkload of expensive lenses is like deciding to play the fiddle and going out and buying a Stradivarius. Almost any adjustable camera in experienced hands will do the job. Go to the limits of cheapo cameras before you stray off into efforts to help the Japanese trade balance. Authoress Eudora Welty isn't the only clever person to have published a beautiful portfolio of pictures taken with an old box camera. (BSA)

MOTOR DRIVES

Amateur photographers love motor drives because it adds an aural quality to their own self-image: Suddenly, they not only *look* like good photographers, they *sound* like good photographers. These expensive accessories send film ripping through your camera at the rate of four to six frames per second. You can use up a whole roll of film in a short burst of feel-good frenzy and end up with thirty-six versions of the same overexposed shot of the family poodle. Except for some special news and sports requirements, professionals don't use motor drives very often. For the average Joe to tack one onto his Nikon is nearly ludicrous. (AR)

BEHIND AUNT MAUDE

Store easily lost negatives behind the appropriate prints in albums. (RTT)

See also *MEASURING LIGHT* **in** *CHAPTER THIRTEEN: MODERN MANURE*.

The Modern Closet

is where it seems your life hangs in the balance and the crucial question is always the same: Does this go with *this?*

Not long ago, the closet was seen as the arsenal in the war for success. No more. While some men dress to avoid arrest and figure they might as well look swell while they're at it, Modern Men cloak themselves in an older garment — *gravitas* — which, in addition to being frequently appropriate, is also comfortable and durable and stylish in every size.

Decorum in dress is common sensical as well as tasteful. Just as many men do not carry ghetto-blasters with which to offend the ear, so Modern Men do not wear junk with which to offend the eye.

C O N T E N T S
Chapter Eleven: *THE MODERN CLOSET*

EYEGLASSES AND CONTACTS

It's a great, big beautiful world out there. You ought to see it.

GET GLASSES TO FIT YOUR HEAD

For some peculiar reason of late men and women have seen fit to wear enormously large glasses. They make women look mousey and men look like wimps. (NGF)

GLASSES FOR THE ELDERLY HIP

Somebody please tell geriatric hipsters — designers, directors, novelists — not to wear oversized eyeglasses with frames in one of the primary colors. It makes them look like old cartoon characters. Ancient baldies are especially prone to do this. (FT)

THE WORLD'S MOST EXPENSIVE LENS CLEANER

American currency makes perfect eyeglass lens cleaners. Old, highly-worn dollar bills do best, but in a pinch you can use a twenty or even a C note. (DR)

LOST CONTACT LENSES

can be easily located by using a vacuum cleaner with a filter (panty hose work well) fitted over the hose end and policing the suspect area. (WR)

SUNGLASSES

You can get them for peanuts or you can get them for the price of a used car. Use sense and save some: the lens is the only part that counts.

THE TINT

of a pair of sunglasses should be sufficiently dark to block 70 to 80 percent of the light. Green, brown and gray are the wise choices; other colors are simply ineffective novelties and can make the visible dimension a very confusing place.

Yellow glasses intensify light on dull, gray days. (SA)

NECKTIES

Prince Charles was once photographed fishing for salmon while wearing a necktie. Modern Men wear them and don't complain about it.

TYING A BOW TIE

Begin by arranging the tie around your neck with one end hanging an inch lower than the other. Next, tie both ends into a simple square knot. Then form the bows by bending first one end in front and pulling it halfway through the knot, then the other end. Finally, adjust the tie by pulling and tightening the looped ends. (AW)

Pretend you're tying a shoelace, except that it's on your neck. Try averting your eyes from the mirror the moment the knot's made and go by the familiar feel of making a shoelace bow. Use the mirror only for adjustments. (AR)

Practice by tying your bow tie around your thigh until you become familiar with the idea of the knot. (FES)

The well-proportioned bow tie will have ends that align vertically with the outside corners of your eyes. (WRe)

Otherwise: Bow ties are affected unless you're famous, in which case they become trademarks. (DB)

COLOR

It's more important for the color of your tie to agree with your shirt and trousers than with your jacket. (GF)

EYE STRAIN

Make sure the patterns on your tie and the stripes or patterns on your shirt are of different scales. (CD)

POCKET STRAIN

You might skimp on other parts of your wardrobe, but don't do it around your neck. Weird, synthetic materials look weird and synthetic. Buy only silk and wool. (HOF)

MORE THAN INTUITION

Women can intuitively spot a cheap tie. (NG)

SUITED TO A SUIT

A tie takes its textural cue from the jacket or suit you're wearing. If the suit is rich and finished, the tie should be too. But if your attire is more casual, say a corduroy sports coat, the tie should have a rougher, more dull luster. (KJ)

MAKING THE GRADE

There's a mysterious grading system that appears in most silk neckties way up inside on the thick, white interfacing, Look for a number of golden stripes woven into the interfacing; five stripes is the highest grade. (PS)

EYE-TIE

Reginald, in the stories by Saki, knew the secret of wearing a tie the same color as his eyes. (AR)

BELTS

The standard width for a belt is one inch, although sizes may vary by as much as a quarter inch from that norm. If you own only one, it should be dark brown.

Be sure to wear a belt of the correct length. If you're wearing your belt on the last hole or two near the end, you're going to look fat; if you're wearing a belt that's too long, you'll look unkempt.

Note: It doesn't work for fat guys to wear long belts. If you're fat, you're fat, and the only thing worse than a belt that's too long is one that's too short, forcing rolls of fat to extrude over your trousers.

As belts wear, they become slightly curved, conforming to the contour of the body. To prevent this blown-out look, reverse the direction of the belt each time you put it on.

Treat your belt like any other leather accessory. Use saddle soap, wax and polish to maintain the belt. (EP)

See also *SUITS AND SPORTS JACKETS* and *CLOTHING CARE,* below.

SUITS AND SPORTS JACKETS

For many Modern Men, it's the daily uniform, like it or not.

Mastering the elements of style often takes no more than a visit to a good tailor. But if you really want to suit up the right way, you should know what the tailor knows:

THE FITTING

In the jacket, the three elements for you and your fitter to watch for are balance through the shoulders, an adequate amount of fabric across the back and a comfortable button closure at the front.

The trousers should feel comfortable in the waist, seat and crotch and look balanced all around. The waistband should touch your navel.

Any trouser pleats should lie flat.

At the fitting, the suit should be "armed" — that is, your wallet, keys and any other items normally carried in the course of things should be in the pockets of the suit — so that the suit can be altered accordingly.

Wear the shoes you're going to wear with the suit, not your basketball hi-tops.

TROUSERS

Cuffs: Whether or not to wear trouser cuffs is a matter of personal preference, although on conventional suit pants, they are traditional. (Generally speaking, formal wear and summer trousers do not take cuffs, while flannel or dress suits do.)

Cuff width varies between an inch and a quarter to an inch and a half.

The break: Fashion-conscious Europeans generally have their trousers break over the fronts of their shoes, while function-conscious Americans are content to have their trousers fall just below the shoe tops.

In determining inseam length, however, err on the side of gravity. Remember that constant daily motion will cause the trousers to ride up a bit, and all material, whatever the quality, will shrink after cleaning.

Bottom slant: In the '70s, it was fashionable to have the bottoms of the trousers slant more severely from the front of the shoe to the back than is favored today. As a rule, cuffed trousers should fall straight, while uncuffed trouser bottoms can slant slightly toward the back of the shoe. (ACT)

THE JACKET

Linen-shoot: The shirt cuff should extend a quarter inch to three-quarters of an inch from the jacket sleeve with the arm at rest. French cuffs, of course, will extend farther.

Vents: Traditional English and American cuts call for a jacket to have a single, center vent, while European custom requires either two side vents or no vents at all. (A man with a large posterior should never opt for side vents.)

Pockets: The style of pocket corresponds to the type of suit worn. A natural-shoulder business suit should have a plain jacket with flaps; a sports jacket should have patch pockets with or without flaps; European-style suit coats should have a flap or besom pocket (straight, and without a flap). Bellows pockets would only be appropriate on a Norfolk or other active sports jacket.

Buttons: The English and Europeans favor three buttons on each suit-jacket sleeve, but any number from two to four is acceptable.

Once the hallmark of a hand-tailored suit, the functional jacket sleeve buttons are now available off the rack. As their function is quite marginal — men ought not roll up their jacket sleeves — they mainly signify the level of care and expense invested in the jacket, although to leave a sleeve button undone is a tasteless affectation. (GP *et al.*)

CHEAP SUITS

will really help you stand out in a crowd. There you are with your crotch riding somewhere between your armpits and your knees and your vest ready to pepper innocent passersby with a shower of flimsy plastic buttons and your inseam twisting gently across your left knee. Still, everyone likes a bargain — if a bargain means you pay a good price for a good product. Paying cheap for a cheap suit is not a bargain. (ACT)

MAKE YOUR OWN TRADITION

in suits. Go for a conservative cut, buy two or three solids and replace one of them each year. The rest of your professional outfit should work the same way: Find a type of shirt that won't be outdated in a year or two. Buy enough to get you through a week, and replace one every six months. (EV)

IF YOU HAVE ONLY ONE SUIT THIS SEASON

make it a dark-colored one, navy or dark gray. (KJ)

VESTS

A suit with a vest is stylistically superior to one without. First of all, the vest itself is optional, so you have greater flexibility. Second, a vest conveys authority. Third, a decent vest gives you four or five more pockets than you had without it. (SD)

THE BOTTOM BUTTON

on a vest is never buttoned, a concession to George IV, who once left his bottom vest button open, an idea whose time had come. (JJ)

SIGNS OF QUALITY

Extra material in the trousers in case of future dietary disasters
Reinforced waistbands keep suit trousers fitting better, longer.
Look for a *second button* and *a tab inside the fly*.
Twist a sleeve (like you did last summer) and hold it that way for fifteen seconds. The material should quickly return to its original shape when released.
Examine a jacket's profile in the mirror; shrug your shoulders while you look at the area on the back near the collar. It should rise uniformly and its configuration should be similar to when it's fitting close to the shoulders. There should be no giant wrinkles.
Lapels and the collar should not pull away from the rest of the suit. (MN)

BLAZERS OF GLORY

The navy blazer is the most practical, hence the most ubiquitous of all sports jackets. It can be worn with anything from blue jeans to gray flannel trousers; depending on the rest of your wardrobe, it can be almost too dressy, or it can be very casual. If you can only afford one sports coat, a standard-issue blue blazer (not a double-breasted job) is the one to get. (HG)

Buttons: Be careful with blazers. Tasteless manufacturers (even some prestigious ones) junk up blazers with a multitude of sleeve buttons and a wad of pretentious embossing in the middle of the buttons themselves. Here's the rule: Three buttons on the sleeve, two or three in front. No breast pocket patch (unless it's one you've earned). No fancy coats-of-arms on the buttons. (ASM)

FORMAL WEAR

Buying a tuxedo is one of those things you do once. The trick is figuring when.

Rule One: If you've rented a tux three times or more in the last four years, it's time to buy one. (SR)

Rule Two: Once you buy a tux, you'll find you use it extremely infrequently, so it will probably last you for the rest of your life. Therefore, it makes very good sense to buy one that is conservatively tailored and not likely to make you look like a lounge lizard in five years. If you just have to look wild, can't help yourself, do it with cummerbunds, waistcoats, scarves, shirts and neckties. (AEW)

Rule Three: Be careful getting carried away with patent-leather dance pumps. Remember, dignity starts at the bottom. (ES)

DRESS CODE

The phrase "Black Tie Optional" is seen with alarming frequency on invitations these days. It's wrong. The whole idea of formal attire is to create a democratic ceremonial style; for this to work, every male must participate. The effect is also somewhat chivalrous in that it allows the varying fashions of women to dominate the social setting. An event should either be Black Tie or not. An event that promotes the optional wearing of formal clothing only makes things confusing, which of course is contrary to good manners. (GG)

MEN'S TRADITIONAL WEDDING-PARTY GET-UP

Day		Evening	
Semiformal	*Formal*	*Formal*	*Semiformal*
Black or gray sack coat	Black or gray cutaway	White tie and tails	Black tie tux
Gray and black trousers	Gray and black striped trousers	Black trousers	
Gray double-breasted vest	Gray double-breasted vest	White vest	
Gray necktie	Gray necktie	White bow tie and wing-collar	
Black shoes	Black shoes	Black shoes	Black shoes
Optional: Gray gloves White boutonnière Gray homburg	*Optional:* Gray gloves White boutonnière Gray top hat	*Optional:* White kid gloves White boutonnière Black top hat	

Remember: Wedding party means primary participants, not guests. (SR)

DON'T BUY ANY FORMAL

or semiformal *day* wear. Unless you're a professional politician, you'll never, ever get your money's worth in wearings. Rent now, rent forever. (FE)

SOCKS

A pair of socks stays together about as long as teenage newlyweds. What's the solution?

Simple. Every few years, go out and buy a large quantity of socks, making sure that the style and color you buy will still be available a few years down the road. When you make your purchase, make certain all the socks you buy are identical. Now when you lose one, set the odd one aside. You'll have another odd sock soon enough, and an instant replacement pair. Incidentally, you can request — and sometimes obtain — a discount when buying socks in bulk. (AR)

COTTON AND WOOL SOCKS

Cotton socks, like all clothing made from natural fiber, are far less likely to cause allergic skin reaction. That's fine. But the good bit is that cotton socks are far more absorbent than socks made from artificial materials.

Wool has all the advantages of cotton, plus the additional virtue of being able to wick away sweat to the outer surface of the cloth, where it will evaporate. (AW)

HATS

For much of the past three decades, hats have been worn only by thugs and Englishmen. Then along came Indiana Jones. Now hats are worn by thugs, Englishmen and unmodern men who don't know how to dress until they see it in the movies.

HATS AND HEAD SHAPES

While there are many different styles and types of hats, the principles of matching the hat to the shape of the wearer's face remain the same.

Three shaping features: There are three primary features governing the shape of any hat. The width and line of the brim, the height and shape of the crown and the width and color of the headband. (**See illustration.**) Even within the restrictions of a given style — such as boater, derby or cowboy hat — the brim widths, crown heights and band widths are variable, and certain key rules are always applicable in determining which hat is best for which head.

A rule: Remember, the shape of the hat should not duplicate the shape of the head.

Brims: Brims may be found in a variety of shapes and widths. They can be large, medium or small; they may droop, turn up on the sides or roll down in front (as with a snap brim). The hat with the irregular, broken brim line is the most universally becoming not only because it may be worn by the majority of men, but also because its varying line softens the lines in five of the most difficult head shapes — round, square, angular, narrow and bespectacled.

Crowns: The crown, too, is important in the selection of a hat. A crown may be straight-sided and high (a style called a "full crown") or it can be short and tapered. Crown shapes can also be altered by the way the top is creased or "pinched."

Proportion: Overall proportion must be considered. Don't choose a hat that is either too small or too large in relation to the size of the face. The crown should be as wide as the face, but the height and shape will vary with the brim and the lines of the face.

Band width: Band width is the third major factor to be regarded in your choice of hats. Bands can be easily and inexpensively changed. Narrow bands give the illusion of a higher crown; wider bands do the opposite, while also creating a more distinct division between the head and the hat, sometimes offsetting the desired effect of an irregular brim line. A hatband in a color contrasting to the color of the hat makes a crown seem smaller, while bands similar in color to the color of the hat cause the crown to appear taller and add importance to the brim line. (AR)

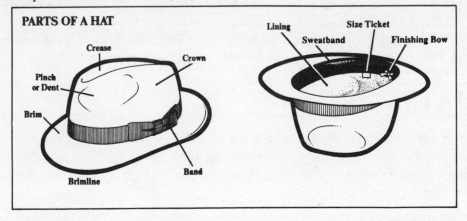

PARTS OF A HAT

Crease

Crown

Pinch or Dent

Brim

Band

Brimline

Lining

Sweatband

Size Ticket

Finishing Bow

HAT POINTS

A hat should be worn firmly on the head, but not so low on the forehead as to obscure the eyes, which are often the most attractive part of the face. It's also an uncomfortable way to wear a hat for very long.

If the hat is pulled too far either to the left or right and the brim is snapped down, the line of the hat will be destroyed and the effect will be comical.

The texture of the material out of which the hat is made is crucial. Materials can visually increase or decrease the size of the hat, so a little self-knowledge, head-shapewise, is important. A guy with delicate features should go for a finished, lightweight material; the man with larger features should select material with more weight and firmness. Fabrics with a dull finish are more easily worn than those with a shiny surface; they also appear smaller and less bright.

Extreme treatment of decorative touches — like feathers or bows — is unbecoming.

A drooping brim or a low back brim decreases the length of the face.

The brow line is the line falling directly over the eyes; it should be given the utmost attention when selecting a hat.

Stand in front of a full-length mirror when making your choice. It is important to see the hat in relation to the whole costume and in relation to the figure. (AR)

HAT MAINTENANCE

Regularly brush your hat in the direction of the nap using a soft-bristled hat brush.

After a hot day, turn out the inner leather band to air it out.

If your hat gets wet, push out the creases and the dents, turn up the brim, turn out the sweat band and rest the hat on its leather. Let it air dry without artificial heat.

Do not rest your hat on its snap brim. Turn up the brim.

Do not stack your hat at home or in public hatchecks.

Do not try to spot clean your hat yourself. You could cause permanent discoloration. Take it to a professional instead.

Always store your hat in a hatbox. (WN)

SHOES AND BOOTS

You can be cheap with almost any part of your wardrobe — except with your shoes and boots. If you wear a cheap shirt, it will look like a cheap shirt and there's an end to it. But if you wear a cheap, ill-fitting pair of shoes, you'll pay the difference many times over, every step of the way.

SHOE TREES

Wooden shoe trees will extend the life of your shoes (except tennis shoes, of course) almost indefinitely. Look for them littering thrift and secondhand shops (if it's possible to litter a secondhand shop), since buying them new can be costly. Use them any time you're not wearing your shoes. You must buy them in your size (although some adjustable ones are now being made). And remember, only the wooden ones work; they absorb moisture from the shoes and keep the leather supple. Those made of cedar are best. (BN)

ALTERNATE SHOES

Try not to wear the same pair of shoes two or more days in a row. If you have enough pairs to be able to alternate them so that any one pair isn't worn more often than every three or four days, all your shoes will last longer. (TSi)

DRYING SHOES AND BOOTS

Don't dry leather goods near heat. That kind of treatment significantly shortens the life of gloves, shoes and boots. (TZ)

Get rid of the white stains that appear on shoes and boots after they've been worn out in the rain or snow by rubbing some mayonnaise into the leather. (AR)

SHINE, MISTER?

Patronize your local shoe shine parlor. A good shine performed by somebody who really knows what he's doing is not only a threatened masculine tradition, it's also a damn fine show — the snap and pop of a buffing rag in the hands of a pro is a unique thing in the world. Besides, loafing for a quarter hour in a shine parlor is good for what ails your ego; you are, for example, strongly advised to visit a shoe shine parlor on your way to a job interview. (AR)

DO-IT-YOURSELF

If you're broke, or insist on doing this sort of thing yourself, here's the drill:

- Don't use mink oil on shoes that need to take a shine; use silicon spray instead.
- Clean the shoe with a rag, followed by a bath in saddle soap.
- Rub on paste wax — no liquid polish — and let it dry.
- Brush first with a rough cloth or brush, then a buffing cloth. (BK)

For a deep shine, try lighting your tin of Kiwi shoe polish (it's flammable). When a nice pool of liquified polish has developed, extinguish the flame and apply the liquid to the shoe. Let it dry thoroughly before you attempt to buff it. (TZ)

COWBOY BOOTS

Cowboy boots are designed to keep your feet in the stirrups, even when your ass is on the ground. They really aren't designed for urban hiking; the high heel with the relatively small contact area can be hazardous to those with weak ankles. Practice will ultimately teach your feet to get along with the rest of your body. (GJ)

SIZE SMALL

Never buy a pair of cowboy boots if they give any indication at all of being too small. Even if the length is right, you'll have big problems with a boot that cramps your arch. There's no good way to check for that without giving them a good test-walk. (SEE)

BREAKER, BREAKER

Bundle up your feet in moleskin, grit your teeth and wear your new cowboy boots every day, rain or shine. Give 'em two weeks. (SEE)

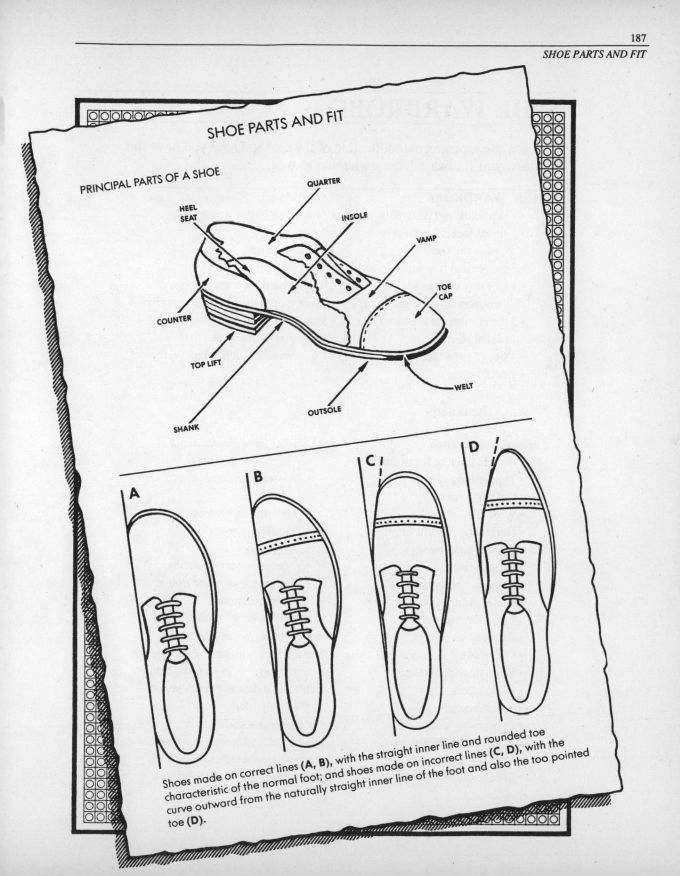

SHOE PARTS AND FIT

PRINCIPAL PARTS OF A SHOE

QUARTER

HEEL SEAT

INSOLE

VAMP

TOE CAP

COUNTER

TOP LIFT

WELT

SHANK

OUTSOLE

A B C D

Shoes made on correct lines (A, B), with the straight inner line and rounded toe characteristic of the normal foot; and shoes made on incorrect lines (C, D), with the curve outward from the naturally straight inner line of the foot and also the too pointed toe (D).

THE WARDROBE

This is the morning menu, the tale of the closet. Once you have the basics, you'll always have *something* to wear.

BASIC WARDROBE

- 1 suit (dark and preferably gray)
- 1 sports jacket (preferably a navy blazer)
- 3 pair casual trousers
- 1 pair dress slacks (or the trousers from the gray suit)
- 5 dress shirts (at least 2 white)
- 4 casual shirts
- 4 ties (1 solid blue or brown)
- 1 belt
- 1 casual jacket or windbreaker
- 9 pair socks
- 9 pair underwear
- 1 pair dress shoes
- 1 pair casual (or tennis) shoes
- 1 pair gloves (depending on region)
- 3 sweaters (at least 1 solid)
- 1 raincoat or overcoat
- 1 woolen scarf (depending on region)

Now for the details.

Fat guys should avoid

- Rough, thick or fuzzy fabrics
- Tight-fitting clothes
- Cuffed trousers
- Wide ties
- Horizontal patterns or prints

Short guys should avoid

- Sport jackets
- Long jackets or coats
- Wide, pleated trousers
- Cuffed trousers
- Detailed tailoring
- Overpadded shoulders
- Wide ties or bow ties
- Wide lapels
- Sweater-vests
- Contrasting shirt and trousers combinations
- Carrying umbrellas
- Shoes with jacked heels

Tall, skinny guys should avoid

- Shiny, smooth fabrics
- Trousers that break above the shoe
- Loose-fitting clothes
- Uncuffed trousers
- Narrow ties
- Vertical prints or patterns
- Same-color shirt and trouser combinations
- Short jackets or coats (TSc)

What all men should avoid

There are men who just haven't gotten the message — even though they haven't had a date in twenty years:

- No polyester
- No leisure suits
- No suits with wild patterns
- No patent-leather shoes with informal wear (RBr)

A COLOR CHART

Color charts are all the rage with the distaff side of mankind, so for those of you who want to dust off all those warm, feminine qualities, here, based on hair color, is a color chart.

Color	Yes	No
Redhead	blue green brown dark gray	red yellow light gray
Blond	blue gray red green	dark brown beige
Black	dark gray beige red green	blue
Brown	gray beige medium brown blue red	dark brown green
Silver	All (except yellow)	

Based on skin tones:

Color	Yes	No
Pale skin	dark blue dark brown	beige light gray yellow
Dark skin	beige light gray	dark blue dark brown

ONCE YOU'VE CHOSEN

your wardrobe for the day, for goodness' sake, leave yourself alone. You chose it, so wear it with dignity. Don't continually fuss with your clothes or fret in front of a mirror. In fact, you may not need a mirror at all, because if it doesn't *feel* comfortable, it probably doesn't look good. (RBr)

USES FOR FASHION

Aside from the dress-for-success fetish that acquired some popularity in the early '80s, the uses for fashion are generally more limited in scope and specific in application.

Bureaucratiques: You can spare yourself a lot of trouble at the motor vehicles hell or at the city business license clerk's office by dressing well. Bureaucrats are intimidated by men (especially tall ones) dressed in tasteful business attire, reserving their sadism for the tieless and blue-jeaned masses. (*Anon.*)

SHIRTS

Here, right off our backs, figuratively speaking:

White collars: The thing about white shirts is that they go with everything, they make your complexion look healthier, they're dignified and convey an aura of elegance regardless of the other crud you might be wearing. (VB)

*Slope***:** The height of the inside collar band, the part that touches your neck, is called the *slope*. There are three classifications of slope — high, medium and low — which correspond to the length of the human neck. If you have a long neck, get a high-slope collar; if your neck is short, wear a low-slope collar. (NGF)

See also *How to Fold a Shirt* **in** *CHAPTER FIVE: MODERN MOBILITY*.

CLOTHING CARE

For most of us, clothing is all that stands between us and the ridicule of the world. Many Modern Men would look terrible on the *radio* and therefore wish to preserve their wardrobe in the best possible state.

AN OLD TRICK

of traveling salesmen, and one you've probably already heard, is to eliminate the wrinkles from suits and jackets by hanging the garments high in the bathroom while taking a shower. Be sure the door is closed. The steam and moisture will eliminate some of the more distressing pleats. (MHG)

A variation: Hang wrinkled clothing in a closet with a wet towel. (AW)

A PAIR OF TROUSERS

will receive a pressing if left between a mattress and a box spring overnight. (MHG)

STORAGE

Don't store your clothes in plastic bags. Natural materials, like wool, cotton and leather, need to "breathe."

A closet that is ventilated is better for storage than one that is kept closed. Leave the door ajar. (SF)

NO WIRE HANGERS, EVER!

Wire hangers are only marginally better than nothing. Use wooden hangers for clothing you care about. (FDS)

HEY, FUZZBALL

Little balls of wool can be removed from a sweater by brushing it lightly with a dry sponge. Use tape to remove lint. (JH)

NEUTRALIZE ACID

spills on clothing by applying a mixture of baking soda and water (this combination also will remove corrosion buildup from auto batteries). (DEW)

DEATH BY DRY CLEANING

Dry cleaning is not only expensive, it also destroys the fabrics it seeks to save.

Brushing won't keep your clothes from stinking of cigarettes, but it will clean them. Get a clothes brush with natural bristles. The best time to brush a sports coat is just after you've removed it. First, brush vigorously against the nap of the fabric, then follow in the opposite direction. (DWA)

Neckties can be a knotty problem for many dry cleaners. If you have a very special, thoroughly stained necktie, you have three alternatives. One, trust the dry cleaner; guaranteed trouble. Two, send it to a place that specializes in neckties; if you live outside a major city, forget it. Three, give it to your sweetheart as a souvenir; she'll give it to Goodwill, where it belongs. (DWA)

Don't try to get away with avoiding your local dry cleaner altogether. Dry cleaning is the only way to get body stink out of delicate fabrics, and dry cleaners try their level best to do the job without damaging the goods. (DWA)

HANG IT UP

Always hang up your clothing as soon as you remove it; the moisture it absorbed from your body will help relieve the wrinkles. (GF)

NEW! IMPROVED!

Life with a washing machine can often resemble a soap opera. The colors don't get along with the whites and the colds hate the heats.

Don't overload the washing machine or the clothes won't get clean. Don't overload the dryer. Separate whites and colors. (HTR)

Gross stains can actually be removed by using the new enzyme cleaners. They're man's best friend.

Commercial laundering and pressing is very hard on shirts; you won't do nearly as good a job, and it's a lot of inconvenience, but your shirts will last twice as long if you wash and iron them yourself. (FES)

Dry clothing at medium or low heat. At high heat, synthetics will pucker and natural fibers will shrink a bit; high heat is hard on any fabric. If you fold your clothes as soon as they come out of the machine, they'll be far less wrinkled. (HTR)

Hand-washing never gets stuff as clean as you'd like. Still, it's cheap: all you need is a sink full of lukewarm water and some mild detergent, like Woolite brand, and a good pair of hands. Soak an item, then gently squeeze it; refill the sink with cold water and repeat, to rinse thoroughly. Squeeze, don't wring (knitted fabrics, especially wool, are extremely vulnerable to rough handling). Shirts should be hung; sweaters should be arranged flat on the floor on a towel. (FES) Or on a drying rack. (DH)

A dissent: You're probably just as well off using Ivory or Joy dishwashing detergent or shampoo or anything that's supposed to prevent dishpan hands. The dish soap is a lot cheaper. For stubborn stains and armpit problems, use a bar of brown soap. (RBr)

EMERGENCY CLOTHING REPAIRS

can be effected by the judicious use of a good Swingline *stapler.* You'll buy about two hours, max, before your rig'll let you down. (TS) If you don't want the staple to show (on a trouser hem, for example), *tape's* your only way. (RBr)

See also Moth Repelling **in** CHAPTER FIFTEEN: MODERN MESSES **and** *Sewing and Clothing Maintenance,* **below.**

SEWING AND CLOTHING MAINTENANCE

Putting together a wardrobe is a lot easier than keeping one together — especially when it's coming apart at the seams. (**See also** *CLOTHING CARE* **and** *EMERGENCY CLOTHING REPAIR,* **above.**)

LET THE CLEANER DO IT

Your local dry cleaner is the logical choice for simple alterations or basic repairs — letting out trouser waists, modifying sleeve and leg lengths, attaching buttons, mending seam tears and fixing linings are inexpensive tasks. (DSA)

AND IF HE CAN'T, TRY THE TAILOR

A tailor should be used to modify suits and jackets; coats can be altered in the sleeve; lapels can be slimmed or widened; back and chest dimensions can be changed. Shoulder and jacket length alterations are generally unsuccessful. (DSA)

WORN OR FRAYED COLLARS

and cuffs can be "turned" to extend a shirt's life. A tailor or local dry cleaner removes the offending collar or cuff, turns it over and reattaches it. It's alot cheaper. (GD)

BUTTON UP

Keep track of loose buttons. If you can't sew them back onto wherever they came from, pin them on the garment so you don't lose them. When you have time to sew them on, here's how to do it:

For shirt buttons push a length of thread through a needle, double it over and knot it at the end. Begin by inserting the needle from the inside of the garment so that the leading half of the needle sticks out where the button goes on the front of the garment. Slide the button on the needle, then pull the needle the rest of the way through the cloth until the knot at the end of the thread stops it. Then aim the needle back at the button, piercing the button through a different hole than the one you used the first time. Keep it up, using diagonally opposed holes in the button until you're almost out of thread, then wind the thread under the button a few times and tie a final knot.

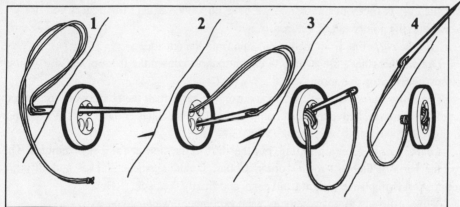

Jacket buttons can be reattached, in an emergency, by a simple needle and thread. But for a lasting repair, you'll need an embroidery needle and some silk thread. The procedure is the same as for shirts, however, except that the pattern of the holes in the buttons should be parallel stitches instead of crisscrossed ones. Leather buttons with a loop are attached by simply looping the thread back and forth between the garment and the button loop.

Patches should be attached from the inside of the garment. Use as much thread and as many small stitches as you can. Figure your repair to be temporary, though, since it seems that only a pro can make a patch stick. Avoid iron-on patches.

For other minor repairs examine the original stitch and try to duplicate it. Note that many seams are made with the garment turned inside out, and you'll have to do likewise to effect your repair. The shorter the stitch, the stronger the mend.

Magic menders, also called reweavers, can repair moth holes, cigarette burns and other wounds made in the middle of the garment and away from a seam. While the effect is truly miraculous, the cost can be tragic. (GRE)

IRONING A SHIRT

The shirt should be *slightly damp* to start with; this allows for a better press. You can use a plant sprayer in place of a steam iron, or you can sprinkle water off your fingertips.

Spray starch isn't bad, if you want a stiffer collar and cuff, but be careful: starch can burn easily and will build up on the iron, where it becomes scorched and then transfers off the iron and back onto the shirt.

Work in sections with the largest areas coming first — the back, followed by the two front panels, working from the shoulder down. Use the tapered end of the board to keep the shoulder area taut as you work.

Iron around buttons, not over them.

To iron the sleeves, make a crease from the shoulder to the cuff; ironing the pleats near the cuff is tricky business, and we have no advice except to suggest you use your noodle and the pointy end of the iron.

Iron the cuffs first from the inside, then from the outside.

The placket (that's the strip with the buttonholes down the front of the shirt) should be pressed from top to bottom.

The collar comes last. Turn it up and iron the back, then the front, working from the middle to the ends. Leave the shirt collar up until the shirt has cooled. This is even more boring to do than it is to read about. (VFE)

Another way: After sprinkling, put the shirt in the freezer for a few minutes. Then iron the parts of the shirt in this order: Collar, shoulder panels, sleeves and cuffs, left front panel (with placket), right front panel and finally the back. (RBr)

A lively dispute. But if you really want excitement, wait till you try

IRONING TROUSERS

The main thing to note is that the creases in the leg go from the crotch to the cuff, front and back. The waist and pocket area is tough to finish, so, except for a pass across the fly, skip it. (VFE)

PRESSING WOOLENS

When doing a touch-up on a woolen item, work with a very slightly damp towel between the iron and the fabric. (VFE)

FOLDING A SHIRT

See *How to Pack a Suitcase* in *CHAPTER FIVE: MODERN MOBILITY.*

DENTAL FLOSS

is better than heavy thread when it comes to mending leather, heavy canvas or Naugahyde. (*Anon.*)

CHUCK IT

Anything not worn within a year should be thrown out — excepting quality classics which will always be fashionable, but not excepting bell-bottoms, which, even when they do come back, will still look horrible. (KS)

SUSPENDERS

For some reason, babes love braces. Maybe it's the avuncular image they convey. Or, more likely, women see suspenders as part of the trappings of paternal masculinity. In either case, braces almost invariably elicit a favorable reaction from girls.

That's not a good reason for buying and wearing the things, though. First of all, they are far more inconvenient than a belt. Second, they force the alteration of your wardrobe (**see below**). And third, they're not for short men or fat men; they look best on tall men of average build. (ATR)

CLIPS OR BUTTONS?

Buttons, no question. The clip-on braces you see around are fine for kids and women, but men's braces should be fastened securely to the inside of the trousers by means of buttons sewn into the waistband. Each pair of pants will require six buttons. They should be attached the way jacket buttons are — heavy duty all the way. (ATR)

SIZING BRACES

The correct width for braces is one inch. If you're taller than average, be sure to get them long enough to fit. Few things look as silly as a guy wearing suspenders which have pulled the crotch of his trousers up into his ass and his cuffs above his ankles. (ATR)

CHAPTER **12**

Modern
Manors

For some Modern Men, fifteen or twenty years ago interior design was a Sealy on the floor and a Mr. Zig Zag on the door. But while it was once acceptable — more, it was *desirable* — to have your decorating scheme reflect your political attitude, these days the social and political atmosphere favors a gooier environment where the inside of your house is supposed to reflect the inside of your head. Indoor decor isn't just decorating, it's a means of self-*expression,* for crying out loud.

Modern Men know that ain't so. To a Modern Man, dressing up the inside of your house or apartment is a *job*, not a catharsis.

C O N T E N T S
Chapter Twelve: *MODERN MANORS*

INDOOR DECOR

Remember your mother's words? "Young man, look at that mess! You call that a room? That's not a room! That's a pigsty."

What you should have said — but doubtless didn't — was that it was *supposed* to look like a pigsty; pigsty was the look you wanted, to be pigsty was to be beautiful.

Indoors is a special place. It's home; it's where your TV lives. And it pays to make it look nice. So the point here is that it will always look just right as long as you execute your decor with a system — a specific *look* — in mind. That way, if pigsty's what you want, pigsty's what you'll get.

THE CLUTTERED LOOK

It's not as easy as it sounds. To properly clutter a room so that it looks at once disheveled and inviting is no easy task.

Start by making an inventory of all your furnishings; be sure to include pictures, posters, collections, all those little pieces of junk that are squeezed onto the bookshelf, the works. This should produce a much longer list than you first suspected.

Go through the list carefully, and organize everything into categories. Then make a judgment call on all your possessions. Is each one interesting on its own or as part of a collection? If not, chuck it. That goes for toasters and chairs as well as for souvenir ashtrays and stacks of junk mail. The end result of this exercise is to create a home or apartment that *seems* to be chock-full of interesting things and pleasant surprises.

Next, look at the space you have available. There are certain areas that you'll want to keep reasonably free of clutter. Make sure, for example, that you have sufficient room around the dining room table to seat guests; try to keep the central portion of the living room open enough to permit free passage. As a rule, you'll want to keep clear those areas that you and your guests most frequently use.

Now, start with the walls (**see** *WALLS AND WALLCOVERING,* **below,** if it applies). Take all the pictures and posters you can find and cover as much wall space as possible. If you have an extensive collection of books, count the bookshelves as part of the wall decor. (Bookshelves are important, here; if you don't have more bookshelves than you need, then you don't have enough. Go get more.) By the time you've finished with the walls, you should be able to justify any bare spots as part of the overall visual effect. If you can't, run out to a junk store and buy a whole bunch of photographs in frames, the older the better. Look for family portraits — instant ancestors — and for pictures of European and American landmarks. Go easy on the obvious things — fruit-box labels and the like.

Once you have the walls done, start on the next visual register — the tables, sofas and chairs that occupy the lower third of the room. Try to find an interesting table lamp for each table, then take all those silly knickknacks and put them in groups around the lamps, as though you were proud of them. Place anything tall and skinny next to the sofa, including at least one lamp and, if you indulge, a standing ashtray; old standing lamps should be placed in the vicinity of the chairs.

Finally, take all the bits and pieces of paper — including newspapers and magazines — that you will invariably accumulate and make them into stacks, neat stacks, stacks that will look important and purposeful when placed on the shelves of your bookcase.

Here's what the cluttered look won't accommodate: no clothes or other objects scattered on the floor; no open closet doors; no bright lights and no overhead lighting (**see** *LIGHTING,* **below**); nothing new made of plastic or painted in bright, primary colors. If you follow these rules, you can pile up the clutter without deleterious effect. (TY)

See also *The Speed Clean* **in** *CHAPTER FIFTEEN: MODERN MESSES.*

THE ECLECTIC STYLE

To successfully pull off an eclectic style of decorating, you must be able to temper the wildest extremes of enthusiasm with tasteful restraint. As in all disciplines of art and design, those who are good at it will know when to stop. Unfortunately, that knowledge is not something that can be taught here; it must be mastered through intuition and experience.

A successful combination of eclectic elements — all those things that you never thought would look right together — depends on the merits of each individual item. Each item in the room must be able to stand alone as a distinctive object.

The eclectic style encourages experimentation — scale, usually crucial in interior design, can be disregarded, and you can shuffle indoor and outdoor furniture at will. It helps to remember that you're never wed to your design. If you do it right, you can alter it easily. (AR)

WIDE OPEN SPACES

The rules here are easy: Remove everything that doesn't get considerable use, and never place more than three large objects (including TVs, beds and chairs) in any single room, and put nothing at all on the floors or walls.

This approach presupposes several things: first, that you have decent, white or off-white walls and attractive floors (no wallpaper, no irregular floor patches); second, that you possess only beautiful or interesting pieces of furniture; third, that you are immeasurably tidy.

White or off-white is the color of choice for all dry goods used in this design.

The desired effect is one of light and elegant spaciousness. If you make it work, it'll look beautiful. If it doesn't work, it'll always look like the bank came and repossessed your furniture.

A final note: you can't do this halfway. You must use the same rule for every room in your house or apartment. (FR)

INSTALLING WALL FASTENERS

Use molly screws or toggle bolts on a plastered wall where strength is needed to hold heavy pictures, mirrors, towel bars, etc.

Molly screws have two parts (fig. A). To install, first make a small hole in the plaster and drive the casing in even with the wall surface. Tighten the screw to spread casing in the back. Remove the screw and put it through the item you are hanging, into casing, and tighten.

For toggle bolts (fig. B), drill a hole in the plaster large enough for the folded toggle to go through. Remove the toggle. Put the bolt through a towel bar or whatever you are hanging. Replace the toggle. Push the toggle through the wall and tighten with a screwdriver (fig. C).

Plastic anchor screws (fig. D) should be used where you want to attach something to a concrete wall. To install, first make a small hole in the wall and drive the casing in even with the wall surface. Put screw through item and into the casing, and tighten.

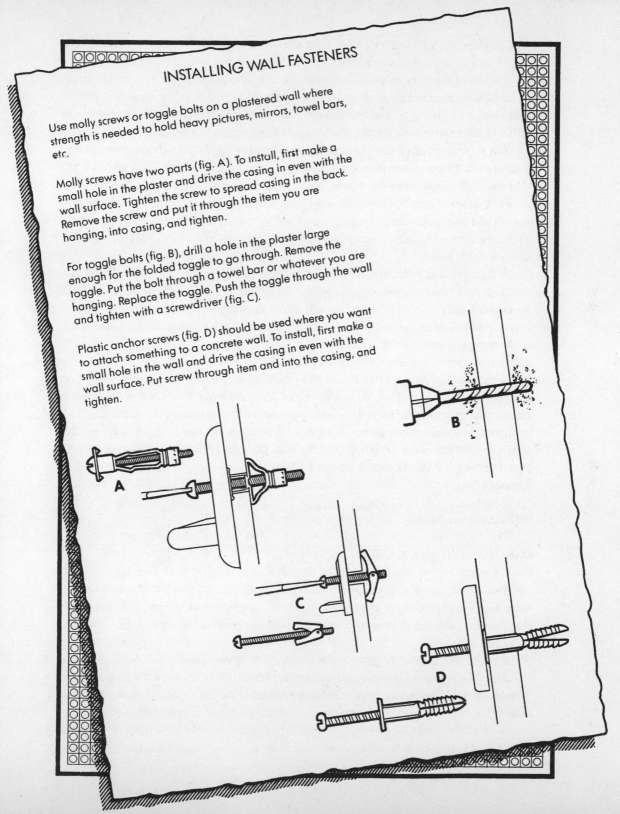

DECORATING A DUMP ON THE CHEAP

There are some alternatives here:

The first one is a variation on the "Wide Open Spaces" theory (**above**), but involving less expensive pieces of furniture. The result is the same, however. The monastic, ascetic style can be so masculine and self-assured that sometimes you can even get away with leaving your walls and other structural elements in a sorry, but clean, state.

The second approach is to visit all the local thrift stores, buying up all the still-inexpensive '40s, '50s and '60s pieces of furniture you need. Next, select two or three Miami Vice pastel shades, such as aqua, pink, coral, lavender or turquoise, and paint each piece one color only. Spend the money on good paint, and do a good job; the finish should be smooth and glossy. Cream or very light gray walls, with a solid-colored area rug, should set off the furniture nicely. Keep your rooms fairly uncluttered. (DBr) (**See also** *PAINT AND COLOR,* **below.**)

A third method is to furnish your house or apartment in new and secondhand outdoor furniture. This produces a pleasantly surprising effect, especially if you don't mix the outdoor stuff with a lot of traditional, indoor furniture. Take this as far as you can stand it: AstroTurf, a gas grill (with proper ventilation, please), maybe some lawn ornaments and some redwood fencing.

For emergencies, there's a fourth way. Let's assume your digs are really horrible, the worst, and your girlfriend hates it, and she won't set foot in the joint. Here's what you do: separate the few halfway decent pieces of furniture from the rest, and set it aside along with the stuff essential to daily life, like your toothbrush. Stack the remaining junk in interesting shapes. Then go out and buy a tremendous amount of inexpensive muslin cloth, the kind artists use for canvas. Get the widest widths available, and double your estimate in terms of length. Drape the muslin over the junk. Your house may resemble a summer home in the off-season, but it'll also look pretty arty, and much better. Be careful, though; you will have made your home into a tinderbox, and a clumsy trick with a match could send your dream decor up in smoke. (AR)

DECORATING AS A CAMOUFLAGE TACTIC

Let's say you're warehousing a lot of really valuable objects in your home — art, antiques, silver, investment quality Orientals, that sort of thing. And let's say you want to keep the inventory a secret from your neighbors, potential robbers, the IRS, the paper boy. And let's say you're as paranoid as one of our anonymous correspondents.

Time to camouflage. Go to a thrift store and buy a quantity of trashy curtains to hang in the windows (if you have gates in the windows, hang the curtains so the bars can't be seen from the outside). On the inside, hang the curtains you really want, so they hide the horrors the neighbors have to see. Clear plastic sheets tacked to the windows not only makes it hard to see inside when the curtains are drawn, but also look pretty bad from the outside. Pick up a beat-up junker for a car and park it in the drive. Use it when you have to make a caviar run. A second car, say a '73 Chevy Nova, might look nice on blocks.

Leave an unfinished project or two in the front yard. You get the idea. The exterior of your house should not betray its contents.

If you're really worried, decorate the downstairs rooms — or at least the living room — in a dull, plebeian fashion, exhibiting nothing in the least bit special. Leave the curtains open, so everybody can see that your idea of luxury is a new beanbag chair. This also provides an area to receive strangers without disclosing your treasure. (*Anon.*)

See also *HIDING THINGS* **in** *CHAPTER NINETEEN: A MODERN MISCELLANY.*

DECORATING WITH ANTIQUES

If you can only afford a few pieces of old or antique furniture, yet want to convey the rich atmosphere an antique decor can provide, select your pieces very carefully.

Your guideline should be to acquire pieces that will stand alone and will not be obscured by things they might contain or display. *Shelves or tables,* for example, ought to be avoided, since they may be hidden by whatever's on top of them. *Chairs and clocks,* on the other hand, are obvious pieces that are not ordinarily cluttered. Attractive *old lamps* can add greatly to the feel of a room, not only because of the soft light they provide, but also because they are quite obvious objects.

Antique couches are rare and expensive and are usually very uncomfortable.

Hatstands are among the cheapest of old items. They're quite useful and easily found. (BR)

See also *ANTIQUE, JUNK AND THRIFT SHOPS* **in** *CHAPTER NINE: CONSUMPTION* **and** *FURNITURE CARE* **in** *CHAPTER FOURTEEN: MODERN MAINTENANCE.*

PAINT AND COLOR

Before you choose a wall color, make sure you have a thorough appreciation of what other elements are going into the room. In addition to furnishings, remember to take carpets, drapes and intended use into account. As a rule, avoid strong colors — blues, purples, pinks, oranges. (The rules here for color choice also go for wallpaper, incidentally.)

PAINT TYPES

Most interior paints fall into two categories: water-based and petroleum-based. Check the container for the appropriate thinner — it's not only something you have to know, it will also reveal the base used.

Water-based (or latex) paint is the easiest to use and, better, the easiest to clean up after you've finished, since everything washes off with water. The price you pay for this ease-of-use is a slight tendency to fade and a less resistant finish.

Alkyd paints require mineral spirits for clean-up. While latex is fine for large wall areas and the like, alkyd paints are more durable and less likely to fade. They're best suited for high-wear areas, like cabinets, molding and trim. (TKJ)

LUSTERS

Paint is best used like a tool: You pick the right tool for the right job.

Flat finishes are best for walls and other large areas. The result is a dull, chalky but warm and unobtrusive look. Drawback: Flat finishes are tough to clean (**see below**).

Semigloss is best for trim, but can be used effectively on walls. Unlike flat finishes, semigloss paint can be scrubbed clean. A higher standard of preparation is required for semigloss finishes.

High gloss paints on a wall will make your house look like an underused disco. Gloss finishes look best on nonmilitary vehicles, but can be used satisfactorily on trim.

No matter which kind of paint you choose, don't skimp. Cheap paint looks like cheap paint. (TKJ)

PRIMERS

Always take the time to seal raw surfaces before applying paint. Unless you're a Zen master, painting is a dull and tedious job; appropriate use of primers will mean you'll only have to do it once.

Primers will also make painting a glossy surface easier. Ask for help in choosing the right primer for the right paint. (FA)

PREPARATION

Painting a room the right way is 10 percent inspiration and 90 percent preparation.

Start by removing the furniture and bringing in a batch of strong lights. Next, find and correct all the surface defects, using sandpaper, premixed spackling paste and primer. Then wash the walls (with detergent, if necessary), rinse and let dry thoroughly. Wipe liquid sandpaper over glossy trim areas that are to be repainted. Mask any glass areas and take off all the switch plates, outlet covers and door hardware before you start.

Remember gravity. Don't paint the floor when you paint the walls; paint spray gets all over everything, so take extra precautions covering the carpets and floorboards with paper, cloth or tarps. (FA)

STORAGE

Keep paint tins tightly capped. Store them in an area where they won't freeze. (TKJ)

BRUSHES

Choosing the right brush is almost as important as choosing the right paint. It's worth spending extra money for a good brush — one that doesn't leave bristles all over

INTERIOR PAINTING

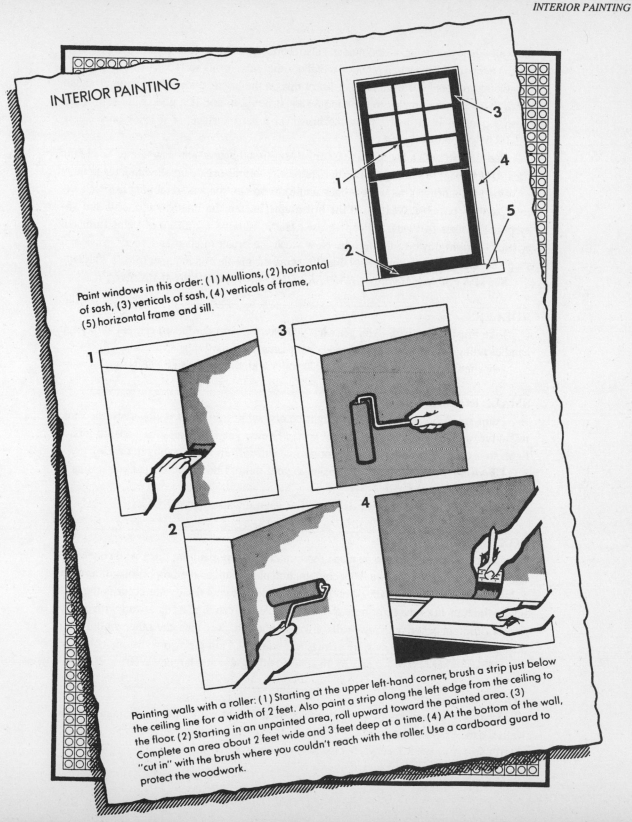

Paint windows in this order: (1) Mullions, (2) horizontal of sash, (3) verticals of sash, (4) verticals of frame, (5) horizontal frame and sill.

Painting walls with a roller: (1) Starting at the upper left-hand corner, brush a strip just below the ceiling line for a width of 2 feet. Also paint a strip along the left edge from the ceiling to the floor. (2) Starting in an unpainted area, roll upward toward the painted area. (3) Complete an area about 2 feet wide and 3 feet deep at a time. (4) At the bottom of the wall, "cut in" with the brush where you couldn't reach with the roller. Use a cardboard guard to protect the woodwork.

the wall when you paint — and thus it's also worth the extra time to clean them properly. This is even more true when painting metal or other nonporous surfaces.

Good brushes have little flags or fuzzy tips on the bristle ends. The ferrule, or metal band, that joins the bristles to the handle should be tight, and is a good indicator of the brush's quality. If in doubt, bang the brush on a hard surface; if it loses only a few bristles, it's probably a good one.

Use a brush with a natural bristle for solvent-based paints, and a synthetic bristle for latex. If you want to see a spreading disaster, use a natural-bristle brush with latex paint.

To clean a brush, first work it back and forth on newspapers, removing as much excess paint as possible. Next, hold the brush upright, fan the bristles, and, with the appropriate thinner (or water, if you've used latex), remove all traces of paint from the bristles — right down to the ferrule. Now wash the brush in soap and water, rinse and shape the bristles, and allow to dry. Finally, wrap the bristle end in paper towels. (TKJ)

See also *Painting Metal* **in** *CHAPTER FOURTEEN: MODERN MAINTENANCE.*

ROLLERS

Like brushes and paint, you get what you pay for. Soft cardboard centers and cheap handles will give you a roller that's no better than a cardboard tube.

Pay attention to the label. Use the right roller with the right paint. (TKJ)

SMALL ROOMS

Paint small or dark rooms with light colors; whites and soft yellows are the most reflective, and will augment a sense of space. Even a very light gray will absorb lots of light, so use darker, grayer shades in rooms that suffer from too much light. (WDo)

Choosing a color: If you can't make up your mind, find the color that you use most often in your wardrobe. (EF)

White, or actually off-white, is the perfect neutral wall color. (ESD)

BOXY ROOMS

Dull, boxlike rooms can be made more interesting by painting three walls one color and the fourth a different one. This combination also changes the proportions of a room; a darker color tends to recede. Generally, the wall that gets the darker color is the wall upon which most of the light from the windows falls. Avoid painting a wall with a window a different color; window walls always appear darker than the other walls, since during the daylight hours they are always in a shadow, Painting two walls one color and two walls another makes a square room appear rectangular and larger. (WNi)

LONG ROOMS

In a long, narrow room, paint one long wall a light color and the remaining three walls a darker color. (BH)

DARK COLORS

Sometimes, guys are afraid to paint a room in dark colors. Screw it. Go ahead.

Medium shades make a room less barren. In large rooms, they convey formal and dramatic qualities; in a small room, they impart a sense of intimacy.

Like wood paneling, dark walls are associated with dignity and masculinity. Dark walls also give other undiluted colors in the room a jewel-like intensity.

Remember, though, that paint almost invariably dries darker, and even a second coat will still have a darker shade than you expected.

If you want to get flamboyant with colors, experiment in the dining room. It's the room used least frequently in an average house or apartment. (GD)

WHITE WALLS

Never use plain white paint for a wall. Always select a softer variation — eggshell or some other off-white color. (GRE)

COAT YOUR HANDS

with Vaseline before starting a painting project and your clean-up will be relatively quick and effortless. (JGF)

See also *STAIN REMOVAL CHART* **in** *CHAPTER FIFTEEN: MODERN MESSES.*

WALLS AND WALLCOVERING

When it feels like they're really closing in:

COST

The most expensive way to deal with a lousy wall is to ***repair the structural deficiencies,*** repair and resurface the damaged areas with new plaster, refinish the thing, then prime and repaint it. That's the right way, so, naturally, it's also the most expensive way. If you're renting, or broke, there are other strategies:

The second most expensive way to cover a bad wall is to ***erect new drywall*** over the old wall. This still involves plaster, taping, painting and a lot of other headaches. But it is somewhat cheaper.

How about ***cheap paneling?*** Not the horrible, two-bit wood paneling, which is out of the question, but some of the other Formica-type sheets that are on the market. Cheaper than wallboard, but not as cheap as

Carpet, glued all over the wall, if you like, from floor to ceiling, or just to chair rail height.

Even less expensive is ***scraping and patching*** the most troublesome spots with plaster, then repainting. (GBMcG)

See also *RENOVATIONS* **in** *CHAPTER FOURTEEN: MODERN MAINTENANCE.*

APPLICATION OF DRYWALL

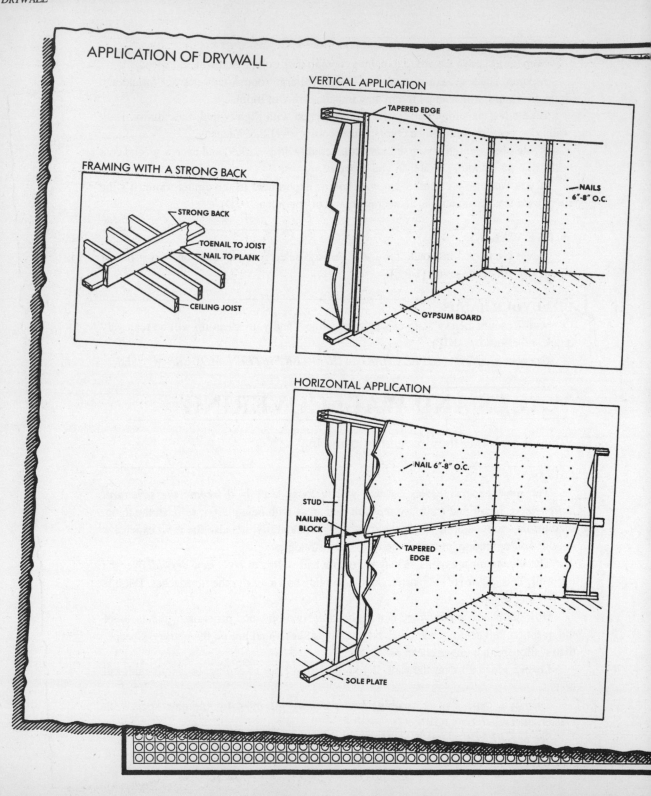

VERTICAL APPLICATION

TAPERED EDGE

NAILS 6"-8" O.C.

GYPSUM BOARD

FRAMING WITH A STRONG BACK

STRONG BACK

TOENAIL TO JOIST

NAIL TO PLANK

CEILING JOIST

HORIZONTAL APPLICATION

NAIL 6"-8" O.C.

STUD

NAILING BLOCK

TAPERED EDGE

SOLE PLATE

CEMENTING AND TAPING JOINT

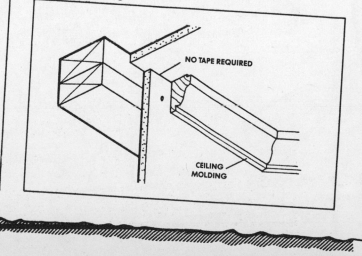

STUD

GYPSUM BOARD

TAPERED EDGE

JOINT CEMENT

TAPE

JOINT CEMENT

FEATHER EDGE

NAIL SET WITH CROWNED HAMMER

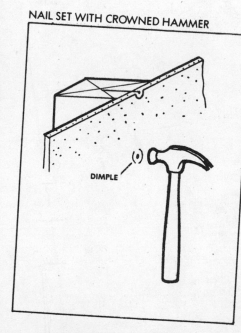

DIMPLE

1. Use a wide spackling knife (5 inches) and spread the cement in the tapered edges, starting at the top of the wall.
2. Press the tape into the recess with the putty knife until the joint cement is forced through the perforations.
3. Cover the edges with additional cement, feathering the edges.
4. Allow to dry, sand the joint lightly, and then apply the second coat, feathering the edges. For best results, a third coat may be applied, feathering beyond the second coat.
5. After the joint cement is dried, sand smooth.

TAPING INSIDE CORNERS

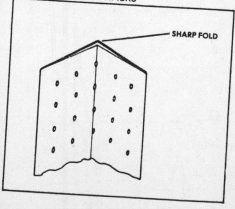

SHARP FOLD

FINISH AT CEILING

NO TAPE REQUIRED

CEILING MOLDING

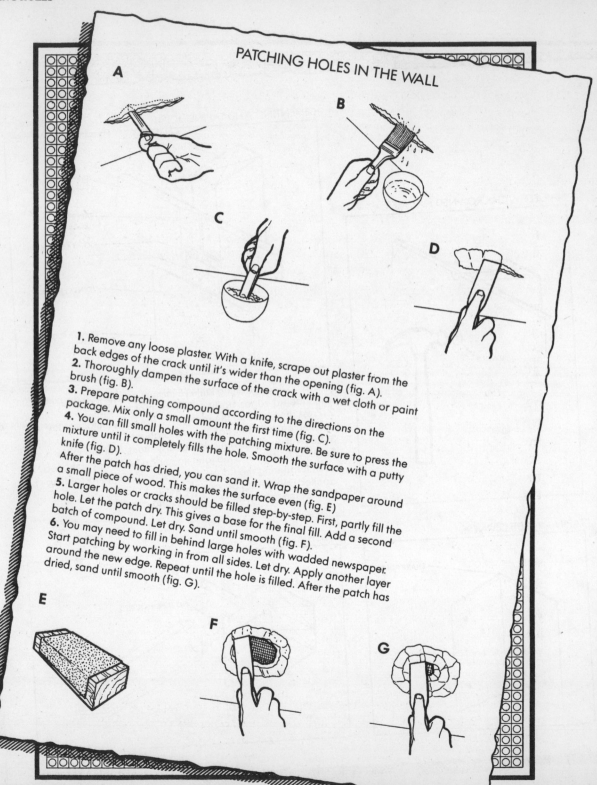

PATCHING HOLES IN THE WALL

A

B

C

D

1. Remove any loose plaster. With a knife, scrape out plaster from the back edges of the crack until it's wider than the opening (fig. A).
2. Thoroughly dampen the surface of the crack with a wet cloth or paint brush (fig. B).
3. Prepare patching compound according to the directions on the package. Mix only a small amount the first time (fig. C).
4. You can fill small holes with the patching mixture. Be sure to press the mixture until it completely fills the hole. Smooth the surface with a putty knife (fig. D).
   After the patch has dried, you can sand it. Wrap the sandpaper around a small piece of wood. This makes the surface even (fig. E)
5. Larger holes or cracks should be filled step-by-step. First, partly fill the hole. Let the patch dry. This gives a base for the final fill. Add a second batch of compound. Let dry. Sand until smooth (fig. F).
6. You may need to fill in behind large holes with wadded newspaper. Start patching by working in from all sides. Let dry. Apply another layer around the new edge. Repeat until the hole is filled. After the patch has dried, sand until smooth (fig. G).

E

F

G

RENTERS

If you're renting or on a short-term lease and don't care to make a major investment in somebody else's property, try hanging curtains from floor to ceiling along the bad wall (**but see** *A Caveat* **below**). A bit pricey, but you can always take them with you when you move. A less costly gambit is to use photographer's seamless paper — available at large photo supply houses — which is sold in a wide variety of colors. You can do a very large wall for less than fifty bucks. It's cheap, but very temporary.

The last solution is, in many ways, the best. Put pictures, posters and graphics all over the offending wall. Framed prints are best, but unframed large pieces will do nicely. Only small portions of the wall should be visible when you're done. (TR)

Take It With You: Use fabric to cover bad walls in a rented apartment. You can go for broke with some expensive material or cut your costs by using bedsheets. Either way, the effect is cozy and you can take it down and fold it up when you leave. (RBr)

A caveat: Covering your walls with fabric may look swell, but it makes your home into a first-rate fire hazard — especially when highly flammable synthetic fabrics are used. This goes for curtains, too. (DH)

See also *PAINT AND COLOR,* **above.**

RUGS AND CARPETS

The first thing you should know about rugs is that rugs aren't carpets. Rugs are woven complete, like a picture, usually with a border framing the whole thing. A carpet, on the other hand, has a uniform pattern (or none at all) throughout; a carpet has no border and is cut to fit. Most of the time it's not a vague distinction: There's a world of difference between a discount warehouse special and a Persian rug.

ORIENTALS

Of all woven floor coverings, Orientals are the best. For decorative use, they're versatile, changing with your tastes in furniture and accessories. And when your tastes outgrow your living quarters and it's time to move, you can take Orientals with you.

Other rugs become practically valueless for resale the moment they're installed in your home. In fact, even with Oriental rugs, it's difficult to actually make money reselling the things. But if you're really strapped for cash, you can at least recover some of your costs by selling the floor coverings. (GF)

PADS

Never use carpets or rugs without a *proper cushion*. A decent pad will not only make your floor covering look better, it'll also help it last far longer. As a rule, the heavier the pad the better, but even a rag of a thing is better than no pad at all.

If *noise* is a factor, use wall-to-wall carpeting with an extra-thick pad.

Small area rugs, especially Orientals, should be carefully padded. A thin quarter-inch no-skid foam pad — cheap and easy to trim with a scissors — will do nicely.

Only *indoor-outdoor carpets* can survive for long without padding. (GF)

HOW TO MEASURE FOR A CARPET

Carpet is usually sold by the square yard. To determine how much you'll need, multiply the length of your room by its width, then divide by nine. (GF)

CARPET MATERIALS

It pays to consider material as carefully as you consider price, color and pattern. Different materials have different characteristics:

Wool carpeting is the most luxurious and durable floor covering material. Hence, it's also the most expensive. While wool is easy to clean, it will need occasional mothproofing. This is the material of choice for smaller area rugs.

Nylon is among the strongest of all carpeting materials. It will take a lot of punishment, hide a barrow-load of dirt and grime and seems inhospitable to insects. Prices of nylon carpeting vary enormously.

Acrylic carpeting closely resembles wool. While it sheds dirt and is somewhat insect-resistant, it sometimes pulls like an old sweater. Acrylic carpeting is moderately priced.

Polypropylene olefin may sound sweet and fragile, but it'll stand up to acts of God, resist frat-house-quality stains and remain impervious to dampness. It's better known as indoor-outdoor carpet, and it is significantly nicer at the higher end of the price spectrum. The cheap stuff looks like artificial grass. In fact, the cheap stuff *is* artificial grass, suitable only for cheap ballparks.

Polyester looks better as a carpet than it does as a suit. It's inexpensive, is dirt- and mildew-resistant and is not congenial to bugs. Spills of oil-based products can cause ugly problems, though.

Carpet tiles come in various materials, and mostly in small square-foot, self-stick pieces. They're often cheap and always easy to install. With a dash of good taste, you can get away with these. Putting self-stick tiles on salvageable wooden floors, however, is an affront that should be avoided.

Regardless of material, remember that a light-colored carpet will make a room appear larger. And while a carpet with a lower pile and an even texture is generally in the best taste, it will show wear and dirt more than a vulgar flecked or multicolored carpet.

If you can't afford good taste, or if you don't have any, buy one of those linoleum rugs — the kind that comes in a big roll and has a picture of a rug on it. Pass it off as a joke. It is. (GF)

INSTALLATION

While installing wall-to-wall carpeting isn't very difficult as a do-it-yourself project, get your dealer to put the carpet down for you. It's very fast, reasonably cheap (some dealers offer it for free as a promotion) and it gives you somebody to be mad at if a mistake should occur. (JHK)

LARGE RUGS

An alternative to wall-to-wall carpeting is a large, room-sized rug. Leave a border of floor a foot or so (not less than six inches) around the rug, but be careful where you put the furniture. Tables and chairs sitting half on and half off a rug look silly. Place the furniture so it is either entirely off the rug or entirely on it.

A large rug is a large chunk of color, so be careful. Gray or green is usually a safe bet (unless the walls are the same color). (GF)

RUG AND CARPET CARE

Vacuum often. Dirt that gets ground into carpets is tough to get out. If you have to call in a pro, locate a company that uses steam, not chemicals.

Orientals pose a special problem. Use care when vacuuming them; if you use a beating brush, don't vacuum at all. You can wash Orientals outside: Use a hose and a mild soap with a soft scrub brush. Remember how much the rugs cost you; don't maul them.

You can sometimes *restore* a fair degree of color in a worthless faded or worn Oriental by using felt-tipped marking pens. Take a color reference to your local art supply dealer and pick up a marker with permanent ink in it. Use care in coloring, but don't worry. It's easier than painting-by-numbers. *More serious restorations* involve the use of permanent inks and small paint brushes.

Nonprofessional restoration will add some vitality to a dead-looking rug, but won't increase its value by a penny. (GF)

See also *Recouping Your Investment* **in** *CHAPTER NINE: CONSUMPTION.*

LIGHTING

In creating ambient light in a room, the rule is pretty simple: if you can't see, it's either too dark, or the light is shining in your eyes.

COMFORTABLE LIGHTING

Small pools of incandescent light, created by individual lamps, create a warmer, more pleasant atmosphere than large, ceiling-mounted fluorescent fixtures, which make your home look like your office.

A room should have suitable lamps to provide *three levels of lighting:* the lowest level should be just enough for intimate chats or watching television. Lamps next to reading chairs should be placed to illuminate the pages of a book without flooding the rest of the room in harsh light; the highest level of lighting should provide sufficient illumination for working and cleaning.

The advantage of using many smaller lamps is the flexibility they provide. Ugly walls can be de-emphasized; unattractive or messy areas can be hidden in semidarkness. In addition, a small room can be made to appear larger by using many small light sources. And remember, you can use light to isolate different areas of a larger room.

Avoid overhead fixtures of any kind, if possible (but **see below under** *Types of Incandescent Fixtures* for a dissenting view). Under no circumstances should fluorescent lights be used in your home, unless you moonlight as a neurosurgeon. Fluorescent lighting causes fatigue and headaches (**see under** *Fluorescent Lighting* **below**). (DFK)

TYPES OF INCANDESCENT FIXTURES

Lighting units mounted permanently in a ceiling or wall are not only expensive, but also difficult and costly to alter. Unless you're really committed to a lighting design, don't mess with them.

Track lighting systems offer a less expensive alternative to built-in units, but they invariably make your home look like a restaurant or art gallery.

Large, overhead fixtures can be used for clean-up or other occasions requiring extreme brightness. (AR)

FLUORESCENT LIGHTING

You'd better have a good reason for using fluorescent lighting, since it is extremely garish and unflattering.

If used in quantity, fluorescent light will reveal the faults of everything it illuminates. A room should be clinically clean to stand up to fluorescent scrutiny. And you'd better be in pretty decent shape yourself. (GH)

MOUNTING A FLUORESCENT FIXTURE

If you must hang a fluorescent ceiling fixture, do not mount it directly to the plaster. Instead, hang it a foot or so from the ceiling so that the light not only projects downward, but also bounces off the ceiling. The result will be a softer brighter effect.

Fluorescent illumination is a cold light. You can further soften it by placing the bulbs in a long box called a trough. Mount it on a wall behind a long, low piece of furniture — a sofa, for example. Fluorescent tubes can also be installed behind a window cornice or curtain valance, but remember that fluorescent light will alter the color of your furniture, carpets, clothing and skin, so test first. (JBi)

See also *Wiring Ceiling and Wall Fixtures* **and** *Wiring Lamps* **in** *CHAPTER FOURTEEN: MODERN MAINTENANCE.*

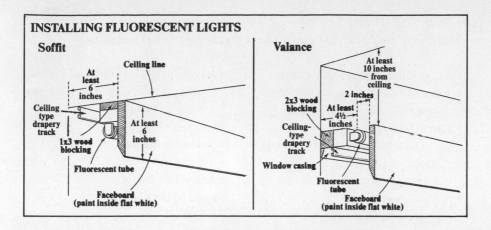

INSTALLING FLUORESCENT LIGHTS

Soffit

Ceiling line

At least 6 inches

Ceiling type drapery track

1x3 wood blocking

At least 6 inches

Fluorescent tube

Faceboard (paint inside flat white)

Valance

At least 10 inches from ceiling

2 inches

2x3 wood blocking

At least 4½ inches

Ceiling-type drapery track

Window casing

Fluorescent tube

Faceboard (paint inside flat white)

OIL LAMPS

Handy in an emergency; make sure the oil lamp isn't the *cause* of the emergency.

Two-thirds full oil lamps draw best. (JH)

Be careful carrying an oil lamp. Remember the bit in the westerns where the bad guys torch the saloon by tossing an oil lamp in the corner? (HDS)

Mineral spirit is the best fuel for an oil lamp. It has less odor and burns cleaner than kerosene. You can get one- or five-gallon cans at dry cleaner supply outlets. (AR)

Trimming the burnt end of the wick with a bit of sandpaper will result in better combustion and more light. (JH)

Preheat all oil lamps by running the lamp very low for the first five minutes. Bright mantle lights need an even longer preheating period — allow ten minutes, at least. (JH)

Mantle lamps give off more light (as much as 40 watts, in some cases) than wick lamps, but they also require more maintenance and operating care. The mantle is a small net "sock" that turns to ash after the first burning, and it's consequently very, very fragile — you'll want to have several spares on hand. The chimneys on mantle lamps can get very hot and occasionally will crack. If this type of lamp isn't watched while it's burning, it may overrun, clog and send an orange flame a few feet above the chimney. If the mantle gets clogged, turn the fire very low and wait until it burns off before turning it back up. A good rule is to operate mantle lamps at less than maximum capacity. (JH)

See also *Lighting in Camp* **in** *CHAPTER ONE: OUTDOORS*.

GUEST ROOM IN HEAVEN

If you've been good your whole life, then die and go to stay with acquaintances, this is what it'll be like:

THE PERFECT GUEST ROOM
This is definitely a top-end guide. The perfect guest quarters will contain

- A bed with a medium-hard mattress
- A bedboard to convert the mattress to a hard one
- Two to four full fluffy pillows
- Very clean but completely broken-in sheets and pillow cases (flannel ones if it's winter)
- A down comforter
- An additional light blanket folded at the foot of the bed for naps
- Plenty of general-interest books and current magazines
- A clock radio
- A color TV
- Daily newspapers
- A bedside reading lamp
- Fresh flowers and/or fruit
- Wooden hangers
- A prebuilt stack of logs and kindling, if appropriate
- Ashtray and matches

In the adjoining bath
- New toothbrush
- Aspirin
- Adhesive bandages
- Hand lotion
- Nail file
- Facial tissue
- Nonscented soap (Ivory is great)
- Shampoo
- Scented soap
- Clean towels and facecloth
- Clothes brush and shoehorn
- White terry robe
- Sewing kit
- Toothpaste   (TR)

THE OTHER WAY
Make your guests as uncomfortable as possible without violating the rules of etiquette. It'll get them out of your hair much faster than if you plead other engagements or business pressure. (*Anon.*)

MORLEY PIX
According to Christopher Morley, if he could have only one book in a guest room, it would be a copy of the works of Saki. His short stories are light and wonderful. (AR)

See also *Houseguest Rules, Gifts* **and** *Pissing* **in** CHAPTER SEVENTEEN: THE DEPORTMENT DEPARTMENT.

MOVING

The only good thing about moving is that you'll never again wonder who your real friends are. They're the ones carrying your sofabed.

PLASTIC MILK CRATES
that have gone missing are desperately wanted back by dairies, who have been

SHIPPING CRATES

Details of basic shipping crate construction.

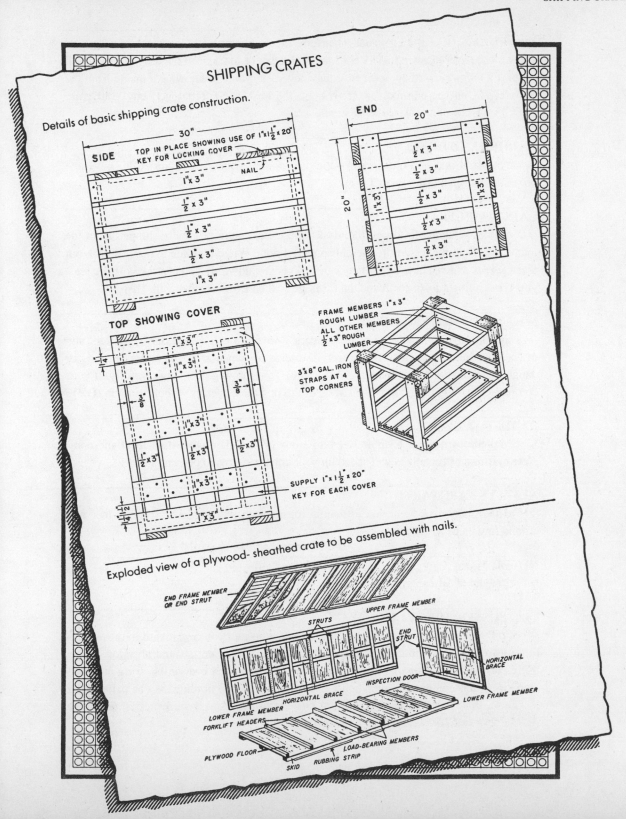

SIDE

30"

TOP IN PLACE SHOWING USE OF 1"x1½"x 20" KEY FOR LOCKING COVER

NAIL

1"x 3"
½" x 3"
½" x 3"
½" x 3"
1"x 3"

END

20"

20"

½" x 3"
½" x 3"
½" x 3"
½" x 3"
½" x 3"

1"x 3"

1"x 3"

TOP SHOWING COVER

1"x 3"
1"x 3"
⅜"
⅜"
⅜"
1"x 3"
½"x 3"
½"x 3"
½"x 3"
1"x 3"
1½"
¼"
3"

SUPPLY 1"x 1½"x 20"
KEY FOR EACH COVER

FRAME MEMBERS 1"x 3"
ROUGH LUMBER
ALL OTHER MEMBERS
½"x 3" ROUGH
LUMBER

3"x 8" GAL. IRON
STRAPS AT 4
TOP CORNERS

Exploded view of a plywood- sheathed crate to be assembled with nails.

END FRAME MEMBER
OR END STRUT

STRUTS

UPPER FRAME MEMBER

END
STRUT

HORIZONTAL
BRACE

HORIZONTAL BRACE

INSPECTION DOOR

LOWER FRAME MEMBER

LOWER FRAME MEMBER
FORKLIFT HEADERS

LOAD-BEARING MEMBERS

PLYWOOD FLOOR

SKID

RUBBING STRIP

penalized by packing their products in one of the most useful personal moving and storage containers known to Modern Man. They can be stacked to the heavens, they will support a *motorcycle,* they never rust, they never rot, you can see what's inside from the outside. If you see one, borrow it. They're the best. (ES) Better yet, buy your own. They're for sale at most large retail stores.

CARDBOARD BOXES

Your best one-stop box supply outlet is probably your local liquor store. Beverage boxes are strong and durable. (TF)

LARGE PIECES

of unupholstered furniture (like desks and tables) were originally shipped from the manufacturer to the retailer in a semidismantled state. When it's time to move, check out these pieces and see how easily they can be knocked down. If you can take off the legs, you'll be saving a lot of room and the furniture will be easier to deal with. (JF)

WHAT THE MOVER DOES

and doesn't do should be a big concern. Movers are not necessarily packers and often they don't even carry the proper insurance to transport art or antiques, guns or dangerous goods. Plan far enough ahead to pick your moving company carefully. If your company is paying for the move, insist on discussing these factors with the mover. (DY)

LABELS

Pour the contents of each drawer into a box or bag, then label it. Careful and complete marking of containers will speed up your unpacking by 50 percent. (WM)

ALWAYS TAPE PARTS

to the main component you dismantle for moving; that way, you'll never lose any crucial tiny piece. (HTD)

NEVER MIX

contents of different rooms. (*Anon.*)

THE POSSESSION RELIEF TIP

You've accumulated a vast amount of possessions and you find it hard to throw anything away when moving, right? Pack a bag with a few essentials and abandon everything else. Get out of town. Arrange for a good friend to sell everything, for a commission, or get a dealer or an auction house to get rid of it. All or nothing may be painful, but it's better than going through everything piece by piece. And it works. (DB) (**See also** *AUCTIONS* **in** *CHAPTER NINE: CONSUMPTION.*)

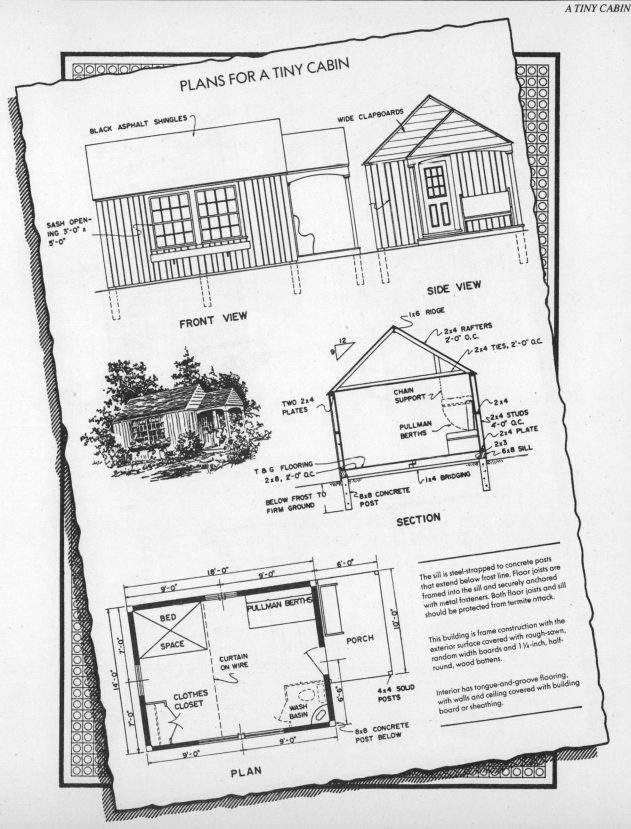

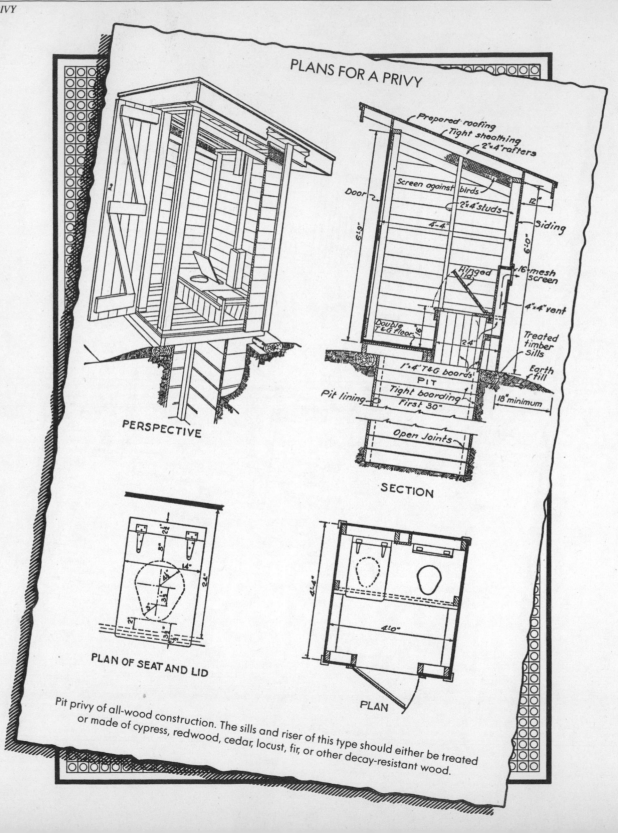

PLANS FOR A PRIVY

PERSPECTIVE

SECTION

PLAN OF SEAT AND LID

PLAN

Pit privy of all-wood construction. The sills and riser of this type should either be treated or made of cypress, redwood, cedar, locust, fir, or other decay-resistant wood.

CHAPTER **13**

Modern Manure

The only way a green thumb will help you grow plants is if you cut it off and use it for fertilizer. Common sense and a dose of modern advice works better.

Modern Men like to goof around in the garden. Gardening is sort of like slow-motion baseball; in a stupid universe, it's one of the few places left where all the old, trusted rules apply. Three strikes, you're out; irrigate or die.

C O N T E N T S
Chapter Thirteen: *MODERN MANURE*

INDOOR GARDENING

The world of plants is divided into two continents — Inside and Outside. We'll start inside.

HOUSEPLANTS AND LIGHT

Next to overwatering or drought, light — not enough or too much — kills most house plants. (**See** *MEASURING LIGHT,* **below,** if you need to determine the amount of sunlight in a room.) Here are the classes of brightness:

Direct sunlight: This means what it says. Sunbeams have to have a straight shot at the plant for at least four hours a day in amounts greater than 800 footcandles (fc). Most flowering plants will require even more. This category includes garden vegetables, wax begonias, bromeliads, gardenias, cacti, coeus ivies, geraniums, orchids, roses, holly and some succulents.

Bright sunlight: That doesn't mean direct sunlight; it does however mean plenty of illumination (say 400 to 800 fc). Great for violets, aralia, crinum, some ferns, crocus, dieffenbachia, a few cacti, cineraria, figs, fuchsia, some ivies, gloxinia, narcissus, nicotiana, okas, palms, schefflera, most succulents, veltheimia and wandering jew.

Medium light: Most rooms we would consider bright in fact only receive moderate amounts (250–400 fc) of light. Medium light will permit the growth of aspidistra, baby tears, rex begonia, "holiday" cacti, calceolaria, candle plants, some evergreens, some dieffenbachia, dracena, most ferns, rubber plants, ginger, grape ivy, love plant, club moss, Norfolk Island pine, lady slipper, bamboo and lady palms, panamiga, philodendron, ruellia, spider plants and Swedish ivy.

Low light: Most daylight illumination in the part of a room most distant from a window is low (100–250 fc). That's not much, but it will support Chinese evergreens, cobra lilies, bird's nest ferns, fittonia, leopard, mother-in-law, nephthytis, parlor palms, philodendron, kite and devil's ivy.

If a plant receives less than 50 to 75 fc, there's a good chance it'll die in the dark.

In the summer, let them go outside to play. (GA)

POTS

Give a plant's roots enough room to grow. Make sure the pot is well drained so water doesn't collect in the bottom (**see** *root rot* **under** *Water,* **below**), and provide a regular (semiannual or annual) soil change. (HFr)

WATER

Without it, all life — including those life forms living in little clay pots — will die. Some plants require moist soil, some don't. No plant requires a swampy pot; overwatering causes ***root rot*** and ***mold***. For many plants, a weekly flush will do nicely. (REd)

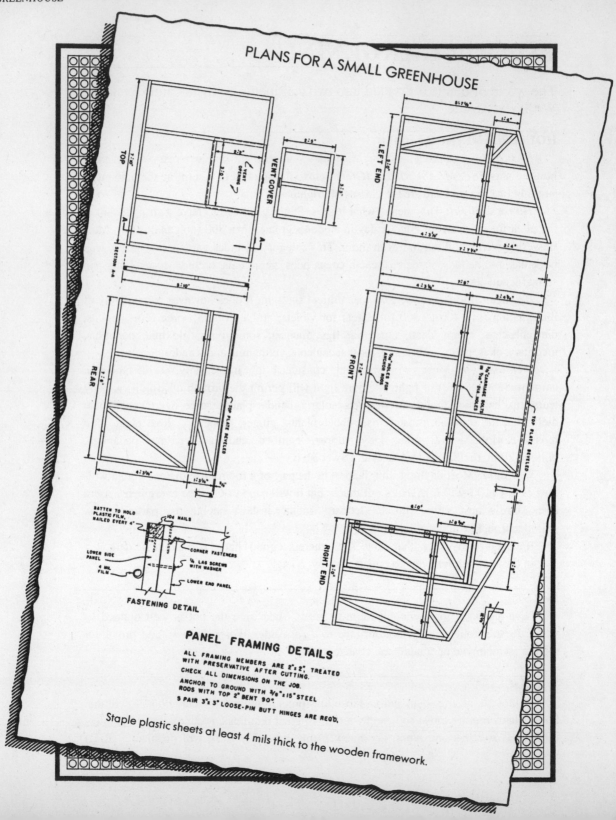

PLANS FOR A SMALL GREENHOUSE

PANEL FRAMING DETAILS

ALL FRAMING MEMBERS ARE 2"x 2", TREATED
WITH PRESERVATIVE AFTER CUTTING.
CHECK ALL DIMENSIONS ON THE JOB.
ANCHOR TO GROUND WITH 3/8"x 15" STEEL
RODS WITH TOP 2" BENT 90°.
5 PAIR 3"x 3" LOOSE-PIN BUTT HINGES ARE REQ'D.

Staple plastic sheets at least 4 mils thick to the wooden framework.

Houseplants like an occasional tepid shower. (JFC) Don't overwater. To see if a plant needs a drink, stick your finger an inch or two into the soil; if it seems dry, water. If the leaves start turning yellow, you're overdoing it. (DU)

NO TASTE

Houseplants love the water leftover after cooking vegetables and eggs, which is why nobody invites them out to eat. Plants also love flat soda water. Maybe "love" is too strong a word here. (KUG)

WATER WHILE AWAY

Rope trick: If you're going to be away for a long time, place a bucket of water over the kitchen door. When the plants go into the kitchen for a drink of water, the bucket turns over and gets them good and wet. It's a joke, okay?

Here's a better way: Put a bucket of water on something so that it's higher than the pots with the plants. Run a rope from the bucket to each of the pots. This works. (KUG)

Hit the bottle: Douse your plants thoroughly before leaving home. Then stick a bottle of water upside down in your planter. The bottle should take days to drain, providing your plants with a ready supply of water. (HKP)

NIGHT OF THE LIVING PLANTS

Florists can sometimes revive dying plants by wrapping them — leaves, pot and all — in a wet newspaper, then stowing them in a cool, dark place for a day or two. (NV)

CHATTER

Talking to your plants doesn't do any good. However, if you *really* believe in that stuff, hire a dolphin to come in for weekly houseplant conversations. (KUG)

FERTILIZE

your houseplants monthly, except during the winter. Do not fertilize an unhealthy plant, and be careful not to use too much. Overfertilizing can burn a plant. (PAI)

TRIM OFF

dead leaves or branches from a houseplant as soon as you see them. They sap life from the plant and can give a home to unwanted fungi. (*Anon*)

CUT FLOWERS

Tulips will retain stem strength and last much longer if you put a shot or so of vodka in the vase with the water. No vodka? Try putting 15 or 20 pennies in the bottom of the vase instead. Also works with some other varieties.

Roses will linger longer if you trim away the diagonal cut at the end of the stem each day and keep the water in the vase very clean. An aspirin in the water helps, too. (NA)

PLANTING DATES

Frost-safe dates for setting started plants in the garden. Seeds should be started indoors no sooner than eight weeks before these dates.

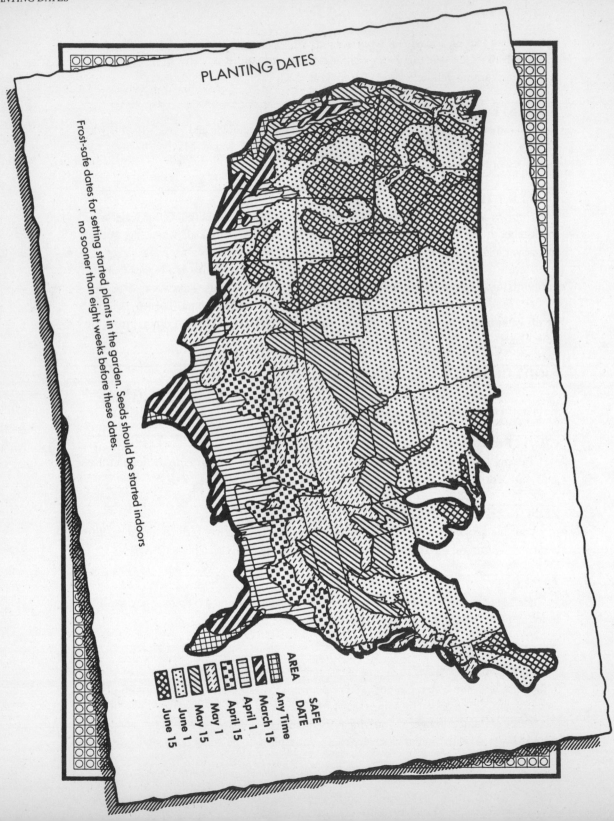

	AREA	SAFE DATE
		Any Time
		March 15
		April 1
		April 15
		May 1
		May 15
		June 1
		June 15

OUTDOOR GARDENING

Plants are a little like pets in that they do best when they have a job to do — like feed the wife and kids. And that's outside work.

OUTDOOR PLANTS

especially those kept on railings or terraces or in other precarious places, should be loosely anchored to the surface by means of a nail driven into the wood. The plant can then be mounted on the nail. (NV)

WOOD ASHES

make great fertilizer. Don't even stink. (KUG)

GARDEN PESTS

are even more ubiquitous than garden gnomes, but not nearly as irritating as garden Venus de Milos.

Gophers have no taste for daffs or narcissus. (NV) Place a half-inch strip of window screen around the bottom of raised beds. This also discourages other burrowers. (KWO)

Outwit the birds by planting sunflower seeds. They'll be diverted from any seedlings you've planted. (FJN) If you make a scarecrow, leave at least one of the arms unstuffed so it will flap in the breeze. If you want to get really involved, you can build a cage to fit over your garden; when covered by a clear, plastic sheet this makes a workable winter frost shelter. (KWO)

Mothballs buried close to the surface discourage small rodents and other garden-devouring mammals. (NV) We hope this doesn't help you grow toxic veggies.

Aphids are repelled by onions and garlic, like vampires and Bryn Mawr girls. (KUG)

Deer can jump any fence under eight feet high. (KWO)

Rabbits are discouraged by the presence of iris, peonies, asters, nicotiana, azaleas and rosemary. (FJN) A fence at least three feet high and at least six inches underground is needed to keep out rabbits. Screen works better than chicken wire. (KWO)

SITING A GARDEN

Here's what you should consider:
- Drainage
- Sunlight
- Soil
- Available area

These are in no particular order, but the key thing is good planning. Once you think you've found the right place for a garden, make a diagram showing what space you will devote to which vegetables or plants. (DSE)

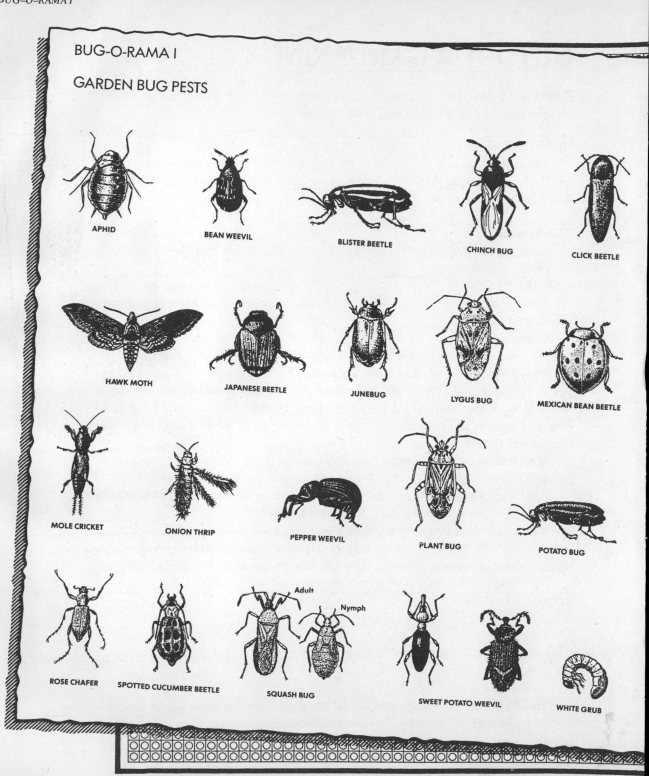

BUG-O-RAMA I

GARDEN BUG PESTS

APHID

BEAN WEEVIL

BLISTER BEETLE

CHINCH BUG

CLICK BEETLE

HAWK MOTH

JAPANESE BEETLE

JUNEBUG

LYGUS BUG

MEXICAN BEAN BEETLE

MOLE CRICKET

ONION THRIP

PEPPER WEEVIL

PLANT BUG

POTATO BUG

ROSE CHAFER

SPOTTED CUCUMBER BEETLE

Adult

Nymph

SQUASH BUG

SWEET POTATO WEEVIL

WHITE GRUB

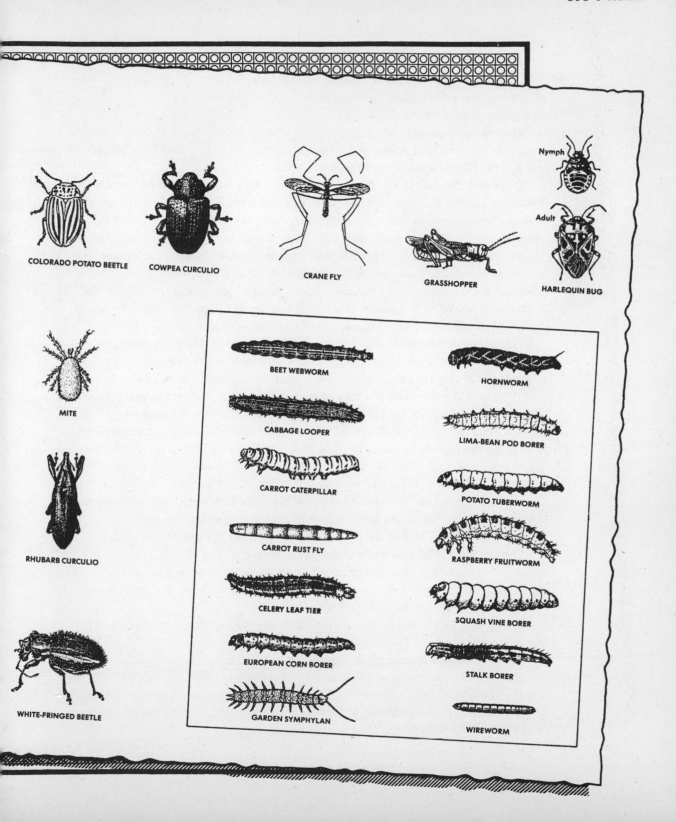

COLORADO POTATO BEETLE

COWPEA CURCULIO

CRANE FLY

GRASSHOPPER

Nymph

Adult

HARLEQUIN BUG

MITE

RHUBARB CURCULIO

WHITE-FRINGED BEETLE

BEET WEBWORM

CABBAGE LOOPER

CARROT CATERPILLAR

CARROT RUST FLY

CELERY LEAF TIER

EUROPEAN CORN BORER

GARDEN SYMPHYLAN

HORNWORM

LIMA-BEAN POD BORER

POTATO TUBERWORM

RASPBERRY FRUITWORM

SQUASH VINE BORER

STALK BORER

WIREWORM

SOIL

Temperature, an important factor in determining the most propitious moment for sowing seeds, can be checked by sticking an iron rod into the earth for sixty seconds. Withdraw it and press it against your cheek. If it feels colder than cool, wait until later in the day, then repeat the test. (DSE)

For vegetable gardens, soil is very critical to success. Once a site has been chosen, factors such as rainfall and sand or clay content must be taken into consideration before making any other decision about the garden. (GMcK)

Preparing the soil: They aren't kidding when they say it's too wet to plough. Anytime a handful of compressed soil keeps its shape instead of crumbling, it's too wet to work. Remember to sample not just the surface soil, but also soil from several inches under the surface. Ploughing wet soil doesn't allow enough aeration to take place. (DSE)

Fertilizer: It really does no good to grow pristine, organic vegetables unless you live on another planet. The ecosystem on this one is so thoroughly fouled that no matter what you plant and no matter where you plant it, it's going to get its share of poison. Still, there's no sense adding to the soup. If you want to shy away from commercial fertilizers and other soil additives, you might want to build a compost heap.

To build a compost heap: Start your compost in the autumn. Place a dozen eight-foot posts in a four- to six-foot-square, four posts to a side, with maybe two feet of each post underground. String chicken wire or loose boards (leave several inches between each board) between the posts until you have an enclosure a couple of feet in height. Spread a layer of plant garbage on the ground in the enclosure. On top of the layer of garbage, sprinkle a cup and a half of fertilizer (a 10/10/10 — a fertilizer with equal parts nitrogen, phosphorus and potash — seems to work okay), add an inch-deep layer of soil, then moisten the heap (but do not flood it). (Check the salinity level — most nurseries sell testing kits — and if you find you need alkaline compost, add as much limestone as fertilizer to the heap.) Add new composting material to your heap every day, repeating the layering process whenever you have eight or ten inches of garbage. An optimum height for a compost heap is five feet. Keep the top flat (or even slightly concave) to catch rain.

Composting accelerates rapidly in the spring. In late July or August, you can speed up the decomposition process by turning the pile with a fork to allow moisture to get to parts that have been sheltered. The whole process takes about a year, so figure the compost will be ready for first use in the autumn.

Start a new heap every year, using the previous year's supply as mulch during the season. Turn it into the soil just like fertilizer.

Compost must be kept moist; decomposition must occur quickly and thoroughly. If this doesn't happen in your heap, you'll have to add nitrogen to speed the process.

If you choose to use *commercial fertilizer,* you should apply it to the soil a few days before planting. To get a good mix, add fertilizer to plowed soil, then harrow or disk it in two or three times. (DSE)

SHADE TREES

TULIPTREE · GINKGO · WHITE SPRUCE · CATALPA · BLACK LARCH · SUGAR MAPLE

RED MAPLE · PAPER BIRCH · YELLOWWOOD · RED MULBERRY · WHITE OAK

WILLOW OAK · HORSE CHESTNUT · CHESTNUT OAK · SWEETGUM

AMERICAN BIRCH · AMERICAN LINDEN · BLACK OAK · SHELLBACK HICKORY

SEQUOIA · SCARLET OAK · RED CEDAR · MIMOSA · HACKBERRY · REDWOOD

Size of mature shade tree in relation to the height of a two-story house. Each horizontal line represents 10 feet.

ARRANGING THE GARDEN

Be careful to plant *permanent crops* — asparagus and rhubarb, for instance — where they will not get in the way of regular garden maintenance.

Any *special seedbeds* should be put in a corner of the garden.

Tall, leafy crops should be planted where they won't interfere with smaller crops.

Tubers and melons should be placed in *low, moist spots;* early crops should be planted where it's high and dry.

Put *corn* near an edge of the garden; remember, when you pick an ear of corn, you have only 12 minutes to get it into boiling water (add a pinch of sugar) before all the natural sugars turn to starch. (You only want to heat the corn, so turn off the heat once the corn hits the boiling water.) The taste difference is remarkable, like a different veg. This is also true of asparagus. (DSE)

Plant tall vegetables (corn, for example, or tomatoes) along the northern side of the garden, and plant short stuff on the southern boundary. Corn should be planted in patches at least three rows deep (as opposed to one long row) for proper fertilization. (DH)

Divide each row into segments less than six feet long so that you don't plant too much of a single variety at a time. Obviously, if you're going to can the surplus, this won't matter, and it also doesn't apply to vegetables like potatoes that can be left on the plant even after they mature. (DSE)

Condiments: Certain plants seem to do better planted in conjunction with certain other plants. The plants listed below on the left seem to grow better when planted next to those in the corresponding column on the right-hand side. The combination also seems to deter damage from insects. You can arrange companion plants in alternating rows or alternate them in the same row.

Anise	Coriander
Beans	Celery, marigolds, potatoes
Beets	Carrots, onions
Carrots	Parsley, onions, sage, peas, beets
Corn	Beans, cucumbers, lettuce
Lettuce	Cabbage, onions, radishes
Marigolds	Tomatoes
Onions	Beets, carrots, lettuce, radishes
Peas	Beans, carrots, corn, turnips, potatoes
Peppers	Basil, sweet chard
Potatoes	Beans, corn, peas
Radishes	Carrots, lettuce, squash, tomatoes
Squash	Beans, radishes, corn
Tomatoes	Carrots, asparagus, lettuce, marigolds, radishes
Turnips	Peas (FPW)

See also *Garden Pests,* **above.**

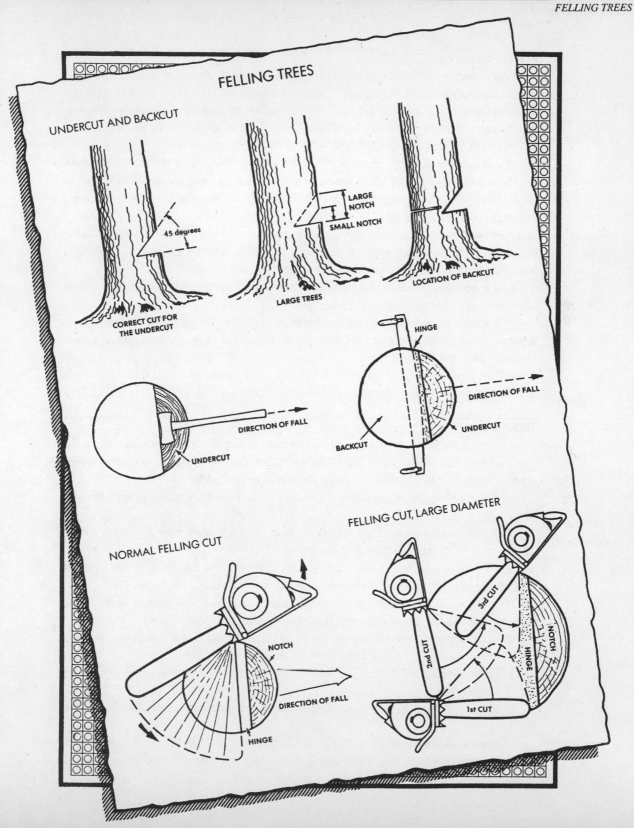

FELLING TREES

UNDERCUT AND BACKCUT

45 degrees

**CORRECT CUT FOR
THE UNDERCUT**

LARGE
NOTCH

SMALL NOTCH

LARGE TREES

LOCATION OF BACKCUT

DIRECTION OF FALL

UNDERCUT

HINGE

DIRECTION OF FALL

BACKCUT

UNDERCUT

NORMAL FELLING CUT

NOTCH

DIRECTION OF FALL

HINGE

FELLING CUT, LARGE DIAMETER

3rd CUT

2nd CUT

NOTCH

HINGE

1st CUT

SOME TOMATOES

Start tomato plants from seeds and keep them indoors for six weeks or so before transplanting them to the big outside. The soil temperature must be above 65F, and the temperature at night can't fall below 55F. You can tell by looking at the plants whether or not it's time for the transplanting: if they're ready to travel, they'll be wearing a half-dozen leaves on their stalks. (DSE)

Plant them in rich soil, protected from the wind but blasted by the sun (sometimes next to a wall works best). Cut off the bottom of a plastic cup and make a little fence for each plant; this'll help keep away insects. Plant the tomatoes near radishes, carrots, asparagus or lettuce. (DSE)

Acclimate your tomatoes before giving them a permanent place in the sun. Put them out a few hours each day — early mornings or late afternoons are best — gradually lengthening the time of exposure each day. (DH)

Use a fertilizer higher in phospates and potash than nitrogen. Apply at planting, then every six weeks or so through the season. (DSE)

If an early frost threatens, pick the tomatoes while they're green and let them ripen indoors. Sample before eating to see if there's the usual tomato goop inside. (KLS) Green tomatoes are good fried. (DH)

Hire a local kid and pay him a buck each for every tomato worm he finds. It doesn't take many of these pests to destroy a tomato crop. (RBr)

TREES

How to grow a tree from a seed: Nothing to it; you could even do it in Brooklyn. In fact, there's more woodland in New England today than there was two centuries ago simply because all the Colonial era farms there have been abandoned.

1. Place a shovelful of rotted leaves on the patch of bare soil where you want the tree to grow.

2. When autumn comes, bury a handful of seeds in a shallow hole in the leafy bed. These seeds will germinate the following spring.

3. Choose two or three of the saplings and let them grow for a year or so, then cut back to just one. This is done as insurance against scab and fungal diseases.

That's that. If you worry about rodents scavenging your fall-planted seeds, store them all winter in an unheated garage, then plant them in the spring. (SOP)

Lots of gentle showers: Trees can use as much as 5 gallons of water a day. That's a lot. Most new trees dies because they don't get enough water. (DH)

How to plant a tree:

1. Get a sapling.

2. Dig a hole large enough to accommodate the sapling's root ball, which must be gently spread out.

3. Put the sapling in the hole. The roots should hang freely and none of them should remain above ground level (they'll simply die). Make sure the tree will stand straight when you repack the hole. Refill the hole gently but make sure the pack is firm; the roots must be in contact with moist earth. To test for a firm planting, give the sapling a little tug; if it resists being uprooted, you've done a good job. Finish with a gentle shower of water. (JRR)

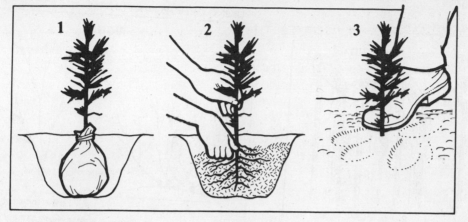

GARDEN TOOLS

Here's a list of essential tools. You don't need many, but these are the one you definitely do need:

- A spade
- A spading fork
- A steel-bow rake
- A seven-inch common hoe
- A wheelbarrow
- A trowel
- A wheel hoe for gardens larger than 2000 square feet. Or a rotary garden tiller for gardens larger than 4000 square feet.

A three- to five-horsepower tractor is suitable for most home gardening uses. (USG)

LAWNS

Five steps to begin a good lawn:

1. Push the top six inches of soil to one side until grading operations are completed.

2. Remove all debris, including stones and sticks.

3. Avoid terracing if possible, since terraces are very difficult to maintain.

4. Install drains if necessary. Some subsoils drain very poorly and, if left untouched, will never support a decent lawn.

5. Protect any trees by not suffocating their roots. Sometimes it will be necessary to construct a small wall around a favorite tree.

Prepare the soil: Loosen the subsoil so it can be worked by careful *ploughing.* Do not plough if the soil is too moist (**see** *Preparing the Soil* **under** *OUTDOOR GARDENING,* **above**).

Slope the subsoil away from your house; it should not exceed a one-foot drop for every 16 linear feet.

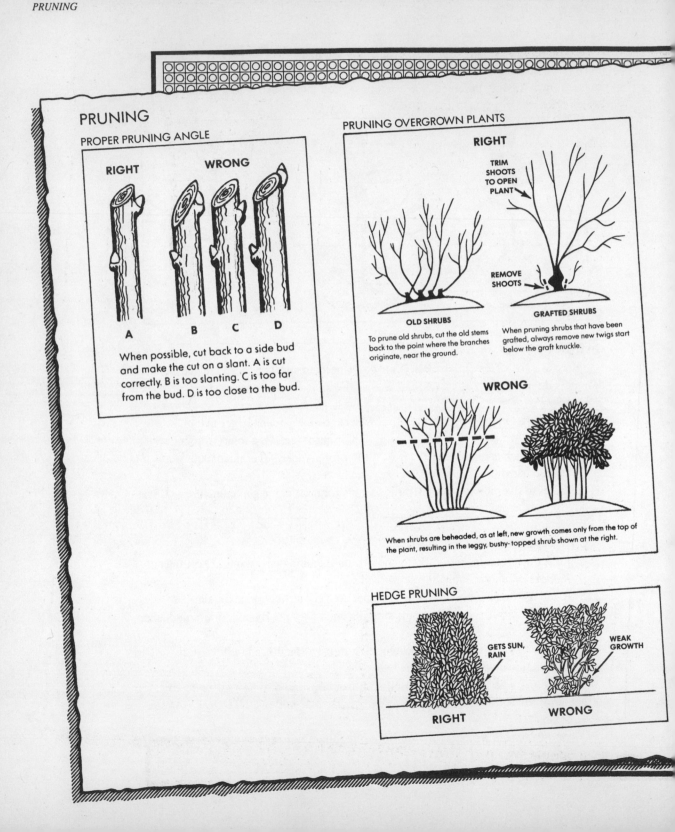

PRUNING

PROPER PRUNING ANGLE

RIGHT **WRONG**

A B C D

When possible, cut back to a side bud and make the cut on a slant. A is cut correctly. B is too slanting. C is too far from the bud. D is too close to the bud.

PRUNING OVERGROWN PLANTS

RIGHT

TRIM SHOOTS TO OPEN PLANT

REMOVE SHOOTS

OLD SHRUBS

To prune old shrubs, cut the old stems back to the point where the branches originate, near the ground.

GRAFTED SHRUBS

When pruning shrubs that have been grafted, always remove new twigs start below the graft knuckle.

WRONG

When shrubs are beheaded, as at left, new growth comes only from the top of the plant, resulting in the leggy, bushy-topped shrub shown at the right.

HEDGE PRUNING

GETS SUN, RAIN

WEAK GROWTH

RIGHT **WRONG**

CONTROLLING SHAPE

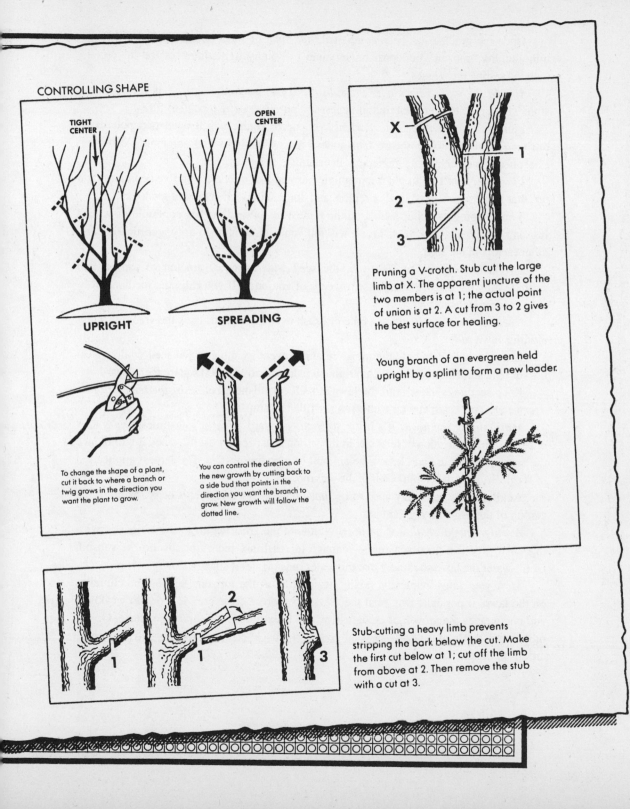

TIGHT
CENTER

OPEN
CENTER

UPRIGHT

SPREADING

To change the shape of a plant, cut it back to where a branch or twig grows in the direction you want the plant to grow.

You can control the direction of the new growth by cutting back to a side bud that points in the direction you want the branch to grow. New growth will follow the dotted line.

Pruning a V-crotch. Stub cut the large limb at X. The apparent juncture of the two members is at 1; the actual point of union is at 2. A cut from 3 to 2 gives the best surface for healing.

Young branch of an evergreen held upright by a splint to form a new leader.

Stub-cutting a heavy limb prevents stripping the bark below the cut. Make the first cut below at 1; cut off the limb from above at 2. Then remove the stub with a cut at 3.

Once the grading has been completed, *add lime or fertilizer,* as needed. To determine acidity, consult your local nurseryman or county agricultural office for recommended testing techniques.

Spread the topsoil back over the subsoil. Try to make the surface as level as possible. Use a rake to even spots out; if necessary, purchase extra topsoil to fill.

Finally, *add whatever soil nutrients* you need; figure you'll need two pounds of nitrogen for every 1000 square feet, unless testing has told you something different. Phosphorus is a very crucial ingredient in establishing a lawn.

Planting: Don't try to plant something that you like a lot after you've been told by a pro that it just won't grow in your region, and don't skimp when buying seed.

You're going to end up with a mixture, most likely, and the bag containing the seed is going to bear a tag. *Read the tag:* It will tell you a lot about the purity, germination and other factors in the seed.

To ensure uniform seeding, mix the seed with an equal amount of topsoil and sprinkle it by hand using crisscrossed sweeps of your arm. If you can't get the hang of it, get a mechanical spreader.

Cover the seed by dragging a rake or brush over the topsoil. Pack the area by rolling it with a lawn roller.

Mulching will help hold the moisture and prevent washing of the seed while watering (or by a surprise rain storm). A 60-pound bale will cover 1000 square feet of yard.

Keep seedlings moist until the lawn is well established, but *resist the temptation to overwater.* You'll just end up with a fungus-filled swamp.

Maintaining the lawn: It's better to *fertilize* a yard three or four times a year than once. A light application of fertilizer in the spring is especially useful, since it will reduce the amount of disease and lessen the amount of mowing needed. The largest application of fertilizer, though, should occur in the autumn.

Acidic, sandy soils may need to be *limed* once every three years or so. Monitor the acidity of the soil with regular tests.

Avoid frequent, shallow waterings. Wait until the grass begins to show signs of wilting, then give it a good soaking — enough to reach six inches or so into the subsoil. Don't water the lawn so rapidly that the water runs off; let it soak in slowly.

Mow your lawn frequently, taking just a little off the top, and leaving the clippings on the lawn, if possible. Don't cut the grass too short; a close crop is prone to weakness and encourages the growth of crabgrass, which is extremely vulnerable to shade. On the other hand, don't let the grass grow tall, then cut it back; such treatment is extremely hazardous to the plant. (DSE, USG)

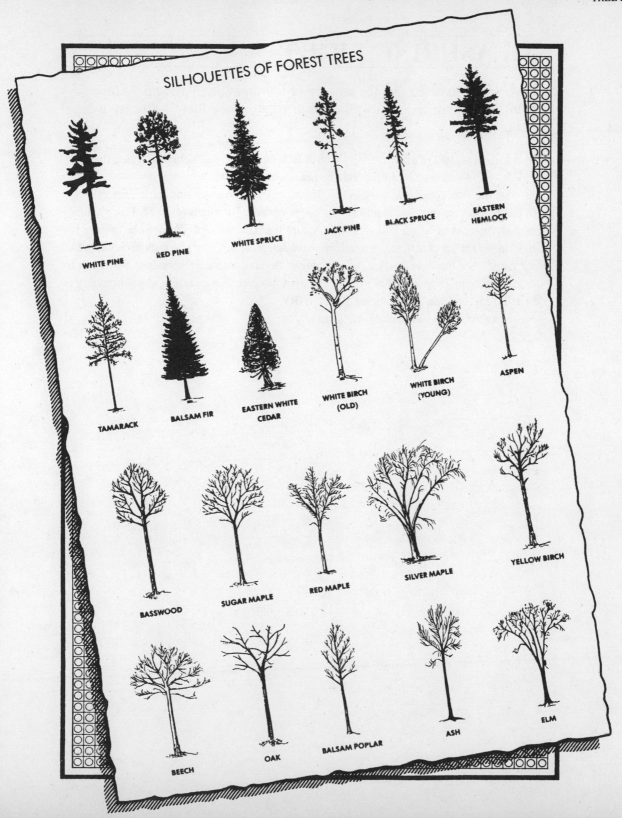

SILHOUETTES OF FOREST TREES

WHITE PINE

RED PINE

WHITE SPRUCE

JACK PINE

BLACK SPRUCE

EASTERN HEMLOCK

TAMARACK

BALSAM FIR

EASTERN WHITE CEDAR

WHITE BIRCH (OLD)

WHITE BIRCH (YOUNG)

ASPEN

BASSWOOD

SUGAR MAPLE

RED MAPLE

SILVER MAPLE

YELLOW BIRCH

BEECH

OAK

BALSAM POPLAR

ASH

ELM

MEASURING LIGHT

If you need to determine the amount of illumination in a room — for plants or to help choose a wall color or whatever — there's an easy way to measure it.

A light meter (or a camera with a built-in light meter) will help you figure the foot-candles (fc) — the unit by which light is measured — in a room.

Set the film speed dial to ASA100. If you're using a newer automatic camera, set it to the aperture priority mode and fix your lens opening (or aperture) to f4. Place a white card in the area in which you wish to measure the light strength. Point your camera (or light meter) at the card to make a reflective reading, making sure you pick up nothing but the card. Take the light reading, and whatever shutter speed corresponds to f4 will indicate the amount of footcandles of light that spot receives. For example, if your reading is f4 at 1/125, then you're measuring 125 fc. (AR)

See also *Houseplants and Light* **above.**

14

Modern Maintenance

There's a lot that needs fixing around this place, what with big piles of poverty everywhere and rotten, putrid heaps of injustice stacked up in the corners.

You have to start someplace. Modern Men know that you have to put your own house in order before you can rib the Russians about their drafty, rattling sash windows.

So for the sake of Modern Mankind, break out those Black and Deckers. This is not a drill. This isn't even an old saw. This is the real thing.

C O N T E N T S
Chapter Fourteen: *MODERN MAINTENANCE*

HOUSEHOLD CARPENTRY

If you want something done right, hire a handyman. If you want to do-it-yourself anyway, here are some tips:

TOOLS

Rules to remember: Get *good tools and use them the way they were intended.* (LL)

Power tools: The same four items seem always to give out on all power tools:

1. The switch breaks from normal use.

2. The cord becomes damaged, especially where it enters the tool.

3. The motor brushes need replacement. As a rule, commutator brushes have standard sizes and can be easily and inexpensively obtained at most good hardware stores.

4. The bearings wear out. Always avoid side loads on a power tool. Power drills — especially when fitted with sanding disks or wire brushes — are often damaged this way.

Whenever possible, buy a variable-speed power tool. (CS)

Brand names for certain tools have become nearly generic, but you can count on the original brand to provide the best service. Some examples: Vise Grip brand locking pliers, Crescent brand adjustable wrenches, Channel Lock brand slotted pliers. (MN)

Household tools can be limited in number, if you choose the right ones. The tools that appear on the Basic Tool Inventory, below, are indispensable; no apartment or house should be without them:

BASIC INVENTORY

- Plain screwdriver
- Phillips screwdriver
- Pliers
- Claw hammer
- Ruler or scale

INTERMEDIATE INVENTORY

- The Basic list, plus:
- Adjustable wrench
- Locking pliers
- Needle-nose pliers
- Crosscut saw
- Drill and bits

THE HANDY-DAD INVENTORY

- All of the above, plus:
- An assortment of screwdrivers
- Hack, coping and keyhole saws
- Flat, rattail, triangle and Swiss files
- Monkey (or Stilson) wrench
- Wood chisels
- Level
- Carpenter's square
- Tape measure
- Bar (or pipe), strap and C-clamps
- Putty knife
- Utility (or matte) knife
- Rubber mallet
- Wire brush
- Propane torch
- Soldering iron

BASIC MATERIALS INVENTORY

- Sandpaper
- Steel wool
- Plastic wood
- Spackling compound
- Electrical tape
- Solvent(s)
- Glue(s)

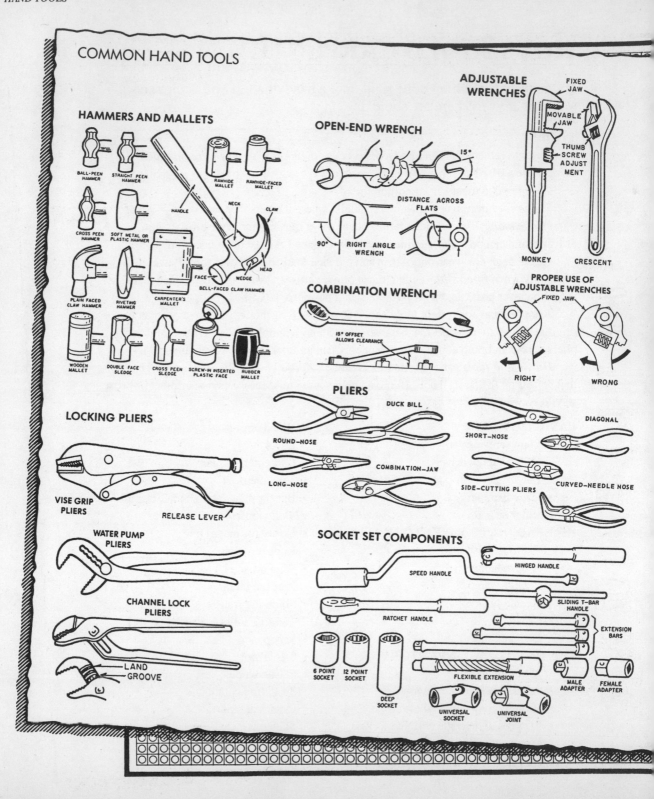

COMMON HAND TOOLS

HAMMERS AND MALLETS

BALL-PEEN HAMMER
STRAIGHT PEEN HAMMER
RAWHIDE MALLET
RAWHIDE-FACED MALLET
CROSS PEEN HAMMER
SOFT METAL OR PLASTIC HAMMER
HANDLE
NECK
CLAW
PLAIN FACED CLAW HAMMER
RIVETING HAMMER
CARPENTER'S MALLET
FACE
WEDGE
HEAD
BELL-FACED CLAW HAMMER
WOODEN MALLET
DOUBLE FACE SLEDGE
CROSS PEEN SLEDGE
SCREW-IN INSERTED PLASTIC FACE
RUBBER MALLET

OPEN-END WRENCH

15°
90°   RIGHT ANGLE WRENCH
DISTANCE ACROSS FLATS

COMBINATION WRENCH

15° OFFSET ALLOWS CLEARANCE

ADJUSTABLE WRENCHES

FIXED JAW
MOVABLE JAW
THUMB SCREW ADJUSTMENT
MONKEY
CRESCENT

PROPER USE OF ADJUSTABLE WRENCHES

FIXED JAW
RIGHT
WRONG

PLIERS

ROUND-NOSE
DUCK BILL
SHORT-NOSE
DIAGONAL
LONG-NOSE
COMBINATION-JAW
SIDE-CUTTING PLIERS
CURVED-NEEDLE NOSE

LOCKING PLIERS

VISE GRIP PLIERS
RELEASE LEVER

WATER PUMP PLIERS

CHANNEL LOCK PLIERS

LAND
GROOVE

SOCKET SET COMPONENTS

SPEED HANDLE
HINGED HANDLE
RATCHET HANDLE
SLIDING T-BAR HANDLE
EXTENSION BARS
6 POINT SOCKET
12 POINT SOCKET
FLEXIBLE EXTENSION
MALE ADAPTER
FEMALE ADAPTER
DEEP SOCKET
UNIVERSAL SOCKET
UNIVERSAL JOINT

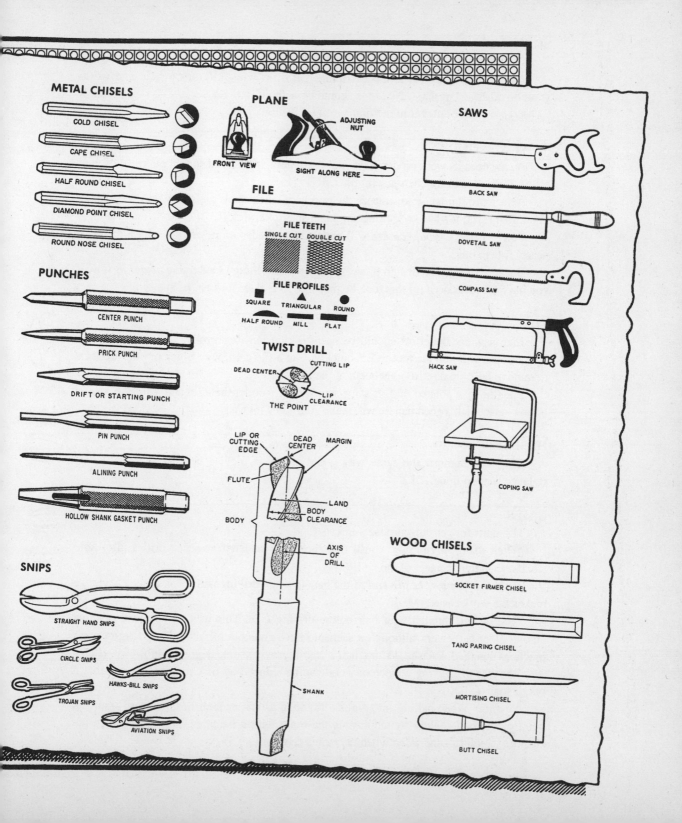

METAL CHISELS

COLD CHISEL

CAPE CHISEL

HALF ROUND CHISEL

DIAMOND POINT CHISEL

ROUND NOSE CHISEL

PUNCHES

CENTER PUNCH

PRICK PUNCH

DRIFT OR STARTING PUNCH

PIN PUNCH

ALINING PUNCH

HOLLOW SHANK GASKET PUNCH

SNIPS

STRAIGHT HAND SNIPS

CIRCLE SNIPS

HAWKS-BILL SNIPS

TROJAN SNIPS

AVIATION SNIPS

PLANE

FRONT VIEW

ADJUSTING NUT

SIGHT ALONG HERE

FILE

FILE TEETH

SINGLE CUT   DOUBLE CUT

FILE PROFILES

SQUARE   TRIANGULAR   ROUND

HALF ROUND   MILL   FLAT

TWIST DRILL

DEAD CENTER   CUTTING LIP

LIP CLEARANCE

THE POINT

LIP OR CUTTING EDGE   DEAD CENTER   MARGIN

FLUTE

LAND

BODY   BODY CLEARANCE

AXIS OF DRILL

SHANK

SAWS

BACK SAW

DOVETAIL SAW

COMPASS SAW

HACK SAW

COPING SAW

WOOD CHISELS

SOCKET FIRMER CHISEL

TANG PARING CHISEL

MORTISING CHISEL

BUTT CHISEL

SOLVENTS

The practical man's alchemical potion.

The universal solvent is lacquer thinner. It dries with little or no stain and works great on oil-based mishaps. No home should be without it. (LK)

Prep-Sol: **See entry under** *Painting Metal,* **below.**

SAWING WOOD

A saw does its work on the downstroke, so that's where you should put most of your effort. Push down hard, then just lift up. (MN)

It's a natural impulse to squeeze the grip hard when sawing. But it won't do you any good. Just relax; it's like swimming: stroke, rest, stroke, rest. (LL)

Power saws: Carbide blades will outlast steel blades on power saws by a factor of nearly five to one.

Because of inherent design flaws, there is no such thing as a durable *power jigsaw.* If you have frequent need for this tool, be prepared to replace it often. (CS)

FILING

Like sawing, the effort should be spent on the pushing stroke. Trying to file with both strokes will dull the tool rather quickly. Use a file card, wire brush or your trousers to remove built-up dust from the teeth of the file. (MN)

Files have a pointed end. It's for a universal wooden handle, and while its use is often overlooked, a good handle will make your job a lot easier. (KH)

HAMMERS

Choose a hammer the same way you'd choose a bicycle or a pair of ice skates: Balance is everything. (LL)

NAILS

Use nails for general-purpose joints.

When using large nails, you'll find the going easier if you first drill a pilot hole smaller than the diameter of the nail.

Hold the hammer at the end of the handle when driving nails. The greater leverage makes the work easier. (MDF)

Drag a nail through your hair before driving it in. This was a traditional practice among older carpenters, although it seems to have gone out of fashion as hair-grooming practices changed. Even so, natural hair oils will provide some degree of lubricant. (LL)

The risk of splitting a piece of wood can be reduced by first sticking the nail into a bar of soap. (MDF)

No-split: When nailing into woods less than a quarter inch in thickness, blunt the point of the nail slightly by tapping on the point with a hammer. This will reduce the chances of splitting the wood when the nail is driven in. (CS)

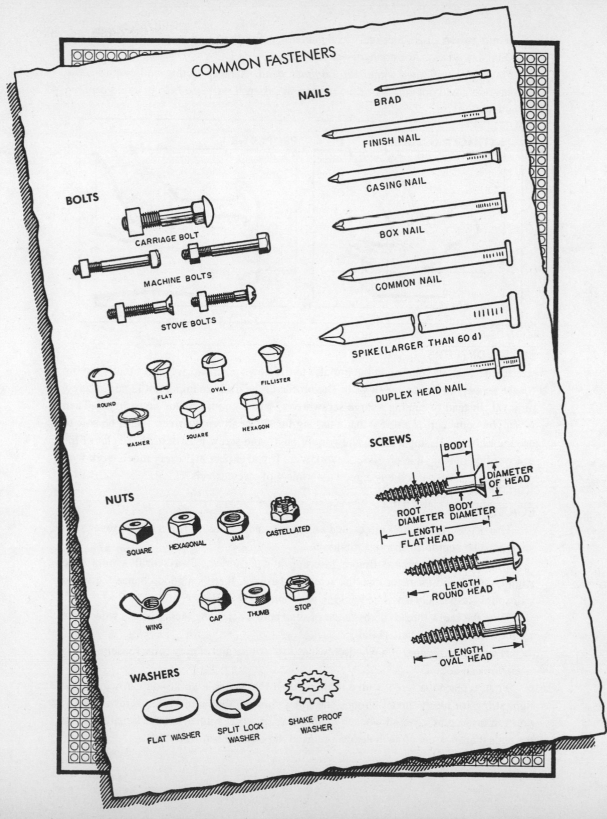

COMMON FASTENERS

NAILS
- BRAD
- FINISH NAIL
- CASING NAIL
- BOX NAIL
- COMMON NAIL
- SPIKE (LARGER THAN 60 d)
- DUPLEX HEAD NAIL

BOLTS
- CARRIAGE BOLT
- MACHINE BOLTS
- STOVE BOLTS
- ROUND
- FLAT
- OVAL
- FILLISTER
- WASHER
- SQUARE
- HEXAGON

NUTS
- SQUARE
- HEXAGONAL
- JAM
- CASTELLATED
- WING
- CAP
- THUMB
- STOP

SCREWS
- BODY
- DIAMETER OF HEAD
- ROOT DIAMETER
- BODY DIAMETER
- LENGTH FLAT HEAD
- LENGTH ROUND HEAD
- LENGTH OVAL HEAD

WASHERS
- FLAT WASHER
- SPLIT LOCK WASHER
- SHAKE PROOF WASHER

Use a punch or another nail to countersink a finishing nail below the wood's surface. Finish with a small amount of putty, if necessary. (LL)

Put a piece of wood under the hammer head when extracting nails with a claw hammer. This will not only make the extraction easier, it will also help to avoid bending the nail. (MDF)

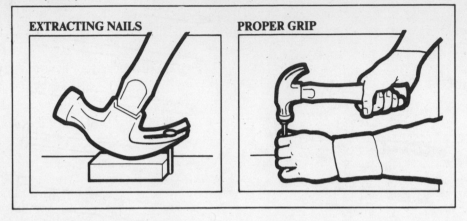

SCREWDRIVERS

Resist with all your might the impulse to file down a screwdriver head that's too big for the screw you want to work with. The profile of the tip is an important factor in screw removal. Instead of ruining a large screwdriver, buy a good, smaller screwdriver. Then when you come across a screw that's too big for the small screwdriver, you'll be able to use the right one. Using a small screwdriver on a large screw may destroy the slot of the screw, often making it impossible to work with. If you expect to do very much work with wood or metal, go out and buy a good assortment of screwdrivers. (LL)

SCREWS

Use screws for joining pieces that will come under unusual stress or wherever slippage must be kept to an absolute minimum.

Installing woodscrews: Before inserting a woodscrew, always drill a pilot hole slightly smaller in diameter than the screw. Otherwise, there's a good chance the wood will split — especially if you're working with hardwoods. (JHG)

Drag the screw threads across a bar of soap before screwing them into the wood. The soap will act as a lubricant. (MDF)

Woodscrew repairs: If a woodscrew has lost its bite and simply turns loosely, here's what you can do:

First, replace the screw with a longer one. If that doesn't work, you can wind some light string (or heavy thread) around the screw threads, then reinsert the screw. Finally, you can insert glue-covered wooden matchsticks or wood splinters in the hole, break off the ends that stick out of the hole, then reinsert the original screw. (KSF)

In a pinch, a vegetable peeler can serve as a poor substitute for a Phillips screwdriver. (LL)

Tight screws can be loosened with a pretreatment of hydrogen peroxide. (LL)

Woodscrews are arcane holdovers from the past. The smooth shank between the head and the threads serves a purpose unknown to contemporary carpenters. *Dry wall and sheet metal screws* are superior for use with wood. Not only do they have more threads than a wood screw of comparable length, but the pitch of the threads is steeper, providing for faster insertion and greater grip. (CS)

Phillips-head screws are better than slotted-head screws; they're easier to drive and less prone to stripping. Perhaps that's why plain, slotted screws are quickly disappearing from manufactured goods. (CS)

For big jobs involving a lot of screwing, get a dry wall gun. Go ahead. It'll make your day. (CS)

DRILL BITS

come in two grades — *carbon,* which are black in color and usually marked with a small "C" near the size indication on the shank, and *high-speed,* which are made of shiny steel and always marked "HS" on the shank. Carbon bits, which are cheaper, are for wood and other soft material. The more expensive high-speed bits are for metal, but can be used on softer stuff as well. (MDF)

DRILLING

Lubricate a spinning bit with a few drops of oil while drilling. This works especially well when working with metal. (LL)

If you need a hole drilled with great precision through a thick piece, use a drill press. If you don't have one, your local machine shop does. (FY)

SOLDERING

There's more to soldering than just dribbling hot metal onto another piece of metal. While different solders and varying amounts of heat are required with different jobs, the principle is the same — heat the parts, not the solder, and work slowly and cleanly.

For any soldering job, you'll need solder, a soldering iron or a propane torch (depending on the application) and some greasy stuff called flux. First, make sure the parts to be soldered are absolutely clean; if you're working with larger pieces, like pipe, for example, thoroughly sand the surfaces to be joined. Paint the surfaces liberally with flux; after heating the parts to be joined, touch the end of the solder wire to the heated surfaces until the solder melts and flows into place along the seam of the two surfaces. A smooth and shiny coat of solder indicates a good job.

Here's an important rule: Keep your solder iron tinned. That means you should always keep the solder iron's working tip covered with solder. If the iron is not sufficiently tinned, solder will be be drawn to the the iron and not the parts being soldered. While

REPLACING A BROKEN WINDOW

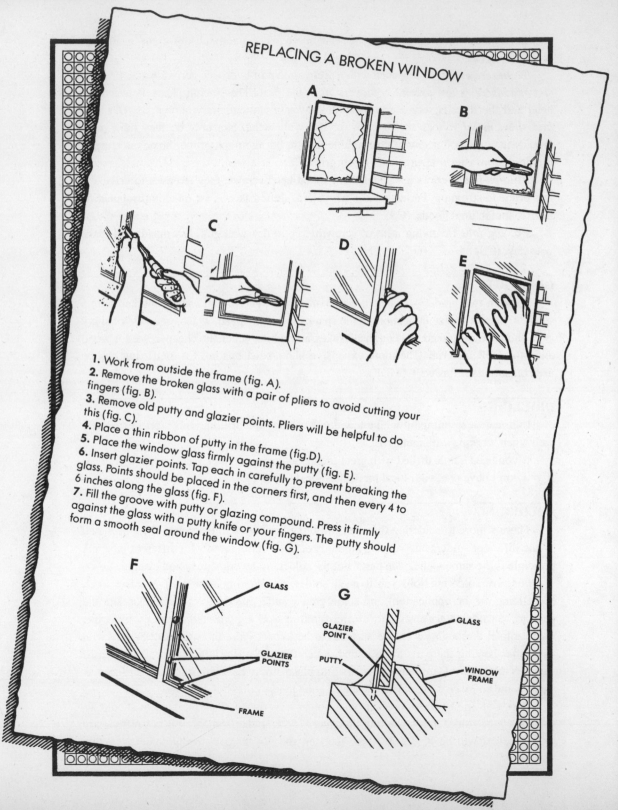

1. Work from outside the frame (fig. A).
2. Remove the broken glass with a pair of pliers to avoid cutting your fingers (fig. B).
3. Remove old putty and glazier points. Pliers will be helpful to do this (fig. C).
4. Place a thin ribbon of putty in the frame (fig. D).
5. Place the window glass firmly against the putty (fig. E).
6. Insert glazier points. Tap each in carefully to prevent breaking the glass. Points should be placed in the corners first, and then every 4 to 6 inches along the glass (fig. F).
7. Fill the groove with putty or glazing compound. Press it firmly against the glass with a putty knife or your fingers. The putty should form a smooth seal around the window (fig. G).

F

GLASS

GLAZIER POINTS

FRAME

G

GLAZIER POINT

PUTTY

GLASS

WINDOW FRAME

working, clean the tip from time to time with a wet sponge, then tin it again by applying solder to the tip until it won't hold any more. (MR)

HOW TO HANG A DOOR

Buy the pre-hung variety. Anything else is too much trouble. (LL, HS)

HOW TO FIX A SQUEAKY DOOR

First, you have to decide what kind of noise the door is making. Is it creaking? A creaking door, like the ones in the haunted house movies, simply needs some oil on its hinges. Is it squeaking? A squeaking door makes the sound of wood rubbing and binding, and in most cases, you'll find the hinges need to be tightened. If the screws turn loosely in the wood without tightening, you may have to rehang the door (although **see** *Woodscrews* **above**). (MDF)

If the door *rattles,* try attaching a felt corn pad or something like it to the lower inside edge. (LL)

DRAFTY, RATTLING SASH WINDOWS

can be set right by using plastic bags from the dry cleaner; roll the bags into a tight rope, then jam them into the space between the window and the frame, using a screwdriver, if necessary. (FR)

TIE PACKAGES

with damp string; it shrinks as it dries. (FR)

PAINTING METAL

Like any surface to be painted, the metal must be clean. When repainting a *previously painted surface,* make sure the original coat is in good enough shape to take a second one. Often, a light sanding and dusting is preparation enough, but if there is rust or corrosion, it must be removed completely by sanding right down to the shiny, bare metal.

Unpainted metal surfaces need to be painted with a coat of metal primer before applying a finish coat. (JHG)

Use a solvent: It's good policy to wipe a piece of metal before it's painted with a solvent called Prep-Sol (preparation-solvent), which is available at most auto paint suppliers. Prep-Sol is the flux of the metal-painting world; it cleans and neutralizes the surface all at once. (SM)

See also *PAINT AND COLOR* **in** *CHAPTER TWELVE: MODERN MANORS.*

REPLACING THE IRREPLACEABLE

Say you break that racing widget on the '39 Olds and you find out they don't make them anymore. What do you do? Sell the car for junk or what?

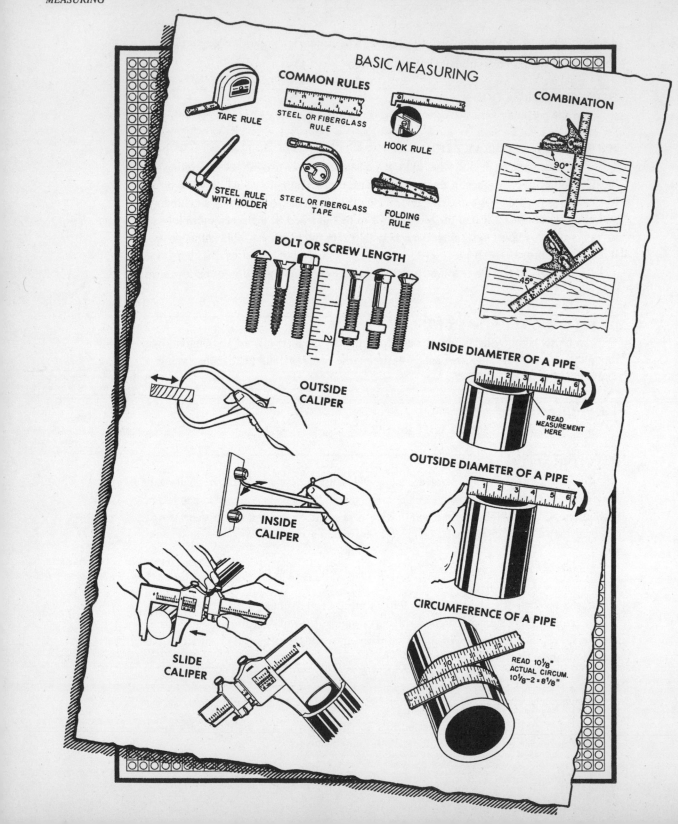

BASIC MEASURING

COMMON RULES

TAPE RULE

STEEL OR FIBERGLASS RULE

HOOK RULE

STEEL RULE WITH HOLDER

STEEL OR FIBERGLASS TAPE

FOLDING RULE

COMBINATION

90°

45°

BOLT OR SCREW LENGTH

OUTSIDE CALIPER

INSIDE CALIPER

SLIDE CALIPER

INSIDE DIAMETER OF A PIPE

READ MEASUREMENT HERE

OUTSIDE DIAMETER OF A PIPE

CIRCUMFERENCE OF A PIPE

READ 10⅛"
ACTUAL CIRCUM.
10⅛ - 2 = 8⅛"

Go for the what. In almost every city and town there are small machine shops willing and able to manufacture a new part for an old car, make up a dummy of the world's greatest invention or reproduce a spare widget so in an emergency you'll have one or two.

Good drawings or the original part are the best guides. *Drawings* can be presented on anything from a cocktail napkin to a blueprint. You needn't be overconcerned about the polish of the artwork, but you must be accurate with dimensions. The more precisely the information is presented, the more likely the finished object will resemble what you wanted. *An original part* should be separated from the assembly in which it fits. Don't show up with your grandfather clock to get a worn gear replicated.

Don't try to tell the machinist how to do his job. He spits these things out all day, and your best approach to him will be a brief and businesslike one, making certain only that you have conveyed an accurate representation of the work you want done. (*Anon.*)

See also *SPARE PARTS* **in** *CHAPTER FOUR: MODERN MOTORS*.

FURNITURE CARE

Take care of your furniture and someday your children will be able to sell it all off in a garage sale.

DROOPING CANE SEATS

can be restored by washing them in hot water. Allow them to dry in the sun. (KJO)

TIGHT DRAWERS

Apply boiled linseed oil to the inside; it will compensate for the expansion and contraction that usually results in balky dresser drawers. (SP)

REFINISHING

Making the old look like new. If a basically sound piece of furniture looks like all it needs is a good cleanup, refinishing is the job. If there's something structurally wrong with the piece, however, make sure you fix it before you start on a refinishing project.

Cleaning: Apply a matching stain to a soft cloth and rub it into any scratched or raw areas where the bare wood shows through. This will darken the wood sufficiently to hide the wound. Prepare a solution of two or three parts boiled linseed oil to one part turpentine. Get boiled, as opposed to raw, linseed oil. They sell it that way, boiled, in the hardware store. Don't try to boil it yourself, as you'll only succeed in blowing the neighborhood to smithereens. Rub this mix into the surface of the wood with very fine steel wool; this will clean and restore the grain and the finish. Restoration purists, who work on valuable eighteenth-century antiques, shun this procedure because the application of the oil is irreversible. (SM)

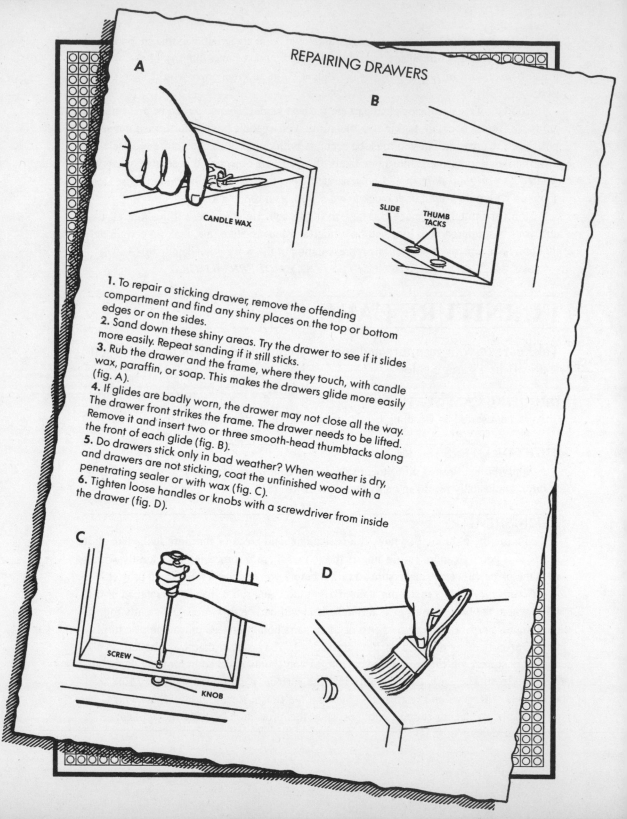

REPAIRING DRAWERS

A

CANDLE WAX

B

SLIDE   THUMB TACKS

1. To repair a sticking drawer, remove the offending compartment and find any shiny places on the top or bottom edges or on the sides.

2. Sand down these shiny areas. Try the drawer to see if it slides more easily. Repeat sanding if it still sticks.

3. Rub the drawer and the frame, where they touch, with candle wax, paraffin, or soap. This makes the drawers glide more easily (fig. A).

4. If glides are badly worn, the drawer may not close all the way. The drawer front strikes the frame. The drawer needs to be lifted. Remove it and insert two or three smooth-head thumbtacks along the front of each glide (fig. B).

5. Do drawers stick only in bad weather? When weather is dry, and drawers are not sticking, coat the unfinished wood with a penetrating sealer or with wax (fig. C).

6. Tighten loose handles or knobs with a screwdriver from inside the drawer (fig. D).

C

SCREW

KNOB

D

Very rare pieces should be handled by professional restorers who will have experience dealing with the various factors — old repairs, patina and the rest — that inform a good restoration; this will also help protect your investment in the piece. (KJO)

Ruined surface: If the finish of the piece has become crazed and looks like reptile skin or something, it can be restored using a substance known as amalgamator, which is available at your hardware store. Brush it on, let it set for a few minutes, then carefully and evenly brush the surface smooth. Let dry. (AR)

Take it off: If the finish is hopeless, you'll have to visit the court of last resort — the neighborhood strip joint. Pay attention. Strippers using a cold solution process should be favored over those using a hot process; while hot chemicals are faster and cheaper, their use can damage glue and joints.

If you elect to undertake the stripping job yourself, get ready for hell. Start by getting more stripping solution than you think you'll need. Buy the thickest glop available, along with some steel wool and a couple of scrapers. Do your work in an extremely well-ventilated area; you'll need lots of newspapers and rags, an empty coffee can, a pair of rubber gloves, if you wish, and an old brush. Apply the solution on the surface as thickly as possible with as few brush strokes as possible. Let it alone for twenty minutes or so, then scrape it off. Repeat as often as necessary, which will be often indeed. Detail with steel wool and a small scraper. If you ever finish, wash the furniture with oil-based solvent (or water, if the instructions so indicate). (SM)

GLUING

If you don't do it right, everything you put together will soon be rent asunder. Start with two clean surfaces. This is important, as dust will not hold an adhesive bond.

Try to make your repairs as soon after the break as possible; sometimes old breaks can be cleaned with sandpaper. While this is effective if done carefully, it can also alter the contour of the two items that must be rejoined, thereby reducing the amount of surface contact.

If you are joining two smooth, flat surfaces, roughening both with sandpaper will give more tooth for the glue to grab.

While the application of a flame is a good method of chemically cleaning a surface, it will not serve to remove residue, and washing with solvents or detergents can leave a microscopic film that may hinder an effective bond but it's better than a lot of old crud on the surfaces to be glued.

In most cases, a thin coat of glue on *each* surface to be joined is far superior to a lot of glue on just one surface. (SM)

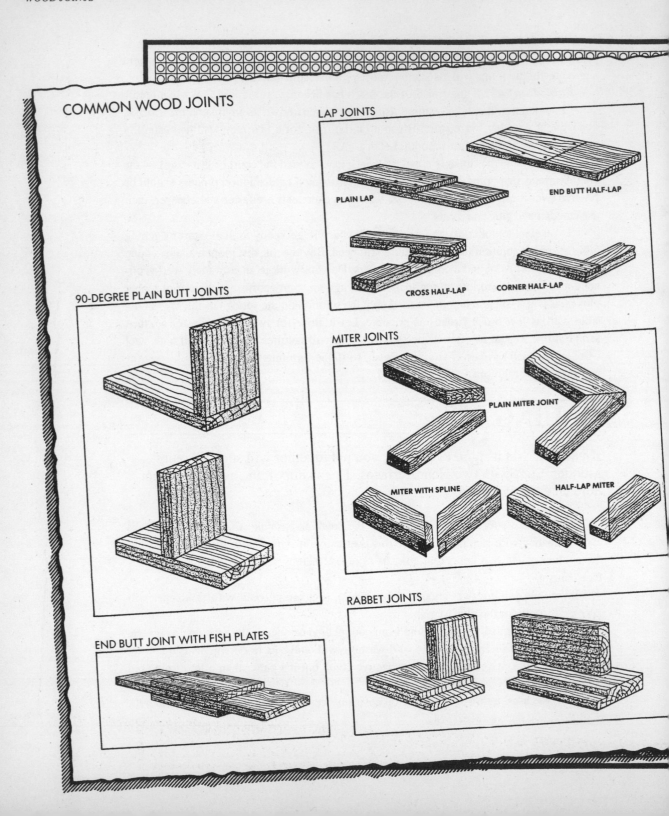

COMMON WOOD JOINTS

LAP JOINTS

PLAIN LAP

END BUTT HALF-LAP

CROSS HALF-LAP

CORNER HALF-LAP

90-DEGREE PLAIN BUTT JOINTS

MITER JOINTS

PLAIN MITER JOINT

MITER WITH SPLINE

HALF-LAP MITER

END BUTT JOINT WITH FISH PLATES

RABBET JOINTS

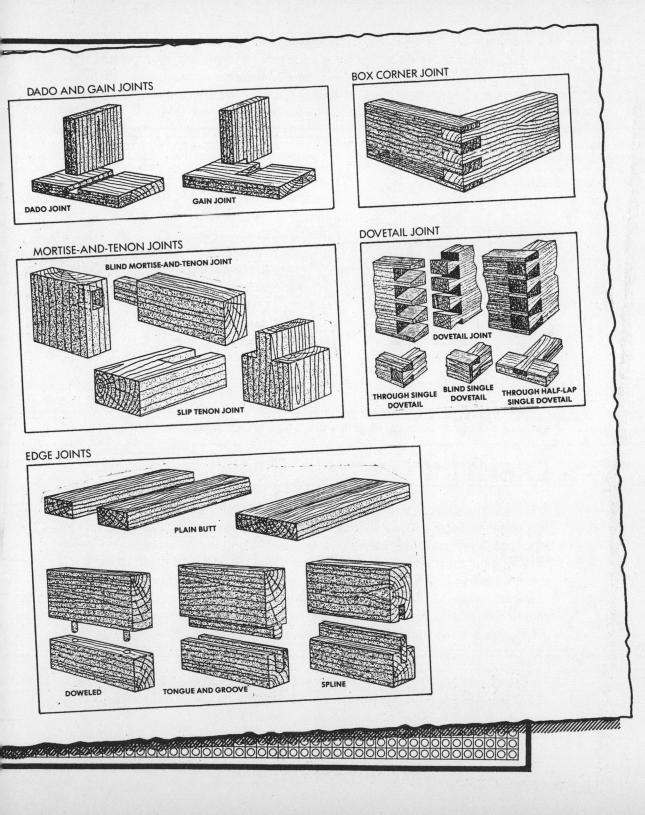

DADO AND GAIN JOINTS

DADO JOINT

GAIN JOINT

BOX CORNER JOINT

MORTISE-AND-TENON JOINTS

BLIND MORTISE-AND-TENON JOINT

SLIP TENON JOINT

DOVETAIL JOINT

DOVETAIL JOINT

THROUGH SINGLE DOVETAIL

BLIND SINGLE DOVETAIL

THROUGH HALF-LAP SINGLE DOVETAIL

EDGE JOINTS

PLAIN BUTT

DOWELED

TONGUE AND GROOVE

SPLINE

CLAMPING

glued parts together while they dry is the difference between a good, permanent bond and a temporary jury-rig. There are different clamps for different jobs — bar (or pipe) clamps, C-clamps, band clamps and spring clamps are the principal designs. It pays to use the proper one. If you aren't sure, ask the hardware store clerk. (SM)

GLUES AND THEIR APPLICATIONS

Metal	Epoxy	*Porcelain*	Epoxy
	Styrene		Super glue
	Super glue	*Fabric*	Barge cement
Plastic	Epoxy	*Paper*	Contact cement
	Styrene		Elmer's
	Super glue		Rubber cement
Wood	Epoxy		Barge cement
	Contact cement	*Leather*	Contact cement
	Elmer's		Barge cement
	Carpenter's / Hide		Carpenter's / Hide
	Barge cement		Rubber cement

EPOXY

Heat helps the curing process of epoxy-based glues. Set the glued parts near a gentle heat source or in direct sunlight while they dry. You'll get a stronger bond. (PNe)

ELECTRICITY

In working with electricity, try not to be intimidated. But do be careful. The basic problem with electricity is that it can't be seen, so it seems a lot more baffling than it really is.

You have think about *everything* when working with electricity. Think about where you're standing, what you're touching, what you're going to touch and what could happen to you if you goof. Always turn off the switch before messing around with the wires to a fixture. Better yet, cut off the juice at the source — at the control box or service panel.

FUSES

are there to blow out before the wiring blows up. A blown fuse can be identified by a darkened or cloudy window; the fuse is a shiny, flat filament of wire that stretches across the diameter of the fuse; that's what blows when a fuse blows.

Find out what caused it to blow before replacing it. Probably, there's an electrical overload — too many appliances on the same circuit, or a defective switch that is causing a short-circuit.

Replace the bad fuse with one of equal amperage. The fuse is a safety device; it'll keep you from burning up and your house from burning down, so never replace a blown fuse with one of a higher amperage. The fuses are all clearly marked — 10, 15 or 20 amps are average. If you put a penny into a fuse slot, as some thrill-seekers do from time to time, you're effectively installing a 500-amp fuse, one that will still happily conduct electricity long after the rest of your life has turned to ashes.

Corrosion can also halt the flow of electricity through a fuse. To clean a corroded fuse bracket, loosen the fuse and tighten it again, repeating the procedure several times if necessary. *Don't try to clean out a corroded socket without turning off the electricity to the fuse box.* Cleaning a fuse socket can give you a hell of a jolt, which, if not fatal, will certainly be memorable. (HJ)

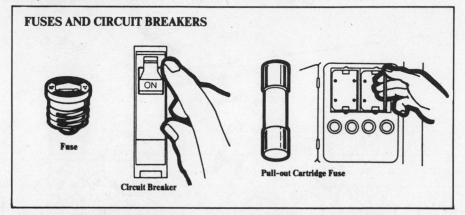

FUSES AND CIRCUIT BREAKERS

Fuse

Circuit Breaker

Pull-out Cartridge Fuse

Verify a dead circuit with a voltmeter. Don't presume anything. (MR)

TURNING OFF THE JUICE

The main switch will either be the biggest fuse in sight or a box containing a breaker activated by a handle on the side, sometimes marked "service disconnect." (HJ)

WIRING CEILING AND WALL FIXTURES

This isn't as mysterious as it seems.

Start by turning on the light you're going to work with. Then go to the fuse box or service panel and turn off the electricity. If the light's off, you've pulled the right switch. You can double-check with a voltmeter.

Remove the old fixture, paying careful attention to the way it's wired and attached. Use the existing wiring and attachment pattern as a model for your effort. Wires are usually color coded, so just match colors. Newer fixtures sometimes have a ground wire; it won't match any color on the old fixture, so attach it to a screw on the box in the wall or ceiling.

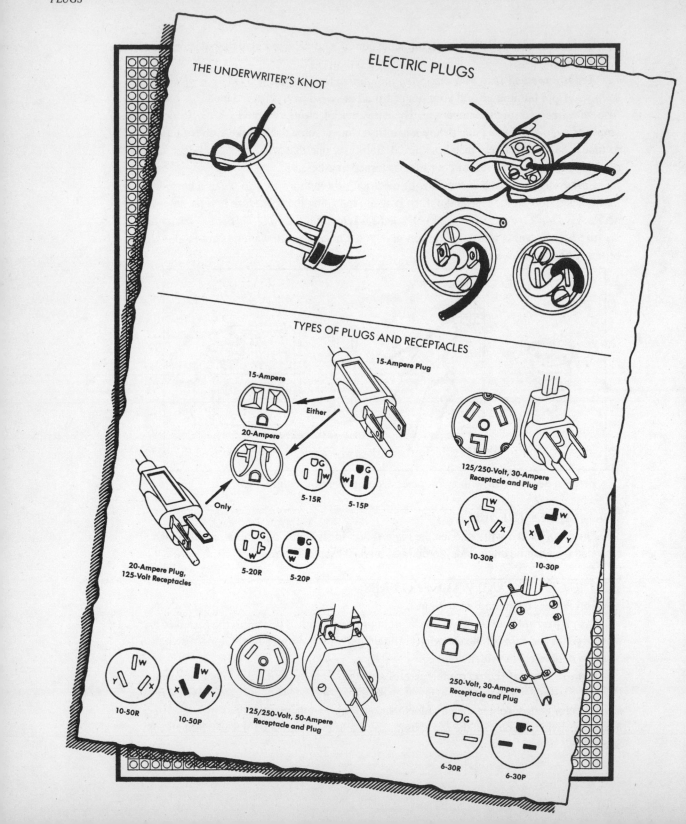

ELECTRIC PLUGS

THE UNDERWRITER'S KNOT

TYPES OF PLUGS AND RECEPTACLES

15-Ampere Plug

15-Ampere

Either

20-Ampere

5-15R

5-15P

20-Ampere Plug, 125-Volt Receptacles

Only

5-20R

5-20P

125/250-Volt, 30-Ampere Receptacle and Plug

10-30R

10-30P

10-50R

10-50P

125/250-Volt, 50-Ampere Receptacle and Plug

250-Volt, 30-Ampere Receptacle and Plug

6-30R

6-30P

When you make your electrical connections, ***secure the splice*** by using twist-on wire nuts, the small plastic bits that look like toothpaste tube tops.

Now test it. If you made a mistake, turn off the power again, and use trial and error to find your fault. Don't try to make it right while the current is flowing. (HJ)

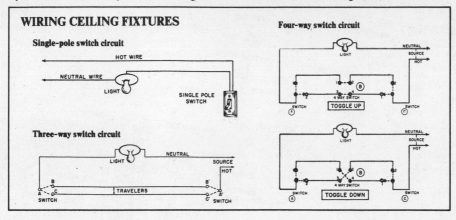

WIRING LAMPS

If you aren't sure of what you're doing, buy the kit they sell in the hardware store. It comes with lamp wire, a plug and a switch, in addition to the parts that hold the bulb. With the pieces supplied, you can make a lamp out of almost anything.

To repair an old lamp, buy lamp wire at the hardware store and simply match the existing wiring. Avoid splices; they aren't necessary, and they can become a danger spot.

If you plan on using bulbs stronger than 60 watts, make sure the fixture on the lamp can handle the additional heat. (HJ)

WEAK FLASHLIGHT

and other dry cell batteries can be rejuvenated once or twice by baking them in the oven for a couple of hours at low heat. (*Anon.*)

See also *Lighting in Camp* **in** *CHAPTER ONE: OUTDOORS*.

RENOVATIONS

Taking an old house and making it new isn't easy. And it's not cheap.

The cost of renovations can vary widely, depending on your location and the type and quality of work required. For a complete renovation, work is often estimated on a square foot basis. In rural areas, prices as low as $30 per square foot can be had; in Manhattan and other urban centers, prices can range from $100 to $250, depending on the specifications of the job.

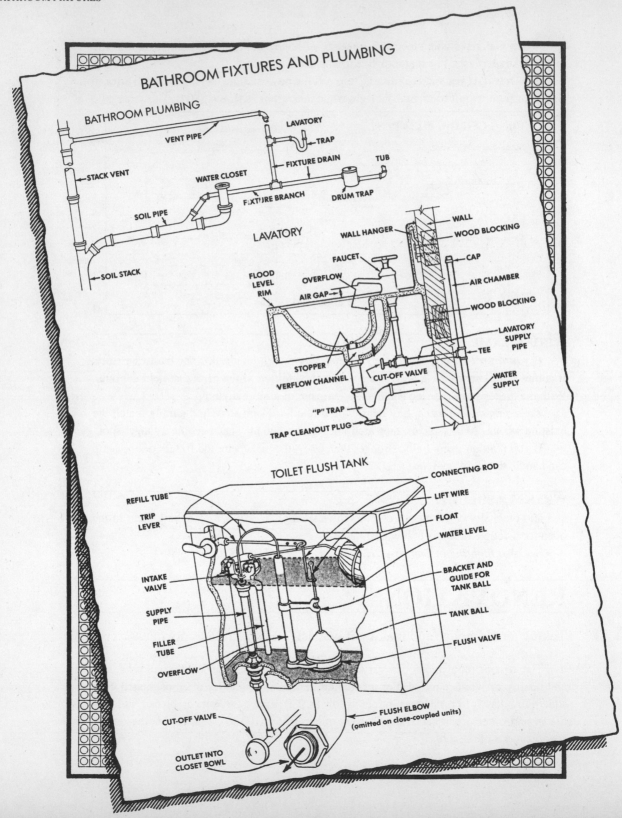

BATHROOM FIXTURES AND PLUMBING

BATHROOM PLUMBING

VENT PIPE

LAVATORY

TRAP

STACK VENT

WATER CLOSET

FIXTURE DRAIN

TUB

FIXTURE BRANCH

DRUM TRAP

SOIL PIPE

SOIL STACK

LAVATORY

WALL HANGER

WALL

WOOD BLOCKING

FAUCET

CAP

FLOOD LEVEL RIM

OVERFLOW

AIR CHAMBER

AIR GAP

WOOD BLOCKING

LAVATORY SUPPLY PIPE

TEE

STOPPER

VERFLOW CHANNEL

CUT-OFF VALVE

WATER SUPPLY

"P" TRAP

TRAP CLEANOUT PLUG

TOILET FLUSH TANK

REFILL TUBE

CONNECTING ROD

TRIP LEVER

LIFT WIRE

FLOAT

WATER LEVEL

INTAKE VALVE

BRACKET AND GUIDE FOR TANK BALL

SUPPLY PIPE

TANK BALL

FILLER TUBE

FLUSH VALVE

OVERFLOW

CUT-OFF VALVE

FLUSH ELBOW
(omitted on close-coupled units)

OUTLET INTO CLOSET BOWL

For less comprehensive jobs, contractors may offer a price based on hourly charges plus materials or on a contractual basis at a fixed price.

No matter which you choose, be prepared for a shock when the estimate comes. It's a sure bet that it will be higher than you anticipated. New computer software is available for those who wish to more accurately forecast costs. (CS)

REQUIRED READING

for anyone anticipating building or renovating a dwelling is Tracy Kidder's *House,* which gives a thorough preview of the ordeal you're sure to face. (CS)

ARCHITECTS

Many people believe that they can save money in a major renovation by being their own architects and working directly with their contractors. While this can work out fine, it's not always true. Invariably, friction will develop between the contractor and the client. The addition of an architect may only add another source of friction to the stew, or he may be able to serve as a competent project manager and deal with the contractor on your behalf.

Many architects have favorite contractors with whom they enjoy working, and while it may cost more to hire these firms, the reward can come with a more rapid completion of a more satisfactory job. For big jobs, architect's fees are definitely money well spent.

As a rule, an architect's estimate for a project will not be as accurate as an estimate supplied by a contractor. (CS)

SHOP AROUND

Many construction projects can quickly turn into ***client-contractor wars.*** Choose your contractor carefully and don't be afraid to keep shopping until you find a man with a personality that suits your own. (CS)

Get references from any contractor. Ask his previous clients about his work. Investigate him thoroughly. It's worth the trouble. (AS)

NEVER TRUST

a contractor (or a plumber) who drives a Mercedes or a BMW. Maybe this'll get me in trouble, but just trust me. Don't do it. (*Anon.*)

DEGREES

Don't treat your contractor and his crew like imbeciles or animals. Many construction workers are college-educated men, just like you. (CS)

INSURANCE

should be one of your biggest questions about a potential contractor. Find out who carries his insurance and request proof of his coverage. (CS)

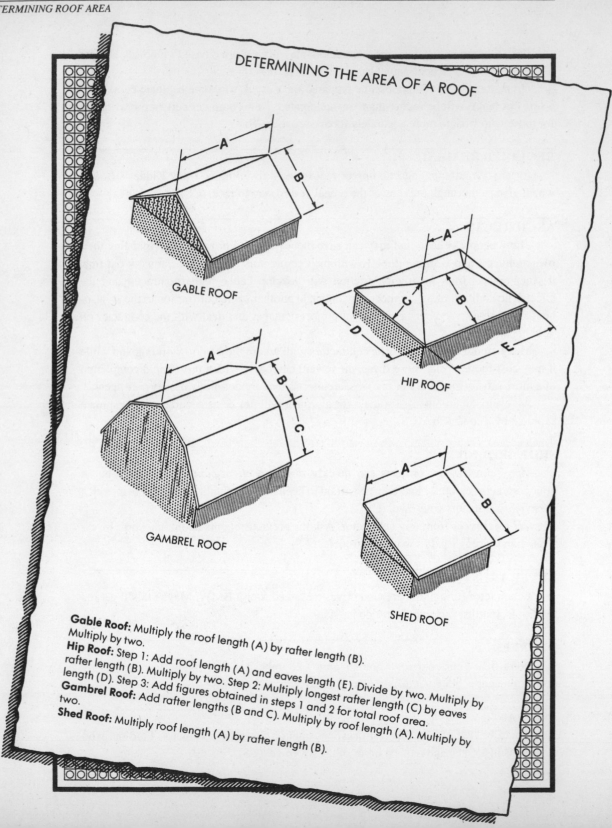

DETERMINING THE AREA OF A ROOF

GABLE ROOF

HIP ROOF

GAMBREL ROOF

SHED ROOF

Gable Roof: Multiply the roof length (A) by rafter length (B). Multiply by two.

Hip Roof: Step 1: Add roof length (A) and eaves length (E). Divide by two. Multiply by rafter length (B). Multiply by two. Step 2: Multiply longest rafter length (C) by eaves length (D). Step 3: Add figures obtained in steps 1 and 2 for total roof area.

Gambrel Roof: Add rafter lengths (B and C). Multiply by roof length (A). Multiply by two.

Shed Roof: Multiply roof length (A) by rafter length (B).

BUDGETS

are not always a good thing. If you press a contractor too closely on a budget that has nothing to do with the actual cost of a job, you'll end up with substandard work and probably a handful of code violations. (CS)

TO BRIBE A NEW YORK CITY HOUSING INSPECTOR

simply hand him an envelope with cash in it and tell him to deposit it to the account of the Policemen's or Firemen's Benevolent Association. There's no secret handshake or anything. Just give him the money. That's it. You have to figure several hundred dollars, minimum. But the actual amount will be based on the extent of the violation.

In New York City, **Con Ed inspectors** can be had for $50 or $100. (*Anon.*)

See also *THE ART OF BRIBERY* **in** *CHAPTER THREE: MODERN MONEY.*

WELLS

The practicality of digging your own well varies not only from region to region, but also according to local geological conditions.

Make thorough consultations before trying this as a do-it-yourself project; you may find that the cost of hiring a well-digger is less than the value of the time and effort required by an amateur.

WHERE

The best way to locate a good well is to use test borings. If you feel like eyeballing it, look for early morning mists, which often occur over groundwater sites. In the South, figs and most species of acacia trees also serve as signposts. The contour of the ground makes a difference; look for low-lying areas, such as valleys or, on a level terrain, a small indentation. Nearby surface water may suggest the presence of groundwater. (WG)

HOW

Dig. You'll be happier if you dig your hole during the driest time of the year, since wet soil creates problems. Some sort of reinforcement is strongly recommended, especially if the soil is loose. The favorite method is to use a well-gasket or curb, a small, circular shelf the same dimension as the hole, but extending beyond the thickness of the brick or stone used for facing. As the hole gets deeper, the bricks placed on the top press the gasket lower down the shaft. (WG)

KEEP IT UP

Always leave the handle of a hand water pump in the raised position on cold nights so it won't be frozen by sunrise. (AJ)

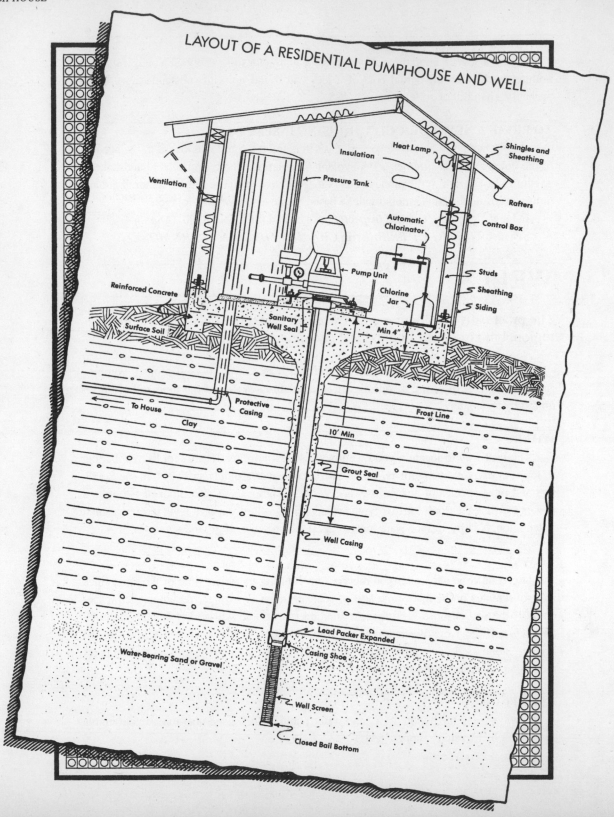

LAYOUT OF A RESIDENTIAL PUMPHOUSE AND WELL

JUNKYARDS

are the vo-tech shopping centers of the mechanical tradesman. They're open to you, too.

We're going to talk about auto junkyards here, but keep in mind that there are junkyards for eveything — boats, airplanes, buildings, you name it.

To get more than a few cuts and bruises out of a junkyard, you need a little mechanical know-how; sometimes you may have to remove a part yourself and in such circumstances the ability to recognize a serviceable component can save a lot of time and trouble.

Many junkyards will strip off the most commonly sought-after parts and keep them in an orderly inventory. Buying these is simple, just like purchasing something at any auto parts store, except the premises might be a little dirtier.

If you ask for something not in the inventory, one of two things will happen. Either you'll cool your heels while a junkyard minion runs to retrieve the part, or you'll be directed to where the part can be found for you to fetch for yourself. This is actually the best case, since it allows you to do a little shopping on the way; you can, for example, try to find the best example of the part you need or a substitute.

You'll need tools to do this sort of thing. If you have an emergency auto tool kit (**see under** *CAR EMERGENCY KIT* **in** *CHAPTER FOUR: MODERN MOTORS*) that'll be enough to see you through. If you don't, here's what you'll need for parts retrieval:

- A slotted screwdriver
- A Phillips screwdriver
- A few common-sized wrenches
- An adjustable wrench
- Cutting pliers
- A hammer
- A hacksaw
- Locking pliers

Often, junkyard operators are dogs, personality-wise. They can be surly and laconic and absolutely humorless. You'll be expected not to be a bother and not to ask to borrow tools. Self-sufficiency is a junkyard prerequisite.

It pays to call first to see if the junkyard has the part you need. (AR)

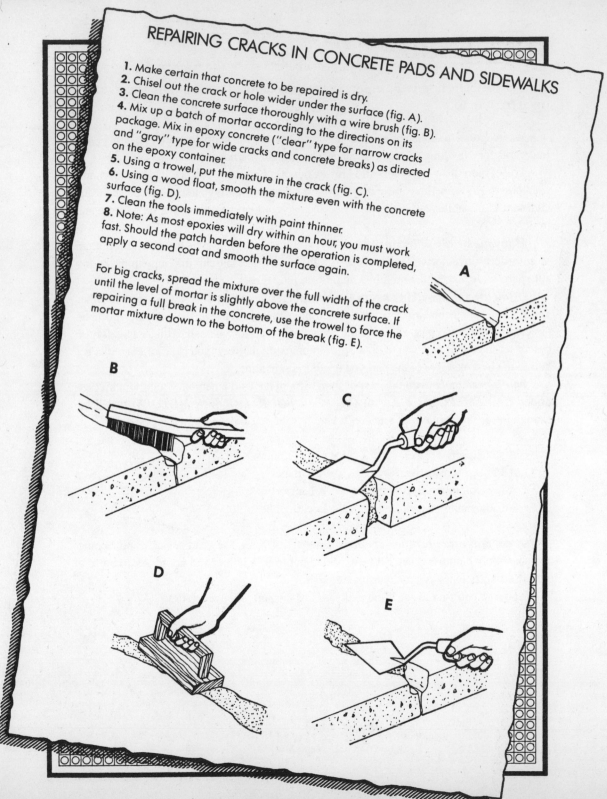

REPAIRING CRACKS IN CONCRETE PADS AND SIDEWALKS

1. Make certain that concrete to be repaired is dry.
2. Chisel out the crack or hole wider under the surface (fig. A).
3. Clean the concrete surface thoroughly with a wire brush (fig. B).
4. Mix up a batch of mortar according to the directions on its package. Mix in epoxy concrete ("clear" type for narrow cracks and "gray" type for wide cracks and concrete breaks) as directed on the epoxy container.
5. Using a trowel, put the mixture in the crack (fig. C).
6. Using a wood float, smooth the mixture even with the concrete surface (fig. D).
7. Clean the tools immediately with paint thinner.
8. Note: As most epoxies will dry within an hour, you must work fast. Should the patch harden before the operation is completed, apply a second coat and smooth the surface again.

For big cracks, spread the mixture over the full width of the crack until the level of mortar is slightly above the concrete surface. If repairing a full break in the concrete, use the trowel to force the mortar mixture down to the bottom of the break (fig. E).

A

B

C

D

E

REPAIRING SCREENS

1. Trim a hole in the screen to form smooth edges (fig. A).

2. Cut a rectangular patch an inch larger than the hole.

3. Remove the three outside wires on all four sides of the patch (fig. B).

4. Bend the ends of the wires. An easy way to do this is by first bending them over a block or the edge of a ruler (fig. C).

5. Put a patch over the hole from the outside. Hold it tightly against the screen so that the small, bent wire ends go through the screen (fig. D).

6. From inside, bend down the ends of the wires toward the center of the hole. You may need someone outside to press against the patch while you do this (fig. E).

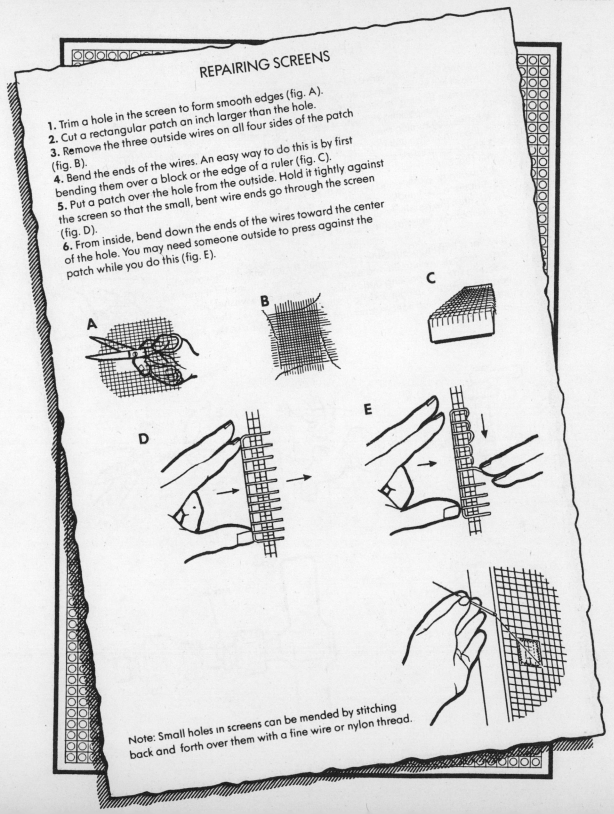

Note: Small holes in screens can be mended by stitching back and forth over them with a fine wire or nylon thread.

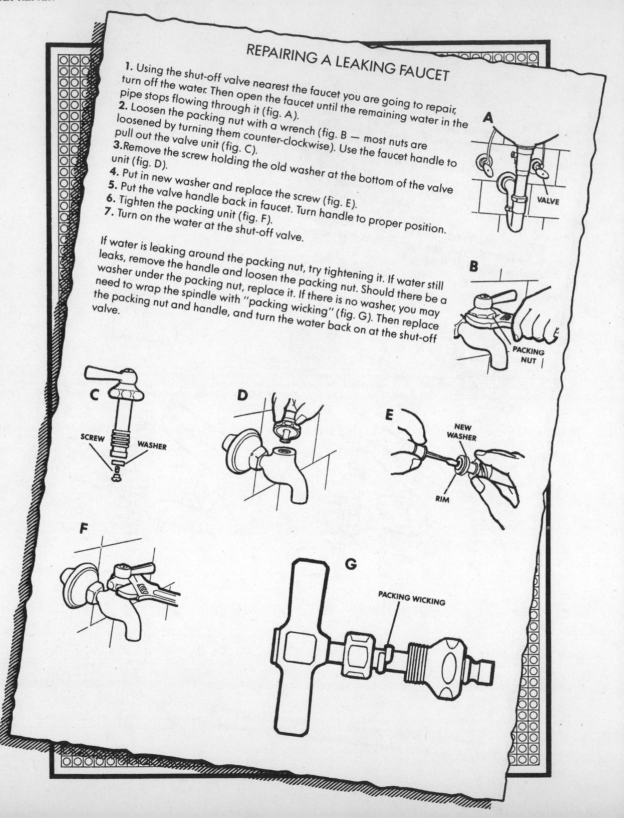

REPAIRING A LEAKING FAUCET

1. Using the shut-off valve nearest the faucet you are going to repair, turn off the water. Then open the faucet until the remaining water in the pipe stops flowing through it (fig. A).

2. Loosen the packing nut with a wrench (fig. B — most nuts are loosened by turning them counter-clockwise). Use the faucet handle to pull out the valve unit (fig. C).

3. Remove the screw holding the old washer at the bottom of the valve unit (fig. D).

4. Put in new washer and replace the screw (fig. E).

5. Put the valve handle back in faucet. Turn handle to proper position.

6. Tighten the packing unit (fig. F).

7. Turn on the water at the shut-off valve.

If water is leaking around the packing nut, try tightening it. If water still leaks, remove the handle and loosen the packing nut. Should there be a washer under the packing nut, replace it. If there is no washer, you may need to wrap the spindle with "packing wicking" (fig. G). Then replace the packing nut and handle, and turn the water back on at the shut-off valve.

A

VALVE

B

PACKING NUT

C

SCREW   WASHER

D

E

NEW WASHER

RIM

F

G

PACKING WICKING

Modern Messes

When we went off to college, one of the reasons we didn't cut *every* class was that we figured that if we passed, we'd never have to clean our own rooms again.

Wrong, of course. So now cleaning is war. And these are the battle plans.

C O N T E N T S
Chapter Fifteen: *MODERN MESSES*

CLEANING

We can't figure out why the oppressed sisterhood makes such a big deal out of cleaning. As a rule, there's not a lot of heavy lifting involved, the emotional investment is low, and you can listen to the stereo real loud while you do it.

THE SPEED CLEAN

Speed cleaning requires that you attend only to those places that an outsider or guest would notice; the rule of thumb is that if no one sees it, it doesn't have to be cleaned.

Determining what others see in order to plan your attack, however, takes a little advance work. Walk slowly through your place to find the lines of sight, and the next time you visit someone else, take note of what you see.

- Most people will see the area immediately surrounding the door they enter. Everyone loiters at an entrance, especially if it's where they say hello and goodbye and wait for their coat.
- Everyone notices the bathroom. After all, what else is there to do in a bathroom but look around?
- Most people are aware of a filthy kitchen.
- Carpeted floors are vulnerable but look clean if they are free of clutter.

There are also some safe areas: No one looks under furniture or at window sills behind drawn curtains. Unlit tables do not show dust. But to really free up cleaning time, you need to establish your lines of sight.

To do this, first determine what rooms will be off limits to all guests; keep the doors to these rooms closed — locked, if you're paranoid. These rooms become free zones, where you can safely store piles of rubbish and anything you don't really want seen.

Next, stand in the doorway to each open room and determine which areas you can't readily see; if you can't see it, don't clean it. Even in bathrooms, remember that with the shower curtain in place you can't see the tub (although girls tend to get friendly with boys who provide a clean tub). It's much easier to close a door than clean a room.

In the kitchen, washing dishes and putting them away is half the chore. Nobody notices waxed floors, so skip that, but pay attention to the line of sight created by counter areas, including stovetops. Keep these clean and the everything else will seem hygienic.

Other handy hints:

- Most people look down, not up, so they'll notice dust rats on the floor before they spot cobwebs on the ceiling.
- If you neatly stack up piles of things they will not be as noticeable and therefore need not be put away.
- Depending on your plans, making the bed is often all that's required in a bedroom, unless clothing — and especially socks and underwear — are on the floor. Put

these things in the closet and keep the closet door closed. If you have sexual ambitions, clean sheets, sadly, are a must, but you can get around tucking them in on the corners if your top blanket is long enough to cover up for you.

- Dust only in rooms you will use, and then only if its thick enough to write in.
- Mopping the kitchen and bathroom floors is necessary only when there are obvious stains and sticky spots.
- Vacuum only high-traffic areas and large exposed surfaces, like an open living room floor.
- Scrubbing, except for the bathroom sink and the toilet bowl, can generally be omitted from any speed clean. (JO)

BEST MUSICAL ACCOMPANIMENT TO A SPEED CLEAN

CBS 35919, Leonard Bernstein and the New York Philharmonic, *The World's 25 Greatest Marches,* cranked up to top volume. (DB)

MOPPING UP

Here's the foolproof method, performance-tested in the Modern Man Bitchin' Kitchen:

1. Get the floor all wet, completely.
2. Take off your shoes and socks.
3. Put an old beach towel under your feet.
4. Turn up the stereo.
5. Get down.
6. Wash feet, wring towel. (KK)

AN AMMONIA ASIDE

Ammonia is good for almost all cleaning chores. The stronger it is, the better it works. The trouble is, by the time you work your way up to the undiluted stage, you're breathing chemical fire. Nevertheless, if it won't come clean any other way, set your ammonia bottle on stun and fire away. (RBr)

THE SUPER CLEAN

This is the once-a-year, just-before-you-sell-the-house cleaning job that separates the men from the home-ec majors. Here are some general hints:

Test any cleaning product in a small and unobtrusive area before applying it to a broad surface. Start with the gentlest stuff you can find and work your way up to the industrial-strength products. (SM)

Stains on various surfaces should be treated separately. A stain is not a stain the way a rose is a rose.

On baked enamel (like stoves and fridges) or *vitreous china* (the sink or the john), use Clorox brand Soft Scrub, which ought to be in the Mild Abrasive Hall of Fame, with a toothbrush. Also useful: cream of tartar mixed with water and made into a paste. Auto paint compound also works. Treat these surfaces gently. (AR)

For metal surfaces: Use automotive chrome cleaner.

Fiberglass: No abrasives. Use auto paint compound.

Plastic laminate: Baking soda and water.

Tile: Oily spots can be cured with a degreaser. Other stains can be removed with a mix of bleach and water at a ratio of one part bleach to a half-dozen parts water.

Unfinished wood: Remove stains with a 50–50 mix of ammonia and water. Rub out any scratches with fine steel wool and apply linseed oil to finish (see *FURNITURE CARE* in *CHAPTER FOURTEEN: MODERN MAINTENANCE*).

On lighter woods, hide scratches by rubbing them with the pulp of a pecan or walnut. *On darker woods,* use iodine.

Wallpaper: Use a degreaser on oil-based spots and a mix of baking soda and water on most others.

Painted woodwork: Easy. Soap and water.

Floor stains: On wooden floors, use a wood cleaner for light duty. Grease stains are trickier: First, place a rag doused with hydrogen peroxide over the stain. Then place a rag dipped in ammonia over the first rag and press down hard for four or five minutes. Rinse. In dire straits, use steel wool and lacquer thinner for grease spots. Black stains on wood, caused by water, for example, are incurable. You have to refinish the floor.

Shower door tracks get clogged with soap film and dirt. Clean them with a soft abrasive and a toothbrush. (NGF)

STRIPPING

a floor as part of a super clean requires the use of a powder product called Mex, an extremely potent cleanser available at all hardware stores. Get a box, dilute some in water (follow the instructions on the box), apply it to the floor and leave it for fifteen minutes or so. Then attack the floor with a scrub brush. Then mop, rinse and go. (AR)

WASHING A WALL

Wash high before you wash low. (GF)

TO POLISH MARBLE

dip a piece of chalk in water and rub it against the stone. (EA)

KEEP SLIPCOVERS TIGHT

on couches and chairs by inserting a rolled newspaper into the back and sides. (EA)

TO KEEP ALUMINUM FROM CORRODING

wipe it once or twice a year with kerosene. (TW)

ARCHIVES

The leather binding on old volumes can be cleaned with heated Vaseline. (EA)

The high acidity in newsprint and other papers can be neutralized by putting the sheet in a large, shallow pan containing a mixture made from a milk of magnesia tablet and a quart of soda water that has been left to soak for a half-day or so. After an hour in the mixture, carefully withdraw the paper and blot dry. (EA)

HOW TO CLEAN WINDOWS

The best tool to use to clean windows is a squeegee, a handy device that looks like a windshield wiper with a handle on it. Apply a nondetergent cleaner (ammonia's good) to the glass and scrape it off with the squeegee. It's quick and easy. (RDY)

If you're a bit tool-shy, here's an alternative: Wash both sides of the glass with a sponge or rag to remove most of the surface grime. Fill an empty plant-sprayer with vinegar and spray one side of the window, then wipe it dry with crumpled sheets of newspaper. Repeat with the other side. This'll use up a lot of newspaper and it'll take an hour or so before your house loses its vinegar smell, but your windows will be very clean — and without streaks. (GB) A mix of ammonia and water is excellent for making your own window spray. (DH)

Avoid cleaning windows in direct sunlight. They're more prone to streaking. (LOL)

Spot your mistakes easily by rubbing windows dry horizontally on one side and vertically on the other. (GB)

TO FIND TINY OBJECTS

on the floor, put a bare light at floor level; the illumination will cause the object to cast a long shadow, making it easier to find. (AR)

HIRE A CLEANING SERVICE

for that really huge, top-to-bottom cleaning marathon. Considering the time and money you'd have to invest (equipment and supplies alone will break you), it will probably be cheaper to have a service come in and do it all. (KLL)

A good use for Moonies: Moonies are great cleaners. They're dedicated to the job and clean like *demons*. (RBr)

PERPETUATE OPPRESSION

and spread the wealth by hiring a cleaning lady. The appointment can range from a full-time, everyday job to a monthly three-hour visit. Let your budget be your guide.

Word of mouth is the best way to find a cleaning lady. Ask around, somebody knows somebody who's been at it for years and knows what she's doing.

If you have no free time, you can use a cleaning lady as a sort of general housekeeper. She can do grocery shopping, errand running, baby sitting and other domestic chores. (MG)

Don't hire a housekeeper, then spend all day the day before she comes cleaning the place so she won't think you're a slob. You're a slob if you have to hire a cleaning lady, so get into it. (KCH)

Fees range from $20 to $50 for a half-day, which is plenty of time to do an average bachelor's place. It's money well spent. Considering that she probably cleans behind the toilet, decokes the oven and changes those crackling-good sheets, it's a bargain. (MG)

FINGERNAILS

can be kept clean during nasty jobs if you first dig them into a bar of soap before you start anything. This makes them much easier to clean later. (HB)

ROOM FRESHENER

Soak a paper towel in vinegar, put it on a plate and leave it out. This works especially well in the kitchen. (FY)

HOUSECLEANING MAINTENANCE SCHEDULE

Daily:
- Air rooms
- Clean range and kitchen counter tops
- Wash dishes

Weekly:
- Dusting, *including*
  - *high cobwebs (use a broom)*
  - *window sills*
  - *base boards*
  - *furniture (use a clean, soft cloth)*
- Wash ashtrays
- Vacuum rugs, floors, carpets
- Clean glass tops *(use window cleaner)*
- Fluff cushions and pillows
- Wash and clean bathroom floor
- Clean the toilet
- Clean the tub and sink
- Mop kitchen floor
- Clean kitchen appliances
- Change towels and bed linens

Monthly:
- Dusting, *including*
picture frames (put spray cleaner on a cloth, not on the frame) and *lamp shades* (dust only)
- Clean and air out refrigerator
- Clean oven *(make this weekly if you do a lot of roasting)*

Quarterly:
- Clean and polish metal fixtures
- Clean bathroom tiles
- Clean medicine cabinet

Biannually:
- Wash bedpads
- Turn mattresses
- Wax floors
- Clean windows
- Wipe books
- Defrost freezer

Annually:
- Wash curtains (except in some cities; in New York City, for instance, this is a monthly chore)
- Clean blankets
- Professionally clean rugs and carpets (SS, RBr, et al.)

HOUSEHOLD PESTS

of a variety smaller than most humans are constant roommates for many unmarried Modern Men. There are ways of forcing an eviction, however.

COCKROACHES

As the previous principal tenants (they've been around for 350 million years, or since long before there were dinosaurs), they *are* going to inherit the earth, no doubt. But not until we're gone. Until then, the little bastards should die. As with mosquitoes (q.v.), we have a special obligation to exterminate as many of them as we can. They spread food poisoning, infection and a welter of diseases.

Battle of the Brains: While roaches are fast, they're not real smart. Sprinkle boric acid around their lairs. Then, when they walk through the powder and stop to clean it off their hairy little legs, the ingested boric acid swells up inside them and they die. With luck, it's a painful and agonizingly slow death.

To do a complete job, empty all the kitchen cabinets and the closets, pull the furniture away from the walls, and get the acid into as many seams and corners as you can. Compulsive readers will yank up the molding and squeeze boric acid into the tiniest cracks in the floorboards. *Really* compulsive readers will first sand the floor, secret the boric acid, then seal the floor with polyurethane. Make the seal reach two or three inches up the wall behind the molding. The room should be able to float.

Remember, *cockroaches love paper and water* more than anything. Standing water is a cockroach spa; a stack of newspapers will support a metropolis of roaches. (LBW)

Roaches can be deterred by using a mixture of equal parts confectioners' sugar and boric acid. Ants won't be put off at all, however. (*Anon.*) (*Note:* This has not been tested by Modern Men.)

Know your enemy: Fun facts about cockroaches:

1. They'll eat anything, including paint chips, pet food and shoe polish. A dozen roaches could live off the glue on a postage stamp for a week. They love oils and proteins and at night they'll eat the lashes and eyebrows off your face. Think about that tonight. They can also fast for a couple of weeks while you're on vacation.

2. They have an early warning system, rather like radar, which allows their body hairs to sense movement, changes in air pressure and fluctuations in temperature.

3. They have clearly defined, individual personalities. They learn from their mistakes and keep cozy nests to which they faithfully return. Male cockroaches stay out later at night than female ones. To get home, they can flatten themselves flatter than dimes and squeeze through cracks.

4. Their favorite places are not under sinks, but around garbage, along kitchen counters and under dining tables. (AW)

BATTLE PLANS

Combat and other pesticides containing hydromethylnon inhibit roach metabolism, causing them to run down like old battery-powered toys, never to reawaken. The chemical is slow-acting, making it less likely that the roaches will develop immunity. (AW)

Endorsement: Combat is all you need to know about getting rid of roaches. Buy some, and remember — it's your home, not theirs. Live your life as you wish. Leave ribs in the sink and cole slaw behind the door. But blast the roaches with Combat, unless they agree to contribute to the rent. (RBr)

Roach-Ender contains the chemical hydroprene, which sterilizes roaches by causing them to produce excessive amounts of their juvenile hormone. Their wings wither and their sex organs never develop before they reach breeding age. (AW)

IN THE BAG

In urban areas, paper grocery bags are a notorious vehicle for cockroach-transfer. Save and use only the plastic ones for trash; get rid of the paper ones ASAP. (*Anon.*)

MICE AND RATS

A house cat is the best mouse removal system known to man. Even a lazy, good-for-nothing puss emits a scent that mice recognize as trouble. (LH) You read it here first.

Chocolate after-dinner mints are the best bait for mousetraps. Traps should be changed and washed regularly, since mice rely heavily on their sense of smell and can easily detect the odor of a dead cousin on a trap. (PEP)

The best bait for catching mice isn't cheese. It's peanut butter or bacon. (ML)

The ashes of a cremated mouse spread near their lairs will keep mice away for a year or so. *To incinerate a mouse,* put the body in a tin can and place the can on a fire. Don't do this indoors, as incinerated mice really stink. (LHMcG)

A complicated but effective remedy for ridding yourself of a major rat infestation calls for the capture of a couple of rats and their incarceration in a deep tub or barrel. Place a microphone in the barrel and tape record the sound of the rats being clubbed to death. Catch every last gasp. Then play the tape on a loop in the infested area. The rats will vacate the premises right *now* and will stay away for a year. Save the tape; it's much easier to replay the tape than it is to club rats in a barrel annually. (*Anon.*)

BAG IT

After setting a mousetrap, place it in a paper bag. This will make disposal of the dead rodent easier and less unpleasant. (ML)

SPEAK UP

Moths are repelled by loud noises. It's good practice to open your closet from time to time and scream at your clothing at the top of your lungs while clapping your hands together loudly. (LA)

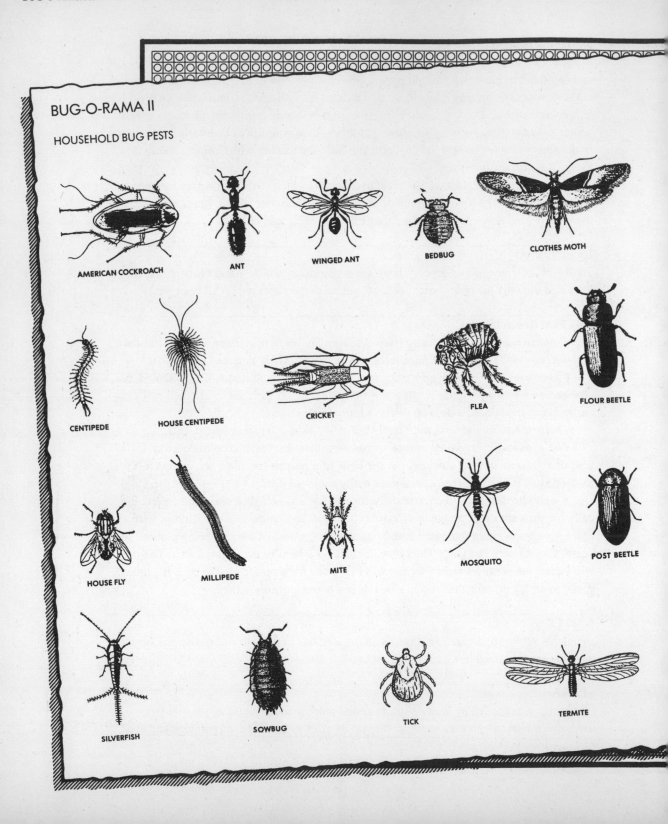

BUG-O-RAMA II

HOUSEHOLD BUG PESTS

AMERICAN COCKROACH

ANT

WINGED ANT

BEDBUG

CLOTHES MOTH

CENTIPEDE

HOUSE CENTIPEDE

CRICKET

FLEA

FLOUR BEETLE

HOUSE FLY

MILLIPEDE

MITE

MOSQUITO

POST BEETLE

SILVERFISH

SOWBUG

TICK

TERMITE

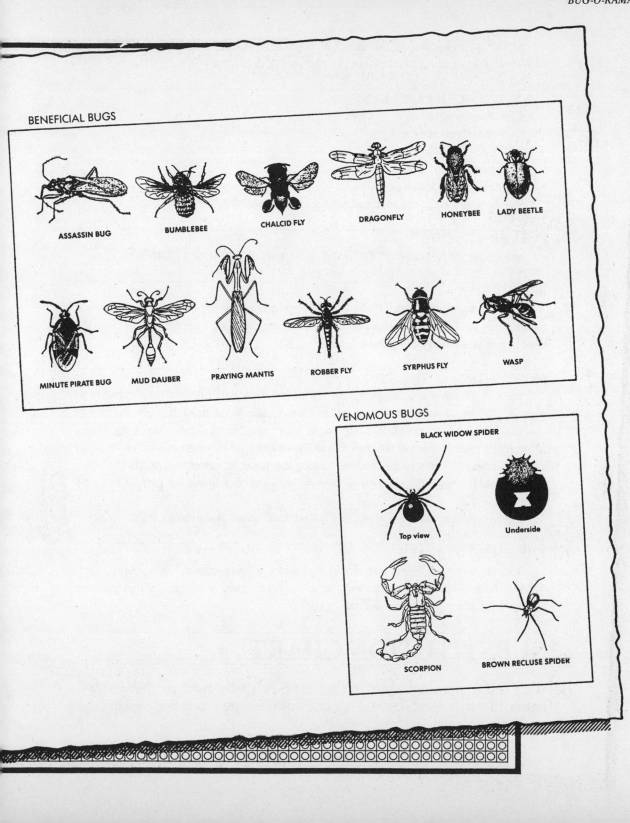

BENEFICIAL BUGS

ASSASSIN BUG

BUMBLEBEE

CHALCID FLY

DRAGONFLY

HONEYBEE

LADY BEETLE

MINUTE PIRATE BUG

MUD DAUBER

PRAYING MANTIS

ROBBER FLY

SYRPHUS FLY

WASP

VENOMOUS BUGS

BLACK WIDOW SPIDER

Top view

Underside

SCORPION

BROWN RECLUSE SPIDER

Moths are more likely to be attracted to woolens that have been stored unwashed, with some slight trace of perspiration still present. (AR)

SUREFIRE MOTH REPELLENT
Combine the following:
- A cup of rosemary and
- a cup of lavender;
- a tablespoon of ground cloves and
- a diced, dried lemon peel.

Put them all into an old sock and hang it in the closet. (PKG)

FLEA REPELLENT
See under *PETS* **in** *CHAPTER NINETEEN: A MODERN MISCELLANY*.

BRIGHT IDEA
To rid a room of a pesky fly or other flying insect, turn off the lights in the room, then turn on the lights in another. The fly will flee to the light. Don't forget to close the door before you turn the lights back on again. (LKH)

MOSQUITOES
are one of those species you must try to kill as a part of your responsibility to mankind. To avoid endless hours of stalking a mosquito in the dead of night, the two of you out for blood, turn on one fairly bright lamp, then methodically check the walls. Mosquitoes prefer to feed in the dark and will wait until the lights are out before buzzing you; the lamp will cast a single shadow, making the mosquito easier to spot. (DB)

Against the wall: Put your ear against the wall and look along the surface to spot a mosquito. (GG)

Cigar smoke repels mosquitoes. (JFQ) And many other living things.

THE SOUND OF DEATH
Vincent Price aside, no one would really buy a "bug-zapper." Notoriously inefficient, these power-sucking devices serve only to annoy everyone within earshot. Sounds a lot like the "better mousetrap." (MR)

SUBSTITUTION CHART

It's a crazy, mixed-up world of choices. Here's a list for a complete alternative life-style. And if you don't like this one, you can make a substitute chart of your own. No hard feelings.

HAPPY HOMEMAKER SUBSTITUTE LIST

For	*Use*
Air freshener	A lit candle to remove farts and stale cigarette smoke
Aluminum cleaner	Silver polish
Brass polish	Catsup
Brown sugar	Equal parts white sugar and molasses
Butter	Shortening, lard, bacon fat or cooking oil
Buttermilk	Lemon juice or vinegar in milk
Cat litter	Shredded newspaper with baking soda
Ceramic tile cleaner	Vinegar; or kerosene for soap scum; ammonia
Chocolate	Three parts cocoa (unsweetened) with one part butter or oil
Chrome cleaner	Vinegar
Coffee filters	Paper napkins (the more expensive, the better)
Colander	Plastic strawberry box
Copper polish	Salt and vinegar Lemon and baking soda
Dental floss	Heavy thread
Egg	One teaspoon cornstarch
Eyeglasses	A pinhole in a piece of paper
Fitted sheet	Flat sheet with knots tied in the corners
Floor wax	One cup cornstarch mixed into one gallon water
Garbage disposal	Toilet
Garment Bag	Old overcoat; or plastic bags from a dry cleaner; or garbage bags
Hair conditioner	Mayonnaise or whole egg
Heavy thread	Dental floss
Hot water bottle	Flat pint liquor bottle
Insect spray	Hair spray
Lucite cleaner	Rubbing alcohol applied with very soft cloth
Powdered cleanser	Baking soda and water
Putty knife	Spatula
Ruler or scale	Dollar bill (6.125" long)
Shampoo	Dish detergent; or egg and borax (wet hair, lather with egg yolk, rinse with water mixed with a teaspoon of borax); or cornstarch (rub in dry; let set ten minutes, brush out)
Shortening	Butter or oil or peanut butter
Sifter	Tea strainer
Soap (body)	Salt and oil; or oatmeal

Sour cream	Yoghurt; or cream mixed with lemon or vinegar; or cottage cheese mixed with a little milk and lemon or vinegar
Spatula	Putty knife
Strainer	Flour sifter; or stretch a cheesecloth over a bowl, secure with rubber bands or clothespins. Panty hose will work, too.
Talcum powder	Cornstarch
Toilet bowl cleaner	Bleach or ammonia
Toothpaste	Salt or baking soda
Window cleaner	Vinegar; or borax and water; or alcohol and water; or ammonia and water (CV, BO, TMcK, DH, REP, et al..)

STAIN CHART

In our lives, it's the blemishes that count. Real wounds heal eventually, but a stain lasts forever.

Unfortunately, there is no miracle remover for stains on one's character. For that reason, Modern Men watch their step and keep constant track of their extremities.

THE STAIN REMOVAL HALL OF FAME
- Hydrogen peroxide
- Chlorine bleach
- Vinegar
- Baking soda
- Lemon juice
- Ammonia   (JV)

IN A RESTAURANT
ask the waiter to bring you some club soda to get a stain before it has a chance to get you. Soak your napkin in the club soda and rub the stain briskly. (DO'R)

OIL PUDDLES
For large oil spills in your garage or on your driveway, sprinkle some "kitty litter," sawdust, or even dirt on the puddle. After it has completely soaked in, sweep it up. This may also be helpful for kitchen oil spills. (MR)

PREWASH PRODUCTS
really do work. They usually remove the most difficult stains from clothes. (VC)

THE STAIN REMOVAL CHART

For liquid stains, always soak up the offending excess liquid right away — and certainly before attempting to treat the stain itself.

To remove	*Use*
Alcohol, from fabric or carpet	Vinegar and water
Ballpoint pen, from fabric	Vinegar and milk (use a sponge and rub)
Beverage stain, from drinking glass	Denture tablet in water; let set. Rinse.
Black coating, from brass	Paste of one part salt, two parts flour and vinegar to moisten. Apply, let dry, wash.
Blood, from fabric	Cold water
Candy, from fabric	Detergent. Rub it in, soak and wash
Catsup, from fabric	Liquid detergent. Apply, let set, wash.
Chewing gum, from fabric	Ice, then cleaning fluid; or put garment in freezer, pick off icy gum.
Chewing gum, from hair	Peanut butter; or olive oil; or egg white; or witch hazel.
Chocolate, from fabric	Borax, then soak in cold water for one-half hour, then stretch fabric over sink and pour boiling water from a height of two feet onto the fabric.
Cigarette burns, from carpet	Rub with edge of silver coin or a piece of raw potato.
Cigarette burns, on wood	Acetone or lacquer thinner. Rub, then stain to match, then apply clear fingernail polish in layers. Let polish dry between applications for a protective buildup.
Coffee and tea, from cups	Vinegar and salt
Coffee and tea, from fabric	See under "Chocolate"
Cosmetic stain, from fabric	Liquid detergent, rub, then wash.
Dark stains in kettles or metal pots	A small handful of cream of tartar added to water boiling in pot; boil for five or ten minutes.
Decals	Prewash spray, let set.
Dirty collar stains	Shampoo rubbed in before washing
Food or utensil stains, from porcelain or enamel	Bleach
Food stains, from plastic	Mix one part bleach with ten parts water; or make a paste of baking soda and water.
Food (cooking) stains, from stainless steel	Ammonia and water; or oven cleaner
Fruit stains, from fabric	Cold water right away; or soak stain in milk, then pour boiling from two feet or more; or powdered laundry starch; let set two hours, wash.

Glass stain rings, from wood	Mayonnaise; or cigarette ash on a licked finger; or wood ash and a raw spud. Rub.
Grass stains, from fabric	Hydrogen peroxide; or naphtha soap; launder in cold water.
Grease stains, from carpet (natural) (synthetic)	Baking soda worked into stain; let set for at least twelve hours; vacuum. Alcohol.
Grease, from fabric	Soda water; or mineral spirits; or lacquer thinner; or shampoo; or a paste of cornmeal and lemon
Grease, from wood	Mixture of vinegar and water
Ink stains, from fabrics	Equal parts water and vinegar; blot, do not rub, repeat.
Lipstick, from fabric	Rubbing alcohol; or salad oil; soak; then wash.
Marble, stains on	Mixture of hydrogen peroxide and ammonia; let set for many hours. Or lemon and salt; rub.
Mustard, from fabric	Vinegar; or hydrogen peroxide
Oil, from fabric	Sugar and water paste; wash.
Red wine, from carpet	Soda water poured over stain; cover with towel; pound on towel to draw up liquid.
Red wine, on fabric	See under "Chocolate"; boil in milk, then wash; or apply table salt right after spill, then wash.
Paint, from skin	Oil
Rubber marks, from vinyl	Toothpaste
Rust stains, from enamel or porcelain	Paste of baking soda and water; or salt and lemon juice; or hydrogen peroxide
Rust stains, from fabric	Paste of cream of tartar and hot water, let set, wash; or lemon covered with salt, set in sunlight.
Rust stains, from metal	Raw onion; or ink eraser; or lemon juice and salt
Scorches in fabric	Sunlight; or baking soda and water paste, leave in sunlight; or lemon juice, leave in sunlight.
Suede, stain on	White bread; rub.
Tape adhesive, on wood	Oil or mayonnaise; rub.
Urine, from carpet	Eight parts water, one part ammonia; let stand, wash with water. Or soda or quinine water; or vinegar and water.
Water stains, on asphalt	Oil
Wax, on fabric	Apply tissue, toilet paper or rags to both sides of fabric; press with warm iron; or use boiling water.

(JV, CV, DH et al.)

CHAPTER **16**

Modern
Mishaps

Oops, you say, a modern mistake. Maybe you catch a genital cold from some modern miss or maybe you have to face the modern mayhem of the local pokey. Woe is you. What to do?

Step right up and look in here. We got your basic first aid, some poison control poop and a batch of briefs from some of the barrister boys.

Trouble can't fool the Modern Man.

C O N T E N T S
Chapter Sixteen: *MODERN MISHAPS*

MODERN MISHAPS

Accidents will happen — and if you're not careful, they'll happen right before your very eyes. Then what do you do?

AUTO ACCIDENTS

First, look out for yourself. Don't become an addition to the casualty list. Wait until all the upside-down sedans have stopped spinning and make sure there isn't another six-pack of Toyotas coming down the road headed for the carnage. If you're crossing the road to get to an accident, what should you do? Right, look both ways.

A damaged car should be secured; the ignition should be off and the wheels should be blocked, if necessary. Send someone for an ambulance, or go yourself. *Don't move any accident victims* unless there's a clear danger from fire or explosion. (KUG)

DROWNINGS

Jumping into the deep end and trying to swim out and rescue somebody is the last resort option. First, look around. Is there a rope or a long pole handy? How about a life ring or a large, watertight container?

Staying on the dry side is not an act of cowardice; it's simply prudent. The chance is fairly high that a drowning man can easily pull under his rescuer.

If you swim to the rescue, carry your shirt in your teeth and extend that toward the victim; then tow him in. If you swim up to a panicked person and try to put your arm around him, buddy-style, you're a goner. If you absolutely must come into contact with a drowning person, *do it from behind* so he can't wrestle you under. With a handful of his hair, move the head backward so he's looking at the sky, then tow him in.

Other techniques include grabbing the head from behind with both hands and forcing it up and keeping it up while kicking toward shore or coming from behind and slipping your arm under the victim's chin, force his head up, then tow him in. Either of these techniques is safer than coming up from behind the victim, putting your arm under his armpit and trying to tow him in; he'll turn on you and you'll both go under. (JGG)

The best towing stroke is a modified sidestroke, using a scissors kick and paddling with your free arm. (KER)

If the drowning man is you, because of fatigue, perhaps, you can take a rest by tilting your head all the way back so that you are facing straight up. Try to relax and let your legs and body maintain a vertical position; stretch your arms out from your sides, palms up, and float. You can safely stay in that position for as long as you like. (JGG)

See *MOUTH-TO-MOUTH RESUSCITATION,* **below.**

ICE RESCUE

Like a drowning rescue, saving someone who has fallen through the ice is best done long distance, using a pole or a rope with a loop at the end.

If you must go out on the ice, take a rope or cloth with you (or, better yet, if there are a sufficient number of onlookers, form a human chain) and proceed by lying as flat as possible on your stomach. If you have formed a chain, everyone should lie down and hold the ankles of the person in front of him. This will distribute your weight over as broad an area as possible. When you are able to reach the victim, grab him by the wrists and wriggle back away from the opening. Treat the victim for hypothermia (**q.v., under** *THE MODERN MEDIC,* **below**). (JGG)

TORNADOES

While your chances of being sucked up by a tornado are rather slim, your chances of being bashed in the head by debris are great. A cellar is the safest place; if you take refuge in a basement, make sure you hide in the corner nearest the oncoming tornado. If you're stuck without a basement, lie low in a closet or bathroom. Outside, your best chance for refuge is in a ditch. *Don't stay in your car.* That works fine in electrical storms, but it's suicidal in a tornado. Instead, seek safety outside. (JGG)

ELECTRICAL SHOCK

Aside from what's happening to the victim, the biggest risk-taker in a situation like this is the person doing the rescuing. If you spot someone who has managed to plug himself into the nation's power grid and you walk up and simply grab his hand (or whatever part of his body is in contact with the electricity), you will become the electrocuted guy. If you work around a bunch of people, all of whom are willing to make this mistake, you could start something interesting. Assuming you can't switch off the power, the best way to get someone out of harm's way is to knock them away — hard and fast. Give them a body block or something. Just don't allow your own body to become a conductor. (JGG)

These shocks can easily kill. The preponderance of injuries, however, will be burns. (For attending to burns, **see the appropriate entry under** *THE MODERN MEDIC,* **below.**)

The bathroom is the most dangerous room in your house for electrical mishaps. If you are exposed to electricity while you are standing in water, the natural resistance of your body is lowered and the amount of current passing through you is increased. (MR)

Shocking youth: The elderly do not suffer from electrical shock as much as young people do; the amount of moisture in the skin affects the resistance to the amount of current conducted through your body. (KLT)

Under 40 volts, it might hurt, but according to National Electrical Code standards, it probably won't kill you. (MR)

See also *Heart Attack* **in** *THE MODERN MEDIC,* **below, and** *ELECTRICITY* **in** *CHAPTER FOURTEEN: MODERN MAINTENANCE.*

CHOKING

The Heimlich Maneuver:

If the victim is sitting:

1. Stand behind the victim's chair and wrap your arms around his waist.

2. Place the thumb side of your fist against the victim's abdomen, slightly above the navel and below the rib cage.

3. Grasp your fist with your other hand and press your fist into the victim's abdomen with quick, repeated thrusts. Repeat this as often as necessary.

If the victim has collapsed:

1. Turn him face up.

2. Face the victim, kneeling astride his hips.

3. Place one hand atop the other, with the bottom hand on the abdomen slightly above the navel and just below the rib cage.

4. Press your hand into his abdomen with quick, upward thrusts. Repeat as necessary.

If the victim vomits, quickly roll him on his side and clear away the vomit to prevent him from gagging on it. (DHe)

LIGHTNING

Indoor lightning strikes can be avoided by keeping clear of fireplaces, power service entries and appliances, including TV sets, during electrical storms. The telephone really *is* as dangerous as popularly supposed. (MR)

Outdoor strikes can be avoided by keeping away from large, metallic objects; bodies of water; high, solitary trees and other obvious points of attraction. Lie low. Get down in a ditch, small valley or a gully for the greatest safety — but watch for flash floods. (JEC)

Not long ago, a few newspapers picked up a small, two-paragraph wire-service story that described how a woman in some remote part of Yugoslavia had been struck by lightning and killed. Turned out that two of her brothers, her father and her uncle had also been struck by lightning. Two thousand years ago, this would be a myth. Today, it's a cautionary tale. Don't let this happen to your family. Don't cuss, don't lie and don't sit under the apple tree in the middle of a lightning storm.

THE MODERN MEDIC

A disclaimer: This stuff is for general information only. Don't try to read this book, then perform neurosurgery, then get mad at us because it didn't quite work out. You won't get a professional diagnosis here. For that, find a high-priced professional diagnostician and leave us out of it. Our assumption is that if you're going to use this section of the book, it's because there's not a good chance of finding competent medical help, so the emphasis is on quick, often temporary, remedies.

PARTS OF THE BODY

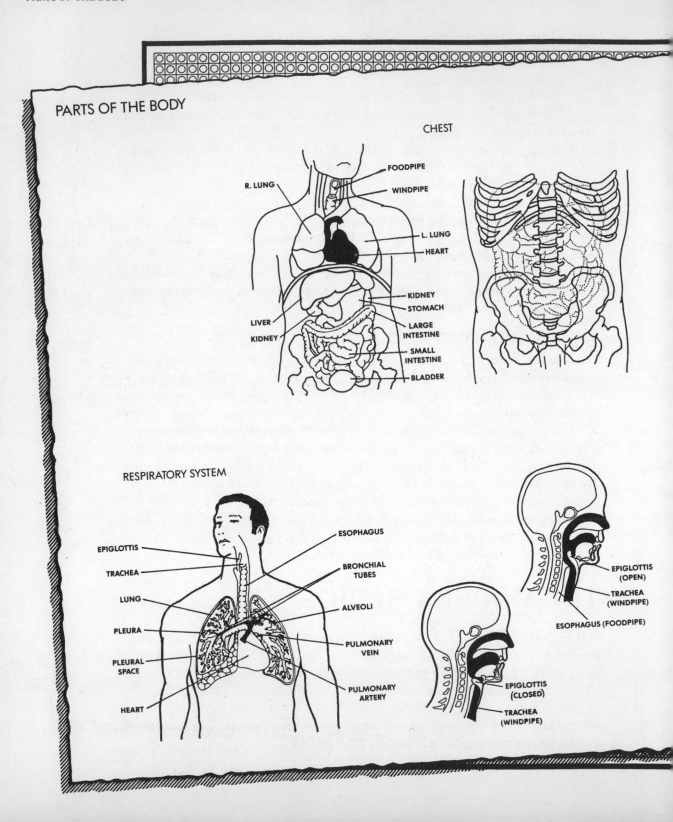

CHEST

R. LUNG

FOODPIPE

WINDPIPE

L. LUNG

HEART

KIDNEY

STOMACH

LIVER

LARGE INTESTINE

KIDNEY

SMALL INTESTINE

BLADDER

RESPIRATORY SYSTEM

EPIGLOTTIS

TRACHEA

LUNG

PLEURA

PLEURAL SPACE

HEART

ESOPHAGUS

BRONCHIAL TUBES

ALVEOLI

PULMONARY VEIN

PULMONARY ARTERY

EPIGLOTTIS (OPEN)

TRACHEA (WINDPIPE)

ESOPHAGUS (FOODPIPE)

EPIGLOTTIS (CLOSED)

TRACHEA (WINDPIPE)

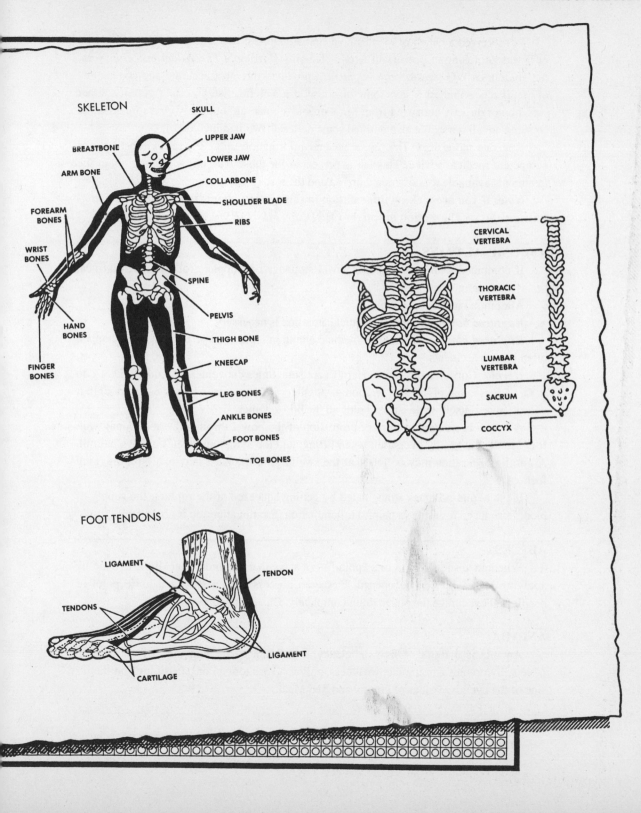

SKELETON

SKULL
UPPER JAW
LOWER JAW
COLLARBONE
SHOULDER BLADE
RIBS
BREASTBONE
ARM BONE
FOREARM BONES
WRIST BONES
HAND BONES
FINGER BONES
SPINE
PELVIS
THIGH BONE
KNEECAP
LEG BONES
ANKLE BONES
FOOT BONES
TOE BONES

CERVICAL VERTEBRA
THORACIC VERTEBRA
LUMBAR VERTEBRA
SACRUM
COCCYX

FOOT TENDONS

LIGAMENT
TENDON
TENDONS
LIGAMENT
CARTILAGE

We received a bunch of medical and first aid entries. Some of it was good, but a lot of it was confusing or downright wrong. Timothy Corfield's *The Wilderness Guardian,* the ubiquitous WG (**see** *Acknowledgments*), provided the most accurate and concise list of MediFacts, so unless it says something else, if it's on this list, you can figure it's either based on or directly borrowed from Mr. Corfield's book, although any errors made in the crossing are all ours. (We also omitted some material WG had included.)

And one more time: This is for general information only. We're no substitute for competent medical advice. This list is presented for those who enjoy reading about the treatments available for common diarrhea and the rest.

Note: **If you are seeking information in this section about first aid** *in the event of an accident,* **see the section devoted to** *MODERN MISHAPS,* **which appears above.**

ABDOMINAL PAINS

If combined with vomiting and bowel stoppage or stoppage followed by diarrhea, see a doctor immediately.

Abdominal injuries include:

Ruptured bowel: Immediate medical attention is necessary.

Ruptured bladder: Immediate medical attention is necessary. This seems to happen often in auto accidents.

Hernia: Consult a physician. Hernias are sometimes conveniently ignored. Don't do it. Get a hernia out of the way as soon as possible. If you detect a hernia early enough, it will often heal itself while a truss holds all the bits together.

A hernia is a common form of protrusion of the bowel through the abdominal wall. It is usually caused by overstrain when lifting, and the symptoms aren't always painful. A gurgling sensation may be felt near the swelling, or the back may exhibit a dragging feeling.

If the hernia becomes strangulated by getting squeezed at the rupture, the supply of blood is reduced resulting in painful inflammation. Prompt attention is critical.

ABSCESS

When an abscess comes to a "point" — a stage that can more quickly be evoked by applying heat — it can be opened. Pierce an abscess with a sterilized knife point or needle and encourage the pus to drain completely. Change the dressing daily.

ANEMIA

Anemia is a result of iron deficiency, a problem easily remedied by taking iron tablets. Symptoms can include weakness, pallor, a sore tongue or pale linings on the inside of the eyelids. Shades of Geritol and Ted Mack.

APPENDICITIS

Symptoms include a sudden severe pain in the lower right region of the abdomen, or

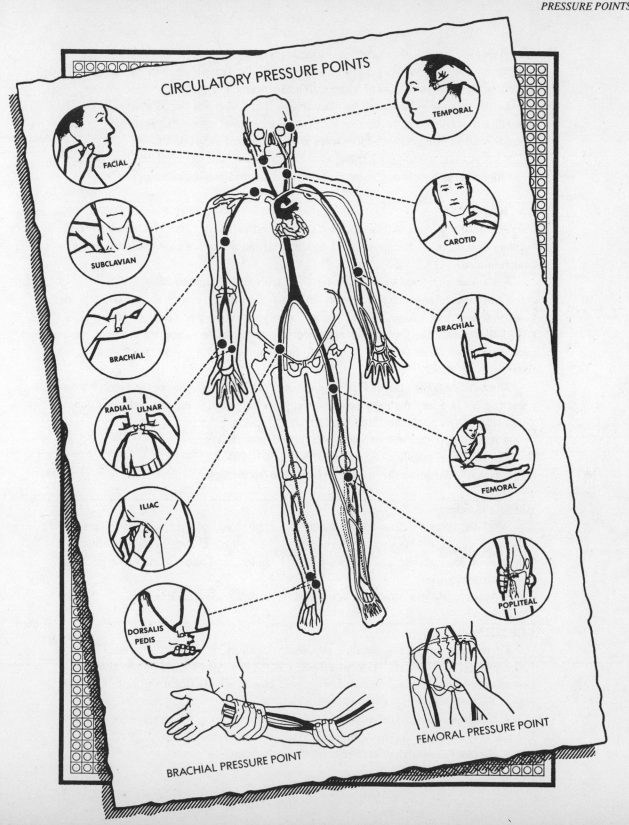

CIRCULATORY PRESSURE POINTS

TEMPORAL

FACIAL

CAROTID

SUBCLAVIAN

BRACHIAL

BRACHIAL

RADIAL ULNAR

FEMORAL

ILIAC

POPLITEAL

DORSALIS PEDIS

BRACHIAL PRESSURE POINT

FEMORAL PRESSURE POINT

loss of appetite, nausea, vomiting and moderate fever.

Never give someone suffering from appendicitis a purgative. Instead, put him to bed and allow him only mouthfuls of water until he's wheeled into surgery.

Recently, a tabloid covered the story of a surgeon who developed a severe case of appendicitis while stuck in traffic. He removed his own appendix, according to the tabloid. We don't suggest appendectomies as do-it-yourself projects.

Note: As one attentive contributor — DH — points out, appendicitis isn't always clear-cut and dramatic. It might sneak up on you disguised as a backache or the flu.

BACKACHE

You have to be sure that the cause of the ache isn't something serious, like a crushed vertebra or something, because there's nothing you can do in that case except have your back removed.

If it's from strain and stress, however, there are some decent remedies.

That's what floors are for: Stretch out on a floor with your arms spread above your head and your legs straight. By slowly twisting your arms, you can roll side to side. Gradually increase the movements until you feel comfortable rolling up in a ball, then rock back and forth on your spine, all the way around to your neck, almost a somersault (NGF).

The tubular pillow: Stressed backs and necks can sometimes be relieved by lying on a thick carpet or a hard mattress, rolling up a pillow into a little tube and stuffing it under your neck so your head hangs backward. (KU)

A sudden pain can be a symptom of a slipped disk. (NB)

Skipping can sometimes help a minor backache. (NB)

For persistent backache, seek professional physiotherapy.

BITES *(Mammal)*

Wash the wound with soap and water, then apply hydrogen peroxide and dressing. Follow-up should include a visit to the doctor, for penicillin and antitetanus injections.

Rodent bites should also be washed and treated, and the victim must go to a physician immediately.

See also *Snake Bites, Jellyfish Stings* **and** *Insect Stings and Bites,* **below.**

BLEEDING

There are three types of bleeding conditions: capillary, venous and arterial. The first two are Band-Aid wounds. *Arterial bleeding* is the one you should worry about. It's characterized by spurting streams of bright, red blood, usually occurring in time to the beat of the heart. To stop external bleeding:

1. Direct pressure at the point where the blood is emerging with a finger or by tightly squeezing the damaged area with the hand.

2. Elevate the wounded part to a level above the heart.

3. Apply heat or cold. Excruciatingly hot water is sometimes effective.

4. Make a tourniquet using a strip of cloth and a stick. Place the tourniquet above the wound, and between the wound and the heart. Wrap the cloth around the injured arm or leg and use the stick to tighten the wrap. A tourniquet *must* be loosened and retightened every fifteen minutes and its use must be abandoned after an hour.

Tourniquets should be used only as a last resort. Get medical help quickly.

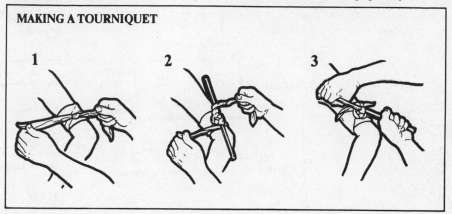

MAKING A TOURNIQUET

1   2   3

Internal bleeding: If there is evidence of internal bleeding (for example, if blood is visible in the victim's mouth), lie the patient down and try to calm him. *Never* administer alcohol. Get medical help as quickly as possible.

Blood in vomit usually indicates a stomach ulcer, although swallowed blood from the nose or throat may also be a cause.

Blood in the urine, which appears smokey and brownish, can indicate kidney disease, kidney stones, very high blood pressure or a pelvic fracture.

BOILS

are annoying, but not particularly dangerous as long as infection isn't likely. Penicillin is immediately effective, while B vitamin supplements can help. Lancing is the traditional treatment.

BOTULISM

Symptoms appear in hours (although there can sometimes be a delay of as much as 24 hours) and include vomiting, stomach pains, difficult and double vision, drooping of eyelids, difficulty in swallowing and breathing, and weakness of the facial muscles. Large doses of antibiotics are helpful, but unless prompt medical attention is given, botulism is usually fatal.

BRUISES

Treat with cold compresses or ice.

GENERAL BANDAGES

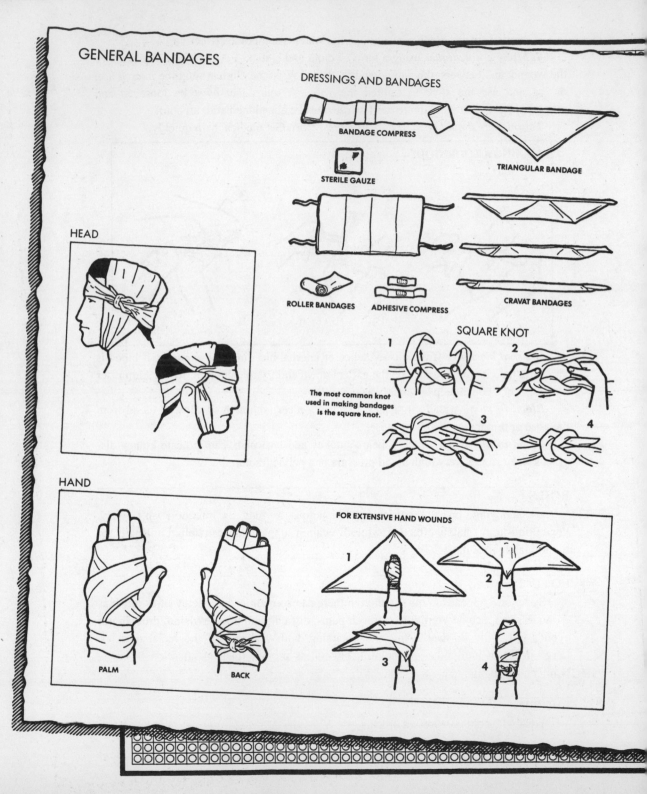

DRESSINGS AND BANDAGES

BANDAGE COMPRESS

STERILE GAUZE

TRIANGULAR BANDAGE

ROLLER BANDAGES

ADHESIVE COMPRESS

CRAVAT BANDAGES

HEAD

SQUARE KNOT

1   2

The most common knot
used in making bandages
is the square knot.

3   4

HAND

PALM

BACK

FOR EXTENSIVE HAND WOUNDS

1   2

3   4

SLINGS

TRIANGLE SLING   CRAVAT SLING   BASKET SLING

SHOULDER

1   2   3

HIP

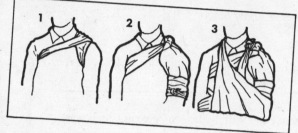

1 SPLIT TAILS OF COMPRESS BANDAGE

2 TRIANGULAR BANDAGE COVER

ARM

1   2

MID-SECTION

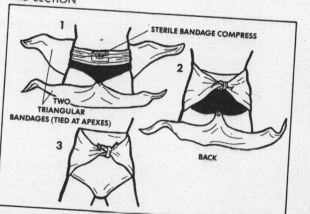

1 STERILE BANDAGE COMPRESS

TWO TRIANGULAR BANDAGES (TIED AT APEXES)

2

3   BACK

ELBOW OR KNEE

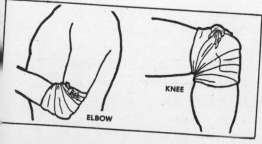

KNEE

ELBOW

BURNS AND SCALDS

In cases of severe burns, shock (**see below**) — due to fluid loss — is the main enemy. Secondary infection must be guarded against.

Cooling or the application of a proper ointment is a way to relieve the pain of minor burns. (Butter, once fashionable as a treatment, seems to have been replaced by ice-packing as a treatment, especially for minor burns.) Dressing for minor wounds should be changed frequently; severe burns should be treated in a hospital. Until the patient can be hospitalized, the burns should be covered with cloth — sheets or towels will do, preferably sterile — wrung out in cold water.

First-degree burns are characterized by redness and slight swelling.

Second-degree burns are characterized by slow blistering and sores.

Third-degree burns are characterized by lost, charred or white, lifeless skin.

Serious second-degree and all third-degree burns should receive medical attention.

Never put grease or oil on a burn. (SJ)

Minor burns can be treated with a cold bottle, snow or ice. (VR)

CRAMP

For muscle cramp, rub the affected area firmly and in the direction of the heart. (SJ)

CUTS AND SCRAPES

Remove any dirt from the affected area and flush with hydrogen peroxide, then wash with soap and water and apply a dressing.

DIARRHEA

The most common form is catarrhal diarrhea; it's caused by inflammation of the bowel and is not serious, although it can sometimes be the symptom of an underlying illness. The best treatment is bed rest and plenty of water. Many over the counter medicines are available for diarrhea.

If the condition persists or is accompanied by blood, see a physician immediately.

The prolonged use of paralytic drugs to treat the symptoms of diarrhea is dangerous.

DISLOCATIONS

are not always painful, but unless the corrective procedure is done carefully, dislocations can be very painful indeed; the sheer violence of the procedure can cause shock. A botched attempt at relocation will damage the blood vessels, nerves or ligaments. After relocation, prevent further movement of the affected area; otherwise, another dislocation may occur. Almost any joint can be relocated by a specialist, but it's not a pastime for amateurs. *Wrist, finger, thumb, knee, spine or ankle* dislocations shouldn't even be attempted. Immobilize the dislocated joint and get the patient to a doctor.

In an *emergency,* where you you can't wait for a professional, proceed as follows:

Shoulder:

1. Lie patient on his back on the floor.

2. Sit opposite the patient's hip on the injured side.

3. Grasp the patient's wrist and place your foot in the armpit on the edge of the shoulder blade.

4. Pull gently, steadily and forcefully downward, toward the patient's hip. If that doesn't work, pull the arm out at a right angle.

5. Ideally, the bone will relocate with a snap. Put the arm in a sling.

Elbow:

Bend the patient's elbow across your knee while pulling on the forearm. Prevent further movement of the arm after relocation.

Jaw:

Put the patient on his back. Relocate by pressing firmly downward on the back teeth with the thumb, while gently pressing the jaw closed. Watch that you don't get your thumb bit.

EARACHE

Look for internal swelling or inflammation (the usual cause) and see a physician, who will usually treat with penicillin or antibiotics.

Sometimes, though, the ear may be blocked with wax. If this is the case, make the patient lie down and turn his head so the bad ear is facing up. Make a solution using two teaspoons of baking soda mixed with a cup of lukewarm water (warm olive oil is a possible substitute). Allow a few drops of the mixture into the ear, and leave it alone for half an hour. Then have the patient turn his head and drain the ear.

EYE TROUBLE

A stye can be treated by applying hot presses. After the stye bursts, apply neomycin ointment.

Conjunctivitis is characterized by redness, irritation and a watery or yellow discharge. Clean the eyes with a mild antiseptic lotion and apply a mild zinc ointment. Do not bandage; sunglasses, though, may provide relief. Get prompt medical attention.

If wounded in the eye by acid, alkali or hot metal, wash the eye under a stream of water for twenty minutes, then pour a drop of castor oil in the corner of the eye, bandage lightly and seek proper medical care.

A black eye can be treated with a pad of cloth wrung out in cold water. A gentle massage also helps.

FAINTING

A person who has fainted *must* be laid down flat or he could die, believe it or not. The best preventive is to have the patient sit down with his head between his knees.

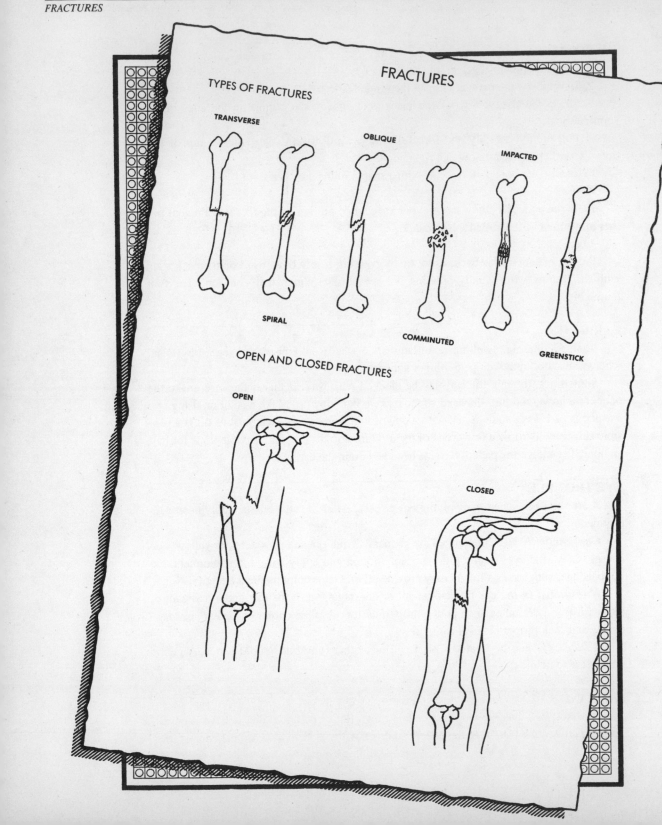

FRACTURES

TYPES OF FRACTURES

TRANSVERSE

OBLIQUE

IMPACTED

SPIRAL

COMMINUTED

GREENSTICK

OPEN AND CLOSED FRACTURES

OPEN

CLOSED

FEVER

If the temperature of the patient exceeds 105°F, the situation must be considered to be very grave, since extraordinarily high temperatures almost always indicate an underlying disorder that requires immediate treatment.

Lesser fevers can be relieved by sponging the patient with cold water or bathing in a warm bath and gradually increasing the amount of cold water.

FRACTURES

A simple fracture is one in which the bone has broken without concurrent damage to the flesh.

A compound fracture is one where the skin has been lacerated, sometimes to the extent that the skin has been penetrated by the broken bone.

When you can't wait for a professional, temporary emergency treatment for either kind of fracture requires three people (not counting the guy with the broken arm or leg) to align the bones. One person steadies the upper area of the limb as the second gently and firmly pulls upon the limb to counteract any muscular contractions; the third man attaches the splint and bandages. This procedure, while daunting, is not *always* painful.

If treated by a professional, get the fracture documented by X-ray to avoid any complications in the recovery. (LEW)

FROSTBITE

is indicated by numbness in the extremities; confirmation comes when the victim's nose, cheeks or ears take on a grayish-white cast.

The first remedy is to thaw the frostbitten area. Hold the afflicted area against a warm and normal area; if the hands are frostbitten, for example, put them under the patient's arms. Next, give the patient something warm to drink, wrap him in a blanket or place him in a warm room. Rubbing cold water against the afflicted area may help. When movement returns to the area, it is recovering. Severe frostbite can result in gangrene, so you should consult a professional. **See also** *Hypothermia,* **below.**

GONORRHEA

See *CLAP, HERPES, AIDS AND OTHER PENALTIES,* **below.**

HEART ATTACK

If you've been trained in CPR, you're lucky. If not, and no one around has had CPR training, you might consider taking a class.

The victim of a heart attack may collapse with severe pain in the chest and left arm. There may also be profuse sweating, obvious discomfort, nausea and vomiting and labored breathing. Do this:

1. Lie patient down and clear his tongue from his throat. Give about five breaths of mouth-to-mouth resuscitation (q.v., at the end of this list).

SPLINTS AND CARRIES

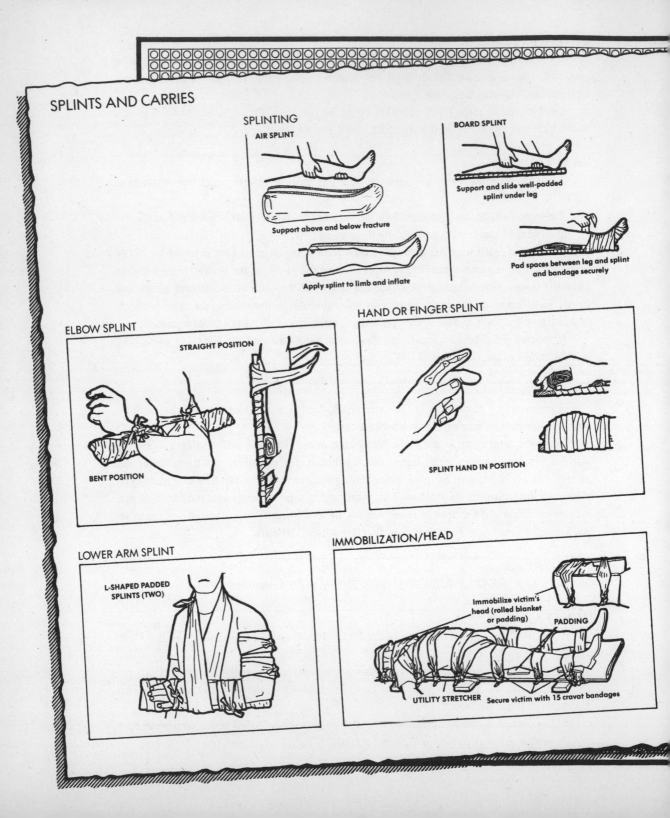

SPLINTING

AIR SPLINT

Support above and below fracture

Apply splint to limb and inflate

BOARD SPLINT

Support and slide well-padded splint under leg

Pad spaces between leg and splint and bandage securely

ELBOW SPLINT

STRAIGHT POSITION

BENT POSITION

HAND OR FINGER SPLINT

SPLINT HAND IN POSITION

LOWER ARM SPLINT

L-SHAPED PADDED SPLINTS (TWO)

IMMOBILIZATION/HEAD

Immobilize victim's head (rolled blanket or padding)

PADDING

UTILITY STRETCHER   Secure victim with 15 cravat bandages

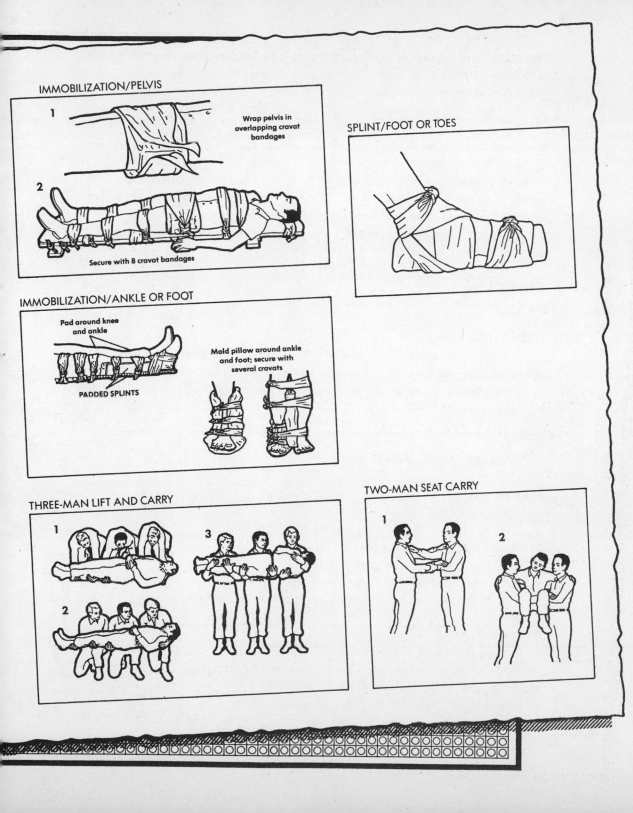

IMMOBILIZATION/PELVIS

1

Wrap pelvis in overlapping cravat bandages

2

Secure with 8 cravat bandages

SPLINT/FOOT OR TOES

IMMOBILIZATION/ANKLE OR FOOT

Pad around knee and ankle

PADDED SPLINTS

Mold pillow around ankle and foot; secure with several cravats

THREE-MAN LIFT AND CARRY

1

2

3

TWO-MAN SEAT CARRY

1

2

2. Feel for a pulse; if the heart hasn't started, make a fist and strike the victim's breastbone with the heel of the fist. This should be an abrupt, exceptionally forceful blow. The blow should be hard enough to shock anybody watching, but not hard enough to kill the poor fellow.

3. If the above two steps are not effective, administer oxygen. After four or five breaths, strike the breastbone again. Repeat as necessary. Leave the oxygen mask in place after the heart has restarted.

4. If the heart *still* won't start, massage it by pressing hard on the breastbone with the backs of both hands and stroking it five times, once per second. Alternate this with a couple of mouth-to-mouth breaths. Continue for fifteen to twenty minutes. Two people working together on these two operations is better than one person doing it all.

5. *Don't move the patient,* unless it's to get him to the hospital. It may be better to bring the doctor to the victim.

HEAT RASH

can be soothed with lemon or lime juice.

HEPATITIS

is a liver infection, usually accompanied by a fever, loss of appetite and weakness. A yellow jaundice (**see** *Jaundice,* **below**) may follow. A physician's care is essential.

Serum hepatitis, a more dangerous variety, is passed by blood transfusions or dirty hypodermic needles.

HERNIA

See under *Abdominal Pains,* **above.**

HICCOUGH

Various remedies include:

Take a long drink of cold water without taking a breath.

Breath in and out of a paper bag. (WG)

Hold your breath for sixty seconds. (DB)

Take repeated, rapid sips of water from a glass until the glass is empty. (SD)

The idea is the same: break the cycle of spasms that cause the hiccoughing.

HYPOTHERMIA

is what you get if you run around in insufficient clothing in cold weather or if you wear wet clothes in windy weather. The first symptoms are fatigue, a slight shivering and irritability. Irrationality and convulsive shivering follow. Get prompt professional care. If left untreated, the patient will die shortly after the shivering ceases.

If the early signs are present, get the victim undressed and in bed under warm blankets. Administer hot, sweet beverages. (JY)

IMPOTENCE

See entry in *MODERN MATING*.

INFLUENZA

Bed rest and aspirin are the best treatments. Antibiotics should be used only to combat serious lung complications.

INSECT STINGS AND BITES

Watch for serious allergic reations to some bites and stings. Get professional help if in any doubt.

Mosquito bites can be soothed with a wet bar of soap. (REW)

Mosquito bites and bee stings respond well to wrapping in a cold towel or rubbing with an ice cube. (*Anon.*)

Itching insect bites or allergic rashes can be treated with a thick paste made of MSG and water. (KJH) You may also try calamine lotion or witch hazel. (DH)

To take the sting out of the stingers (including scorpions), mix yourself some paste made from meat tenderizer and spread it on the bite. (JAG)

For bee stings, rub on vinegar. It takes the pain away and stops swelling. (SMY)

Baking soda and water applied to stings and spider bites will ease the itching. (KQ)

To remove a tick: Apply heat to the exposed part of the tick with a hot needle; the tick will pop out. (JGG)

Cover the tick with grease or petroleum jelly for forty-five minutes or an hour. Eventually, he'll come out. Turpentine also works. (HWe)

Either way, make sure the tick's head doesn't remain embedded in your skin. If this happens, treat it like a splinter (q.v.).

JAUNDICE

is characterized by a yellowness appearing first in the eyes and later over the entire body. Treat with plenty of rest; eat plenty of carbohydrates and protein — but no fats. See a doctor.

JELLYFISH STINGS

can be treated with ammonia or piss (VR) (unlike shit — a vile and dangerous substance — piss is sterile and safe, for whatever *that's* worth). (WRu)

LICE AND PARASITES

See also *Crabs and Lice* **under** *CLAP, HERPES, AIDS AND OTHER PENALTIES,* **below.**

Local redness and persistent itching may indicate the presence of lice; visual inspection is the best way to confirm the presence of lice.

Treat by boiling any exposed bedclothes and garments and dusting the body with a mild insecticidal powder three times per week.

For *crab* or *head lice,* wash the affected area with a commercial product, such as A-200, or with a more powerful, prescriptive drug shampoo, such as Kwell.

Disinfect buildings and furniture of fleas, lice and bedbugs by spraying or dusting with a pyrethrum-based insecticide.

LIGHTNING
See under *MODERN MISHAPS,* **above.**

MEASLES
can be identified by watery, red eyes, sometimes accompanied by diarrhea, high temperature or a cough. Confirmation comes with a rash on the face, then the body, followed by facial puffiness. Respiratory disorders, like bronchitis, can follow. There may be no specific treatment other than bed rest, but a doctor should be consulted when the symptoms start.

MUMPS
is a viral infection causing swollen salivary glands; in males, the testes may be inflamed and may partly atrophy; however, there seems to be little risk of sterility as a result. You should consult a doctor if you have these symptoms. Treatment often consists of a week's rest and another week (following the onset of swelling) of confinement.

PNEUMONIA
is a lung inflammation evidenced by pains in the chest, shivering, rising temperature and labored breathing. A hacking, raw cough that brings up blood or rust-colored phlegm may also be among the symptoms of pneumonia. At the critical point, the temperature may drop, sweating will start and the pains will ease. The patient must lie flat and receive competent nursing; sponge baths to reduce temperature (**see** *Fevers,* **above**) and administration of oxygen are important. A bluing of the face and lips indicates a need for oxygen. You should get a doctor. Antibiotics are often effective, but a very long period of convalescence is essential.

POISONS
If it's not on this list, you can't handle it. Get the patient to a hospital. Call a physician or your poison control center in *any* case of poisoning.

Emetics: First, see if the poison container has instructions for cases of accidental poisoning. In some cases, administration of an emetic (something that induces vomiting) is necessary. Useful emetics include warm salty water, mustard in water, or baking soda in water. Do not use an emetic unless you are sure it's the right thing to do. We only suggest the need for an emetic in some of the entries that follow (if we don't mention it, we obviously don't suggest it), but this list is only for general information; your doctor or your poison control center should be your ultimate guide. Call them first.

Acids (hydrochloric, nitric, sulfuric): Administer lime water, oil, magnesia, chalk or bicarbonate of soda in water, followed by albumin water.

Alcohol: Flush the stomach and administer stimulants.

Alkalis (caustic soda, ammonia): Administer vinegar in water or lemon juice, followed by olive oil.

Camphor: Administer an emetic followed by stimulants.

Carbolic acid (including Lysol): Administer magnesium sulphate, then milk. Wash out stomach.

Cocaine: Wash out stomach; administer artificial respiration.

Digitalis: Administer an emetic; wash out stomach with permanganate of potassium.

Ether: Wash out stomach; follow with cold douches.

Iodine: Mix flour (or some edible starch) in water; wash out stomach.

Laudanum (including morphine and opium): Administer an emetic; wash out the stomach with permanganate of potassium; give strong coffee; keep patient awake; administer artificial respiration.

Lead acetate: Administer magnesium sulphate; wash out stomach; follow with albumin water or barley water.

Mushrooms: Give an emetic followed by injections of atropine and nikethamide.

Oxalic acid: Administer magnesia or chalk — but *not* bicarbonate of soda. Wash out stomach; follow with milk.

Phosphorus (matches, for example): Use sulphate of copper as an emetic; wash out the stomach with potassium permanganate; administer albumin water. Avoid oils.

Silver nitrate: Administer salt water; wash out stomach. Follow with milk.

Turpentine: Administer an emetic, then follow with milk.

Zinc chloride: Wash out the stomach; follow with milk.

RABIES

Rabies is often signaled early by difficulty in swallowing and copious salivating. Contact a doctor immediately. When pelvic convulsions begin, accompanied by labored breathing, the patient will die in about four days.

Prevention is your best shot. *Try to capture the animal* that delivered the bite; if the animal lives for more than ten days, it probably doesn't have rabies. A dead animal can be analyzed to determine if it has rabies.

Rabid bites should be thoroughly washed with detergent and flushed with strong antiseptics; fang punctures should be probed with a swab. *Do not stitch wounds closed.* If rabies is thought likely, antirabies serum must be sought immediately.

SCURVY

is indicated by tender or bleeding gums, persistent halitosis, anemia and bleeding from mucous membranes. The ailment responds quickly to consistent doses of vitamin C.

SHOCK

Shock can be caused by a number of factors, including extreme pain or fear. Somebody suffering shock will appear sickly, pale and weak; he may have chills and he might vomit; his skin will be cold and clammy.

If the victim is conscious, have him lie down with his feet slightly elevated. If the outside air is cool, keep him warm. A little water is okay. If the victim is unconscious, lie him on his side.

Shock can be quite dangerous. Prompt medical attention should be sought.

SNAKE BITES

Snake bites are rarely fatal, but rapid attention is important. Have the patient lie down and make certain that the bite is lower than the rest of the body. Apply a tourniquet (**see under** *Bleeding,* **above**) a few inches above the bite to slow the poison's spread. Don't make it too tight, or gangrene can set in. (In most parts of the world, the local snakes will give you enough time to get to some competent medical help.) Advice is often given to incise the snakebite wounds and drain the poison along with about two or three cups of the patient's blood, and among some tropical species, like the African mamba, for example, maybe that's a good idea. But for most snakes in North America and Europe, it's safer and faster to get to a doctor.

SPIDER BITES

The most venomous spider is probably the black widow, whose bite is fatal some 5 percent of the time. The best short-term treatment is to prevent panic or shock (the relatively harmless tarantula has killed virtually all its human victims by fear) and try to convince the patient to stay very still.

SPLINTERS

Pluck them out with a tweezer; wash thoroughly. If the splinter is buried in the skin, sterilize a needle and dig it out or cut with a sterilized X-acto knife. (EP)

SPRAINS

Ankle sprains are always accompanied by swelling and pain. To effect treatment, leave the shoe on the patient and wrap a bandage tightly around the shoe and ankle. If the sprain is severe, have the patient lie down, raise his leg, and wrap the sprain in a cold, wet towel or rag. Seek medical attention.

SUNSTROKE

is indicated by giddiness, tiredness, fainting, heat cramps and severe headache. Treatment is best effected by resting in a shady place, eating a little salt and drinking lots of water.

SYPHILIS

See under *CLAP, HERPES, AIDS AND OTHER PENALTIES,* **below.**

TOOTHACHE

Oil of clove can be a relief, as can a mouthwash made from baking soda, and sometimes a cotton swab soaked in whiskey can make it easier. Aspirin helps; Tylenol doesn't. A dentist cures.

We know a guy who was stuck in the African bush and developed a horrible abscess in his front tooth. He put up with the pain for a day or so, then finally broke out his Black and Decker, attached the smallest bit he could find, drilled it out and plugged up the hole with candle wax until he could get to a dentist. He said the pain of drilling couldn't be worse than the pain he was already in. He was probably kidding. Don't do it.

ULCERS

Early symptoms of *stomach ulcers* include pain (generally when the stomach is empty) at the lower part of the breastbone or in the middle of the back. Later, vomiting may commence; the presence of blood may be noticed. Treatment is largely a dietary adjustment: eat many small meals, instead of three big ones. Add an abundance of mild dairy products to your menu. Licorice is useful and so is milk of magnesia.

Perforated ulcers are life-threatening and require immediate medical attention.

External ulcers often have a visible, well-defined bottom edge, sometimes bluish in color. This is where the healing takes place.

To treat an external ulcer if you can't wait for professional help, first remove the badly contaminated tissue with a sharp, sterilized knife. Clean the area with a mild antiseptic or antibiotic preparation. After purification, cover the wound with a light dressing and a boric ointment. Change the dressing every three days. When removing the old bandage, very carefully soak it off so the healing edge of the ulcer is not damaged.

MOUTH-TO-MOUTH RESUSCITATION

As easy as 1-2-3.

1. Clear debris from the victim's mouth, lay him down on his back, tilt his head way back and place one hand under his neck and lift. Use your other hand to pinch closed his nostrils.

2. Make a seal between your open mouth and that of the patient, then blow into his mouth until you see his chest rise as his lungs fill.

3. Take your mouth away and watch to see if his chest falls slightly as he exhales, then repeat.

For an adult, this should be repeated every five seconds or so.

For a child, the interval between breaths should be every three seconds.

If you have trouble getting the patient to breathe on his own, turn him over on his side and pound his back very hard four or five times with the heel of your hand. Then repeat mouth-to-mouth exercises. Don't give up; your breath is having effect. If you've had no luck after forty-five minutes, you can assume you've done all you could. (JGG)

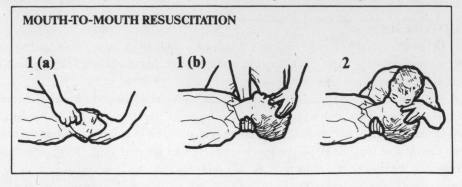

MOUTH-TO-MOUTH RESUSCITATION

1 (a)   **1 (b)**   **2**

FIRST AID KIT

It's better to have it and not need it than it is to need it and etc. While you can buy a complete first aid kit, packed and ready to go, you can also assemble one yourself. Either way, here's a list of essentials:

- Adhesive tape
- Adhesive bandages
- Cotton balls
- Antiseptic spray and/or disinfectant
- Razor blades or a knife

- Sterile gauze
- Soap
- Scissors
- Thermometer
- Antibiotics
- Tweezers

- Ace bandage
- Hydrogen peroxide
- Merthiolate
- Alcohol

(APT)

FIRST FOLK AID REMEDIES

Try the official stuff first (**see** *THE MODERN MEDIC*). Then try these. Who knows?

FIRST AID/FOLK REMEDIES MEDICAL SUBSTITUTE LIST

Symptom	Use
Bee stings	Onion or onion juice
Blisters	Sew a piece of cotton thread from one side of the blister to the other. This will let pus drain more easily
Burns and oozing cuts	Half a tomato pressed against wounded area
Corns, Cracked lips, Cuts	Cut a cranberry and apply or rub with ear wax. Ugh. Hold inside area of an onion skin to cut until it stops bleeding

Food (hot): Burns on mouth and tongue	Dip tongue into vinegar
Food (spicy)	Eat yoghurt or cucumbers; or breathe through a piece of bread held over your nose and mouth
Poison ivy	**See** *Poison Ivy Supplement* **below**
Sewage infections	Sulfur tablet
Warts	Milky sap from a dandelion stem; or spit
Whiteheads	Rub gently with fingernail for thirty seconds daily.
Worms	Bread rubbed with garlic, olive oil and salt (GHJ)

POISON IVY SUPPLEMENT

Put several *jewelweed plants* into a blender with a little water. Blend thoroughly and reserve the liquid. Soak gauze in the liquid and apply it to the affected area. Repeat two or three times daily. Recovery will be underway in a few days.

(*Note:* The following has never been tested by the Modern Men; we take no responsibility whatsoever for the consequences of its use.) *Eating poison ivy* is a remedy that some folks swear by. They say it helps your body develop an immunity to the plant, or at least a tolerance to its effects. Here's how it works:

Eat only the fresh, red three-leaf rosettes that appear in the springtime. The total size for all three leaves combined should be no bigger than a dime. *Never, ever eat a big, green leaf.* Handle the rosettes carefully, and eat about one cluster per week while they're in season. The only side effect you may notice is a slight rectal itch that will persist for a few days after eating the plant. Your poison ivy worries for that year will be vastly reduced; local infections will not spread and will disappear quickly. (RRa) If you're severely allergic, don't even think of trying this. In fact, we wouldn't think of trying it ourselves. It's here for general information, as they say.

See also *LIVING OUTDOORS* **in** *CHAPTER ONE: OUTDOORS*

DENTAL CARE

Nothing's worse than really sinking your teeth into something and leaving them there.

The nags are right: Brush after meals, see your dentist regularly, floss like crazy. Here are the details:

PROPHYLAXIS

With the use of fluoridated water and toothpaste, proper home maintenance and biannual professional check-ups, generally speaking, no one need fear dental emergencies or the loss of their teeth. (MBW)

HOW TO BRUSH

Move the toothbrush from the gums to the end of the teeth, one way only. Sawing back and forth, up and down will only erode the enamel coating on your teeth. Brushing the right way takes longer; maybe that's why dentists say you should brush your teeth for a full three minutes — five would be better. (AR)

A dissenting view: Brush with a side-to-side motion with the bristles angled at 45° to the base of the tooth. This is the most effective way to remove tartar. (DNO)

And another: Brush in a circular motion, paying special attention to the base of the teeth. The brush should hit the base of the tooth at a 45° angle. (NHG)

And a variation on a dissenting theme: The *direction* that you brush is less important than the requirement that you use a soft-bristled toothbrush at a 45° angle against the gumline. (WCG)

TOOTHPASTE

Fluoride, definitely. The stuff's a wonder drug, aspirin for the teeth, and, despite the scares of the late '50s, won't make you into a commie. (VNF)

A dissent: Adults can expect to enjoy few benefits from fluoridation as only maturing teeth assimilate the chemical. (WCG)

The new gel-type toothpastes can remove any of the bonding material now so popular in cosmetic dentistry. (RBr)

Dentists hold the new *antitartar dentifrices* in high regard, but caution they are ineffective unless the dentist has just cleaned your teeth. The new toothpastes are no good against hardened plaque, but they will prevent buildup on a clean tooth. (RY)

Most available brands of antitartar dentifrice are effective only against the tartar known as "supragingival calculus," the stuff that forms above the gumline at the base of the tooth; the mechanical action of the brush removes most of this. But it is the tartar that forms *below* the gumline that fosters gum disease, and the majority of antitartar toothpastes provide the consumer with no more prophylaxis than standard dentifrices. One antitartar brand of toothpaste that actually does seem to live up to its advertised claim is sold under the name Viadent. Viadent contains a natural agent that has been shown to be *chemically* effective against the formation of dental plaque. (WCG)

TONGUE BRUSHING

is a learned skill, but one you ought to master if you're ever going to get the demon of halitosis behind you. To ward off the involuntary gag reflex, stick your tongue out and, while looking at what you're doing in the mirror, brush it like crazy. (FDS)

A dissent: Tongue brushing is largely ineffective against actual halitosis, which is caused by stomach acids and gum disease. (WCG)

FLOSSING

is the second most important element in home dental care. Brushing's first. (WCG)

CHEAP CARE

You can get competent dental care at a low cost — or sometimes even for free — if your local university has a dental school. The students are carefully supervised, and in some states the work is even guaranteed. Difficult or unusual problems are especially welcomed. Because of the quality of the work and the low price, there may a long delay after you've signed up. But once you're on the program, your dental care problems are history. (NW)

A dissent: As dentistry is as much craftsmanship as anything else, experience counts a great deal. The patient who goes to a dental school for treatment is there as a teaching dummy, and, in exchange for what can only be adequate care, will be subject to long waits — if he is taken at all. While this and other forms of low-rent dental care may seem beneficial in the short run, the quality of private, professional care makes it not only the healthiest, but ultimately the most cost-effective way to go. (WCG)

THE BIG SQUEEZE

To get the last bit of toothpaste out of the tube, put it on the floor and step on it. Gently. (JKG)

THE ALL-PURPOSE, YEAR-ROUND FITNESS KICK

This is a progressive, nine-week program of basic exercises designed to make sure you don't end up looking like a chunk of furniture. You do it five times a week, preferably at the same time each day. It is not amusing. It is in fact quite boring. But it works.

Note: Use your noggin. If you're sick or something, don't do this stuff without asking your doctor for permission. And don't attempt to do more than you think you can *comfortably* get away with; the number of repetitions are only suggestions.

When you reach the performance level suggested for the ninth week, maintain that level or slowly increase it for as long as you stay with the plan.

1. Warm-up exercises should be done before every workout.

Distraction: Stand erect in front of your TV or stereo. Reach down and turn on the power switch. Tune in a game show or the top 40. These exercises are so dull, you'll want a little distraction as you proceed.

Bend and stretch: Stand erect with your feet shoulders'-width apart. Bend down and forward while flexing your knees. Try to touch the floor; return to a standing position. Repeat ten times.

Knee lift: Stand straight with your arms by your sides. Try to lift first your right knee as high as you can, grasping and pulling your leg up and toward your body. Repeat with your left knee. Once is enough.

Wing stretcher: Stand straight with your elbows out at shoulder level and your fists clenched in front of your chest. Without arching your back, vigorously thrust your elbows back. Keep your head erect and your elbows level with your shoulders. Once or twice will do.

2. Conditioning exercises: These are the ones that make your muscles bigger.

Toe touch: Your feet should be slightly apart, sort of in line with your shoulders, and your arms should be extended overhead with your thumbs interlocked. Twist your trunk to the right as you bend over and try to touch the floor inside your right foot with the fingers of both hands. Then touch the floor on the outside of your right foot. Return to the starting position, bringing your arms up in a slow sweep, then go for the left foot. For the first three weeks, repeat this humiliating exercise 10 times; 20 times the second three weeks; 30 reps the third three-week period and thereafter.

Sprinter stretch: Squat with your hands on the floor, fingers pointed forward and with your left leg extended behind you. In a bouncing motion, reverse the position of your feet, bringing your left foot up and under you as you extend your right foot backward. First three weeks: 12 repetitions; second three weeks: 18; third three weeks: 20.

Sitting stretch: Sit on the floor with your legs apart and your hands resting on your knees. Bend forward at the waist, extending your arms as far forward as possible, then return to a sitting position. Repetitions: same as for *sprinter stretch,* above (12, 18, 20).

Push-ups: You know how it works: lie on the floor with the palms of your hands pressing against the floor under your shoulders. Make sure your fingers are pointing straight ahead. Push your body off the floor by extending your arms and keeping your body straight so that all your weight rests on your hands and toes. Lower your body until your chest touches the floor. Don't let your belly sag and keep your ass down. Do this 4 times a day for the first three weeks, 10 times for the second three weeks, then 20 times.

Sit-ups: Lie on the floor with your legs slightly bent and your toes pointed and your arms extended beyond your head. Bring your arms forward, over your head and down toward your toes as you lift your back into a sitting position. Try not to "roll forward"; let your stomach muscles do the work. Slide your hands down your legs until they grasp your ankles. Then *slowly* bring your arms back over your head and return to a lying position, again letting your stomach muscles do the work. Do this 5 times a day for the first three weeks. During the second three weeks, do it 20 times, but instead of holding your hands over your head, lace your fingers behind your head and bend forward extending your elbows. During the third three weeks, again extend your arms, but bend your knees so your feet are flat on the floor; stretch and twist to either side of your feet 30 times.

3. Circulatory exercises are the ones that make your heart and lungs healthy.

Walking: Set your pace for 120 steps per minute and tramp a mile a day for the first three weeks. During the second three-week period, travel the same mile, but this time, alternate 100 jogged steps with 100 walked ones. During the third three weeks, go a mile and a half, alternating 200 jogged steps with 200 walked ones.

Or, *skip rope* for 30 seconds, then rest for 30 seconds, repeating twice a day during the first three weeks. During the second three weeks, alternate for minute-long periods and repeat 3 times; do the same during the final three weeks, but repeat 5 times. (JAG)

THE PC WORKOUT

You'd never think it, but a good round of PC (for *pubococcygeus*) muscle exercises will do more for your sex life than almost anything else.

The PC is the central muscle of the pelvis. Suspended like a hammock from front to back, it keeps in a straight line when it's fit — a condition that doctors have found to be rare. The proper exercise of the muscle, originally intended to help overcome incontinence, will help you enjoy:

- *More frequent erections;*
- *An increase in sexual endurance by as much as 50 percent;*
- *Reduced or cured urinary tract infections.*

Simply finding the PC muscle will give you an intuitive understanding of how this works. To locate the PC, sit down on the toilet with your legs spread and urinate. The PC muscle is the one you use to start and stop the flow of urine. Do this three times or until your bladder is emptied. Now that you've found it, you can exercise it — without pissing.

You exercise the PC simply by contracting it according to the following variations:

- *"Flicks,"* which are rapid, regular and best timed to a beat.
- *"Holds,"* which are maximum contractions held for 10 seconds or so, then relaxed for 10 seconds, then repeated.

Exercise the PC twice daily for about 15 minutes per session, gradually increasing the flicks and holds as you progress. You might want to start the first week's program with five or six flicks, followed by five or six holds, followed by a half-dozen more flicks. Gradually, you should work yourself up to the point where you're doing the same sequence 30 times apiece (30 flicks, 30 holds, 30 flicks). By the way, women will find the PC exercise will help them achieve orgasm more easily. (PM)

SLEEP

The hidden world of reality where we find refuge after daily struggles with the American Dream.

INSOMNIA

In a world with less medical carnage, insomnia would rank as a big one, a nocturnal tragedy that afflicts millions. Jerry Lewis would do a telethon for it and you could put Snooze Stamps on your Christmas mail. But as it is, the remedies come folk-style:

On cool nights, pull back the covers until you feel cold, then crawl under the covers and relax in their warmth. On warm nights: Stay under your blankets until you can't stand it anymore, then flip them off and you'll feel cool enough to doze off. (AR)

Put a pillow or a folded-up bunch of blankets between your knees, lie on your side and try to get some shuteye. Hospitals use this remedy. (BC)

Hypnotize yourself. Lie perfectly still in a comfortable position and tell yourself that you're not going to move no matter what. Concentrate on keeping still. (ASw)

Never exercise within six hours of bedtime. The increase in heart rate and oxygen content will fool your body into staying awake. (KUG)

HOW MUCH?

It doesn't matter, so long as it comes in 90-minute sleep cycles. Six or seven and one-half hours per night is a good quantity. (BB)

Less: Three hours a night, max. (BA)

THE DEEPEST REST

is essential to good health. Rest is the basis and fundamental principle of activity; you must take at least an hour a day for deep rest, even if you think you don't need it. Meditate, if you know how. Snooze if you don't. Or just soak in a hot tub. (FF)

THE SHORTEST NAP

is the best kind. Try grabbing ten or twenty minutes every day sometime between four and six o'clock. The difference it makes is remarkable. (*Anon.*)

THE MODERN MAN FOOLPROOF DIET

This is it, the perfect diet, the one that doesn't fail — so long as *you* don't. Here's how it works:

You figure you're an average guy doing an average job. Every pound of horrible, ugly fat on your Jell-O-like body is equal to 3500 calories. You burn up maybe 2000 to 2500 calories per day. If you require 2500 calories per day but only eat 2000 calories per day, you'll lose a pound every week, no problems, absolutely and positively.

Get a calorie-counter booklet and keep track. In three months, you can lose more than ten pounds; in a year you can shed over fifty pounds; in ten years, *you can lose more than 500 pounds,* safely and effortlessly. This is the diet you've waited for. This is science. (*Anon.*)

CLAP, HERPES, AIDS AND OTHER PENALTIES

Who says there's no such thing as Divine Order? When the Lord giveth, it's usually because something else has been taken away.

When morality and fidelity became unfashionable, for example, we were given a new inventory of sexually transmitted diseases. Science is putting in overtime trying to cure them, even though it seems quite inevitable that they will be replaced by newer, tougher strains of hideous ailments. Adopting sensible patterns of sexual behavior is plainly out of the question. So we lose a little on the ethical front, but we gain gobs on the frontiers of medicine.

WHOSE MESS IS THIS?

The only way to avoid sexually transmitted, incurable diseases is to avoid fucking people about whom you know little. (Although, actually, to be safe you don't need to know very much. Forget names, interests, points of view. Just get a good medical dossier on your prospective partner and rut away to your heart's content.) (SO)

THE CONDOM

Put your future in a good rubber if you want to pursue irresponsible acts without accepting responsibility for them. No other prophylaxis exists that deals with so many sexually transmitted problems (including surprise babies) as a trusty Trojan. Figure a 1-to-5 percent failure rate. Be careful during withdrawal; you could spill the beans. (JFP)

See also Condoms **in** *CHAPTER SEVEN: MODERN MATING*.

VEEDEE VOODOO

The symptoms of a venereal disease vary slightly according to the nature of the ailment, but you can figure something's amiss if you experience any of these:
- Painful urination
- Watery or thick, dripping discharges from your penis
- Skin changes in the genital area, including blisters, sores, rashes and warts
- Acute itching
- Lower abdominal pain

It's quite possible to have a whole mixed salad of these symptoms.

If you have any of these symptoms, contact your doctor to determine whether or not you've got a transmittable disease. If you don't have a doctor, call the National VD Hotline at

800/227-8922 toll free
800/982-5883 in California

415/327-5301 Bay Area local
800/200-8922 for herpes

If subsequent tests prove positive, you *must* also inform your bed partners.

AIDS is an acute viral illness transmitted both sexually and through the sharing of contaminated needles. Drug users and homosexual men are in the highest-risk groups, but the disease has recently spread to heterosexual males and females. The virus causing AIDS is carried in body fluids — especially in semen, blood and vaginal fluid. The disease has a high mortality rate and is likely to become a major epidemic; at the time of writing no cure has been discovered. In fact, the exact cause of the disease is still a subject of dispute. If you think you have AIDS or if you have had intimate contact within ten years with someone who now has AIDS, call the United States AIDS hotline at

800/342-2437.

You can also contact your local county or state health department.

Common venereal diseases are increasing in frequency, largely through public ignorance. Early treatment of these common illnesses will make their cure much easier — and will make you a safer sexual citizen:

Candidiasis (moniliasis, yeast or thrush). Males develop an inflammation at the tip of the penis from women who exhibit symptoms that include itching, odor or cheesy discharges. Cures are not complex, but must be effected by both partners or you'll be giving it to each other forever.

Gonorrhea symptoms appear between the third and the eighth day following exposure. Watch for pain during urination and a secretion of pus. Although these early symptoms disappear, the disease doesn't and if left untreated may eventually become quite serious, threatening mucous membranes, including in the eye. Women with gonorrhea will transmit the disease to babies during childbirth.

Syphilis, a.k.a. Old Joe, pox, syph, bad-blood, haircut and lues. A chancre appears ten to ninety days after exposure, followed three weeks later by a rash. Left untended, patches of hair will start to fall out; a mild fever may set in, accompanied by a sore throat, headaches and similar symptoms. In time, these symptoms will disappear, but the disease will continue, eventually attacking the heart, spinal cord and brain. Ultimately, untreated syphilis is life-threatening.

Herpes progenitalis or herpes simplex or genital herpes is a disease shared by 20 million Americans, and is characterized by recurrent bouts of painful itching sores or blisters and pain during urination. The sores heal after two or three weeks, but the disease is with you for life and the symptoms may reappear at any time. Herpes is extremely contagious while the sores or blisters are present. The disease is incurable.

Monogonococcal urethritis (MGO) is most commonly caused by an organism called *Chlamydia,* by which name the disease is often known. Symptoms include pain during urination and, occasionally, during ejaculation. This disease is on the increase, and if left untreated may result in sterility caused by inflamed and blocked sperm ducts.

Pediculosis pubis, better known as crabs or lice, are oval, grayish-colored insects that turn brown when engorged with blood. They attach themselves to the pubic hairs and are easily spread by close contact or by exposure to contaminated clothing or bedding. Persistent itching is the principal characteristic of crab infestation. Treatment is painless: use a medicated shampoo (the best is available only by prescription) and clean all exposed areas, bedding and clothing completely.

Scabies is characterized by persistent itching caused by mites burrowing under the skin and laying eggs, especially on wrists, elbows, underarms, ankles and genitals. Like crabs, scabies can be defeated by using a medicated cream and cleaning all exposed clothing and bedding.

Trichomoniasis is caused by a microscopic single-celled organism. Although primarily transmitted by sexual contact, it can also survive for a few hours in damp environments, like soiled towels.

Venereal warts are cauliflowerlike growths transmitted by sexual contact that flourish on the genitals and around the anus. The favored treatment is with a mild acid under medical supervision, but a permanent cure is not always possible. (AW)

See also *Lice* **in** *THE MODERN MEDIC,* **above, and** *Impotence* **and** *Condoms* **in** *CHAPTER SEVEN: MODERN MATING.*

TROUBLE

usually comes in a uniform, wearing aviator sunglasses, asking you for your license or knocking at the door before breakfast.

What's a poor Modern Man to do?

IF YOU'RE ARRESTED

keep quiet and get out. Never say more than you have to, and once you hear the Miranda warning (the speech about how what you say will be held against you), clam up and *stay that way*. Name, rank, serial number, period. There will be plenty of time later to talk, so don't rush. Besides, once things have gotten this far, you're not going to be able to talk your way out of trouble. You will be allowed a single phone call. Use your call to get out of jail. Call someone who can help you raise bail or come pick you up at the station. *Do not waste your call talking to some lawyer's answering service.* You need help *now,* not at 9:00 A.M. on the next business day. Call the lawyer when you get home. (JO)

The question, "What should I do if I get arrested?" is not nearly as interesting as the question that should be asked first, which is, What did I do to get arrested?

If you know the answer to the important question, you've probably already thought about how to answer the less interesting one. But if you're like most of us, you simply blunder ahead in pursuit of happiness, and for many of us, happiness lives on the other side of the zone of social prohibition. Whether or not you can find happiness with your head buried warmly in the bosom of your desires can't be addressed here; as you well know, most pursuits of happiness lead to unhappiness.

Just as most people disregard that truth, so most people disregard the advice of their lawyers. Which is fine with the lawyer, who waits for calls from locked-up clients.

So here's some more advice to ignore, this time in the form of scenarios ranging from a rather insignficant roadside waltz with a traffic cop to a full-scale, tilt boogie with a federal drug enforcement officer as your fated partner.

Driving while stupid: Let's say you and your old lady are quietly mushrooming along after a dinner party in the next suburb over. The radio's just right; the rear-speaker separation is just how you want it, and your wife is feeling warm and plushy by your side; the babysitter has the kid dead asleep and has her own car to get home after you do.

A siren framed in blue light suddenly tears at you.

What would your lawyer advise?

Imagine yourself a Republican, then come down. If you are drunk, say as little as possible. Get your wife to ask the kind officer if she can drive for you. Let her get out and walk around the car; you keep your mouth shut and don't let your feet even *think* about touching ground.

If you're high on something other than drink or Jesus, and nothing interesting is visible inside the car, be cool, be humble and be guilty of a traffic offense. If dope is visible, and you think you can make it invisible by really *concentrating* on it, try that. If you can smoothly whisk it out of sight without attracting attention to the gesture, do that.

The policeman has a great deal of latitude when he stops you even for a minor traffic infraction. Secure in your house you may be; secure in your car you ain't. So saith the Supreme Court. The policeman can use any excuse under the sun or moon to arrest you, including the suspicion that you won't show up in traffic court. And a search follows an arrest. Usually, the search reveals nothing, the arrest vanishes and you are left by the side of the road feeling violated, angry and terrified. Tough.

Let's say, however, the search is fruitful, and you find yourself spread-eagled against your car. Listen to what the policeman says, because he means it: What you say can be used against you. Be nice, but be quiet. Be mindful that to the policeman, you are nothing but meat and the promise of overtime. Politely refuse absolutely to discuss the facts of the case. You can ask what will happen to your car, whether or not you can call the babysitter, if he thinks it will rain tomorrow, but don't cooperate, even when he promises to go easy on you. *No deals offered by the police alone will stand in court. Only bargains made by the prosecutor — and I advise you to have them made in the presence of your lawyer — will hold up in court.*

If the trouble is big enough, cool your heels until dawn and call an attorney and refuse to say anything until he arrives. If the questioning gets intense, simply remain calm and ask every fifteen minutes for the exact time and whether you can have an attorney. Remember, you are in the land of the enemy. Go to sleep; it's all a dream; you will wake up tomorrow in your own bed.

Indeed, if the mess is minor, be cool. It's simply an expensive inconvenience and you won't be thrown into jail.

If held overnight and a bail is set before release, point out your stable ties in the community (if you have any) and try to get the amount of bail reduced. If, at your first appearance the next morning, the prosecutor offers you a plea bargain that you think sounds good, first ask if he can make it a sweeter deal, then accept. The courts want cases disposed of as quickly as possible, so be nice and respectful and see what kind of deal you can make.

But what if there isn't a deal? Do you need a lawyer? Probably. Do you *want* an attorney? You won't really know until you're standing all alone in a courtroom and a very embarrassing question is asked of you by some stern face and the courtroom suddenly gets very still and the afternoon light falls into the room making the dust dance and suddenly you wish you were dancing with it on the happy side of the zone. (RHW)

IF YOU CANNOT AFFORD A LAWYER

and most people cannot, ask for a public defender. Every jurisdiction — local, state and federal — must supply you with an attorney. Most public defenders are overworked, so some tend to become lazy — they won't hold your hand and they won't answer your phone calls. Even so, they know what they're doing, since all they do all day long is defend the likes of you. They're a lot cheaper than the dudes in the Italian shoes and sleek suits and a hell of a lot better than the fool who decides to defend himself. If your defender suggests pleading guilty behind a plea bargain and you don't think it's a good deal, check out your case with the most expensive lawyer in town; if he says the same thing, then the public defender can handle the job quite nicely. (RHW)

WHAT A LAWYER DOES

during office hours is counsel and represent.

Counseling is when the lawyer sits down and tells you your options under the law and the consequences of each option. A lawyer may tell you why some options are better than others, but the final choice is always yours. In a sense, a lawyer tells you what the winning cards are, then leaves it up to you to play the hand.

Representation means that lawyers "take your place" in certain circumstances. In court, they organize your side of the story into the specific form that courts require in order to consider your evidence and try to convince the judge or the jury that your side of the story is the right one.

Out of court, they can make things more convenient for you by making deals or signing papers so that you need not tie up your time.

Finally, lawyers are hired guns. You are paying not only for legal expertise when you retain a lawyer, but also for a loyal ally. (JO)

CHOOSING A LAWYER

The best way to find a lawyer is through word of mouth. The worst way to find a lawyer is through the Yellow Pages. If you are at a complete loss, call the lawyer referral service run by your local, state or county bar association. They'll refer you to someone who specializes in the area of law that most concerns itself with your sort of problem.

Be wary of choosing a lawyer on the basis of credentials alone. Not every lawyer went to Harvard or Yale and a lot of the ones that did are no better than a lot of hard-working lawyers who went someplace else. Look instead for someone accomplished in the area of law that is of most interest to you. If you're facing a trial, get a member of the trial lawyer's association; if you want to transfer property, look for a conveyancers association member. Don't be convinced by community affiliations; lawyers will join anything to get extra name recognition. And watch for fancy offices; if you find a lawyer on the thirtieth floor surrounded by oak antiques, ask yourself who pays for it.

Big versus little: Big firms can afford to have a legal specialist on staff full-time to handle just the kind of case you have. Solo lawyers tend to be more generalized, but their charges are also more modest. If you're going after Multiple General Amalgamated Corp., get a large partnership; if your quarrel is with Doctor Bob, go for a smaller outfit.

The first one is free: Most lawyers will give you a free (or very cheap) initial consultation. Use that first visit wisely. Bring all your papers, contracts, receipts and any other appropriate documentation for your case. Be ready to describe your problem in just a few sentences, Leave all the rest of your problems out of the discussion. Ask questions about what the lawyer plans to do for you, and ask for referrals so you can check his work with other clients who have had similar cases. Make sure you understand *exactly* what the fee arrangement is and what services you will get for your money. Most important, make a character judgment. You will be working closely with the lawyer and confiding in him, and it's important you like him as a *man*. Don't take the first guy you see, either. Make appointments with two or three and shop around. (JO)

PAYING THE LAWYER

There are four principal payment structures favored by lawyers:

1. Flat fees.

2. Hourly fees. Remember that the lawyer will have the meter running on *everything* that affects your case, including the briefest of phone calls. There's usually a quarter- or half-hour minimum, too, and at $200 per, that can run up the tab in a hurry.

3. Contingency fees: On a contingency basis, the lawyer will take a chunk of whatever he wins — but will have no right to anything if he loses. The advantage here is that *the lawyer has a great incentive* to perform and you aren't out any cash; the disadvantage is that the lawyer can win all, unless you structure the agreement with care.

4. Retainers: A retainer is a fee paid up-front to the lawyer as a sort of advance deposit on the fees anticipated in dealing with your case. Sometimes these are combined with contingency agreements.

Fees and costs: Remember, a fee is the charge for handling the case. Costs are for all the odds and ends associated with handling the case — things like stamps and photocopies and telephone calls. The costs of a case can be astonishing, so be sure to keep track — and ask for an accounting after the smoke clears. (JO)

GETTING BY WITHOUT A LAWYER

There are three options here:

1. Mediation, in which you agree to the findings of an independent third party. Mediators are trained professionals (they're listed in the Yellow Pages, if not as "Mediators," then under "Dispute Resolution"). Mediation only works with rational people willing to compromise.

2. Small claims court: This is where Judge Wapner reigns. In some states, no lawyers are allowed here, but there is a ceiling on claims — usually somewhere between $1000 and $2000 (depending on state laws). When you go for your hearing, make sure you have all the documentation possible; often these cases are one man's word against another, so paper counts.

3. Self-help kits: These are risky. Some are good, some aren't but since you can't tell which is which without being a lawyer yourself, it's a shot in the dark. (JO)

THE WEIRD PROFESSION

Lawyers are trained by rote, then given a booster shot of forensics. Their profession exists because existing laws were framed by other lawyers. Reasonably intelligent people have a right to expect that the laws of a reasonable society should be able to be read and understood by other reasonably intelligent people. Law is the language of bureaucrats aspiring to mediocrity. (*Anon.*)

FIXING A TICKET

Traffic tickets are almost impossible to beat. When it comes to court, the policeman who wrote the ticket will be there to swear you really did do what he said he saw you do, and unless your car was in a different city, or it isn't your license number — and you can prove it — you'll be out of luck. The best you can hope for is getting the ticket fixed.

A traffic ticket is handled by a long chain of people starting with the guy who wrote it, to the judge who makes you pay it. If you know even one person in this chain, you can get your ticket fixed by just showing up at his house with some good Scotch and a smile. He can erase, lose or tear up the ticket and you're home free. If you don't know somebody, pay the fine and make some new friends; trying to pay someone to fix a ticket could cost you a lot more than the traffic fine. (JO)

See also *The Art of Bribery* **in** *CHAPTER THREE: MODERN MONEY.*

LOOK FOR TROUBLE

In a mugging or while dealing with civil servants in the Third World, you can substantially reduce your chances of getting shot or stabbed by looking your assailant right in the eye. (RK)

FIGURE THE ODDS

Anyone who threatens you with a gun or knife and without producing it is very likely bluffing. (RK)

CHAPTER **17**

The Deportment Department

Social behavior is one of the principal concerns of this book, since Modern Men find modern manners appalling and aren't afraid to advocate more traditional criteria for determining acceptable behavior.

Old-fashioned courtesies cause serious distress among the very hip, however. There's not much Modern Men can do to relieve that situation, except to tip their hat and politely hold the door.

C O N T E N T S

Chapter Seventeen: *THE DEPORTMENT DEPARTMENT*

THE CARDINAL RULES

On behalf of all men everywhere, please observe the following rules of behavior at all times:

- Do not whistle, shout or make animal noises at females in public.
- If you are over the age of forty, do not make suggestive remarks or double entrendres as part of a flirtation ritual with a younger woman.
- Do not make rude or suggestive comments to any females with whom you have a less than intimate acquaintance, and especially if you are in the company of one or more other males.
- Never touch a female with whom you have a less than intimate acquaintance in any way differently from the way you would touch another male.

Women who wish you to violate these rules will make their wishes known to you in unambiguous ways. Until then, assume that every woman — along with all Modern Men — will find the violation of these rules grotesquely offensive.

That takes care of some basics, the kind of stuff that will elevate you out of the world of kennels. But there's more. For those who want to be modern and civilized, there're

COURTLY MANNERS

These are traditional tasks that Modern Men are expected to perform as a part of everyday life:

- You should open doors for women.
- You should offer to light a woman's cigarette.
- You should offer a woman your seat if she otherwise must stand.
- You should stand when a woman approaches the table at dinner or supper, or when she approaches a group of seated gentlemen of which you are a member, or upon being introduced to a woman at any time, or when a woman takes leave of a group of companions.
- You should remain standing until all women at table have been seated.
- You should never publicly answer any public rebuke, however false or foolish, made by a woman companion.

These small gestures are not subject to negotiation and should never appear ostentatious and do not really merit much discussion. (In fact, if remarked upon in public, they should be dismissed.) They must, however, never fail to be observed, despite any contrary claims by fashion or vogue.

The world is a graceless and ill-mannered place. Courtesy and gallantry may fall in and out of fashion for some, but they always fit the Modern Man like a glove.

See also the more comprehensive entries in *THE DEPORTMENT DEPARTMENT,* **and** *SEX AND SEDUCTION* **in** *CHAPTER SEVEN: MODERN MATING.*

THE DEPORTMENT DEPARTMENT

*The world is going to hell. All we can do is behave
in a way that makes us look good on the trip.*

— P. J. O'Rourke
Modern Manners (1983)

When it comes to etiquette, Modern Men are blindly obedient soldiers in
the service of Consideration, the grand wazoo of society.

What follows, then, are marching orders. You don't really need to know why these
things are done the way they are (although if you want to deal with causal matters, read
almost any etiquette handbook in the world). All you really need to know is that these
things are done and that if you don't do them too, you're doing your bit to make the
world a slightly uglier place than it already is.

We received many suggestions for inclusion here. (Indeed, many submissions appear
elsewhere in this chapter.) But etiquette is the expressed accretion of arbitrary social
rules, so we decided the smart tack was to canvass a bunch of other, older etiquette
books, do an exit poll of our own experiences and list the consensus. Seemed sort of
democratic.

Meanwhile, the chances are pretty good that somebody, enchanted by a new, improved idea of how people should behave this year (**see** *The Modern Conceit* **in the
INTRODUCTION to this book**) will seek to introduce some sort of unisex, one-size version of new manners. We say that courtliness and grace are still in vogue and that gallant
social gestures still define the Modern Man.

SIX EXAMPLES OF GENDER BURDEN or HOW TO HANG AROUND IN PUBLIC WITH A WOMAN

Many of the rules of etiquette involve deferential behavior toward women. It must
be sadly said that some modern women don't merit such deference, and if there were an
acceptable way of granting the exemption from this deference they so ardently desire, it
would be a very good thing indeed. But social and political fashions change and the courtesy shown to women in many of these rules is perhaps more necessary now than at
other, less inelegant times. It is, after all, quite ungentlemanly to assume that most
women are not also ladies, and quite pessimistic to assume that society will always
tolerate the present confusion.

On the street: According to tradition, you're supposed to walk on the curb side of a
woman, and it still looks swell. There's been a recent vogue of walking on the building
side of a woman to offer better protection against muggers. That's bogus; a mugger can
cross the street as well as you can. Stay vigilant if you live in Metropolis, USA.

Walking with two women: Walk on the outside of both of them, not in the middle.

You should always allow your companion to lead the way, indoors and out, except on staircases and when the travel becomes perilous or obstructed by crowds.

Open all doors for women. This is gender burden at its apex, and there's nothing for it but to stand there taking insolent abuse from every passerby (and probably including more than one modern woman). In a busy doorway — at the entrance to a department store, for example — you may let go of the door if an *unencumbered* woman is several yards away, and especially if your civility is inconveniencing your companion by making her wait. You are completely justified in releasing the door to the next man on the scene.

You may enter a door first if it opens inward; once inside, you must hold the door until your companion enters. In a revolving door, it's a near split, with a slight edge going to the idea that a man should enter first and push the door for his companion. Allow a woman to enter an electrically operated door first.

Always open a car door for your female companion, even if you've been married for half a century. Open that door and hold it open until she has been comfortably seated; watch for fingertips, dress hems and raincoat belts before you close it.

In an elevator, allow ladies to exit the car before you, unless your gesture would obstruct free passage out of the car.

Tote that bale: In the company of a woman, you must carry the heaviest packages and the most packages and, if possible, all the packages. This goes for suitcases, too.

If you encounter a female stranger burdened with a heavy load, offer her your assistance. Offering similar assistance to another man is optional, but quite appropriate.

In a restaurant, carry a woman's drink from the bar to your table (unless the staff offers to do this, as they should) or from one table to another. Your companion should follow the maître d' and precede you on the way to a table in a restaurant.

Hold the chair for a woman when she sits at a table. If you are with more than one woman, seat whichever one is nearest you first — or, when applicable, the guest before your wife.

Help a woman with her coat. After removing it, hang it up or drape it over the back of a chair. In a restaurant, check your own things, but carry your companion's stuff; only check her things if she asks you to. To help her put on her coat, align the sleeve holes and guide the coat up and over her shoulders, where your responsibility ends.

WHEN TO STAND

Women often say, "Don't get up," or "Sit down," and they usually don't mean it. That's women for you.

It doesn't matter. *It is not the job of women (or of other men) to determine which social conventions deserve observation or when they should be observed.* Obviously, when mannerly behavior causes distress, it should be suspended, but that should occur only in the company of ill-mannered folk. (**See** *Situational Etiquette,* **below.**)

So on your feet, no questions asked:

- *When a woman enters or leaves* a room or a table where you are sitting. Remain standing until she has left the area of the table or the room.
- *For your wife* in public places or at social events.
- *At a table* until all women present have been seated.
- *When shaking hands* with another person, or when being introduced.
- *When people pass in front of you in a row of theater seats.*
- *When you're in a public place and being addressed by a woman.*

Half-stand any time a full and formal rising would seem ostentatious or would be awkward because of something like the placement of the table.

See also *Duties of a Host,* **below.**

TAKE OFF YOUR HAT

- *Anytime you're indoors,* except in public areas like lobbies, hallways, airports and railway stations and the like; when in crowded elevators; in a church or synagogue (except when without a yarmulke).
- *When you're speaking to a woman* and certainly when you're kissing one (unless it's part of your favorite French-maid-and-chauffeur routine).
- *At any religious ceremony,* including outdoor burials and weddings.
- *As a matter of patriotic protocol,* such as the passing of the flag or the singing of the National Anthem.
- *As a general gesture of respect.*

Tip or slightly lift your hat with your left hand (leaving your right hand free for a handshake or to offer assistance). This sort of half-doff is appropriate when exchanging courtesies, to indicate a response (such as "you're welcome"), when offering assistance to a woman or at almost any informal, outdoor conversational exchange.

SHAKE OR OFFER YOUR HAND

- *At all introductions* and farewells to other men.
- *On congratulating other men.*
- *Whenever a handshake is offered.* This must be done without hesitation.
- *With a woman,* but only if she offers her hand first. Never offer a woman your hand first. On shaking hands with a woman, use a light (but not limp) grasp.

Take off your gloves before shaking hands.

Offer your hand, palm up, to assist a woman up or down on entering or leaving a car, boat, train, bus, carriage or other conveyance.

More hand jive: Don't touch a woman's waist or put your hand under her elbow to guide her. Women don't like to be steered around any more than you do, and this particular gesture is especially obnoxious.

If, however, the situation calls for you to offer your elbow to a woman, crook your arm so it's parallel to the ground. Don't be creepy about it, though.

Don't keep touching your face, hair, etc. Don't jam your mitts in your pockets.

WHAT TO DO WITH YOUR EYES

Use them exclusively to watch your step or to look at your female companion when involved in conversation. *Never* gape at another woman. If you aren't happy with your companion, you shouldn't have invited her out. The barbaric practice of drooling over another woman will not only offend your companion, but also the other woman. You'll look like a chump to both of them.

INTRODUCTIONS

Introductions are often more than simply a matter of manners. Nothing's worse than being left unintroduced before a group of strangers. A bungled introduction is much better than none.

The primary rule for introductions is that a man is *always* presented to a woman. The first name mentioned is that of the honored woman, followed by that of the man being introduced. For example: "Miss Chastity Smith," [I'd like to present] "Mr. Modern Jones."

There are two supplements to the primary rule — introduce the young to the old and the significant to the less significant — but they're tough to apply; the first makes no one happy, while the second appeals primarily to women vice-presidents and the mayors of small towns.

Introductions should include the honorific, first and last name; this not only conveys the proper respect for both people, but also provides each the ability to remain on either formal or informal terms.

Feminine honorifics: Who knows? Strictly speaking, you should avoid the whim of the week and go trad: If you're introducing a woman and you aren't aware of her marital status, "Miss" is still the preferred form of address (unless she has a professional honorific). The recently fashionable "Ms" is not an abbreviate form, but a contrivance invented by committee, as it were. As an artifice, it thus demeans and patronizes women — while also providing the use of honorifics with a wholly inappropriate dimension. (It is, however, impolite to refer to a woman as anything other than "Ms" if she has asked to be addressed that way.) If you are aware that the woman is married, use "Mrs."

The other way is to use "Ms" until told to knock it off. The situation is ludicrous, of course. Modern Men are caught in a crossfire between the well-intentioned and the well-bred. How absurd that the use of *any* feminine honorific should have political implications — or that a woman's marital status should be the subject of rhetoric.

Women at the bar: The use of "Esq." by women who are lawyers is funny, sort of like Pavarotti calling himself a diva. Perhaps somebody will introduce the professional honorific "Msq" and thereby move civilization one step closer to perfection.

If you introduce yourself, mention your name first. If you are re-introducing yourself to someone you've previously met, give your full name; don't ask, "Remember me?"

Going blank: If you're making an introduction and you find you've forgotten one person's name, about the only thing you can do is to introduce that person by description (for example, "I'd like you to meet my macramé merchant" or whatever). If that person doesn't pick up on your hesitation and instantly volunteer his name, you're stuck. You should then immediately confess that your mind has gone to California, that you can't remember anything — including most of what happened to you in the '60s — and confess that you've forgotten his name.

If the situation is reversed, offer your name directly it becomes obvious that your host has let your name slip.

Don't be offended if someone forgets your name, and don't worry too much if you're the one doing the forgetting. It is quite possible to forget your own mother's name.

Introductory don'ts:

* *Don't* offer business leads and job descriptions as part of an introduction; names are enough.
* *Don't* repeat the introduction in reverse (i.e., "Miss Chastity Smith, Mr. Modern Jones; Mr. Jones, Miss Smith").
* *Don't* introduce people by first name only (unless one is a family member).
* *Don't* add commands — such as "shake hands with," or "say hello to" — to your introduction.
* *Don't* introduce a person to a large group all at once.
* *Avoid* introductions any time it's socially or physically awkward.

See also *Duties of a Host,* **below.**

CONVERSATIONAL ETIQUETTE

It is extremely useful to consider the content of your thoughts before giving them form in speech. In the language of bumper stickers, you should be sure your brain is in gear before engaging your mouth.

Conversation is as close as most Modern Men get to dancing the ballet. A well-mannered discussion is a masterpiece of improvised, exquisite choreography in which each participant is allowed a turn. Polite conversation is not the verbal equivalent to arm-wrestling; a Modern Man does not seek to turn a conversation into a competition. After all, almost any conversation can be dominated by whoever has the loudest voice.

Do	*Don't*
Bring people out by asking for advice or by gracefully fishing for a topic of mutual interest or by asking your partner about himself.	Abuse the first person singular pronoun or talk ceaselessly about yourself.
Look your partner in conversation directly in the eye.	Discuss your problems or misfortunes (except with close friends — and even then in private).
Listen as well as speak.	Boast.

Do	*Don't*
Talk in turn. Don't dominate the conversation.	Inquire about money matters — especially about specific amounts for specific items.
Credit the source of ideas.	Make critical or insulting remarks to anyone present or behind any mutual acquaintance's back.
Relax and be natural. Don't be overly concerned about controversial opinions, grammar, vocabulary, pronunciation, accent or profanity.	Whisper to one person in a group.
Keep prejudice and bitterness out of an argument.	Seek desperately to fill in every moment of silence in a conversation. Let a conversation develop a pace of its own. Don't force it.
Give compliments privately.	
Respond forthrightly when receiving a compliment,. Simply say thank you, and never belittle the compliment.	Finish the sentences for someone else who's telling a story. Also avoid correcting details of the narrative, interrupting or trying to complete the tale and attempting to correct grammar or syntax.

So much for the basics.

SPECIFICS

Many of the specific rules that constitute courteous behavior are quite situational — stuff that comes up once in a blue moon. Others are more frequently encountered.

We chose to start where, in our own personal histories, manners were born —

AT THE TABLE

We assume your mom taught you how to eat. But the world of table manners is a big, hazy planet and most men, no matter how Modern, have not yet explored all the terrain. Etiquette as part of Real World Navigation and Exploration is a bit different, that's all. So if you encounter the unexpected, here's all you need to know about polite eating in three words: be *neat, quiet* and *discreet.*

Honestly, most of this stuff is common sense. A table is the physical world where all gaffes live. We figure if you know the landmarks, you'll be able to find your way around.

The napkin:

Do	Don't
Place it on your lap when you sit down.	Attatch it to your neck.
Place it on your chair when you leave the table.	Leave it on the table.
Place it to the left of your place when you've finished.	Use it to clean the silverware or china.
Use it to discreetly remove food from your mouth.	
Use it to "blot" your mouth, not rub at it.	

The silverware:

Do	Don't
Work from the outside in. Use the outermost utensil for the first thing brought to you, then use them up until there's nothing left..	Use it as a pointer during conversation.
Place the knife and fork (or whatever utensil is appropriate) together at a 45° angle when not in use. (In Europe, this also signifies to the help that you've finished the course and that the plate may be removed.)	Clatter the stuff while you're eating.
	Use your knife as a saw.
	Put dirty silver on the tablecloth.
	Use utensils to eat food that would more neatly be eaten using your fingers (see *Tricky Food* in *MODERN MEALS*).
Use the silverware to bring food to your mouth; don't hunker over your plate. Sit up, boy.	Use the stuff like construction tools.
Use a knife to cut your salad. This was once an error; now it's okay.	Use your soup spoon like a little cup. Eat from it, don't drink from it.
Use your soup spoon by moving it away from you while filling it with soup.	

A note on silverware: Americans use a crisscross eating system in which (for right-handed people) the knife is held in the right hand when the food is being cut; after a bite has been cut, the knife is set down and the fork, which had been used in the left hand to hold the morsel of food while it was being cut, is transferred to the right hand; the piece of cut food is then placed on the fork and eaten. Everyplace else in the world (or at least that part of it where people use silverware), the fork remains in the left hand, tines down, while the knife is used to both cut and push food onto the fork. While both are correct, the "foreign" method is quickly gaining acceptance among Americans who find it both easier and more efficient. It's certainly more elegant.

Your mouth:

Do	Don't
Chew your food throughly; swallow before taking another bite.	Talk, chew or drink with the thing full of food.
Wipe it off before drinking.	Stick your fingers in there to suck on them.
	Use to gnaw on bones, slurp soup or announce that you are "full."
	Belch through it.
	Blow through it to cool your food.

Your hands and arms:

Do	Don't
Place your elbows on the table when you *aren't* eating, if you so choose.	Eat with your left arm around the plate.
Eat with your fingers if using silverware would be messier.	Stick your pinky in the air when drinking from a teacup.
	Pick your teeth with your fingers
	Eat with your elbows flapping
	Use your finger (or a piece of bread) to push goop onto your fork.

Your chair:

Do	Don't
Lift your chair a bit when pushing it away so it doesn't scrape across the floor.	Lean back in your chair so that the front legs are off the floor.
Hold the chair of the woman to your immediate right.	

Note: The host and hostess sit at opposite ends of the table. The female guest of honor sits on the host's right; the male guest of honor sits on the hostess's right.

The crackers and bread:

Do	Don't
Put crackers into your soup unbroken.	Use your bread as a mop for getting all the gravy. If you want to sop up some gravy or sauce, place a small piece of bread on your plate, then eat it with your knife and fork.
Break bread into pieces before buttering	

The plates and serving dishes:

Do	Don't
Use your bread plate for bread and butter, relishes, celery, olives and so on	Push your plate away when you've finished eating.
When serving, pass plates counter-clockwise.	Reach in front of another diner to get something. Ask that it be passed.
Tilt your soup bowl away from you if you're trying to get the last drop, not toward you.	

Your nose:

Do	Don't
	Touch it. And don't stick it in the food so you can take a good sniff.
	Blow it on the napkin.

Salt and pepper:

Do	Don't
	Sprinkle it on your food until after you've tasted it.

Women:

Do	Don't
Wait until the hostess and most other women begin eating before you dig in.	
Talk to the one on your right. Then talk to the one on the other side.	

UPMARKET MANNERS

At *formal dinners,* everyday manners go to the moon. The elaborate ritual outlined below (in roughly the order in which these things might occur) is museum-quality stuff.

The servants: Be polite and cheery, but try to keep your exchanges brief.

Envelope, please: A servant will offer you an envelope. In the envelope is a card, and on the card is the name of the woman selected to be your dinner partner.

Before dinner, your host or hostess will introduce you to your partner. If they don't, it won't matter much; she'll be the woman sitting on your right. If you spot her before the host has a chance to introduce you, feel free to introduce yourself.

If you're served a drink before dinner, down it before you go into the dining room.

When dinner is announced, offer your partner your right arm and follow the host and hostess in to the table.

The butler may give you a clue where you're supposed to sit. Listen for the one-word hint: "Right." Or "left."

Hold your partner's chair, which will almost invariably be the one to your right (this varies sometimes, but you'll figure it out). Seat your partner right away, but remain standing until the other women have been seated.

On your feet: Never sit down before the hostess and most of the other women have also been seated.

Once you sit down, put your place card above your plate, your napkin in your lap and start yakking to your partner.

Watch the hostess. She sets the pace for the party. She will be talking to the person on her right, but at some point she will switch and start talking to the man on her left. When this happens, you must do likewise. It's sort of like a square dance or something; if you don't turn to face a new partner, you're going to make a mess. Wind up your conversation as quickly as possible, then turn to the woman on your left and chatter. This is called "turning the table."

Service: You will probably be served on your left by a footman (or a substitute). Take the serving spoon provided in your right hand and the forklike tool in your left. Put the spoon under the food and the fork over it and transfer it to your plate. Keep talking to your companion — and don't acknowledge the server. (He knows the rules; if the tables were turned, he'd treat you like a damn servant, too.)

Dessert may appear with a fork and spoon on the plate. Put them to one side.

A finger bowl may accompany the fruit bowl. Place the finger bowl (and the doily that came with it) above your plate and slightly to the left. Transfer the silverware that came with the fruit to a position on either side of the plate. When you use the finger bowl, do so unobtrusively — and don't splash.

You may decline a dish or glass of wine by passing a discreet word to the server.

Dinner's over when the hostess rises. Stand and hold your partner's chair. Watch the host; he'll tip you as to whether or not to escort your partner to another room or to remain standing in the dining room until the women leave, at which time you will be expected to join the other men.

Get out: Unless the hostess indicates otherwise, you're expected to leave within a half-hour after dinner.

What not to do: Don't smoke. Don't ask for seconds. Don't pass a dish or plate. Don't ask for a bread dish.

Odd bits: There may be no *bread plate;* you'll be expected to place your bread on the tablecloth.

Salt might be placed in a neat pile on the tablecloth to pinch and add to your food.

Clean up your plate. It's good form; don't leave little pieces of food.

If the dinner party is quite large, you don't have to wait for the hostess to begin eating before you do.

This might sound insipid, but the most important rule of good manners in these situations (or indeed in most situations) is a simple one: relax. You can make the biggest social goof in history, but if you do it with charm and with obvious consideration of those around you, it will be seen as a social triumph.

For formal wear tips, **see also** *Formal Wear* **in** *CHAPTER ELEVEN: MODERN CLOSETS.*

DINNER AT HOME

At the other extreme are the small dinners to which you may be more frequently invited. These informal affairs are usually held at the home of the host and hostess; although the routine of the event is less liturgical, the more casual social obligations are far more pronounced.

- *Don't yak* to the host and hostess if they are busy in the kitchen (unless invited to do so, of course).
- *At dinner, talk* to the diners seated on either side of you.

- *No shoptalk.*
- *Don't talk about yourself.*
- *Don't ask for seconds,* although you may accept a second helping if it's offered.
- *If you must refuse* certain foods or drink, mention it to the hostess quietly before dinner; if served, say simply "No, thank you."
- *Keep your napkin* in your lap and don't put it on the table until the hostess (or host) does.
- *Offer to help* with the dishes and with cleanup — but don't insist.
- *When it's time to go,* simply thank your host and hostess and leave without loitering around the door.

If you're the guest of honor at dinner, you'll sit at the hostess's right. Traditionally, you will be the first to leave the party, although that obligation is slowly falling by the wayside.

From a guest's point of view, the easiest social functions to attend are the ones that don't involve feeding. Compared to the stresses of a formal dinner, a stand-up, get-drunk, talk-to-your-enemies cocktail party is a snap.

See *Conversational Etiquette* **and** *Table Manners,* **above.**

AT A COCKTAIL PARTY

- *Don't request* goofy specialty drinks.
- *Offer to help* the host or hostess, especially if the gathering is a large one.
- *Don't get drunk.* At least, don't get so drunk that you will cause alarm or concern to your host or hostess.
- *Easy out:* Be sensitive to the mood of the party. When you think it's time to leave, simply thank your host and go. Don't loiter.

Modern Men at dinner, like Modern Men at drinks, work hard to see that every social event goes smoothly. An attentive guest is concerned for the success of his host. But it's not easy, and after a serious tour of other people's dining rooms, you may want to stay home with a Big Mac & Brew and chat politely with the TV. (**See also** *LIQUOR* **in** *CHAPTER EIGHTEEN: MODERN MISBEHAVIOR.*)

However, if you think the rigors of *attending* dinner and cocktail parties are substantial, imagine how burdensome are

THE DUTIES OF A HOST ENTERTAINING AT HOME

In the order of likely occurrence when entertaining at home:

1. Greet your guests. See that their coats and wraps are taken care of and that they feel welcome.

2. If there is no hostess, the host will be responsible for organizing the servants, if any, and for ensuring that during the dinner, he will have nothing to do except play host.

In the absence of a hostess, he will also be called on to *make and serve predinner cocktails, announce the seating for dinner* and *decide on the seating arrangement.*

3. At the table, the host must carve the meat (this also can be done beforehand), serve the guest of honor, make certain all glasses are refilled and, to signal the end of the meal, place his napkin on the table.

Informal buffet dinners are the easiest to host because of the do-it-yourself nature of the event. At a buffet, the host's only jobs involve seating the guests, keeping the conversation going and topping up the glasses.

THE DUTIES OF A HOST AT A COCKTAIL PARTY

1. If there is no hostess, the host must organize the help, if any, and ensure that the drinks, mixers, glasses, hors d'oeuvres, cocktail napkins (plain white ones, without golfing and sex jokes on them) and coasters are all ready. *During the party, the host should have nothing else to do except entertain his guests (see number three below).*

2. Welcome the guests. Take their coats and wraps and direct them into the party.

3. Serve drinks and run the bar. This can be part of the guests' entertainment.

4. Make introductions. Involve the wallflowers; chat a little with everyone present. Stay alert, appear relaxed, be tireless. Watch for drunks; if a guest appears to be drinking too much and losing control, intervene immediately. As the host, you are the authority figure — and besides, a rampant drunk will destroy a good party unless he does something truly scandalous.

5. Offer coffee to signal the approach of the end of the party. *Make every effort to convince anyone who's had too much to drink not to drive.* Offer, if necessary, to pay for taxis or organize rides for them with other, more sober guests.

6. Say good night to every departing guest.

See also *Introductions,* **above,** *The Drunk Driver* **in** *CHAPTER FIVE: MODERN MOBILITY* **and** *LIQUOR* **in** *CHAPTER EIGHTEEN: MODERN MISBEHAVIOR.*

THEATER PROTOCOL

When escorting a woman to a play or film, here's the proper form:

What You Do	*While She*
You wait in line for tickets.	She waits in the lobby.
You hold open the door to the auditorium, then escort her to an usher. She follows the usher; you follow her.	She leads through the auditorium door, then waits for you to escort her to an usher. She follows the usher; you follow her.
You sit in the chair nearer the aisle.	She sits in the chair farther from the aisle.
You make sure her view is not obstructed. If it is, you must make the necessary adjustments.	She will tell you if she can't see the stage or screen.

At intermission, you must not leave her alone in the lobby. If you go to the washroom, you must first escort her back to her seat. If she goes to the washroom, you must wait for her in the lobby.	At intermission, she joins you in the lobby for refreshments or a cigarette.
If the show is bad, it's up to you to suggest an early departure.	If the show is bad, she will wait for your cue to leave early.

Theater courtesies: Here are a few sensible rules governing theater attendance:
- *If you arrive late,* wait in the back of the theater and take your seat between the first and second acts, or during a chorus or a prolonged round of applause.
- *No hats.* This goes for women as well as men.
- *No talking* during the performance.
- *No photography,* especially if you are using a flash.

*A **theater party host** has a number of added responsibilities:
- *Tickets.* The host must arrange for advance purchase of tickets.
- *The guests pass* the ticket-taker first, followed by the host.
- *Allow the women* to precede the host down the aisle.
- *The host sits on the aisle.*
- *At the end of the performance,* the host stands in the aisle, waits for his date, then escorts his party out of the theater.
- *Dinner:* The host should have prearranged dinner at his chosen restaurant for a pretheater dinner. He should also have made arrangements for after-theater drinks at the same or another establishment.
- *Black tie* is required only at the request of the host or hostess on the opening night of the performance.

POST-THEATER RESTAURANT ETIQUETTE
If you're entertaining guests at a restaurant:
- *Select the restaurant* and book the table in advance.
- *Wait at the bar* or at another designated area for your guests to assemble before going to the table.
- *Precede* your guests to the table and assign them seats.
- *You may wish to pre-order the meal.* Often guests enjoy being relieved of this responsibility, but be careful of visiting vegetarians and the like. The alternative is to find out each individual's preference, then order for everyone.
- *Pay up.* If you're the host, pay the check. to avoid an awkward, but well-intentioned dispute, leave the table and settle the bill in another part of the restaurant.

RECIPES AND RESTAURANTS

Restaurant recipes, perhaps not surprisingly, are often quick and simple.

If you enjoy a dish at a restaurant, ask to see the cook, compliment him, and ask how he made your dish. Occasionally, chefs are uncooperative, but a large number of them will be glad to share the secret of their success — although sometimes they'll leave out an important, though not crucial ingredient in order to protect their culinary invention. You've got nothing to lose by asking. (AR)

A dissent: Please do not ask for the recipe for dishes you enjoy at a restaurant. The recipes a chef uses are his stock in trade, his livelihood. Asking for them is rather like asking for permission to shoplift. (KHG)

See also *RESTAURANTS* **in** *CHAPTER EIGHTEEN: MODERN MISBEHAVIOR.*

SMOKING ETIQUETTE

When not to smoke: Near a "no smoking" sign; in church or at religious ceremonies, including funerals and weddings; anyone's home or office if you see no ashtrays; in theaters; at formal dinners; in hospitals or sick rooms; when dancing; on city transit vehicles; in stores and supermarkets; in someone else's automobile; in a restaurant, unless you first ask permission of those seated next to you. If you aren't sure, ask.

Light the cigarette of your female companion. When lighting up, light hers first if you're using a lighter, yours first if you're using a match (to spare her the sulfurous taste). If you are with more than one woman, go in order of proximity. Never light more than two cigarettes on the same strike of a lighter or on the same match.

Cigars: Don't smoke a cigar in any public area or room.

When a guest: Extinguish cigarettes in ashtrays only, and make sure they're completely out.

Don't carry a lit cigarette to a dining table.

See also *TOBACCO* **in** *CHAPTER EIGHTEEN: MODERN MISBEHAVIOR.*

SENDING INVITATIONS

Don't waste your time and energy trying to make your invitations cute when it's the gathering itself that needs your attention. Instead, make sure your invites bear the following information:

- *Names* of the host and hostess.
- *Address* of the gathering. The postal code isn't necessary.
- *The date* and time of the event, as well as the reason for it.
- *Activities,* including things like cocktails, dancing, dinner and so on.
- *An r.s.v.p.,* although that's optional (**see below under** *Responding to Invitations*). If the r.s.v.p. is supposed to be sent by post or to a different address, be sure to indicate the proper postal code.
- *Dress code.* This is optional and should only appear if the gathering is formal. The only choices are for black tie or white tie.

- *Misleading terms* like "black tie optional," "semiformal," "dressy" or "casually elegant" are meaningless and should never be used. If you want people to dress formally, say so. If you don't care, then don't say anything. As for formal day clothes, the likelihood of your conducting or attending an event requiring their use is rare. Such clothing is appropriate for members of a formal wedding party, pallbearers at a funeral or guests at a formal diplomatic reception.

A *good printer* will have samples of formal invitations, along with paper and type samples. Follow the standard form for invitations unless you have a compelling reason to break with precedence.

Visiting cards, those seemingly useless things that carry only your name (and occasionally a street address) are often used for informal invitations. The information about time, place, date and reason are handwritten on the card. A charming old-fashioned touch is to strike a line through your name and sign your first name below the line.

See also *STATIONERY* **in** *CHAPTER NINETEEN: MODERN MISCELLANY*.

RESPONDING TO INVITATIONS

R.s.v.p.: R.s.v.p. stands for *répondez, s'il vous plaît,* which is the way Frenchmen ask each other to let them know if they're really going to show up at each other's *fêtes.* Sometimes, the more appropriate "Please reply" is used, but either way, the rules are the same: You must promptly notify the sender whether or not you plan to attend. *Not responding is not the same as sending your regrets.* You must say so if you cannot attend; not to reply is inexcusably rude.

If you decide to accept an invitation, you *must* go. That's all there is to it. No last-minute dodges and no lame excuses. The rule in the world of party invites is like the one in the world of work and wife: Always do what you say you're going to do.

Form of a response: The proper form for a reply to a formal invitation is in handwriting. Repeat the salient portion of the invitation and send it off. Here's an example:

The invitation reads:

> Mr. and Mrs. Smith
> request the honor of your presence
> at the marriage of their daughter
> Chastity Hope
> to
> Mr. Modern Jones
> on Saturday, the Fifteenth of June
> at three o'clock
> Saint Alonzo Martyr Church
> and afterward at the reception
> 311 Maiden Lane
> R.s.v.p. Baltimore, Maryland

your acceptance:

> Mr. Modern Johnson accepts with pleasure the kind invitation of Mr. and Mrs. Smith to the marriage of their daughter Chastity Hope to Mr. Modern Jones on Saturday, the fifteenth of June at three o'clock Saint Alonzo Martyr Church and afterwards at the reception 311 Maiden Lane

your regrets:

> Mr. Modern Johnson regrets that owing to (insert excuse here) he is unable to accept the kind invitation of Mr. and Mrs. Smith to the marriage of their daughter Chastity Hope to Mr. Modern Jones on Saturday, the fifteenth of June and to the reception afterwards

Another use for those name-only visiting cards is sending informal replies to invitations. Send your brief handwritten reply on the calling card; again, the traditional form is to strike out the printed name and insert a first name signature below the line.

HOUSEGUEST RULES

The houseguest is an invited invader, a person in whom a tremendous amount of trust has been placed. If you are invited as a houseguest, remember that your invitation extends only to the premises; you have a concurrent responsibility to protect the privacy of your host. The best houseguest is a flexible one, ready for anything. The rules governing behavior here are commonsensical:

- *Arrive* when you say you will.
- *Bring* a small gift for your hostess. Don't get carried away, here. Flowers or chocolates will do, or a bottle of wine.
- *Never bring uninvited guests.* This means no surprise kids, girlfriends or pets.
- *Be adaptable* to the habits of your host and his household. If everyone seems to rush the showers in the morning, for example, lay low and stay out of the traffic. Take your shower last or at night before retiring.
- *Self-amusement:* Don't tag around after your host expecting him to offer you constant amusement. Entertain yourself and allow your host some privacy.
- *Offer* to take your host and hostess out to dinner.
- *Clean and tidy:* Don't make a mess; don't leave a trail of household chores in your wake.
- *Replace* or arrange for the repair of anything you might break or damage. Don't offer cash as a replacement.
- *Telephone:* The most considerate way to handle long distance calls is to charge them to your number. If that's impossible for some reason, pay promptly for any phone charges.
- *Duck* any domestic disputes. If called on, offer sympathy, but not advice. *Never take sides.*
- *Leave* as planned; don't overstay your welcome.
- *Send flowers* or a thank you note when you get home.

See also *Guest Room in Heaven* **in** *CHAPTER TWELVE: MODERN MANORS,* **and** *Gifts,* **below.**

ETIQUETTE IN MOTION

Public transport: Progress is riding shotgun on the nation's subways and buses, so Modern Men are not absolutely required to jump to their feet the moment a public conveyance is filled in order to afford a woman a seat. *They are however urged to do so.* Giving up your seat to a woman is an act of grace and social faith, subject to ridicule, maybe, but always worth the risk. (**See also** *COURTLY MANNERS* **at the beginning of this chapter.**)

Modern and other Men should however *always* relinquish their seat to those more in need, namely:

- *Pregnant women*
- *The elderly*
- *Invalids*
- *People obviously ill or enfeebled*
- *Mothers carrying infants or tending their children*
- *Anyone with a lot of baggage or wrestling with a large parcel*

(**See also** *When to Stand,* **above.**)

Conversation with strangers on intracity public transport should be avoided, since the wrong word could get you shot in this country. On intercity trains and coaches, some polite conversation is permissible. On an airplane, be careful: If the person seated next to you seems to not want conversation, don't force it on him. If he tries to collar you in a coast-to-coast chat and you don't want to talk, mumble a perfunctory response and immediately start to read or pretend to fall asleep. On cruise ships, cheerful chatter is a major preoccupation and everyone is expected to participate. (**See also** *Conversational Etiquette,* **above.**)

At the airport: Don't expect your host to pick you up or drop you off at an airport. Airports are built for airplanes, not for cars, and even the briefest visit to one is a dreadful inconvenience to a motorist. Among all public places, airports are best served by public transportation. Have your host pick you up at a convenient spot near his home or office.

Tip a porter at least a dollar a bag. Most baggage handlers are paid the minimum wage to bust their backs; the quarter-a-bag rule went out with Ike.

Foreign tips: In the literal sense, that is. Remember to tip theater ushers (approximately 10 percent of the single ticket price) and the ladies that guard the urinals. More figuratively speaking, here are other foreign hints:

Do not demean foreign customs or traditions. Never make a value judgment on a foreign custom; to do so is to reveal an enormous reservoir of provincialism.

Do not compare foreign values, sights, buildings, institutions or anything else with their American counterparts.

Learn the language: Not the whole thing, of course. But if you can pick up the words for "wonderful," "beautiful" and "pleasant" — in addition to the usual thanks, hello and goodbye stuff — you'll gain points galore.

In hotels: There is a class distinction in hotels. If you're checking into a cut-rate, roadside motel, don't ask for service; as a rule, there isn't any. The guy running the motel is also running a family in a small room behind the desk and your dinner desires are not interesting to him. At larger establishments, however:

- *Tip the room service waiter* by adding on to the total or in cash when you sign your food bill on delivery. Don't add on a gob of money for room service when you check out.
- *Place the cart* with the dirty dishes on it in the hall when you're finished eating.

- *Tip the maid* by leaving her some cash when you check out of your room. Five percent of the total bill is adequate.
- *The desk clerk,* once one of the rare untippables at a hotel, can now be given a gratuity for any special favors, especially if they involve room placement and the like. In foreign hotels, the concierge is the guy to see to arrange special stuff. Tip him or die.
- *Do not be intimidated.* The job of a good hotel is to cater to the conventional desires of its guests. Checking into a good hotel is like moving into a house already equipped with hot and cold running servants. If the man who does the shoes doesn't do a good job, say so. A polite but firm insistence that people meet minimum standards of competency is always in good form. By and large, most hotel staffers are more competent at their jobs than most politicians or journalists are.

WHY FOREIGNERS ARE RUDE TO YANKEES

Don't attract attention to yourself or confirm foreign prejudice against Americans by indulging in public drunkenness, vulgar behavior or loud conversation. It is important to always remember that in Europe especially Americans are despised. This attitude is not only the result of example, of course; the new empire is cultural not political and as Americanization, now a global phenomenon, continues to gain ascendancy, nationalism will continue to find a release in the form of irrational xenophobia. At the beginning of this century, the British were everyone's favorite targets, and the Japanese are next, so don't take it personally.

The term "American gentleman" is not an oxymoronic pun, but rather a phrase referring to one whose behavior falls somewhere between Fred Allen's dictum that a gentleman wearing a hat should never hit a woman and the demands of the spinster who ran his high school library.

If an American man needs grand models for his conduct, he can find them in Washington's sense of sacrifice, Jefferson's intellect, Lincoln's geniality, Theodore Roosevelt's manliness, Kennedy's poise and Carter's compassion. But the most appropriate qualities can be found in the national character itself: Only a typical American can combine heartiness, openness, honesty and generosity.

The existence of these virtues should come as a relief to the American man who has the persistent impression that the word "gentleman" itself implies something foreign, that a true gentleman should ape either British formality, German precision or Gallic ostentation — all fine qualities, but all slightly inappropriate to proper conduct, anyway.

An American gentleman embodies the five qualities outlined by Emmett John Hughes: A gentleman is first a man; second, a useful man; third, one who respects women; fourth, one who respects other men; and fifth one who is himself and does not affect being a gentleman. (*Anon.*)

TELEPHONE ETIQUETTE

The telephone is the modern replacement for thoughtful communication. Because of the transient, one-dimensional nature of telephone conversations, considerate behavior often gets lost someplace along the line.

The same rules of etiquette apply whether you're dealing with somebody in person or on the telephone. Don't assume that because it's easier to be rude to someone on the phone (or by not returning their calls) you aren't seen as an asshole. If you have bad phone manners, you're a jerk, that's all.

Turn it off: Don't have the TV or radio blasting away when you're trying to talk. It sounds unprofessional — and it's very confusing.

If you are disconnected, it's the responsibility of the caller to call back.

Don't take calls if you have a visitor in your office, unless it's an emergency. If you're in someone's office when a call comes through, give the person some privacy. Either get up and wander out to the hall or pick up a magazine and at least *pretend* to read. If the call seems emotional or personal, leave the office at once.

Don't enter someone's office if he's on the telephone.

Identify yourself as soon as the party you're calling answers the phone. If you're at the office on the answering end, identify yourself *and* the company when you answer. Even if you're calling Mom, have the courtesy to identify yourself to your caller. Never assume that you are as important as a nameless caller should be.

Shouting on the phone only causes distortion. If the connection's bad, dial again.

Don't dial a number, then ask the person who picks up the receiver to identify himself before you do. It is considered good sense to simply hang up the telephone on a caller who asks you to identify yourself before he tells you who he is.

If your call is coming through your secretary, the first thing you should tell your caller is that you appreciate his waiting.

When answering, asking the name of the caller is not impolite. If you're the caller, never assume that the person you are calling has nothing else going on in his life except your phone call.

It's the responsibility of the caller to end a telephone conversation.

When saying goodbye, wait for the return goodbye before hanging up.

See also *Business Calls* **in** *CHAPTER TWO: MODERN MAN AT WORK* **and** *Phone Contact* **under** *CHAPTER SEVEN: MODERN MATING.*

GIFTS

are tricky things. Too often gifts come wrapped in fancy obligation with guilt trim. Always bear in mind that the giving of a gift is a simple gesture; don't make it a complicated one.

If asked what you want for a gift (for Christmas or a birthday, for example), offer a suggestion by broadly indicating your hobbies and interests. Do not suggest a specific item, unless it comes up in conversation with a family member.

Ostentatious gifts are rude.

Joint gifts are fine. Two or more givers can pool to give a gift for a wedding, birthday, retirement or as a special token to a co-worker. You can also put together a gift pool to give a family a Christmas gift.

Include whatever paperwork the recipient needs to be able to return the gift.

Be polite and enthusiastic about a gift you receive, no matter what your private thoughts may be.

When gifts are appropriate: There are certain occasions when giving a gift is expected or at least appropriate.

- *On engagement announcements,* but only from close friends or family.
- *Wedding gifts:* The best thing to do is have the gift sent to the bride's home before the wedding, but bring it along to the reception if there's no other way. Gifts may be sent to the couple up to a year after the ceremony.
- *Second marriages:* Always assume that somebody is getting married forever, even if it's the seventh time around. Previously, gifts for those marrying for the second time did not need to have the notion of permanence that attached itself to gifts for those marrying for the first time. Liquor, food, tickets were all acceptable. Continued observance of this triviality may be acceptable (the reasoning is that the couple already owns four of everything from previous marriages), but it's difficult to endorse.
- *From the groom* to his ushers at a wedding. Small, personal items are appropriate.
- *Between the bride and groom:* The exchange of gifts between bride and groom is a lovely tradition that has almost vanished. That's too bad. The appropriate time for the exchange of these gifts is after the reception and in private or the presence of the immediate family or members of the wedding party.
- *Anniversaries, or when attending an anniversary party.*
- *Housewarmings:* These gifts should be expensive and permanent.
- *On christenings* and to celebrate the arrival of a new baby.
- *Birthdays,* of course, and
- *Graduation.*
- *Houseguest:* Give a gift when you're a weekend houseguest. Flowers, food, a book or a bottle of wine or spirits will do.

When to send flowers: Send flowers anytime a woman's involved and you're confused about what to do. Otherwise:

- *To accompany* a thank you note.
- *To a hostess* who has put you up for the weekend.
- *Before or after* a date. Traditionally, you should take a corsage, if you're giving flowers before a date, or you can take cut flowers. If you're sending them later, send roses. Really, it doesn't matter. Just send or bring flowers, then send or bring more. If you haven't the knack for romance, a handful of posies can work wonders for you. It is almost impossible to give flowers gracelessly.

- *Beforehand* to the hostess of a dinner party where you are the guest of honor.
- *To women in shops,* stores or other places if they have done you a special favor or provided outstanding service.
- *To sick people.* Tell the florist; he'll know what to do. Potted plants are preferable.
- *To funerals:* Send them to the funeral home or church. Do not send flowers to an orthodox Jewish funeral; only the immediate family sends flowers to the church for a Catholic ceremony.
- *For friends' anniversaries,* if you're a close friend.

Do not send flowers to a memorial service.

Gifts at a dinner party: Don't show up with food, unless you've first discussed it with the hostess. Wine is good, though; one bottle is enough. The host has the option of saving it for later or serving it. Don't bring gifts to formal dinners.

Business gifts: This is gift-giving at its most odious. Clients get gifts and don't give them. Suppliers seek to bribe buyers. It's terrible. Here's how it's done:

- *Make it impersonal.* Make it commensurate with the occasion. It's always best if the gift is given as a gesture of appreciation for a past favor or after a successful transaction, but it usually isn't. Usually, it's a bribe. That's the occasion.
- *Don't neglect the secretary* of the person or company to whom you're giving a gift. This is especially important if she has had to put up with your outrageous requests.
- *Around the office:* Don't give gifts to someone in a higher position than yours. If you're socially involved, exchange gifts outside the office. Give a gift to your secretary, but don't make it work-related or obnoxiously personal.

Postmen, doormen and others who provide year-long service should be remembered at Christmas with a simple card and a suitable tip.

SAY THANK YOU

The form of a thank you note is less important than the *fact* of one. The rule is to send one to whoever has done you a good turn, especially:

- *After you've been a houseguest.* The note should be addressed to the lady of the house.
- *After you've received a gift* from someone or such expressions of their goodwill as sympathy or congratulations. Handwritten sentiments should be answered in kind and never by means of a preprinted card.
- *In response* to being granted a business or professional favor. Such correspondence should be in the form of a typed business letter.

SPORTS ETIQUETTE

Play it as it lays.

THE RULES

Learn the rules of any game in which you participate and abide by them until invited to do otherwise. Never propose changing the rules of a game if it seems it will benefit you.

At a spectator sporting event, never intrude on others around you. Don't lean forward and shout in somebody's ear and don't drink so much you spill beer all over your neighbors. If you can't control yourself at a sporting event, don't go.

If the vicitm of a cheat, don't make a fuss. Simply leave the game and scout for another, less vulgar game.

At game's end: A loser should compliment the winner on his skill, while the winner should console the loser for his lack of luck. Never ask, Who won?, rather, Did you have a good game?

Underplaying in an effort to equalize a game — or out of sympathy for a poor player — must be kept absolutely secret. Both winner and loser should be able to maintain that they played their best games.

Pay up: Even if it means walking home naked, pay your gambling debts *on the spot* and without fuss. A bet is an agreement that must be honored.

POKER PLEASURE

Poker is perhaps the most masculine of all card games, one that most women seem to avoid. Unlike most sports, which may be played without consideration of gambling, there is no other way to play poker — and certainly no other reason to.

If you've lost more than you have, go ahead and write a bad check. Then stay up all night or until you figure out a way to cover it. Never welsh on a poker debt.

Deceit: Despite the fact that the most deceitful poker player is often the best poker player, certain rules of etiquette do apply:

- *Don't play out of turn.* As Hoyle says, "A player must pass, bet, raise or fold only when it is his turn to do so." To do otherwise is to tip your hand, a gross gaffe.
- *Pay attention:* Don't daydream. If you don't know what the bet is when your turn comes, you have no business playing.
- *Never lie.* Bluffing, of course, is part of poker. But verbalizing a lie is unfair.
- *Don't sandbag.*
- *Don't freeload.* If the game is held regularly at the home of one player, make sure you do your share by bringing food, drinks and so on, or by adding to the kitty.
- *Be quiet.* Don't sit around the table chatting with other players while play is in progress.
- *Take the trouble* to understand house rules before you play. If you are a visitor or a new player to a well-established game, it's impolite to ask for rule changes.

SAILING

The rules of etiquette surrounding sailing have a double purpose — first, to support the primacy of the captain and second to ensure the welfare of the craft.

Getting aboard: Always wear *soft rubber-soled shoes* on a boat; never go aboard a boat or small ship wearing leather- or hard rubber-soled shoes.

Get permission from the captain before going aboard any vessel.

Watch your step: The procedures for boarding some vessels in some circumstances may not be strictly logical.

On board: The captain is the absolute master of his vessel. Boats and ships are not democratic places; there is a tyrant on board and *everything* he orders or requests that deals with the operation of the boat or ship must be strictly and promptly obeyed.

Keep your belongings *stowed and tidy.* Space aboard most boats is at a premium.

Never alter the arrangement of the ship's equipment unless asked to do so by the captain or his mate.

Clean up any spills for which you are responsible. Don't hang wet towels or swimming costumes on the rails or in the rigging.

Always offer to help with a day's chores. Be prepared to have your offer accepted.

Smoking: On a sailboat, be especially careful if you smoke. Never light up when furling the sails. Watch your ashes; don't let the wind blow them into someone's face.

The watery deep: Although obvious, remember that the worst offense on a ship or boat once it's under way is to fall overboard. *Be careful and wear nonslip footwear.*

When *swimming off a boat,* swim against the current.

SHOOTING

This isn't concerned with etiquette as much as it is with safety.

The main thing is to consider every gun or rifle to be a loaded gun or rifle.

Carrying a weapon: When transporting a firearm, it must be unloaded (of course) and either taken down or packed with the action open in a case.

If the gun is loaded, carry it in such a way that you will always have control of the direction the muzzle is pointing. Leave the safety in the on position until just before it's time to fire.

Don't fire until you're sure of your target, and never point your firearm at anything unless you intend to shoot it.

When hunting: Have some consideration for others in your party. Don't smoke upwind of your prey, and keep quiet and still when stalking. Shoot in turn or only in your assigned area. Don't try to control or command dogs belonging to another hunter.

Three don'ts: One: Don't kill more than your limit. Two: Don't kill females (and it's dreadful form to kill a pregnant female). Three: Hunting dumb animals with high-powered weapons is easy enough. Don't further tip the balance in your favor by making easy kills such as sitting ducks or birds on landing.

And a fourth: Don't kill the dog.

If you wound an animal, you are duty-bound to go to *any length* to find it and finish it off. This is an ironclad rule, a no-matter-what rule.

FRESH-WATER FISHING

Don't take more than a few fish per day — especially trout. Acid rain and some kill-crazy trout fishermen are severely depleting stocks of trout. Most fishermen value conservation efforts.

Fly fishermen are snobs in funny boots. Avoid them if your intention is to fish for a small catch or relaxation. If, for some implausible reason, you find it necessary to join a group of fly fishermen, *don't use a worm* for bait. To fly fishermen, the use of a worm is a violation of stellar magnitude and will gain you naught but their enmity.

Give a fellow fisherman a seventy-five-foot-radius circle in which to try his luck. Don't encroach on his territory. In fact, the best move is to avoid fishing within sight of another fisherman.

Get permission to fish in private ponds.

Never ask to borrow another fisherman's rod.

See *Fishing* in *CHAPTER ONE: OUTDOORS.*

TENNIS

First serve: Decide who's first by flipping a racket. Call "rough" or "smooth" to determine the winner, who receives his choice of *either* service or court.

Switch courts on each odd-numbered game (third, fifth and so on).

Don't return balls served to you that go out of bounds.

Avoid shouting. Tennis is a quiet game. Especially dodge the boorish habit of yelling decisions regarding an opponent's shot (such as "Good!" or "Out!").

Don't call the score after every point.

Finish a singles game before starting doubles.

See also *Tennis* in *CHAPTER EIGHTEEN: MODERN MISBEHAVIOR.*

GOLF

The two most important rules are to avoid damaging the course and to avoid impeding the progress of the game.

Don'ts:

• *Don't play* until the players playing in front of you have left the area.
• *Don't raise your voice.*
• *Don't grant* certain unplayed putts to yourself.
• *Don't keep asking* everyone's score. Try to keep an approximate mental record.
• *Don't give advice* unless asked.

Tip caddies and the locker room attendant, but *not* the pros or the caddie masters.

See *SPORTS* in *CHAPTER EIGHTEEN: MODERN MISBEHAVIOR.*

Contributors to **THE DEPORTMENT DEPARTMENT** and **SPORTS ETIQUETTE:** ACT, AR, AW, BDa, BN, BPy, CCP, DA, DB, DO, DW, GFr, HGF, JD, KER, KH, LHMcG, PAT, PC, SD, SFE, SK, SO, TNR, TSc, TT, VB and YB.

CUTE MANNERS

The ostentatious observation of simple rules of etiquette is rude. (CD)

ERUDITE COROLLARY
Immodesty in erudition sucks. (HGF)

SITUATIONAL ETIQUETTE
The rules of etiquette may, within reasonable limits, be waived if observing them would cause distress to those unaware of such rules. (TFY)

INTIMATE PARTNERS
and friends need not (indeed, often must not) stand on ceremony. (AW)

FAILURE

In all human endeavor, failure is the result about half of the time. So it's probably a mistake to appropriate failure as a personal characteristic.

USES OF FAILURE
Fear of failure is a handy, self-fulfilling device for justifying indolence. If you're inclined to need a lot of sympathy, fear of failure will get you nowhere with your friends. Actual failure, on the other hand, will get you a lot of mileage. (TRD)

HEROISM

Heroism comes from a strong desire — pursued at any risk — to do the right thing.

It will be seen, then, that heroism as a circumstance peculiar to a single event (say, saving a child from a burning building) is not something that one seeks; rather, it is a circumstance created by the event itself.

Rarely do men and women live their entire lives dramatically manifesting the quality of heroism. Despite the precepts imposed by the Modern Conceit (q.v.), lives of a less dramatic but more profound form of heroism more frequently are dedicated to the preservation of families and the rearing of children. The exploits of scientists, athletes, politicians and businessmen are often confused with heroism, so extraordinary has simple competence become. (*Anon.*)

EUROGREETINGS

The elaborate and, to an American or English sensibility, effusive greetings exchanged by Europeans on meeting and departing have a protocol that requires strict observance.

While normal people shake hands, Europeans do a pantomime "kiss" — actually a sort of cheek-rub. In France, men do this to each other twice, once on each side; if the greeting is between a man and a woman, then kisses are exchanged four times, alternating side to side. In Belgium, the rule is three times regardless of gender. Germans don't smooch at all, but Italians have a free-form arrangement that usually results in two kisses, along with hugs and loud and effusive verbalizations. The Dutch kiss twice, except in Amsterdam, where they kiss once if at all. English people shake hands or ignore each other, while Scotsmen bang their foreheads together in an apparent effort to dislodge morbid Calvinist tendencies. (YB)

GOSSIP

Gossip? Not you, right? Sure, sure. That's not what *we* heard.

THE LESS YOU GIVE, THE MORE YOU GET
It is usually best never to gossip. People will respect you for your discretion and tell you even *more*. (HH)

EQUAL OPPORTUNITY
Gossip is not a sex-linked characteristic. Despite appearances, women, as well as men, are predisposed to gossip. (GE)

There is a difference between male and female gossip. Men tend to gossip about general topics; women tend to gossip about specifics. They both gossip the same amount, however. (ALo)

COMPLAINTS

Listen, this is the free world. You've got a right to complain, but you've also got to complain right.

ACTION DIRECT
You have something to say, come out and say it. Nothing's worse than moping around, threatening emotional havoc, until somebody forces the complaint out of you,

girlstyle. In dealing with friends, especially, be direct — within the bounds of common sense — but be just. Simply because someone's a pal doesn't mean you can endlessly bewail the state of the universe or something.

On the other hand, friends have a right to be heard on general woes. These are not complaints, of course, but they sound very much like them. Actually, they are direct descendents of foxhole whispers: Sometimes it's good to know you've got company. (KJC)

THE RIGHT OF JUST COMPLAINT

Within limits, you have the right to unburden yourself to your friends on the subject of the woes that beset you. This should be done, however, with the understanding that a good friend will invariably be upset by what you have to say, since he will feel some compulsion to try to set things right — an impossible task, almost by definition. This can lead to resentment.

You should seek to ease your friend's distress by making him understand that he is being of great value to you as a sounding board. His sympathy and advice are welcome — but he is not being asked to *solve* your problems. (FM)

BLUE RIBBON COMPLAINTS

The nature and effect of personal problems makes them too subjective a matter to be compared like heifers at a county livestock show. Resist the temptation to continually remind a friend that *his* situation's not so bad because *your situation's worse*. (CGF)

TOIL AND TROUBLE

Above all, don't confuse your day-to-day woes with real suffering. The chances are that no matter what's bothering you, it's largely something you've invented or something you could control if you really wanted to. Real anguish, pain and suffering — objective, verifiable phenomena — are strangers to most of us. Suffering is *not* being bummed out. So make sure your complaint is in tune with your woes. (GT)

See also *Conversational Etiquette*, **in** *THE DEPORTMENT DEPARTMENT*, **above.**

THE PROPER PISS

One thing that separates the boys from the girls is the relative flexibility of our urinary habits. But the seeming advantage our gender enjoys is not without its perils — especially given the occasional unpredictability of the equipment.

Modern Men of good taste and virtue know that good marksmanship is an essential component of smooth living.

AVOIDING THE TELLTALE DRIBBLE

The horror of the postpiss dribble can be easily avoided by firmly pressing one or two fingers up and out on the area immediately behind the scrotum after urinating. This forces a tidy evacuation of the urinary tract and prevents the surprise that appears after closing the zipper on trousers of unusually light color.

If, for some inexplicable reason, that doesn't work, simply walk to the basin, sprinkle water all over your chest and lower abdomen and, when rejoining your companion, place the blame on faulty plumbing in the men's room. Better their plumbing be bad than yours. (WY)

KEEP IT DOWN

Please, on behalf of all women everywhere, *please* put the seat down on the toilet when you've finished using it. This is important. Nothing will kill true love faster than getting up in the middle of the night to piss and nearly falling in because your formerly favorite man has forgotten his manners and left the seat up. More than that, it's also dangerous. (RBr) Sometimes, it seems, not dangerous enough.

THE RADIANT URINARY PHENOMENON

Gingerly spreading the opening in the tip of the *glans* will prevent the occurrence of the radiant urinary phenomenon, the most obvious manifestation of which is the uncontrolled and simultaneous discharge of urine in two or more different directions. The result is usually a small, unsightly puddle on the floor (or, worse, on your shoes). (WY)

Modern Misbehavior

Say you work all day monitoring account budgets for the marketing and promotion departments of InterWidgCo. You start at nine in the morning, pushing those numbers, drumming those digits. You grab a chick. sal. sand. for lunch, then rush back into the final edit on the sales/marketing ratio charts, and bingo, before you know it *damn* if it isn't five o'clock and even though you aren't finished, it's time to quit. What do you do?

You get *serious,* that's what. You strap on an old motorcycle helmet, round up a few of the guys and put together a pick-up game of typist's chair hockey or a down-and-dirty round of Nazi Truth. A Modern Man knows what counts, right? That's why we keep score.

Moreover, Modern Men are amateurs in the grand sense. We could, for example, make a career out of driving in demolition derbies, but that would only provide us with unsuitable employment while somehow degrading a noble sport by making it into a *job*.

No. If we are going to sully a pastime, let it be in commerce, education or government, where the stains won't show.

C O N T E N T S
Chapter Eighteen: *MODERN MISBEHAVIOR*

AMUSEMENTS AND DIVERSIONS

Sometimes, a Modern Man's gotta do what a boy does — screw around and have a good time.

DEMOLITION DERBIES

A good demo derby can provide a relaxed and amusing way to pass a languid summer afternoon. There's something intrinsically rewarding about wrecking cars. It makes all those traffic snarls and neighborhood brawls fade into insignificance.

Rules: The rules are simple: First, all contestants must wear appropriate protective headgear. Second, all collisions must occur when the automobile is traveling in reverse; forward collisions are grounds for immediate disqualification for life. Third, all collisions must be to the *side* of the opposing vehicle. Fourth, the last car moving is the winner.

Materials: It doesn't take much to organize a demolition derby. You'll need a few acres of vacant land and a "second" to serve as a pit man. Cars can be obtained for less than a hundred bucks from your local junkyard; ask for a car that will still move under its own power. If law enforcement officials are touchy, you may also want a trailer to get the car from the junkyard to the site of the derby — and subsequently back again, where you can sell it back to the junkman. Maybe the junkyard will tow it away for you.

Safety: Health is on everyone's mind, and never more so than in the heat of a good demo. Wear a helmet, use a seatbelt and get rid of those troublesome windows, door handles, knobs and anything else that might break your heart — or worse. No rearview mirrors, no headlights, no radio antennæ; common sense will help you out here. (*Anon.*)

See also *CAR CARE* **in** *CHAPTER FOUR: MODERN MOTORS* **and** *JUNKYARDS* **in** *CHAPTER FOURTEEN: MODERN MAINTENANCE.*

WIFE FOR LIFE

In this game, women are not only treated as sexual objects, but also as profoundly threatening human beings in their own right.

The principle of WFL is to choose, by various means, your eternal partner.

The basic game: Stand in a crowded barroom with a pal; look around until you find your ideal WFL. The variation is to find your friend's WFL before he finds yours. That's it. Not much, huh? Then try these intriguing modifications:

Blind WFL: This is a much more complex game, requiring careful consideration of time and place. The ideal location is in a café or coffee shop where a window table provides seating for two people facing each other, each with a clear view of oncoming pedestrian traffic. Each player scouts the oncoming pedestrian traffic and, when he thinks he's found a potential WFL, asks his opponent to declare his intentions — before he's had a chance to see the object of the game, of course — according to the following table:

Blind Wife for Life Basic Declarations
Pass
One-night Stand
One-year Affair
Wife for Life

Blind WFL with an option: Played exactly as *Blind WFL,* with an important exception — a player is allowed to make his declaration contingent on an option clause that allows for instant upgrading, although not without risk of penalty (as indicated on the following table) should he choose not to exercise his option:

Blind Wife for Life Declarations with Options and Penalties

Declaration	Option	Consequence of Refused Option
Pass	None	N/A
One-night Stand	None	N/A
One-night Stand	One-year Affair	She'll call you every night for one year.
One-year Affair	None	N/A
One-year Affair	WFL	She'll call you every night for the rest of your life.
WFL	None	N/A

A player may elect, for example, to select a girl as a one-night stand with an option, in which case he is agreeing to accept her for a one-night stand, but, if she is desirable enough, he can exercise his option to *upgrade* her to a one-year affair. If, however, he refuses to exercise his option, he *must* accept the penalty (in this case, she will telephone him every night for a year, ask him what he's doing, how come he treats her so badly, when is he going to grow up, the usual).

Other Blind WFL versions: Once the basic premises of this riskier version of Blind WFL are understood, you may wish to try your luck at the following variations:

- *Countdown WFL:* This version has you seated in a busy restaurant or airport waiting room. You choose a number between one and whatever you have time for and count the women coming through the door. When you get to your number, you've got your number.

- *WFL with upgrades:* This is an acceptable variation to Countdown WFL, but the best version is played on the street. During a long walk, you make a declaration on one block for someone unseen on the next block. That is, you say to your pal, "I'll take a one-nighter with an option." By the time you've completed your stroll down the block in question, you must find someone to become that lightly spoken one-nighter (or someone with whom you feel comfortable having a one-year affair, or someone with whom you think you can converse every night for a year). Now, established with a solid one-nighter, you can trade up, making upgrades or lateral moves until you spot your WFL. You're stuck with whomever you picked last. If you don't make it to WFL, but remain stuck at, say, a one-year affair, after the year's over, you must remain celibate for life.

- *Other variations:* There's *Give-Your-Wife-a-Quarter,* in which you must persuade the object of your matrimonial intentions to accept a 25¢ coin from you. Similarly, *Give-Your-Wife-a-Smile-Button* requires you to persuade your intended to pin on the Have-a-Nice-Day smile button you give to her. Or *Direct-Eye-Contact WFL,* in which you are required to first make your declaration, then consummate the relationship by achieving direct eye contact (a smolder means that you'll also have perfect children with perfect teeth). The variations are endless here. One advanced eye-contact version stipulates that if you declare a one-night stand, for example, but then fail to get eye contact, you must then escalate to *Voice-contact WFL,* in which you must *exchange* polite greetings (nothing weird; something on the order of "Hello. Nice day, isn't it?" is sufficient) with the next one-night-stand candidate before you can continue. If you declare, then fail to get voice contact, you are then at the mercy of your companions who can stipulate the subsequent one-night candidates until you get one that will return your greeting.

Variable rules include banning animals, members of the same sex or street bums from blind versions of the game. Various location restrictions can also be imposed. Be careful, for example, playing WFL at a bowling alley.

Both ways: Finally, it should be noted that women seem to enjoy playing the distaff versions of these games. *Hubby-for-the-Weekend* is a great game, tailor-made for boring Sunday doubleheaders at the local ballpark. (*Anon.*)

If you get completely carried away, **see also** MARRIAGE in *CHAPTER EIGHT: MODERN MATRIMONY*.

CLASSIFIED LIFE STYLE

For this game, you need a publication with an abundance of classifieds, preferably a magazine specializing in such ads. To play, select a prophetic figure who assigns each player a life-style based on numbers chosen at random. For example, the game leader turns to the section advertising jobs available. There are six columns of help-wanted ads, so the first player must choose a number between one and six. He chooses four. In column four, there are twenty-three jobs listed, and he chooses number 17, which turns out to be a vacancy for a family therapist. Next, he needs a home, a hobby, a mate (if there's a personal sections), a boat, a car, the works.

This also works, although less comprehensively, using a Spiegel catalog. (WST)

CLASSIFIED PRICE IS RIGHT

is a game in which an emcee reads out all the information in a given classified ad except the price of the object advertised for sale. The contestants then have to guess the price; the person coming closest without exceeding the advertised price wins. (AR)

NAZI TRUTH

This is a congenial game in which the players are given an opportunity to learn a little more about each other.

To play, the players sit around a table. A lit cigarette is passed around the table, each player taking a puff, until the ash falls off. The person holding the cigarette when the ash falls off is "it." (If there are nonsmokers, you can spin a bottle, cut cards, roll dice, draw straws, pick a name out of a hat, whatever.)

The person selected as "it" may then be asked *any question whatsoever* to which he is *bound* to answer fully and truthfully. When all the other players have asked a question, the cigarette is passed again.

Warning: This game has broken up marriages. (*Anon.*)

WHAT'S MY PROBLEM?

In this game, a player is selected at random to leave the room. While he is out, the other players agree on what his biggest problem is — perhaps he's a liar or a compulsive thief or boring. When the group has decided what the exiled player's biggest problem is, he is then recalled to the room, where he must try to guess what problem the others ascribed to him. Follow the format used by the old TV program, *What's My Line?* (MR)

SEXY FOLLIES

This game is based on one actually broadcast on French television. Three couples are segregated according to gender. One group leaves the room. In the first round, for example, the three men must take off all their clothes and stand in a row. The three women are meanwhile blindfolded. They then reenter the room. One at a time, each player must attempt to identify which of the men is her partner using only her sense of touch and smell. The partner cannot move and cannot make a sound. The player may touch any part of the men's bodies, but she may not touch their faces or their hair. After each player has made her choice, she can remove her blindfold but she may not assist the other players. During the second round, the roles are reversed, and the men are blindfolded.

This game works best if you have one person or one partner to guide the others into the room, enforce the rules and moderate the play. (FDF)

This is a *game?* **See also** *SEX AND SEDUCTION* **in** *CHAPTER SEVEN: MODERN MATING* **and** *DIVORCE* **in** *CHAPTER EIGHT: MODERN MATRIMONY.*

TYPIST'S CHAIR HOCKEY

Typist's Chair Hockey is a game designed to be played in large, uncarpeted reception areas or conference rooms.

Equipment: A typist's chair, a little masking tape, a motorcycle helmet, a puck (see below) and four folding chairs. The typist's chair is the most crucial piece of equipment; it must have a low center of gravity and a set of very good wheels. If you can find one with arms, you're golden.

Playing area: Clear all the furniture out of an uncarpeted, level room at least forty feet long and fifteen feet wide. Place two folding chairs four feet apart at each end of the room. Mark the center ten feet off with masking tape. The floor should be smooth and should be uncarpeted.

The puck is a volunteer who sits in the typist's chair wearing a motorcycle helmet.

Play is divided into four ten-minute quarters, with the first team to have possession of the typist's chair decided by the flip of a coin. The puck is pushed forward by one team toward the other team's goal area — the space between the folding chairs. Any part of the puck passing through an imaginary straight line drawn between the front side of the folding chairs (including the chairs themselves) constitutes a goal. The team with the most goals wins.

As few as three people can play (counting the puck).

Rules: It is against the rules to run while pushing the chair, and all push-offs — either toward a teammate or toward the goal — must be made with one hand raised in the air. Defensive players may not enter the center area; offensive players may not cross the center area's forward line (the line closest to the opposing goal). Violations of the rules are punished by awarding a free shot to the victimized team.

The puck's feet may not touch the floor. If this happens, the puck is returned to the offensive team's goal area and play is resumed from that point.

Free shots are taken by pushing the puck toward the opposing goal without crossing the forward line.

Strategy: Typist's Chair Hockey is a game rich in strategy, as even a brief pregame experiment or two will show. For example, should the puck be a fat guy or a short girl? Weight has a lot of effect on the spin and delivery of the puck. And don't forget about fear. Since a goal can be scored by any part of the puck passing the goal line, try to terrify the puck into stretching his arms out to defend himself as he hurtles toward the folding chairs. Practice will help you develop strategies and techniques of your own. (AMP)

CONFERENCE TABLE HOCKEY

is played on a large conference table by two or more players, armed with hair dryers, who attempt to drive the bottom of a polystyrene cup through a goal set up at each end of the table. (WF)

PARTIES FOR GROWN-UPS

Cocktail parties, to paraphrase Chinese Gordon, are social events where people who don't like each other stand uncomfortably in a room they don't want to be in eating things they don't want to eat and drinking things they don't want to drink. No wonder everyone gets drunk and acts like a jerk.

There's not a great deal about cocktail parties in this book because there's nothing you need to know about cocktail parties that you don't already know. Think of boredom on the bottle and you've got a perfect cocktail party.

But for something a little different, try

A BUS PARTY

Charter a bus, overstock it with food and drink and a couple dozen of your friends and do the town; (AR) or

A BAR PARTY

To entertain massive amounts of people on an annual basis, find a sleazy, near-bankrupt bar in a horrible part of town. Tell the owner you want to buy ten bottles of whiskey, thirty of vodka, ten of bourbon, ten of gin, maybe twenty-five liters of white wine and half as much red and twenty or twenty-five cases of beer — all at bar prices. This will set you back about a grand and will make the guy think he's struck gold. Then tell the guy that the only way you can manage to drink it all is if you invite some friends in. Tell him you want his bar for the night, and you'd rather he wasn't around except to unlock the place at eight and lock it up again at dawn, and that when it's all over, everyone in town will know about his tavern.

Find some partners, four or five guys who have more than two friends, and who will be willing to act as bartenders. All the partners should spend a day or two on the phone calling everyone on their Rolodexes, telling them to come to the party and to bring as many other people as they want. You should end up with 600 to 800 people. Plug in a good stereo, rustle up some decent tapes and watch everyone get thoroughly stinko.

One very charming aspect of this sort of thing is that the buffoons invited by your partners, all people you don't know, will treat you like crap while you stand behind the bar refilling their glasses for hours on end. (DB)

See also *Bar Lore,* **below.**

ENEMIES

Always invite a few sworn enemies, divorcing couples or people with profound professional or personal differences to your parties. They can always be counted on to squabble and cause a scene, providing entertainment for the others and helping to make your party a memorable event. (*Anon.*)

NEVER AT YOUR OWN HOME

This is the first rule of party-giving. Who wants to baby-sit a bunch of drunks determined to wreck your personal property for the sake of a good laugh? (DN)

KILL-YOUR-DINNER PARTY

This is great if you have a rambling old house or an acre or two of ground. (We tested it once at an MM dinner held in a warehouse and it worked like a charm.)

Before the guests arrive, prepare (or purchase) a separate dinner for each guest. Make them varied — everything from a Caesar salad to a steak with a lasagne stop in between. Some dinners should be spectacular — lobster, say — while others should be quite mundane — a Moby Jack fishwich, maybe.

On separate slips of paper, make a note of each dinner. Put the slips in a box.

From a toy store, purchase a supply of water pistols; each guest will need one.

Next, prepare the targets for the hunt. If you have ten guests coming, write a number on a separate slip of paper. *You must use water-soluble ink.* Stick a safety pin through each slip.

When the guests arrive, allow them time to sip a drink and relax. Then distribute the numbered slips of paper and tell each guest to pin the slip on his shirt. Finally, hand out the weapons, loaded and ready to go.

The hunt: Everyone must be allowed enough time to find a position that allows not only for protection but also for the possibility of a stalk. The best way to do this is to play "Brain Damage" from Pink Floyd's *Dark Side of the Moon* and let the hunt begin when the music ends.

The object is to kill your dinner. You stalk another guest, fire with your squirt gun, and attempt to hit your prey on the numbered tag, making the ink run. When this happens, you take his tag, put it in your pocket, give him *your* numbered tag and retire from the hunt.

When everyone has successfully killed his dinner, serve and eat.

See also *The Speed Clean* **and** *Mopping Up* **in** *CHAPTER FIFTEEN: MODERN MESSES* **and** *LIQUOR,* **below.**

LIQUOR

is not an aphrodisiac nor is it a stimulant. It is a depressant that may induce significant vapidity and a consequent lowering of inhibitions and common sense.

It is, in the words of (PJO), "liquid idiot." Among alcohol's impressive list of dreadful side effects is the likelihood that severe drunkenness will impair your ability to achieve an erection, while prolonged periods of alcohol abuse will reduce the amount of testosterone, the male sex hormone, resulting in loss of body hair, added girth around your ass, increased flabbiness in the tits and a sudden compulsive desire to subscribe to *Esquire.*

PROOF

Once, the alcohol content of a solution was tested by an old method of soaking gunpowder with the solution and then attempting to ignite it; if it lit, the alcohol was said to have "withstood the proof."

There is no international standard for proofing, so different countries enforce different measures. Basically, however, all proof spirits contain about 57 percent alcohol. That is, a bottle of 100 proof spirit contains about 57 percent alcohol; 80 proof contains approximately 45 percent, and so on. (CW)

Alcoholic Beverage Percentage Table

Liquor	Percentage of Alcohol
Spirits (including rum, whiskey, brandy, gin and vodka)	40 to 50 percent
Liqueurs	15 to 50 percent
Port, sherry, Madeira, vermouth	15 to 30 percent
Table wines	9 to 10 percent
Ales	8 percent
Beers	2 to 3 percent
Cider	2 to 3 percent

EAT FIRST

The old tale is true: you really can drink more (and lessen the impact of a potential hangover) if you eat first. When the pyloric valve, which is the avenue between your stomach and your small intestine, is closed, the alcohol must slowly pass through the walls of the stomach. Before a big binge, eat either a big slab of beef or a dairy product.

Yoghurt is ideal for coating the stomach and slowing the absorption of alcohol. If it's an after-work cocktail party, scarf up on whatever hors d'oeuvres are handy. (CW)

HANGOVERS

are a voluntary illness — a sign, a message left for you while you were out, that drinking too much alcohol is drug abuse and is bad for you. After a night on the bottle, your insides are dehydrated, your stomach's cooked, your liver's working overtime, your nervous system has been blasted and you've been executing brain cells by the million.

While there is no cure for a hangover, there are some ameliorating steps you can take. Carbonated drinks (cola is particularly good) will help your stomach, caffeine will stimulate your nervous system and water will help rehydrate your dried-up body cells. Protein will give you some staying power and carbohydrates will give your stomach something to do besides get mad at you. Eat as much as you can if you are suffering from a hangover. But don't fall for the "hair of the dog" gambit. Drinking a shot of alcohol to cure a hangover will often do more harm than good and may make you puke.

Prevention is the best remedy. *Eat first* (**see above**) and you'll reduce the chance of getting a hangover. A more certain prophylaxis is *water* — one eight-ounce glass before bed for every drink you consumed. This is not easy, but it works, especially if you eat a slice of bread while you're downing the water, and it works even better if you double the amount of water and consume it at a more leisurely pace before retiring. Not only will the water help you combat dehydration, it will assist in flushing out your system and give you some help in riding a bucking bed or worshipping the white porcelain god.

If you're certain you aren't going to puke, take some multi-vitamins; B-complex is particularly helpful. (DB)

The hangover heirarchy: Liquors vary in their ability to cause hangovers according to their chemistry. As a rule, the darker the liquor, the more profound the hangover.

In descending order of danger: Brandy, whiskey, beer, red wine, tequila, gin, white wine, vodka. Mixers (soda, tonic and the rest) make no difference. (*Anon.*)

SUGAR, SUGAR

Most spirits contain a large amount of sugar. Adding even more sugar to your drink may get you drunk quicker, but it may get you sick quicker, too. As a rule, girls like sweet drinks more than guys do. (SR)

MIXING YOUR DRINKS

will not make you drunker or sicker. Your limit is your limit, no matter how you get there. (*Anon.*) As predicted, this observation drew

A dissent: Drinking the same spirit all night will not make you as sick as when you mix wine, brandy, vodka and the rest. (RBr)

WHISKEYS

There are four main types of whiskey:

1. Scotch: Scottish blended whisky has a smokey, medicinal taste and does not work well in most cocktails. Unblended Scottish whisky is noticeably smoother and should not be chilled or mixed with anything.

2. Bourbon is an American whiskey with its origins in Kentucky. Like Scotch, it is best drunk on its own and not used as a base for cocktails.

3. Rye whiskey has come to mean many things to drinkers. American blended whiskey, Canadian blended whisky or straight rye whiskey are all distilled from rye grain.

4. Irish whiskey has a taste more similar to American whiskeys than Scottish ones.

Irish and Americans drink whiskey; Canadians and Scots drink whisky. Most people can't tell the difference between two Scotches or two bourbons, so be careful you don't pay for a label. (SR)

OTHER SPIRITS

Vodka is a neutral grain spirit. Buy the cheapest filtered stuff you can find. There is absolutely no difference between any domestic vodka except the piece of paper stuck on the front of the bottle. Imported vodkas do vary enormously, however, and your own taste will steer you right. Vodka should be stored in the freezer.

Gin is one of the few spirits that are made better with money. Juniper is the primary ingredient here and the real thing is more expensive than the phony "extract."

Brandy is distilled wine and is marked according to its origin. The most expensive stuff comes from Cognac, but don't be gulled. Ratings like "VSOP" and "VS" are nearly nonsensical, while bottle aging means nothing in brandy. Cask aging is what counts, so don't pay a ton of money for a dusty bottle of Armagnac. Money is a good guide to quality, but try several varieties and choose for yourself. (SR)

MIXING DRINKS

is not a particularly mysterious art. As in cooking, the most important thing is to get an idea of proportion, rather than spending a lot of time and effort getting measurements exact. Common sense tells you that if you add too much booze or too little mixer, your drink will taste strong; experience will help you learn the rest.

Measures and glasses: There are two basic type of *drink glasses:* The smaller variety is called an old-fashioned glass and measures approximately 4" in height and 3" in diameter and holds about six ounces. The second and larger type is called a highball or Collins glass; measurements vary, but an average highball glass holds about eight ounces of liquid and is about 5.5" high and a little less than 3" inches in diameter.

Drink recipes call for *measures* in ponies, jiggers and shots; this sort of thing is basically bunk, and you can just as easily *use your fingers*. A "finger" of alcohol is measured from where the liquid sits on the bottom of the glass. The following chart may provide some guidelines:

Bar Measures

Name	Volume	Fingers
Pony	1 ounce	One-half finger in an old-fashioned glass shot
Jigger	1.5 ounce	Slightly more than a half-finger in an old fashioned glass; one finger in a highball glass
Large jigger	2 ounces	One finger in an old-fashioned glass; just under one and a half fingers in a highball glass.

The standard ratio for a mixed drink is one to one; in other words, use half liquor and half mix. (DRA)

THREE STANDARD DRINKS

The dry martini is a true grown-up drink. For some reason, kids under thirty just don't understand the virtue of a great martini. This drink is served well chilled, so either keep your spirits in the freezer or mix your martini in a pitcher, then strain off the ice. Under extraordinarily rugged conditions, martinis can be served on the rocks. Mix two fingers (four ounces) of gin or vodka in an old-fashioned glass with just enough vermouth to cover the bottom of the vermouth bottle cap. Stir slightly; add a twist of lemon peel or a couple of olives. If you add cocktail onions instead of olives or a twist to this drink, it becomes a *Gibson*. If you add a few drops of bitters instead of lemon or olive, the drink is known as a *Nigroni* and tastes much better than it sounds.

A **Bloody Mary** uses about two fingers (two and a half ounces) or more of vodka in an eight-ounce glass. Add less than a teaspoon of horseradish, a teaspoon of lemon juice, a few shakes of Worcestershire sauce, tabasco or hot sauce, some red and black pepper, ice and top up with tomato juice. Squeeze in a quarter of lime, stir and serve.

In *A Farewell to Arms,* Hemingway talks about a drink called a **French 75,** which is half cognac and half champagne. The drink might be better called *A Farewell to Legs* since it's a ruthless killer, fortunately much beloved by drinking ladies. (SFR)

THE WELL-STOCKED BAR

Even if you're not a big boozer, keeping a decent bar for guests is always well-advised. Here's a basic shopping list:

- One-half gallon vodka
- One-half gallon gin
- One-half gallon whiskey
- One liter bourbon
- One liter rye
- One liter rum
- One fifth (750 ml) tequila
- Wine and beer, if you like
- Nonliquor items, including olives, bitters, soda water, quinine water, ginger ale, cola, fruit juice, lemons and limes
- One fifth (750 ml) brandy

One quart yields 21 one-ounce jigger glasses (of one and a half ounces each). Figure three drinks per person and you'll get seven people on a bottle. (DRA)

THE CHEAP OPEN BAR

Get one fifth bottle each of top-shelf gin, vodka and the rest but keep bottles of cheap, generic liquor in reserve. Nobody will be able to tell the difference after an hour or so anyway, so either stonewall it or refill the bottle with the expensive label with the cheap stuff whenever necessary.

Beer and wine are not significantly cheaper to serve than mixed drinks, so keep only a small supply on hand for those who insist on either one.

Spend money on top-of-the-line mixers. Brand names always look good, but brand-name soda is lots cheaper than brand-name Scotch.

Limit your selection — don't cater to those with affected tastes in liquor. If you feel you must have a liqueur on hand, make it a dry one (like cognac) and not a sweet one (like Grand Marnier); people drink sweet cordials faster and in greater quantities.

Serve salt-free snacks to munch on. Salty snacks only make people want to drink more of the booze for which you are paying.

With the current attitudes about drink and driving liability, the best plan is to reserve several tables at a bar, where someone else's insurance is on the line. (JO)

SUBDUING UNRULY FRIENDS

who are drunk can be a daunting task. Here are four methods, in ascending order of risk and difficulty:

1. Feed a drunk and the chances are he'll get sleepy and docile. (JO)

2. Accomplice: Pretend to be willing to aid and abet his misbehavior. Tell him you know of a place with better girls (or booze or music or whatever seems to be his interest of the moment), get him in the car, then drive him home and either force him out of the car or refuse to drive any farther. (KJP)

3. Dare a rowdy, drunk friend to eat a raw egg. Then duck. It will make him puke, ridding his system of some excess alcohol and leaving him exhausted. (JO)

4. The most dangerous method of subduing a drunk — if his life is threatened by his actions, for instance — is to delivery a hefty blow to the side of his head. It'll knock him out. This is for emergencies only. (*Anon .*)

DRUNK WOMEN

Since you must never abandon a drunk woman companion no matter how disgusting her behavior, *try your best to remain civil* with her; it's important that she not perceive you as the enemy or as a patronizing authority figure. Rely on one of these two methods to bring her under control:

1. Get her dancing. Girls love to dance. Wear her out. Sure, she'll fall all over the place and make you look like a jerk, but the exertion will eventually subdue her. (JPK)

2. Don't stop: Feed her more alcohol, while you guzzle soda pop. She'll get sick or pass out before too long. If it gets tedious, regard it as a scientific experiment: How much booze can a small human hold? (EDM)

See also *The Duties of a Host at Cocktail Parties* **in** *CHAPTER SEVENTEEN: THE DEPORTMENT DEPARTMENT* **and** *Parties for Grown-Ups,* **above. And see** *Drunk Drivers* **in** *CHAPTER FIVE: MODERN MOBILITY.*

BAR LORE

Bars, cafés and taverns are like far-flung outposts of the Smithsonian, harboring specific and regional artifacts of popular culture.

DRINK UP, MAT DOWN

If your beer mat sticks to the bottom of your glass, sprinkle a few grains of salt on the mat. (RF)

GO QUIETLY

Never bang your glass on the bar to get a bartender's attention. (TI) Never whistle at a bartender or waitress to get their attention. (JYF)

SOLO

Look lonesome, never lonely. This takes years to learn, and you may lose your liver in the process, but it's worth it.

Never smile to yourself. (GC)

AND ONE FOR YOURSELF

In most bars outside North America, one commonly accepted form of tipping is to ask the waiter or bartender if he'd like a drink for himself. (NVB)

GETAWAYS

Be sure both the front door and the men's room are never more than ten quick steps from your barstool or booth.

Never drink at a bar that has a uniformed city cop as its doorman.

When in a booth, never sit next to the wall; sit on the outside. (GC)

THE LIPLESS LIGHT

To light a cigarette from a candle or other open flame without bending over the flame, hold the cigarette between the thumb and middle finger with the end of the cigarette in the flame. Tap the filter end of the cigarette with your index finger a few times, and the cigarette will light evenly. (BC)

RESTLESS NATIVES

Bar fights: According to Daniel Lessa, whose International Bartenders School has trained thousands of barmen (including Sid Vicious) since the end of Prohibition, the *first signs of a bar fight* are when the patrons begin sitting uneasily at the bar, then begin prowling around like cats. The first real red flag, though, is when the jackets come off.

A bartender should immediately go and "stand" on the situation, imposing his presence on the antagonists. He should slowly clean the bar in front of the unruly patrons, washing glasses, emptying ashtrays — anything that could serve as a missile — and remove it or put it out of harm's way.

Some 90 percent of all bar fights involve juveniles, and most fights are between people who have come into the bar together but whose differences have been exaggerated by alcohol. (DLe)

WOE, PARTNER

There are two stories bartenders hear on a nonstop basis: One involves the bad-news girlfriend or wife; the second has to do with employers.

A good bartender knows that patrons look to a bartender for sympathy and don't expect a solution to their problems. A good bartender doesn't suggest one, either. (KG)

See also *COMPLAINTS* **in** *CHAPTER SEVENTEEN: THE DEPORTMENT DEPARTMENT.*

YEAH, HE'S HERE AND HE'S DRUNK

If you're a bartender, never tell a lie for *anybody,* especially somebody involved in a lovers' spat. Eventually, they'll make up and you'll be the bad guy. (DLe)

THE LOUNGE VULTURE:
STICK AROUND UNTIL NOON THE NEXT DAY

The later the hour, the more approachable the women. (*Anon.*)

A corollary: Girls get prettier at closing time. This is a phenomenon witnessed by more than one customer, who generally learns his lesson and asks the bartender to cut him off when the woman at the end of the bar starts looking good. (AMcA)

The vulture: Every bar has a lounge vulture in its inventory of regulars. He's generally disliked by other men at the bar, and never seems to be able to find a date of his own. He waits forever for a couple to have a squabble, and if the man leaves, he's the first one over to offer the woman sympathy. Similarly, he's ready with a shoulder for the woman whose husband has just left her and has come to a bar trying to drink through her confusion. He doesn't score very often, but he never stops trying. (AMcA)

NO MONEY DOWN

The habit of leaving your change on the bar is unacceptable at first-class watering holes. It's also not a good idea in any bar where you're not a regular. (KG)

CYCLES OF DISCONTENT

Don't enter any bar which has a row of choppers parked outside — unless your chopper is bigger and faster. (AI)

ONE- DRUG BARS

Alcohol is usually the only drug sold in a bar. Don't get the bartender fired by asking him for drugs. If the bar owner's sitting nearby, you could make a guy's life miserable. For the most part, bartenders are not drug dealers. (SW)

THE BROTHERHOOD OF BEERS

All domestic lager beers are created equal. Here's a simple test to prove it:

Set up a blind taste test using six or more different domestic brews. The tasters should try to identify the brands and arrive at an agreement on preference. Repeat the test with six or more imported lagers.

Most likely, the result will be that all domestic lagers will taste the same, just as all imported lagers do.

You can run taste tests with other drinks — Scotch, gin, vodka. Nobody can identify their brand and no group of tasters will be able to agree that one is better than the others. This is a great way to burst pretentious balloons.

Good head: A good head on a beer releases carbon dioxide and gives the beer a more genuine taste while lessening the fart- and belch-inducing qualities of more gassy brews. (DST)

SMOOTH SIP

The harshness of straight-up drinks can be at least partially eliminated by inhaling when you sip and exhaling as you swallow. (NG) Don't choke.

THE SPIDER

An old ginmill tradition is that of giving a free drink to the man who got the final pour — the spider — from a bottle. Most bartenders are too young to have heard of this one, but at least for thc customer, it's a tradition that deserves to be kept alive. (AW)

OLD BUSHWA

The dreadful affectation of ordering fashionable brands of whiskey by name is enough to give most men the dry heaves. Avoid pretentiousness by calling for your poison by its generic name; if you want a bourbon, ask for bourbon. It'll make no difference to your palate (although your wallet will feel better for it) and the directness involved is appropriate to both the setting and the occasion. (AW)

RESTAURANTS

Proper restaurants are a shockingly late development in the history of civilization, so it is perhaps not surprising that we are still trying to figure out how they *really* work.

DINNER DATES

If you invite a woman to lunch or supper, you are bound to pay for her meal. This is not an optional arrangement (except in the case of business engagements). On the other hand, if a woman invites you to dinner, you may be justified in understanding that she wishes to assume the responsibility of the bill (**see under** *The Dinner Guest,* **below**). Any private variation to this conventional arrangement should be made in private and remain there. (NF)

BOOKING A TABLE

It's really easy. Call in advance, be polite, don't ask for the moon and don't try to be a big shot. (HMJ)

CHOOSING A TABLE

Try to get the wall or the corner of the room directly behind you. All mammals are at their greatest ease with their backs protected — especially while foraging. (DO'R)

GROUP DINNERS

Requesting separate checks or itemizing a single check is unusually bad and graceless form. In a group situation, the rules are quite clear.

If it's a *social occasion,* the total amount of the dinner check, plus any other charges or gratuities, is divided by the number of male diners. A gentleman pays for his guest or date; if there are women present who are neither guests nor dates, it is your responsibility to temporarily "adopt" one for the purpose of paying her share.

For business meals, a different rule applies. *The Female Responsibility Act of 1971* is waived and it's every expense account for him- or herself. (SM)

See also *Post-Theater Restaurant Etiquette* **in** *CHAPTER SEVENTEEN: THE DEPORTMENT DEPARTMENT.*

THE DINNER GUEST

If you are taken out to dinner (in a social context) by someone else, you are required to offer to pay for a nonfood portion of the meal (i.e., the bar tab or the tip). You'll probably be refused, but the offer must be made — and with sincerity. (AR)

Guests at a business lunch or dinner need not make such an offer. In fact, to do so would be a minor breach of etiquette. (JK)

If you're not sure whether or not your host is writing off your meal as part of his expense account, ask. (FES)

75¢ AND THREE STAMPS. WHY?

You finish your meal, get the bill, reach for your wallet and it's not there and all your date has are quarters to call Mom. Now what?

You have a choice:

1. Beard the check. This is an act of unconscionable sleaze, and you'll get caught for sure if there're more than two of you.

Here's a typical bearding maneuver: Party of two, Mr. A and Mr. B. Dinner's over and the check comes: forty bucks. A says, "I'm off to the john, B." B says, "Right you are, A." B goes outside while A is in the can. A emerges from the men's room and walks out the front door. A and B vanish around the corner.

Meanwhile, back at the restaurant, a waitress making minimum wage and starving on tips gets stuck with the forty-dollar tab.

Some restaurants will split the difference with the waitress. (SW) But even so, bearding a check is the worst, and Modern Men don't do it. Instead, if they can't pay, they choose option two:

2. Give yourself up. Find the manager or owner and throw yourself on his mercy. He'll probably ask for some identification and some assurance from you about the date and manner of payment, and then he'll probably let you go. (SW)

Incidentally, most customers in this tacky situation don't pay up. Modern Men are not among them.

WHO ARE THOSE GUYS?

The maître d' is the guy standing at the front of the restaurant asking you if you have a reservation. He controls the seating and booking of tables. If he doesn't like you, he'll seat you at a table next to the entrance to the kitchen or the restrooms. Nothing personal.

The captain works amongst the tables and supervises the waiters. Sometimes he'll also assume the role of the now-rarely-seen

Sommelier, or wine steward, who carries a little tasting cup around his neck and routinely refuses to take back bottles of brackish vinegar.

The waiter is the man who picks up the tip after he's dropped off the food. (SW)

TIPS

Fifteen percent minimum (but don't be afraid to grossly undertip for sullen or arrogant service). Once upon a time, the waiter was tipped 15 percent of the food bill, not including wine; the sommelier was left 10 percent of the wine bill. That was too confusing, especially when restaurant tabs started peeking into three digits.

In restaurants this side of coffee shops, don't leave change; instead, round up to the next dollar.

The waiter collects tips and in most cases contributes them to a common pool which is split up at the end of the evening with preassigned percentages going to various staff members, including the bus boys. This is called "tipping out" and is done by the waiter.

Although the captain gets a percentage of the tips, if you want him to remember you in the future, or if your dinner companion has made bizarre requests or been foolish, you should tip him separately. Credit card slips leave a space for captain's tips, but palming the guy some bills (see below) is the preferred way. The captain gets 10 percent in this case.

The maître d' gets his tip — or, more properly, "bribe," given to persuade him not to seat you next to a box of onions in the scullery — in the form of a ten or a twenty (or more) folded into your palm and transferred in the course of a hearty handshake. (SW)

THE MAN

to know is obviously the maître d'. If you haven't booked a table, he can get you one. If you're trying to be a big shot, he can help you out by getting you a good table.

A good table in a popular restaurant is likely to be near the front door, in order to see and be seen. The worst tables are usually near the kitchen.

The palmed bribe to the maître d' is never discussed, but it's the essential ingredient in getting the "right table." Figure twenty bucks average. (SW) Modern Men shouldn't bother trying this hard to impress themselves.

THE BARTENDER

in a restaurant is tipped at the bar for his services before or after dinner. (SW)

THE COOK

gets nothing in the tip department, but you can offer to buy him a drink. (In fact, you can offer any member of the staff a drink and be within the bounds of good taste.) (SW)

CHINESE DINNER DRILLS

An empty teapot placed on the service side of the table with the top open is the Chinese signal to request another serving of tea. (PSW)

Family style: Chinese food is perfect for family-style dining. You can use this quality as a way of preventing everyone in a group (say, six or more) from ordering too much food.

When you first order, order only one or two dishes. Divide them and eat them, then order one or two more, then one or two after that, until everyone has had enough. The waiters hate this, but Chinese food cooks fast, and it's a wonderful way to pace a dinner. Discuss each course before you order, or play it surprise-style, with each person taking a free hand at the menu. Because this requires an inordinate amount of service, your tip should be more generous than usual. (NW)

SPORTS

No matter which professional sport you follow, it's important to remember that what you think you see on the field is probably the least important aspect of the game.

FLATFOOTED NUANCES

The true sports spectator knows that every sport has lots of carefully hidden nuances, small things that constitute the reality of the game (as opposed to the large gestures that make up the appearance of the game). This is especially true of pro sports, since those who play the games are, in theory, the very best. The rule of thumb, then, is watch carefully; the most meaningful part of the game might pass in an instant.

On the other hand, participating in sports is to slow time to a crawl — especially if you're over forty and out of shape.

HOW TO WATCH PRO SPORTS ON TELEVISION

Most of us follow pro sports on television, a peculiarly disjointed way to watch such variations on pastoral themes.

When watching a sport on TV the idea is to try not to focus on any individual (although TV has a bias toward personal conflict). Instead, try to familiarize yourself with the game sufficiently to allow for movements that take place off-camera so you can "see" everything at once.

On TV, every major spectator sport has a degree of subtlety that, apart from more obvious factors, sets it apart from the others. The list that follows is in descending order :

Baseball: Baseball is primarily an intellectual game, at least compared to basketball, football, hockey and the other "back-and-forth" sports (although it pales in comparison to cricket, perhaps the most beautifully structured field game in the world). In baseball, all the movement is circular and there are no time contraints. Baseball is also the only American game in which the defense controls the ball.

There are two key players on the field during a baseball game that must be watched carefully. The pitcher, of course, is crucial, since, in theory, he is the only defense a team needs. The course of the game hinges on the way he grips and delivers the ball. Watch the series of moves that inform his delivery; if there is a runner on base, watch the way that fact influences the pitcher. The other key player to watch is the shortstop; his initial movement during the pitcher's delivery will signal the general direction of play if the ball is hit. If the ball passes beyond the infield, a spectator at the park or in front of his TV can best judge the depth of outfield flies by watching the outfielder, not the ball, since his movements will indicate exactly how hard a ball is hit.

Television is especially adroit at displaying the two most interesting elements of baseball: the tense relationship between the pitcher and the baserunner and the balletic quality of most infield plays. Beyond that, one of the nicest things about baseball is that it is a tremendously cerebral game played by semiliterates whose off-field tawdriness and misbehavior can easily pass unnoticed by those who are devoted fans of the sport, if not the sportsmen who play it. (DB)

Baseball also enjoys the best officiating; the calls of umpires are right far more often than are the decisions of other referees in other sports. Basketball, football and hockey have so much contact that refs can't see every violation and must overlook others in order to avoid needlessly extending game times. (WR)

Basketball and hockey: Basketball is a difficult game to take seriously, since it can only be played successfully by men with severe physical disorders. Nevertheless, it is a fast game, and one that can be enjoyed on television because of replays from optimum angles; the replays alone put you in the best seat in the house.

Hockey shares many of basketball's characteristics. It too is a fast-paced game, except the players carry sticks and have no brakes. (WR) The other difference is that hockey is perhaps the most ludicrously violent sport this side of dog-fighting.

Football is better on TV than it is in person. In a freezing stadium, football is an interminable game of discontinuous action; TV fills in those dead spots with replays, including the marvelous reverse-angle shots, which are sort of mirror-image replays. (WR)

Bowling and golf: These games are only interesting to watch if you are also a player; golf, for example, is one of the only sports with almost no continuity and in which every situation is different. Spectators watch these sports mostly to gain insights into various shortcomings in their own game. (WR)

PARTICIPATORY SPORTS

The choice of a sport is based first on childhood experiences and individual physical advantages, and second on cost and convenience — if you live across the street from a tennis court, chances are you'll be a better tennis player than a tobogganer.

Your success, however, will be based largely on your temperament. Your personality will help you chose a team sport over an individual or a one-on-one sport. (WR)

Tennis is a great sport for indoor play and for those who seek a sport for sheer exercise. But remember, you can play it in cut-offs and old sneaks; don't let the game turn you into a fashion snob. Work on your backhand, instead. (JHP) (**See also** *Tennis Ball, below.*)

Ping-Pong is surprisingly intellectual and physically demanding. I seem to be able to fool myself all the time. (SF) Ping-Pong is the ideal indoor paddle or racket sport. Who can afford an indoor tennis court? Almost anybody can put up a Ping-Pong table, and if you play the game well, you can get a real workout. If you're on a weight-loss kick, put the table in the basement next to the furnace and play in your sweatsuit.

Swimming is the best sport for exercise, bar none. And it is far less damaging to your body than running. (RE)

COED SPORTS

The best coed sports are volleyball and tennis, games in which the sexes can compete most evenly (men can deliver a much stronger serve in tennis, however).

There is a good reason for segregating most sports. Men are simply stronger than women and most coed contests cannot be played on a basis of equality. (WR)

Thank you. Now for a fun fact:

TENNIS BALL

revitalization can be accomplished in the privacy of your local launderette.

Wash the balls in the washing machine (with your clothes, if you want) on regular cycle. Then toss them in a dryer and run them through on medium heat. Be careful they don't overheat. The original bounce will return. (NW)

THE PONIES

The track is the lottery in motion, where week after week you can stand in the shade and watch your retirement income die prematurely on the home stretch.

A SIMPLE SYSTEM

There's no need for fancy racing forms here. All you need is a good look at the tote board and the track form.

At a time as near as possible to post time, examine the odds for each horse in a given race. Next, divide the bet into the payoff. For example, if a horse is going off at five-to-two, divide two into five for two and a half. Next, add the resulting figure to the jockey's weight. To continue our example, you would add two and a half to say 120, giving you 122.5. You bet on the horse with the lowest total. If more than one horse has the same total, bet on the larger horse. (MBe)

SOME REASONS WHY YOU SHOULD READ THE RACING FORM

The form will tell you:

- The horses most recently raced
- The horses that finished out of the money, but within five lengths of the winner
- Horses frequently worked out by trainers prior to the race
- Horses with recent changes in their equipment (with blinders added or removed, for example), their jockey or their trainer (SL)

WHERE YOU CAN'T WIN

If you have to gamble, stick with the track. You absolutely cannot win at two-table casinos and after-hours joints. (*Anon.*)

MOTOCROSS

See *Motorcycle Madness* in *CHAPTER FIVE: MODERN MOBILITY*.

TOBACCO: SMOKE, CHEW AND SNUFF

Tobacco is great stuff. You can do things with tobacco you can't do with money or women. You can chew it, smoke it and stuff it up your nose. It'll cool you out and calm you down. Too bad it kills you.

It's sort of overrated, too. The stuff doesn't *really* calm you; in fact, it makes you more nervous. It also doesn't taste real good; in fact, it destroys your senses of taste and smell. Even as a killer, it isn't particularly efficient: death by cancer takes far too long and is generally a tasteless episode for everyone concerned.

STOP SMOKING

But not now. Wait for a while. If you stop now, you'll only be stopping because your wife or mother or girlfriend has jumped on your back and ridden you over the edge of Red Butte Mesa. You'll never stick with it, so ignore all those well-meaning knee-jerks. Strike a match and light another.

When you get good and ready, get good and sick — something that makes your throat feel like bad road and makes the thought of a cigarette seem almost funny. It'll make stopping for the first two days a snap.

After that, it's maintenance. Quit for an hour at a time; never admit to yourself or to anyone else that you've really stopped.

Don't expect to feel great; in fact, for the first month or so, you'll feel like you have a low-level, persistent cold. You'll cough up big, black goobers and blow yellow rope out of your nose. You won't really be dying for a smoke, but the idea will have a certain charm. Let it pass. Wait for another hour. Don't complain. Take a deep breath. Be a Modern Man.

Eventually, you'll be an ex-smoker. Then you can put your self-righteousness all over your sleeve and browbeat those unfortunates too healthy to catch cold at the right time. Brag about how you've reduced the chances of heart disease and cancer and all the rest. Drive your friends nuts. (DB)

Forget about substituting any other tobacco product. If you smoke just one teeny, little puff of *anything* you'll be hooked again, and that's a promise. (SJP)

CIGARS

Smoking a cigar can be so offensive to others that the vice *demands* consideration on the part of the smoker. In a curious way, smoking a cigar will *force* you to become a gentleman. Aficionados, however, claim that a man has to go a long way before finding a habit as satisfying. Besides, *anything* George Burns does must be okay. (ESt)

Cuban cigars are considered to be the world's best — perhaps because they can't legally be imported into the United States (although they are available in Canada). Both Dominican and Jamaican stogies are comparable, however. (ESt)

Sumatran wrapped cigars — especially those marketed as "Wilde Esprits" — are smoother and more satisfying than any small Havana. (DB)

Punch a hole in the tip of your cigar with a toothpick at dinner, a sharpened pencil at your desk. (ESt)

Never, under any circumstances, light up a cigar in a restaurant or in someone else's automobile. You may be a great lover of cigars and swear that yours are the sweetest-smelling cheroots ever, but you'll likely ruin somebody else's hundred-dollar meal. Cigars are best enjoyed as a private pleasure.

Holding a cigar: Never hold a cigar by the label; it looks too prissy. Throw the damn things away. On the other hand, use of a cigar holder saves the stogie's end from being chewed into something resembling road kill and makes cigar smoking more pleasant both for the smoker and for those around him. (ESt)

A dissent: Never use a holder with a cigar. The enjoyment of a cigar comes as much from the juices in the leaf as from the smoke. (DK)

Let it burn: Never stub out a cigar; the smell is monstrous. Just place it in an ashtray and let it go out by itself. Don't flick the ash from the cigar, either. Keep about three-quarters of an inch of ash on the tip and let the rest fall off on its own. (AB)

When a cigar goes out, and you decide you want to smoke it later, be sure to blow gently into it to clear the smoke trapped inside. (*Anon.*)

PIPES

are tweed for the mouth. Like tortoise shell specs, a pipe can make a tuna look intelligent. So a smart man looks after his pipe.

Breaking in a pipe can be a painstaking process, if it's done right. The idea is to slowly coat the inside of the bowl with a fine layer of "cake" — the residue left after a smoke. The best way to evenly coat the bowl is to work from the bottom up, smoking just a little at first, then gradually increasing the amount of tobacco on successive smokes. *Be careful not to smoke the tobacco too hot.* This is especially easy to do with a short bowlful. Burning a new pipe can destroy it. (JCC)

A dissent: To break in a pipe, fill it up and smoke it all the way down to give an even cake inside. (GVS)

Thoroughly clean and empty your pipe after a smoke. Swab it with a pipe cleaner and periodically remove the carbon from the bowl with a pipe tool or a small penknife. Take particular care that the heel of your pipe is free from the dottle remaining in the bowl after a smoke. And be careful not to use instruments so sharp they'll leave the cake uneven — or, worse, cut into the briar.

Never bang the pipe against anything harder than your hand when you're cleaning it out. And never remove the mouthpiece if the pipe is still warm. When you do remove the mouthpiece, use a full grip and always turn clockwise.

It's best to let a pipe rest for a day after a thorough cleaning.

Fill your pipe gradually. The operative maxim here is, "First with the hand of a child, then with the hand of a woman, then with the hand of a man."

Polish the briar on your pipe by simply running it down your cheek or alongside your nose from time to time.

Tobacco: Flake tobacco should be smoked in a narrow, tall pipe into which the flakes should be inserted *vertically*. A flake tobacco will not smoke satisfactorily in a wide-bowled pipe. (DM)

Tobacco types:

Virginia — Strong and sweet. May burn slightly hot. A favorite for blending.

Burley — Rich and sweet, with a mild bite.

Latakia — A strong and smokey flavor with some bite.

Perique — Spicy and very strong, with a pronounced bite.

Cavendish — A dusky, aromatic tobacco, often used in blends.

Watch out for *fruity tobaccos*. These blends usually burn so hot you can't taste them, and when you can you wish you couldn't. They are for children, for the most part. (DM)

Don't mix tobaccos in a pipe. Reserve a pipe for each type of tobacco. (*Anon.*)

Children are completely and utterly incapable of understanding the value of a good pipe. If you expect kids to visit, get all your pipes up and out of reach. To a child, a pipe is what a normal person uses for blowing bubbles, that's all. If you are careless, all you can do is shrug and go out and buy another pipe. The kids won't understand until they're older, at which time your restraint will guarantee you a lifetime of endearment. (RBr)

Cigar and pipe smokers trade the threat of lung cancer for throat cancer, jaw cancer and other grossly disfiguring ailments. (MC)

See also *Smoking Etiquette* **in** *CHAPTER SEVENTEEN: THE DEPORTMENT DEPARTMENT.*

CHEW AND SNUFF

Perhaps the most peculiar way to imbibe tobacco is to shove it up your nose. A full snuff addict is so far gone that you can substitute instant coffee for tobacco and be reasonably certain he won't notice for the first two or three sniffs. (HE)

Chewing tobacco is for baseball players who never went to college and for those whose work prohibits them from entering structures inhabited by human beings. (SPN)

And not into the wind: Try not to spit in the direction of the person you're talking to.

Cup one: Indoors, pretend like you're drinking out of a paper cup; spit into it, then throw it away. (RR)

DRUGS

are the perfect booster for those who have trouble getting stupid naturally.

LUXURY TAX

Ounce for ounce, drugs are among the most expensive consumer goods on earth. Snorting Platinum is cheaper — and is less likely to transform you into a paranoid driveling bore. (*Anon.*)

OVERDOSES

In all situations where symptoms of serious drug overdose appear, *immediate medical attention should be sought or death may result.*

The information that follows is not designed to replace competent medical assistance. The "street" remedies presented here have been around since the '60s, and a lot of druggies have died since then.

Don't try to act like a doctor for your dying pal unless you really *are* a doctor, and unless you really are straight at the time. There is a natural reluctance to refer a friend to a hospital in the event of an overdose, and that's too bad, since that's often the only measure that will save a life. If you decide to treat an overdose yourself, get ready for some serious legal complications if your patient dies.

Don't attempt to treat anyone in a coma. Get help fast.

TO COUNTERACT THE EFFECTS

Drug	*Try*
Marijuana	Eating and exercise will help decrease the high.
Cocaine and other stimulants (*Dexadrine, amphetamines, Benzedrine*	Tylenol can help. Balancing a speed overdose with downers — most commonly codeine — is done, but we certainly wouldn't recommend it.
Sedatives, barbiturates or downers (*Doriden, Equanil, Librium, Luminal, Miltown, Nembutal, Pentothal, Quaalude, Seconal, Valium*)	A mild stimulant, like coffee, may diminish the effects. *A sedative overdose is extremely dangerous and requires careful medical attention.* Sudden withdrawal from barbiturate addiction can be more dangerous than kicking heroin cold turkey. Unless the intake is diminished gradually under medical supervision, the effects of sudden withdrawal can be deadly. *Don't let them sleep.*
Hallucinogens (*LSD, peyote, mescaline, psilocybin, STP*)	A mild tranquilizer can help calm an anxious psychedelic user. In effect, however, there is no reliable antidote for a hallucinogenic overdose, and, since most "trips" last eight or more hours, you can only look forward to a long night of nursing. Stay nearby to keep the victim from harming himself.
Volatile substances (*glue, solvents, nitrous oxide*)	The highs brought on by sniffing and inhaling this stuff are short-lived — although the victim can sometimes become violent, in which case physical restraint is necessary. If the overdose is acute, the victim may pass out, forget to remove the bag and thereby inevitably suffocate. So let him have plenty of fresh air. If required, administer mouth-to-mouth resuscitation (**q.v., under** *THE MODERN MEDIC* **in** *CHAPTER SIXTEEN: MODERN MISHAPS*).
Narcotics (*morphine-based heroin, Percodan, Dilaudid; synthetic-based: Demerol, methadone*)	Walk 'em and walk 'em some more. If the victim *stops*, the whole show's over. They'll simply sleep *to death*. Make them take a shower, give them coffee, and give them a quick ride to the hospital. Narcotic overdose is *extremely* dangerous, and requires prompt medical attention.
PCP	Restrain until hospitalization is possible.

TV METAPHYSICS

Tune in and tune out.

STAR TREK
Trust Sulu before Chekov.

DICK VAN DYKE
Never rearrange Rob and Laura's furniture.

BONANZA
Never ask Hoss. Hoss doesn't know.

FATHER KNOWS BEST
Father knows second best. (FW)

KIDDIE PARTIES

Easy on the rental ponies and the clown suits. Kids have simple tastes, and for a birthday, ice cream and cake is good to eat and good to wear and good enough.

THE BIG GETAWAY
from the house: take the kids to a local amusement park or the movies or to a picnic. It'll save wear and tear on the house, but probably not on you. (KHG)

PARTY FAVORS
Give away the party favors as the kids leave. It's a nice note to end on, and the children won't leave the stuff behind. (KHG)

AND ONE FOR YOU
Have plenty of liquor handy for the grown-ups. It'll keep them calm, thereby reducing some of the youngsters' frenzy. (KHG)

A Modern Miscellany

This chapter includes weird stuff that seemed interesting when we received it, but didn't fit anywhere else. If books had attics, this one's would be here.

C O N T E N T S
Chapter Nineteen: *A MODERN MISCELLANY*

PETS

Aside from their rather obnoxious personal habits, pets can make swell companions — Modern Man's best friend and all that.

FLEAS

are petdom's incurable disease. Be careful of flea collars; their toxins can sometimes do more harm to Rover than his teeny guests. A good bath in salt water is better. (LJ)

Natural flea repellents include powdered rosemary, tobacco, citronella and eucalyptus. If you use these, or their chemical equivalents, do it outside. Otherwise the fleas will infest your house. Fleas can live in a dormant state in carpeting for years, then revive moments after sensing the presence of a warm-blooded host. (KHR)

A swim in the ocean or a salt-water bath can help for a flea infestation. (FC)

Flea-related skin problems on your dog can be soothed and often cured by applying a concoction made by adding one sliced lemon to a pint of rapidly boiling water. Allow the brew to steep for twelve hours, then apply it to the afflicted area daily, letting it dry thoroughly after each application. (SLa)

SKUNKS

and dogs don't mix. When they do, give the pooch a strong vinegar bath to eliminate the odor. (WJ) Tomato juice will cancel the odor of a skunk on a dog. Apply the juice, let it dry for a half-hour, shampoo and rinse. Repeat if necessary. (NLN)

FUN WITH PETS

Actually, having fun *with* pets is difficult. You can have fun with a monkey, for example, under almost any circumstance, but you can have fun with a dog only if you have sufficient real estate. You can never have fun *with* a cat, ever.

It's much easier to have fun at the expense of your pets. Modern Men don't get cruel with hearts so true as those beating in the furry chests of their pets. On the other hand, the Ken-L-Ration's on you, so if you get bored, try these:

Cats: Many people who own cats have been hoodwinked by the animal's cunningly instinctive reactions to various stimuli into thinking the small beasts actually have measurable intelligence. In fact, cats are a lot dumber than most of the things they eat. You can, however, use your cat for fun in a number of imaginative ways.

Displays: Cats are heat-seekers and will automatically find those places in the house that provide comfortable warmth. In the winter, try substituting that boring creche with a nice cat-bed display on top of a warm TV. In the summer, a cat on a windowsill can replace a troublesome herb garden. Look around your home; there are many funny or picturesque spots to display your cat at rest. Like the kitchen freezer.

Ordeals: Cats have the ability to quickly develop survival instincts, and you can amuse yourself by inventing "ordeals" which will help your feline pet develop those skills which will serve it well in times of tribulation. Try The Ordeal by Kitchen Cabinet or The Ordeal of the Giant Shopping Bag. You can spend many happy hours devising dire situations for your cat, secure in the knowledge that what you are doing is more for the cat's benefit than yours. Think of it as cat boot camp. After all, teaching your cat to swim in the pool can only be prudent. What if it fell in when nobody was at home?

Domestic Survival: To remind your cat of its instinctive responses, let your cat watch a TV show with lots of close-ups of insects. Cats love this. (SLa)

Dogs: If dogs looked and smelled better, they would deserve to inherit the earth. God has made no creature more noble than the dog, who exists only to make more pleasant the lives of others. As a result, you are encouraged to treat your dog the way your dog treats you.

We all know, however, that dogs are prone to making fun of their owners. In cities like New York, in fact, dogs have successfully induced their masters into acts of public humiliation. On a good day, you might catch this month's *Vanity Fair* cover subject squatting in the middle of a Fifth Avenue sidewalk picking up her dog's excrement. You can turn the tables on old Rover by dressing him up in clever disguises (dogs love sunglasses) or teaching him to tango.

If you neglected to train your dog when he was a pup, you can still convince him to do a variety of humiliating tricks if you wait until just before suppertime and use food as a reward. Remember, dogs love cheese and will do *anything* for a morsel. (RER)

Birds, rabbits and fish: Most members of these species make better dinners than pets. Don't play with your food. (DB)

Winged houseplants: Birds have traded light for flight. (SD)

Rabbits: Bunnies make fine house pets. They can be housebroken and litter-trained just like a cat, and, if your house also contains a dog or cat, they will assume many of the characteristics of these other animals. Remember, though, that rabbits are not cats. While cats aren't real smart, nobody calls them dumb bunnies. And be forewarned: unlike cats, rabbits cannot be left unattended for long periods of time. So if you bring a rabbit home, your traveling days are over. You might as well get a dog. (AR)

Pets and fun: The notion of a "fun pet" is oxymoronic. You should own pets only when you have a job for them to do. Make them work for their dinner: some cats are useful at controlling vermin; dogs are good hunters and sentinels. Pets are happy if they are gainfully employed. Birds and fish are never happy. (DB)

MAD DOGS

and Englishmen are both easily confused. When one comes at you, Thoreau said of mad dogs specifically, whistle. This is good advice even in a nonmetaphysical sense, as a friendly "Here, boy!" or two seems to puzzle pernicious pups. If you'd feel better carrying hardware, fill a water pistol with highly-diluted ammonia. One squirt will send both mad dogs and Englishmen running out into the midday sun. (AW)

BREEDING

Bitches are usually in heat for about three weeks. The interval between the eleventh and the fourteenth day is the most fertile period. Ovulation is also indicated when the bitch makes unmistakable presenting behavior. (*Anon.*)

ID

Many dog owners identify their pets by having their social security number (the owner's, not the dog's) tattooed painlessly on the inside of the animal's hind leg. Your local vet or kennel can give you more info on this, but the program is run by the National Pet Registry who collects a one-time fee for the service. (*Anon.*)

CAT PERILS

You can run through all nine lives of your cat by feeding it toxic houseplants, such as poinsettia. Insecticides will also do the job, as will mothballs and lead-based paint. The radiation that comes from your TV or microwave may give you a domestic *chat de Tchernobyl*. (NLN)

BIRD CARE

Do: Talk to your bird daily, provide a safe area for rest and relaxation, provide a warm and nurturing atmosphere, provide regular cleaning and grooming.

Don't: Make loud noises, expose the bird to smoke or noxious odors, overcrowd the bird, tease or harass.

Don't push or expect too much too soon from a new bird.

Essentials: Here is a list of bird basics:

- *Seeds*. Freshness is of primary importance since seeds form about 75 percent of a bird's diet.
- *Vegetables*. Almost any vegetable will do, but the best are corn on the cob, celery, spinach, alfalfa, broccoli, carrots, endive and cabbage.
- *Fruits*. Again, most will do fine, but pears, bananas, grapefruit, dates, cherries, apples, oranges and plums should be considered first.
- *Table foods*. Some table scraps are okay, but avoid hot, spicy foods.
- *Liquids*. All birds need plenty of liquids.

Also important: Vitamins, pelleted food, minerals and grit. (PSp)

BIRD FEEDING

Many birds become fussy about the food they eat. Poor eating habits are one of the chief causes of nutritional problems. Owners are often helpless in correcting this dilemma. Birds will often eat only one or two types of seeds (sunflower seeds will usually be one) or peanuts or they totally avoid fruits and vegetables.

Birds depend on visual recognition more than on taste or smell. Until they become familiar with the appearance of food they will be reluctant to try anything new. The answer is to be persistent. If your bird doesn't seem to like a new food immediately, don't give up. Keep offering it — but make sure it's always fresh.

Avoid abrupt changes in diets. *Never starve your bird into eating new foods*. Here are some other suggestions:

- For fussy seed eaters, try removing most — but not all — of the one or two types of seeds that your bird seems to prefer.
- Remove the preferred seeds at night. *Do not* put them back first thing in the morning. If necessary, add them later in the day.
- Mix new foods with regular foods.
- Place new foods near a favorite toy or at the end of the perch.
- Sweeten foods with a *small* amount of molasses or brown sugar.
- Try hand-feeding new food, but don't allow the bird to become dependent on this method. You can also try offering food as a part of a game or as a reward.
- Feed the bird in favorite areas outside its cage.
- Try feeding new foods in new forms (i.e., chopped). Try warming the food.
- Use your imagination — where there's a will there's a way.

Always be sure the food is fresh and is changed frequently while your bird is becoming accustomed to it. (PSp)

HIDING THINGS

Got something valuable? Never mind, stick it next to the meaning of life. Nobody'll spot it.

SO OBVIOUS

Many times, the most obvious place is the best place to hide something. Imagine you were assigned the task of "searching the premises" to find something of value. You'd probably rush in, take apart the lamps, check down the goldfish's throat, look in the frozen food, empty the closets and sift through the flour. But would you look in the handkerchief pocket of a sports coat thrown in a heap in the middle of the floor? (APS)

OLD SMUGGLERS KNOW

you should try to hide the goods in something that would not normally be regarded as being hollow. Most people will think of looking in an object where a cavity exists or could easily be created. Change your way of thinking — and seeing. If you were able to change the shape of the material you wish to smuggle, then you could, for example, sandwich it between two sheets of wood veneer to make a tabletop, or you could attach one fender inside another on an automobile with the illegal stuff in between. (Don't use these ploys; they've already been used to death by many smugglers, including me. But this should give you the idea.) (*Anon.*)

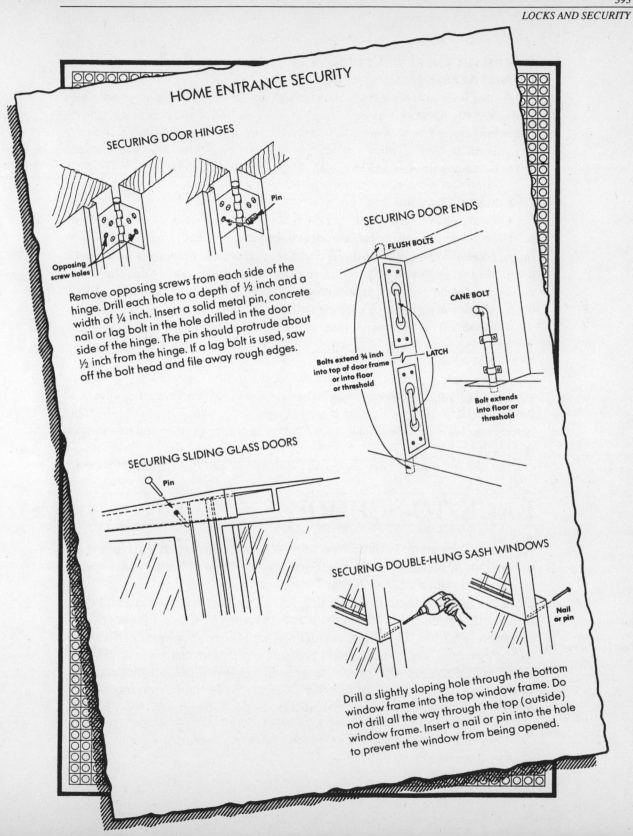

HOME ENTRANCE SECURITY

SECURING DOOR HINGES

Opposing screw holes

Pin

Remove opposing screws from each side of the hinge. Drill each hole to a depth of ½ inch and a width of ¼ inch. Insert a solid metal pin, concrete nail or lag bolt in the hole drilled in the door side of the hinge. The pin should protrude about ½ inch from the hinge. If a lag bolt is used, saw off the bolt head and file away rough edges.

SECURING DOOR ENDS

FLUSH BOLTS

CANE BOLT

Bolts extend ¾ inch into top of door frame or into floor or threshold

LATCH

Bolt extends into floor or threshold

SECURING SLIDING GLASS DOORS

Pin

SECURING DOUBLE-HUNG SASH WINDOWS

Nail or pin

Drill a slightly sloping hole through the bottom window frame into the top window frame. Do not drill all the way through the top (outside) window frame. Insert a nail or pin into the hole to prevent the window from being opened.

WHERE, OH *WHERE* CAN I HIDE THAT
HESTER BATEMAN TEA SERVICE?

Or that troublesome chest full of silver bullion? Or the collection of grandfather's gold coins? Big problems, you say? We say, "No sweat." What you need is a hole in the cellar floor. Dump the goods in the hole and recover it with concrete. Of course, it will be inconvenient to fetch it when you want it. But everybody else will have the same problem. Just beware of Avon Ladies carrying jackhammers. (*Anon.*)

CAR CAMOUFLAGE

Camouflaging the interior of your car is the best way to deter thieves looking for locked-up valuables. Since most competent thieves are delayed for only a moment by locked doors or alarms, you want the inside of your car to look like it's just not worth the trouble. Leave newspapers in the back seat, along with an empty can of Road King motor oil; dirty coffee cups and a cheap swim fin will all help convey the desired image. Use an old, moldy shower curtain to hide the big stuff.

This ruse will not work well if your car is a late-model Euro-import. (PNe)

GIVE 'EM AN IOU

Carry cash in your front pocket instead of in your wallet. This will help you increase your odds against pickpockets. It can also be used as a foil against muggers — just show them your empty wallet — although if you're caught out, it's considered rather bad form (street thugs have the same attitude toward hidden income as the IRS) and may result in severe injury. (RDK)

See also *Decorating as Camouflage* **in** CHAPTER TWELVE: MODERN MANORS.

BACK-TO-SCHOOL

Access to the pleasures of college life — without the expense of tuition, the tedium of meaningless lectures and the boredom of homework — can be obtained with a college ID card.
Get a friend who's actually attending school to lend you his card and take it to another friend, this one in the graphics trade (a printer, maybe, or a commercial artist). They'll help you negotiate the miraculous corridors of superphotocopy machines, instant presses, plastic laminators and all the other tools that can help you create a phony ID. Then the familiar world of first-rate libraries, swimming pools and gyms, student discounts and even college mixers will reappear. It'll be like you never left. (NW)

Many Modern Men feared that they'd never be *able* to leave.

COMPUTERIZED TELEPHONE DIALERS

The times that try Modern Men's souls are when the telephone rings on a Saturday night. You pick it up and find that a computer has called you to try to sell you some aluminum siding.

Listen to the message. At the end, you will be given an opportunity to express your interest in the product. Lie, and tell the machine it's a swell idea, you'd love some.

Eventually, somebody will contact you — this time, a real person. Play along through the sales pitch; in fact, do everything possible — but don't sign anything. What you're trying to get here is simple: You want the name of the company and as much information about the firm and its management as you can get. If you're extremely lucky, you may even get the name of the manager or president (although once you have the company name and the city in which it's located, you can get that information through the local government or through the Better Business Bureau).

Once you have the name of the president, get his number from the directory and call him at home and tell him you'd like to discuss his product. Repeat this at all hours. Tell him how much you love his computerized telephone-dialing machine. (KCC)

MAGAZINE SUBSCRIPTION CARDS

The loose cards, called "blow-in" or "drop" cards, used by magazine publishers to push subscriptions are becoming an environmental hazard. They litter parking lots and roadsides. And they're damn irritating. It's time to put a stop to them.

In every magazine, there are at least two of these dreadful nuisances. They all bear prepaid reply postage so you can apply for a subscription and be billed some other time. Forget that. Here's what you do: Every time you get a loose card in a magazine, simply drop it into the nearest post box. *Do not write anything on it.* The magazine will be obliged to pay the postage — sometimes a substantial amount — and after a while, they may be persuaded to drop the drop cards. (PP)

STATIONERY

To the entrepreneur, stationery is the first step in transforming fantasy to reality. A letterhead makes you whoever you wish to be.

These days, of course, practically anything that's printed on paper constitutes stationery. The guidelines here are for the most conservative forms of business and personal stationery:

Paper: A high-quality, smooth-finish letterhead stock with matching envelopes should be used; the best colors are white, off-white (including cream and ivory) and gray.

Ink: Remember, we said *conservative*. The best choices are black, dark red, dark blue, dark green or gray.

Printing methods: Engraved (or intaglio) is the most conservative and formal; it's also the most expensive. An inexpensive version of intaglio printing, called thermography, is now popular. Thermography involves the use of heat-sensitive inks in an offset process. After printing, the ink is exposed to heat and rises on the surface of the stock. Thermography is so obviously a cheap version of intaglio that it should be avoided. If intaglio is too expensive, then go with simple offset lithography.

Type: For gentlemen, the type should be simple, straightforward and, above all, *small*. Eight-point type should be the maximum size; seven-, six- and even five-point type is not uncommon. **(See illustration.)**

TYPE SIZES:	
6 point type	THE MODERN MAN A Guide to Life THE MODERN MAN A Guide to Life
8 point type	THE MODERN MAN A Guide to Life THE MODERN MAN A Guide to Life
10 point type	THE MODERN MAN A Guide to Life THE MODERN MAN A Guide to Life

BUSINESS STATIONERY

The dimensions for business letterheads in the United States are 8.5" x 11"; in Europe the standard size is A4. The name of the organization or business should appear at the top of the sheet, along with the address and telephone number, including all appropriate codes; occasionally, an individual's name and title will also appear on personalized company letterhead. The name should be at the top, but set aside from the rest of the information.

The matching business envelope measures 4.5" x 9.5" and is called a number-ten envelope. The return address should appear in the upper left-hand corner.

Personal stationery often has only the sender's initials at the top of the letterhead, although another equally acceptable practice is to show only the sender's address and sometimes the telephone number centered at the top of the sheet. On the envelope, only the sender's address appears on the envelope flap.

The sizes for personal stationery have been standardized. The most common size is called "Monarch" (7-7.25" x 10-10.5"), which folds twice to fit a number-eight envelope

(3.875" x 7.5 "); Monarch-sized stationery is often used for informal business correspondence. The other standard size is called "Baronial," and measures 6" x 9"; it's folded once to fit a number-six envelope (4.75" x 6.5"). Baronial-sized stationery is favored mostly by women.

Business-sized letterheads are suitable for personal use, although the style of personalized stationery should be observed.

Cards: Traditional personal cards carry only the user's name, a practice that substantially reduces their practicality. Vulgar moguls have adopted the name-only principle for their business cards; the assumption is that they're so well-known that no further information is necessary. You can go them one better by being so well-known you need no card at all.

Business cards should bear the information that appears on the letterhead, along with a scaled-down logo (if any), and, of course, the appropriate name and title and, if desired, direct line. (KDO)

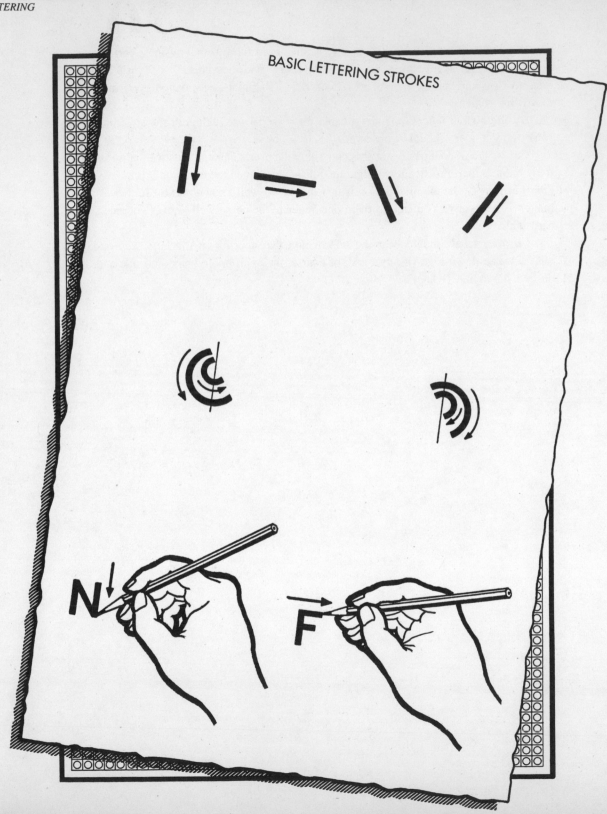

BASIC LETTERING STROKES

CHAPTER 20
Modern Meals

Something's always cooking in the Modern Man's Bitchin' Kitchen.

We've got easy recipes for bamboozled bachelors. (You can't miss.We tried all these ourselves, and we're here to tell the tale.) And we've got the inside poop on frying pans and menu-planning and beer storage and all the rest.

Maybe it doesn't seem real modern to strap on an apron after a hard day arc-welding U-boats. But Modern Men are made in the kitchen. If you can feed yourself, all other domestic arrangements become completely optional.

A Modern Man at Mess is a Modern Man at liberty.

C O N T E N T S
Chapter Twenty: *MODERN MEALS*

Part One: KITCHENS: The Kitchen Credo — How to Look Like You Know What You're Doing — Fun with Food and Other Facts: Lloyd Bridges, Pan Flips and Better Rice — Drains — How to Sharpen a Knife — How to Sharpen Scissors — Hot Knives — Bottle Drips — Stinky Fridges — Silver Salvage — Recycling Charcoal — Mending Cracked China — Greasy Pots — Cleaning an Oven — Literary Shelf Liners — Glasses — Kitchen Control — Kitchen Safety: *Gas / Oil and Water / Chopping Food / Fire* — Kitchen Design — Kitchen Tool Inventories: *Basic / Intermediate / Advanced* — How to Use a Frying Pan — Grocery Inventory — The Refrigerator — The Freezer — Microwave Ovens — Tablecloths — Part Two: MODERN MEALS: Cooking for One — Cooking for Girls: Budgets and Tactics — Cooking for Many: Carving a Turkey — *Plan Ahead / How to Blowtorch a Tenderloin / Keeping Beer in the Washing Machine / Budgeting* **— Part Three: ENTERTAINING WITH FOOD:** *Menu for One / Menu for Two / Menu for a Crowd* **— Part Four: WINE: Red and White — Ignoring Pretentiousness — Vintages — Wine Merchants — Wine and Asparagus — Breathing — Serving Temperatures — Storage — Broken Corks — Opening Wine — Opening Champagne — Labels — Quick Chills — The Surefire Wine List — Three Great Italian Wines — California Wines — Advertising — Part Five: TRICKY FOODS: Finger Foods and Gravy Mops — Foods You Should Buy and Not Try to Make — Part Six: RECIPES FOR MODERN MEN: An Intro — Spices — Explanations and Apologies — Quality Counts — Timing Dishes — Flavorings to Avoid — Ten Great Meat Dishes —** Filleting a Fish **— A Perfectly Adequate, Functional Sauce — Ten Great Vegetable Recipes — Ten Great Breakfasts — Soups, Salads and Stews — Bread — Pasta — Wines, Cheeses and Desserts**

Part One: KITCHENS

are Modern Man's final frontier, the last place many of us head when we're hungry.

All that's changing now, of course. The new sensitivity has taught us that a Modern Man should know his pots and pans and that it's not unmanly to cook for himself. Plus, it saves a lot of money, and what with girlie magazines now going for four and five bucks, every little bit helps.

KITCHEN CREDO
Wok like a man. (AW)

The kitchen is a world of mystery and mayhem, a world where, especially in the company of guests, what you really want to know is

HOW TO LOOK LIKE YOU KNOW WHAT YOU'RE DOING
And, of course, the answer is to *actually* know what you're doing. But that only comes with experience. In the meantime, here are some hints to help you disguise your shortcomings:

Stick to what you know or have already practiced. Don't try out a new dish with guests hanging around. You'll just ruin your image and their appetites. On the other hand, if you do something you've already done successfully before, go about your business with the unconcerned air of the supremely confident chef. (AR)

Most food prep involves a lot of tedious chopping, skinning and mixing. The actual cooking part is a brief, dramatic crescendo of fiery activity in a smokey hellhole fit only for the brave. So do as much of the boring stuff as possible before turning on the heat, or during the inevitable intervals that occur when dishes are cooking. Keep the various chopped and premixed ingredients in some orderly fashion and near to the stove. When the flashy bit happens, make sure somebody's watching. (AR)

Remain visible. Don't disappear into the kitchen for hours. Instead, do as much as possible before anyone arrives, then whip it together in short order. It'll seem like you made the whole meal in minutes. (DB)

Give your kitchen that pro smell by sautéing some garlic cloves in a skillet with some oil. (AR)

See also below: *Cooking for Girls, Plan Ahead, Meat for Many, Entertaining with Food* **and** *Pan Flips.*

FUN FOOD FACTS
Water boils almost twice as fast with the pan covered. (BGF)

Prevent sticking by heating a pan before putting anything in it. (EDV)

Thicken a sauce that won't behave by mixing some cornstarch with water, adding the mixture to the broth and cooking a little longer. This mean trick has saved many a cook's ass. (OG)

To skin a garlic clove, simply press down firmly on the clove with the tines of a fork. The skin can then be easily removed with the fingers. (RB)

Chopping an onion can be most easily accomplished by first cutting away the tips of the onion, then making a layer-deep incision from the top to the bottom and thereby removing the outermost layer. Next, slice off enough of a side to allow the onion to rest on its side without rolling. Make a series of horizontal slits from the top of the onion almost to the bottom. Then slice off another side, turn the onion 90 degrees and make another series of slices. Finally, slice the onion and presto! you've got it diced. (TE)

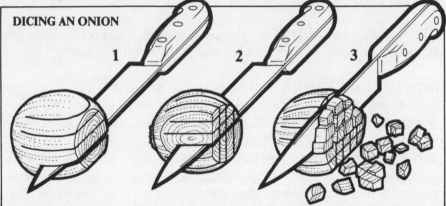

DICING AN ONION

1   2   3

Lloyd Bridges never cried: Soak onions under water before chopping to avoid tearing and crying. (JT) If you keep onions in the fridge, you won't cry when you cut them. But don't try putting garlic in your icebox. (DH)

Gravies and sauces generally comprise equal amounts of flour and grease (including butter, oil, drippings, fat and the like) mushed into a paste called a *roux* to which liquid is added. The whole trick is that the liquid should be quite hot and stirred into the roux in small amounts. (REJ) To give gravy a darker, more appetizing look (while adding some color to a name), mix in a small dash of instant coffee and call it "redeye." (RB)

Proficiency at the pan-flip, the hallmark of a gastronomic acrobat, is all in the wrist. Try it: Hold the pan by the handle and, without removing it from the top of the stove, give it a sharp jerk back and toward you. Practice with sliced raw vegetables until you have it pat. (AR)

If you're cooking for an audience, sling food and utensils around with decisiveness and authority. Embrace a flash in the pan. Bang a few pots, stir up some smoke; lots of high heat and sizzle adds to the drama. (MHG)

Produce will ripen quicker if put in a paper bag in a closed area, like a drawer (JKJ)

Stale bread can be made civilized again by placing it in a wet paper bag, then placing the bag in a 300° oven for a few minutes. You can also microwave stale bread for a few seconds on high to give it an all-day chewy consistency. (TKY)

Egg whites will froth higher when beaten if they're at room temperature. (JKJ)

For better rice with a professionally "dry" consistency, put a piece of dry bread on top of the serving dish. Take it off before anyone sees it, though. (TKY)

Frozen fish will taste much better if you let it thaw in milk. (TKY)

Bad canned food is what's inside any tin can that exhibits

- Leaks
- Rust
- Bulging

What makes bad canned food really bad is that the badness is poison and the poison is one of the baddest — botulism (**q.v., under** *THE MODERN MEDIC* **in** *CHAPTER SIXTEEN: MODERN MISHAPS*).

DRAINS

often can be unclogged by pouring in a half cup of salt with some boiling water. (PT)

HOW TO SHARPEN A KNIFE

The easiest way to keep knives sharp is to take them to a sharpener about four times a year. Otherwise, the following:

Regular honing on sharpening steels or rods will keep your knives sharp. Longer steels (12" or more) are easier to use than shorter ones (9"). Draw the knife edge across the rod while simultaneously bringing the blade down the rod and toward you. The edge of the knife should be kept at a 30° angle.

Steels and rods are good for edge maintenance, but not very useful for sharpening a dull knife. (BH)

Use a whetstone on a flat surface to sharpen knives the old-fashioned way. Press the edge of the blade against the stone at a very acute angle, so the blade is nearly flat against the stone. The sharpening action seems complex at first, but basically it consists of the following steps all done at one time: First, hold the stone in place; second, hold the knife handle and press down the knife edge against the stone; third, draw the knife across the stone from the handle to the tip; fourth, while drawing it across, you also have to pull the knife along the stone's length. Remember to keep your fingers below the level of the work. Repeat this action as many times as required on both sides until it's sharp.

A whetstone, incidentally, is not a wetstone. Use it dry, without any oil or water. There are modern devices available for knife sharpening, and they work easier and do just as good a job. But they lack the satisfaction of working with a stone. (ATH)

A dissent: Never use a whetstone without first applying a film of oil or water. (DC)

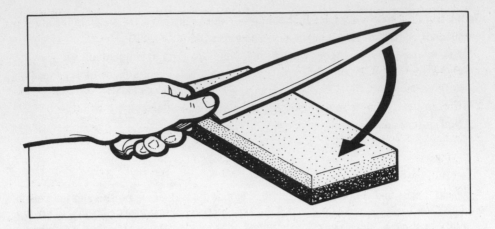

A HOT KNIFE

cuts fresh bread easier. (*Anon.*)

SHARPEN SCISSORS

by cutting a piece of fine sandpaper twice — but no more. (EA)

BOTTLE DRIPS

Immediately after pouring liquid from a bottle, wipe the lip of the bottle across the back of your hand to prevent the inevitable dribble. (TKY)

REDUCE FRIDGE ODORS

by storing either of the following inside: Charcoal, baking soda or coffee. (TKY)

THINGS TO KEEP AWAY FROM YOUR SILVER

Rubber, citrus, salt, eggs, guys with panty hose on their heads, mustard, batteries and detergent. (FTM)

CHARCOAL

can be reused once, even twice after its first use.

Close the lid on your charcoal grill immediately after the cooking is completed. Without oxygen, of course, the coals go out, leaving plenty of unburned charcoal for the next time. (NW)

CRACKED CHINA

can be mended by immersing the damaged piece in boiling milk for forty minutes or an hour. Not only will the cracks vanish, but the piece will be significantly stronger as a result. (CSD)

TO CLEAN GREASE-ENCRUSTED POTS

and pans, fill them with soapy water and let them simmer while you eat. (AW)

CLEAN YOUR OVEN

by diluting ammonia with water in a ratio of about one to five. Paint the mixture on the inside of the oven and leave it for about a day. Wipe clean using warm water. (GVO)

HONEY, WHERE'S MY MANUSCRIPT?

Typing paper makes excellent shelf liner. (TKY)

GLASSES

To unstick stacked glasses, put the two glasses in hot water; put ice inside.

Store glasses upright. They'll require more frequent washings, but they won't be as apt to develop a musty odor. This is especially critical with wine glasses.

The weakest part of a glass, particularly a crystal one, is its rim — another good reason to store them upright. (TKY)

KITCHEN CONTROL

Basically, the way to keep a busy kitchen under control is to keep it clean while you work. When making a meal, there are always lulls in the process, and since you're already humping through the mix-and-stir stage, you might as well keep going through the slow-simmer stage. Wash a few dishes or pots; put some food back in the pantry; wipe a counter; shine that stove knob, soldier. If you do it right, when dinner's over all you have to clean is the eating dishes.

Dishes and counters should be washed daily. Wash the kitchen floors weekly. (ML)

Dishes should be thrown away daily. (GR)

Always run some water into a hot pan or skillet the moment you're finished cooking. It makes later cleanup much easier. (TF)

Organize your spice rack alphabetically. (TKY)

KITCHEN SAFETY

Boring, right? How about

NUDE KITCHEN SAFETY WITH NAZI DOGS

How about paying attention?

Gas is definitely the preferred means of cooking. The heat is easier to control; an electric ring can look the same no matter how hot or cold it is. (JG)

Gas does present some problems, however:

Número Uno rule for gas appliances: Unless you smell something funny, light the match before you turn on the gas. If Sylvia Plath had followed this simple rule, she'd be alive today. (JG)

More gas facts: Although propane and natural gas are both odorless, they are scented with garlic to make leaks easily detectable. Valves along a gas line are turned on by rotating them in the direction of the pipe's travel. A valve perpendicular to the pipe's travel is in the "off" position. (FFC)

Looking for a leak? Follow your nose until you've narrowed down the location of the leak, then paint the suspected area with soapy water; bubbles will form over the source of the leak. (FFC)

If you suspect a big leak, or can't find the source of a small one, open all the windows and shut off the main valve on the gas meter or on the propane tank. It's best to call your local gas company for repairs. If you want to attempt minor corrections yourself, make sure the gas is off and the system is purged. (PF)

Instructions for *lighting pilots* appears on most appliances. If the instructions aren't handy, locate the thermocouple, a sensor that must be heated by the pilot before the main burner will ignite. Before lighting the oven pilot, heat the thermocouple with a match. With most hot water heaters, first turn the burner knob to the pilot position, then press the reset button, and light the pilot while holding the reset button. After sixty seconds or so, release the button and if the pilot stays lit, turn the burner knob to the on position. (FFC)

Burners on gas appliances often become clogged. On a stove, grease is the usual culprit; rust and combustion debris attack oven burners, heaters and furnaces. In either case, remove the burner and clean all of the ports with a needle or an unbent paper clip, then tap the burner and shake out the crud. (FFC)

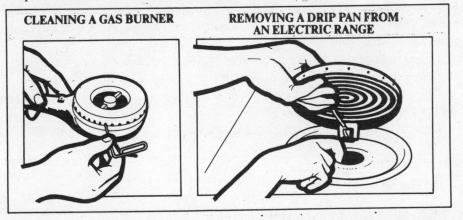

CLEANING A GAS BURNER

REMOVING A DRIP PAN FROM AN ELECTRIC RANGE

OTHER HANDY SAFETY TIPS:

Get all the water out of a pan by heating it before you heat any oil or grease in it. You heard it here first: Oil and water don't mix. Even a few drops of water trapped inside a pool of heated oil can cause a mini-explosion. (MHG)

When cutting or chopping hold the food with your fingers tucked under at the first joint so your hand looks like Fido's paw. This takes a little getting used to, but all the food-hacking pros do it, so it must make sense. (MHG)

If you're confronted with a fire in a pan the best remedy is to cover it immediately. The second best idea is to sling some baking soda at it. The single worst idea is to douse the fire with water. (JG)

Deep-fat frying is potentially a big fire hazard. In restaurants that do a lot of deep-fat frying, local codes usually require the installation of a profusion of extinguishers, sprinkler systems and the rest. So when you're cooking in deep fat at home, at least make sure the utensils you're using are safe. The pan should extend at least five inches above the level of the fat, since when cold food is added to hot fat, a large quantity of foam rises for the first few seconds. If the foam rises over the edge of the pan and reaches the burner, it's curtains. The place'll go up like a house a-fire.

If this should happen, try to cover the pan. Next, turn off the exhaust fan, since the flames can ignite the greasy fan filter, the filter can ignite the greasy flue and so on.

It's a good idea to have a decent *fire extinguisher* (q.v.) in the kitchen. One rated for class A, B and C fires is the ticket. Ask anyone who has been able to get in on the ground floor of a great house-fire opportunity what they think of fire extinguishers as a good insurance investment. (KJT)

If you hurt yourself, **see** *The Modern Medic* **in** *MISHAPS*.

KITCHEN DESIGN

Restaurant kitchens are good models of food preparation efficiency. If you want to see how a good kitchen should be designed, look backstage at your favorite diner. You'll see easily washed floors and counters; pots and tools will be well-organized and stored within easy reach. You'll also be surprised how few tools there are; a good cook knows that aside from the essentials (**see** *Kitchen Tools*), many tools are just useless clutter. If dinner is being prepared while you're taking your tour, you'll note that most of the cooking takes place on top of the stove; there are warming shelves above the stoves, and there is a broiler. But the oven is seldom used. (HG)

Conserve space on counter tops by relocating all those electric appliances — can openers, knife sharpeners, coffee makers, toasters — to a less-used area. (HGF)

Common sense and tradition stipulate that good kitchen design places the three primary work areas — the stove, the sink and the refrigerator — in a triangular pattern. If these areas are in a line, the number of steps between them increases significantly; when two of these areas are adjacent, that part of the kitchen becomes clutter-central. Busy kitchens are confusing enough without having confusion as part of the design. (SJH)

A sink should be surrounded by open counter space. (HGF)

THE REASONABLE KITCHEN

Rule One: Avoid gadgets.

Rule Two: Kitchen utensils are not pieces of construction equipment.

TOOLS

Basic
- Sharp knife with an 8" to 10" blade
- 12" iron skillet with lid
- Saucepan 7" wide, 5" deep, or 6" wide, 4" deep
- Mixing bowl
- Spatula
- Aluminum foil
- Can opener
- Corkscrew and bottle opener

Intermediate
- Everything on the basic list, plus
- Additional knives
- Another skillet
- Another saucepan with lid
- Another mixing bowl
- Large stewing kettle
- Colander
- Cutting board
- Baking sheet
- Loaf or bread pan
- Coffeepot
- Tea kettle
- Roasting pan
- Roasting pan rack
- Measuring cup and spoons
- Egg beater

- Meat thermometer
- Four-sided grater
- Vegetable scraper
- Serving and slotted spoons
- Assorted plastic containers with lids for leftovers

Advanced
- Everything from the first two lists, plus
- More knives and pans
- Soufflé dish
- Casserole dish
- Large wooden bowl
- Baking pans
- Muffin tin
- Cleaver
- Steam rack
- Cooking fork
- Wooden spoons
- Ladle
- Rolling pin
- Funnel
- Teapot
- Food mill sifter
- Electric blender
- Kitchen towels

FRYING PANS

Make 'em hot and make 'em of cast iron. Nothing's worse than trying to cook in a paper-thin, 25¢ frying pan.

Flash in the pan: To heat food in the blink of an eye, put a cast iron frying pan over the fire until it becomes very, very hot — hot enough to turn water to steam instantly. Take a half-shot of water (or more, depending on the quantity of food to be added), toss it in the pan, quickly add whatever food you wish to heat, and slam on the lid. Give it a minute or two of this kind of treatment and it should be done. (FF)

INVENTORY

A list of grocery store items you should keep on hand if you plan on cooking often.

Stage I
When you're first getting underway:

Grains
- Flour
- Sugar
- Baking powder
- Cornstarch
- Breadcrumbs
- Bisquick
- Cornmeal
- Salt

Liquids
- Cooking oil
- Olive oil
- Vinegar
- White wine

Dairy
- Butter
- Milk
- Parmesan cheese

Spices
- Pepper
- Thyme
- Oregano
- Basil
- Rosemary
- Tarragon
- Cayenne
- Chili Powder
- Cloves
- Nutmeg

Condiments
- Mayonnaise
- Catsup
- Mustard
- Worcestershire sauce
- Soy sauce
- Maple syrup

Fresh Items
- Garlic
- Onion
- Lemon
- Ginger
- Parsley
- Scallions

Nonfood
- Aluminum foil
- Paper towels
- Food storage bags
- Trash bags
- Dish detergent
- Sponges
- Scouring pads

Stage II
Grains
- All Stage I items

Liquids
- All Stage I items, *plus*
- Red wine
- Sherry
- Vermouth
- Brandy

Dairy
- All Stage I items, *plus*
- Heavy cream

Condiments
- All Stage I items, *plus*
- Chili sauce
- Tuscan peppers

Spices
- All Stage I items, *plus*
- Sage
- Curry powder
- Fennel
- Fines Herbes
- Caraway
- Marjoram
- Bay leaf
- Dill
- Cinnamon
- Celery seed

Nonfood
- All Stage I items, *plus*
- Waxed paper
- Clear food wrap

THE REFRIGERATOR

This is the big, bulky item once called "Where the Beer Is" but which they have recently renamed after a football player. The best way to keep a refrigerator running is to keep it full. Even if you don't have a lot of food in there, a fridge (and especially the freezer, q.v.) will run better if it's kept loaded. In a pinch, a bag of leaves or a stack of newspapers will do. Rotate weekly. (KH)

THE FREEZER

is the part of the refrigerator with the ice cube trays in it. Guys often underestimate the value of a freezer, but since you're paying for it anyway, you might as well use it.

Here's a list of freezer foods and the stuff that will keep in those Arctic conditions:
- *Nuts* keep far longer and are easier to crack when they're frozen.
- *Popcorn* pops better when it's put in the pan frozen.
- *Candles* stored in a freezer burn slower.
- *Ground or instant coffee* will keep fresh and frosty.
- *Plastic wrap* isn't as likely to stick to itself. (KH)
- *Vodka* won't freeze — the colder the better. (MR)

MICROWAVE OVENS

appeared on the market at about the same time women decided cooking was an act of political subservience. A bad girlfriend's not worth a good microwave. (RG)

TABLECLOTHS

Got a wrinkled tablecloth and company on the way? No prob:

Spread the tablecloth over the dining room table. Get out your plant atomizer and apply a mist of water to the tablecloth. Let dry. If you have an expensive mahogany table, this will promptly destroy the finish. So if your wooden table's worth more than a nickel, use some plastic protection — a couple of trash bags, maybe. (KK)

Part Two: MODERN MEALS

Nothing says lovin' like somethin' from the oven.

COOKING FOR ONE

Don't taste the food while you're cooking it; you'll spoil your dinner.

There are two schools of thought about solo cooking: One holds that you shouldn't let your eyes trick your stomach. When cooking for one, it's quite easy to cook more than you can possibly eat. Besides, if you're still hungry, you can make some more. The other holds that you should cook as much as you can stand so you'll have plenty of leftovers and thereby reduce your cooking chores next time. (AR)

Divide and devour: Many men dining alone never feel really full until all the food in sight has been eaten. You can save a little money — while fighting the good fight against gluttony — by simply wrapping normal-guy-sized portions in tinfoil or whatever and tossing them into the freezer. (AW)

A dissent: Single guys shouldn't cook. That's why we have coffee shops. (DB)

COOKING FOR GIRLS

Don't be confused. The idea here is to cook for the benefit of a visiting girl, a gesture not without charm, and one that deserves serious deliberation.

First, there's money: You can save a serious amount of money by cooking at home for a date, rather than picking up her chow bill at the local eatery.

Second, girls go goopy for a guy who confidently crosses what she considers to be traditional gender boundaries.

Third, you don't have to go through a lot of trouble to invite her home after dinner.

Fourth, and this is a problem, dinner at home takes the place of dinner out, so things like meatloaf and hotdogs are out. (**See** *Recipes for Modern Men,* **below.**)

Now, for some guidelines:

- Know your diner. Is she a vegetarian? Does she like fresh blood? You got to figure a menu for two.
- Keep it simple.
- Do as much as you can in advance.
- Practice everything once. Most girls are familiar with a kitchen, even if they later give up cooking for political reasons, and they have a general idea of what is supposed to happen and when. So you don't run the risk of looking like a jerk, keep the time she has to watch you cook to a bare minimum.
- Always refuse help. It all starts with a little help and before you know it, she's doing the cooking and making you feel bad. Instead, give her a drink and ask her to chat with you while you work. This does two things: it reduces tension, and it dulls her taste buds, just in case.
- Always leave the dishes for tomorrow. Never solicit help with the dishes, and refuse it if it's offered immediately after dinner. If she's still there in the morning, she can help with the dishes, but never after dinner. (JO)

A dissent: Be a klutz in the kitchen. Conveying the impression of absolute mastery in the kitchen squanders brownie points which can be earned through the impression that your cooking battles manfully against the Jurassic role-modeling that once tied her to the stove. So feign a bit of incompetence if you have to, just like she would if her oil filter needed changing. (AW)

COOKING FOR MANY

Plan for trouble. Something's going to go wrong; a kitchen error is hiding in the trees staring at the back of your head through a deer scope. So relax. Do your best. And duck.

CARVING A TURKEY

1. Carving position—First move turkey comfortably close and turn it on its side, breast away from carver.

2. Remove wing—Next raise wing and cut it off at the second joint. Set wing aside.

3. Bare thigh bone—Slice dark meat off drumstick and thigh until thigh bone is exposed.

4. Remove drumstick—Lift drumstick with napkin and cut off at thigh joint, leaving thigh on bird.

5. Meat from drumstick—Slice away dark meat from drumstick.

6. Cut away thigh bone—Cut around thigh bone with knife and remove from bird, as pictured.

7. Slicing dark meat—Slice dark meat away from turkey just above removed thigh bone. Arrange on platter.

8. Base cut—Make deep vertical cut in breast just in front of wing joint to serve as base for all breast slices.

9. Breast slices—Start from center of breast and cut toward you, removing slices one by one as shown.

Planning ahead is the name of the game. Do as much as you can in advance. Most of the Modern Man stew recipes are good for large groups because they can be prepared early and will benefit from sitting around for a day or two. Also, they're basically one-dish meals, a consideration for reducing the number of cooking and serving dishes and tools. Buy the dessert at the store (along with the appetizer, if you plan to have one). That leaves only a salad to be made while everything else is heating up. (AR)

MEAT FOR MANY

Get a tenderloin of beef, a whole one, a primo cut of meat about the size and shape of a fat man's arm. Have the butcher cut off the fat and sinew.

Because a tenderloin is a great cut, cooking is a cinch. You *can't* screw it up: Apply heat and serve. You can cook a tenderloin over coals, fry it in a giant skillet, roast it in the oven (350° for 20 minutes per pound; use a meat thermometer). You can, for example, quite successfully cook a tenderloin with a blowtorch: Place a fireproof plate on the table, take two blowtorches and, working on both sides at once, move the torches slowly back and forth along the length of the tenderloin. It's okay to char the outside; the inside will be pink. Twenty minutes ought to do it, although a discreet slice with a knife will reveal the state of the inside. (Serve with ears of corn with the husks on and wrapped in foil. Five minutes per ear under the torch will suffice.) Welding torches will also work. In fact, the only mistake you can make is to overcook the meat. Don't add any salt or pepper until after the cooking is complete. Fast food: heat and eat for eight. (SM)

PARTY CYCLE

Stow beer and other cold beverages in a washing machine with lots of ice. After the party, use the spin cycle to expel the water. (SLT)

Add lettuce to your washing machine, no soap. Put it on rinse cycle, wash the lettuce, spin it dry. This is a little tip for making big salads. (KUG)

WHAT'S IT COST?

Figure about ten bucks per person (at 1987 prices), including all foodstuffs, excluding all wine and other beverages. (AR)

Part Three: ENTERTAINING WITH FOOD

You have to do more than juggle small casabas and sing camp songs. You have to be smooth and self-assured and seem like you know what's going on. Entertainment doesn't just happen; it's always scripted.

MENUS

Making a menu is a great example of careful planning. Here are four extremely useful ones, the recipes for all of which can be found under *Recipes for Modern Men* **below,** except where noted:

1. Entertaining yourself: This is quick and easy.

Steak

—

Asparagus
or
Green Beans

—

New Potatoes
in Burnt Butter
or
Pasta Carbonara

—

Green Salad

2. Entertaining a girl: Caution. Girls often know a lot about how food is supposed to taste, so you're not going to go far on your ability to impress her foodwise. Instead, stress presentation. First, here's the menu:

Pistachio Nuts

—

Champagne, Valpolicella, *or* Beaujolais

—

Smoked Trout
(Buy the smoked trout; leave it whole or cut it
into two-inch pieces and present them on a leaf of lettuce
with a dab of mustard and sweet pickle on the side.)

—

Veal Piccata
with
Broccoli with Polonaise Sauce
or
Sautéed Zucchini and Onion

—

Greek Rice

—

Strawberry Sherbet

—
Coffee
(The trick is to have the coffeepot loaded so all
you have to do is turn on the heat.)

Presentation: The food's a snap. All the recipes are around here somewhere, and they've all been through the wringer in the Modern Man Bitchin' Kitchen. But *presentation,* well, presentation is the crucial bit.

Get cloth napkins. Hide those paper towels you've been stealing from Exxon. Buy or borrow a real tablecloth, preferably an off-white one. Have some flowers handy somewhere nearby, although not necessarily on the table. No candles. Piling candles and flowers all over the table makes it look like an altar (on which you seem to be willing to sacrifice your self-esteem).

The table should be set when she arrives, and the wine should be open. Put the pistachios in one bowl and leave a smaller shell-bowl alongside. Go easy on putting together the ranks of silver and all that. You will want to try to have matching silverware, stem glasses and plates, with separate plates for the appetizer and the salad. But get rid of as much table clutter as you can. One plate at a time, one glass at a time.

Put the portions on the plates in the kitchen, then bring them to the table. Keep the serving dishes in the kitchen, too, and clear away each course before setting out the next one.

Make a modest wine toast, nothing flowery, and be attentive to wine refills. Never force a drink on someone who doesn't want it.

When you serve the coffee, don't do it in mugs. Use cups and saucers; put the cream in a creamer and the sugar in a sugar bowl. (BD, et al.)

3. The general purpose, feed your-brother-in-law-and-your-parents special:

Black Bean Soup
or
Spicy Shrimp
with
Bread
or
Lox on Buttered, Toasted Pumpernickel
with
Lemon
—
Roast Duck
(allow one duck for three people)
or
Grilled Leg of Lamb

—

Cucumber-dill Salad

—

Greek Rice
(optional)

—

Red Cabbage

—

Zinfandel

—

Uncle Rick's Cherry Goo

—

Coffee

Presentation: This meal takes about four hours to put together. The presentation is the same as for the meal above, but this time you can put flowers on the table, you can haul out the salad forks and you can jam the table full of serving dishes.

If you've got the eye and the china, your dishes should be in color-contrast to the food you're serving.

See also *Tablecloths,* **above.**

4. The dinner party, where disaster's always on the menu. We favor the blowtorched tenderloin here, but, in case you've got grown-ups on the guest-list:

Nuts

—

Cioppino

—

Caesar Salad

—

Warm Rolls

—

Chianti

—

Fruit Tarts
(Buy these.)

An alternate:

Nuts

—

Choucroute

with
Boiled Potatoes
served with
Mustard, Bread and Pickles
—
Endive Salad
—
Moselle or Mâcon Wine
—
Store-bought Dessert

Presentation here is the least of your problems. Just try hard to make sure it doesn't look like a church social; avoid folding chairs, paper plates and cardtables.

Part Four: WINE

It's a beverage, nothing more. They make it from grapes. You buy it, then you drink it. If you drink a lot of it, you get drunk. Until wine can be discussed without pretentious side-effects, that's really all you need to know.

If battery acid had the same effect on the brain as wine, people would probably wax as enthusiastic about Sears Die-Hards as they do about Pouilly-Fumé '76. (MR)

DON'T SWEAT IT

Unless you're courting a wine steward, don't worry about it. A standard 750 ml bottle looks better than a jug (although it may not taste better), and you should figure a bottle per person for big drinkers.

If you don't know what wine goes with what, don't bother to learn. Find a wine you like and drink it with whatever you want. (JO)

DON'T SWEAT IT II

You can forget the riff about red wine with meat, white wine with fish and fowl. These are simply traditions, and justifiably some people insist on upholding them. But it's perfectly right and correct to drink any wine you wish with your meal. (AR)

DON'T SWEAT IT III

More esoteric jive has been written and said about wine than any other ingested substance (with the possible exception of marijuana, about which more ponderous garbage was written and spoken in a single decade than in the millennia that man has been cultivating the grape). Ignore the pretentiousness and learn to appreciate wine simply by drinking different types and formulating your own preferences and theories. Which you should keep to yourself, thanks. (JYG)

DON'T SWEAT IT IV

Too much importance has been placed on vintages of wine. Vintages are really only of importance in discussing certain expensive red wines and have little or no significance in determining the worth of most wines.

An "important vintage" occurs when ideal climatic conditions prevail for particular kinds of grapes. A good vintage year also reflects a wine's ability to withstand prolonged storage. Putting away wine for years and years is valid only for particularly great wines, and even then only after a period of maybe fifteen to twenty years. So, unless you're fooling around with "investment quality" wines, don't clutter up the basement. *Almost all wines suffer from prolonged storage and should be consumed when purchased.* The notion that wines get better with age is bunk. A truly great wine will not suffer from storage as much as a lesser wine, but it won't improve, either.

For white wines and light red wines, like Valpolicella and Beaujolais, vintage dates have a more immediate value, since these wines are not "keepers" and suffer most from storage. White wines should be drunk when young; light red wines should be consumed within the shortest possible time from the date of bottling.

If you do have to store wine, remember that air and fluctuations in temperature are harmful to wine. Keep wine on its side with the top slightly higher than the bottom; this ensures the cork will stay wet and swollen and that the seal will remain intact.

Wine is best kept in a dark area where the temperature is not likely to vary beyond a 50° to 60° range. Storing wine near heaters, stoves or in the sunlight is trouble. (JHG)

The Best Years: Here's the top of the pops since '76:

Bordeaux, Red	1976, 1982, 1983
Bordeaux, White	1976, 1983
Burgundy, Red	1981, 1985
Burgundy, White	1976, 1985
Cabernet Sauvignon	1985
Chardonnay	1980, 1985
Chianti	1985
Moselle	1983, 1985
Rhine	1983

As a rule, the more recent the vintage, the better the wine. (WRa)

LET SOMEONE ELSE SWEAT IT

Among the first things a new connoisseur of wine should do is cultivate the good graces of his local wine merchant, who will be your single most valuable asset in helping you negotiate the complex maze of wines. (JH)

NEVER MIND, GO AHEAD AND SWEAT IT, AFTER ALL

Never drink wine with dishes containing asparagus, artichokes, citrus or curries or other foods containing a lot of vinegar, like salads. (HMG)

BREATHING SPELLS

a controversy among most œnophiles. Some say uncorking a wine and exposing it to the air is essential, while others say pass the bottle quick. You decide. Most proponents of breathing say an hour for reds, twenty minutes for white. You decide. (AR)

SERVING TEMPERATURES

for wines varies according to type. Here's a general guide:

Heavy reds	Room temperature, but not much above 75°F
Light reds	Cool
Whites	Chilled
Sparkling wines	Cold (WRa)

UNFINISHED WINE

can be recorked and kept in the fridge, but the quality will steadily diminish, so a couple of days is the maximum storage time.

Save a plastic cork from a cheap bottle of bubbly; it can be used to reseal a more expensive bottle, but not for more than a day. It's bad form to try to recork champagnes or other sparkling wines. It can be done, but it'll not taste nearly as good as it did when you opened it the first time. (HG)

IF YOU BREAK A CORK

when opening a bottle of wine, try again, this time inserting the corkscrew at an angle. If this fails, your best bet is to use a "bootlegger" opener, a two-pronged gizmo that is worked in along the outside edges of the cork, twisted, then withdrawn, usually with the cork in tow. If all else fails, push the cork into the bottle, then strain out the bits and pieces as you decant the wine.

Many wine lovers advocate the "bootlegger" opener over the traditional corkscrew as the best choice. (NHG)

CORKSCREWLESS

Sometimes, a still wine can be opened without using a corkscrew by violently whacking the bottom of the bottle with a book or the bottom of your shoe.

Note: Don't do this with champagne, expensive wines or rare first editions. (AR)

TO OPEN CHAMPAGNE

or other sparkling wines, hold the bottle at a 45° angle (top up, natch) and slowly twist the cork without pulling. Natural pressure will force the cork out. (HG)

OUT OF HIDING

Don't serve a wine with the bottle wrapped in a napkin. It looks like you have something to hide — like a Thunderbird label. (HG)

COLDER QUICKER

Need to give a bottle of wine a quick chill? Instead of using the freezer — a risky proposition, especially with sparkling wines — use a bucket filled with ice and slightly salty water. Water is a better conductor of temperature than air and the liquid will ensure that the coldness comes in contact with most of the bottle's surface. Make sure the bottle is thoroughly dried before serving; a few drops of salt water in a glass of wine is a terrible idea for a spritzer. (FB)

THE SUREFIRE WINE LIST

Sparkling wines: Almost any sparkling wine that has both the phrase *"Blanc-de-blanc"* anywhere on the label and is capped with a natural cork is likely to be a fine alternative to champagne, even if it costs only three bucks a bottle. (NW)

Red wines: Practically any brand of California Zinfandel, considered by many to be the most robust of all wines, is a safe bet, and can be obtained at a reasonable price. (HG)

Red cabernets from Yugoslavia and Chile are good wines at bargain prices. (NW)

White wines: If white, slightly sweet German wines are to your taste, stick to the green-bottled Moselles or the Rhine wines (Rhinehessen, Rhinegau or Rhinepfalz) that come in brown bottles. Give Liebfraümilch a wide berth.

French white Burgundies from Mâcon are nearly as good and far cheaper than Pouilly-Fumé, Pouilly-Fuissé and other Loire valley whites.

Muscadet and the other Loire valley wines are the most reliable white wines. (NW)

Rosé wines: Modern Men should avoid rosé. It's sweet, so it wrecks the taste of food, and is often favored by young girls who are going upmarket from Colt .45. (NHG)

See also the list of wine-and-cheese combinations in *Desserts,* **below.**

THE THREE MUSKETEERS

of Italian wines — Bardolino, Valpolicella and Soave — are among the most trustworthy wines. Lambrusco, on the other hand, will give you an Italian headache before you've finished the first dreadful glass. (NW)

ALL CHANGE

When you find what you feel is a good California vineyard, switch to their table wines. You'll find that as a rule they're as good as their premium wines. (NW)

ADD ADS

You'll contribute nearly twice as much to the advertising budget of a heavily promoted wine than to the equivalent bottle from a less heavily promoted vineyard. (NW)

Part Five: TRICKY FOODS

The menu of the world is too big. Here's how to handle the items you haven't tried yet. (For cooking tips, **see** *Recipes for Modern Men*.)

THE MODERN MAN'S MASTER LIST OF FINGER FOODS

If it's here, grab it. If you want details, see elsewhere below.

Artichokes (**see below**)	Mussels
Asparagus	Olives
Bacon (**see below**)	Oysters (on half-shell; **see below**)
Cheese	Pizza
Clams (on half-shell; **see below**)	Potatoes (French fried, except in
Corn on the cob (**see below**)	many parts of Europe)
Crackers	Sandwiches (except in many parts
Fondue	of Europe)
Fowl (roast or broiled; **see below**)	Shrimp
Fruit (fresh)	Snails
Lobster	(KF)

ARTICHOKES

Pull the leaves off one by one. Hold the pointed end between your thumb and forefinger. Dip the pulpy end of the leaf into whatever you have handy — melted butter, melted butter with lemon, mayonnaise — and scrape the soft pulp off with your lower teeth (or, if you're worried about propriety, nibble the pulp off the leaf until you reach the stringy bit of the leaf). Ultimately, after all the leaves have been removed, you will come to a portion of the vegetable abundant in small, hairy fibers. Scoop these out. What's left is called the heart, and it's the best. Slice in quarters, dip in condiment and pop in your gob.

Artichokes should be served with a small bowl for disposing of leaves. (KF)

CHERRY TOMATOES

Select one small enough to place in your mouth whole. Close your lips tightly and chew. If they're all too large, break the skin with your front teeth before biting into one. Be careful — they squirt like crazy. (JTh)

CHICKEN

Unless served in a sauce, chicken can be eaten with your hands. Princess Margaret eats chicken that way, so it must be okay. A finger bowl is handy. (HF)

Roasted or broiled chicken must be eaten with a knife and fork at any formal dinner, although the use of your fingers is permissible at less formal gatherings. The same rules apply for frogs' legs. (JTh)

CLAMS AND OYSTERS (Raw)

When served on the half shell, these should be speared with a shellfish fork, dipped into whatever condiment is offered, and eaten in a single bite. Don't cut them up before eating them. At picnics and clam bars, forks may be dispensed with and the shellfish can be simply sucked right off the shell.

It's okay to crumble oyster crackers into the cocktail sauce. (DNO)

CORN ON THE COB

The whole idea here is to be neat. Whether you use little holders stuck in the end or your fingers, go easy on the butter and don't ravage the cob like a Hun. Take your time. Don't serve this at a formal dinner. (JTh)

BANANAS

At home, you can eat these the way the monkeys do. But out with other humans, you're meant to peel a banana, then eat it off a plate with a knife and fork. (JTh)

GRAPES

Break small bunches off the cluster; it's okay to dispose of the pips by shooting them into your fist. (JTh)

GRAVIES AND SAUCES

If you want to dunk your dinner roll into the gravy and slop it all up, you have to do it by the rules. Place a small piece of bread in your plate, then cut it and eat it with your knife and fork. This is meant to be a compliment to the cook, and it is. (JTh)

FOODS YOU SHOULD BUY AND NOT TRY TO MAKE

There are limits to industry, and when it comes to certain kinds of foods, the frontiers are here:

Chicken stock	Tea bags
Marinated ribs	Catsup
Pizza	Mustard
Mayonnaise	Ice cream
Bread	Candy
Cole slaw	Cooked corned beef
Hot sauce	Peanut, or any other kind of butter
Pickles	Cheese
Soft drinks	You get the idea. (JGF)

Part Six: RECIPES FOR MODERN MEN

The recipes here share some common characteristics. First, they're easy (although soups, salads and stews tend to be a little trickier than most dishes). Second, most of them can be made on top of a stove or on a hotplate. Third, they all taste pretty good; we know, we checked.

We do have some comments about recipes in general, though.

In baking breads and making cakes and things like that, exact **measurements** are important because of the chemical interaction of the ingredients. But for most other recipes, precise amounts don't amount to much. The measurements we give, for example, only provide *an indication of the proportion* of one ingredient to another. Where we say, a teaspoon of sugar and a big bag of beans, what we mean is that there are a lot more beans than there is sugar in the recipe. If you like sugar more than beans, though, have at it.

Improvise: In all these recipes, you should sort of wing it; you won't end up far wrong. The following rule suggests the best way to deal with measurements in recipes:

SPICES

If you can identify the spice in your dish, you're using too much of it. (BD)
See also *Tasteless Flavorings,* **below.**

And the next rule is probably the best way to deal with violations of the first rule:

NEVER EXPLAIN, NEVER APOLOGIZE

When presenting your guests with your efforts, don't go on about kitchen mishaps, about how the food's undercooked, overcooked, all over the floor, whatever. The taste of food is so completely subjective that without another similar dish with which to compare, few will be able to judge your competency.

If you keep up the dissembling remarks, you'll finally convince your guests to dislike a meal they quite probably would have otherwise enjoyed. (HGO)
See also information on presentation **in** *Entertaining with Food.*

GRADE A

In cooking, quality counts. Buy the best ingredients you can afford. If you're low on dough, inferior products won't exactly ruin your efforts, but quality shows. (GI)
See also *Food You Should Buy and Not Try to Make.*

TIMING

Timing is the toughest part of cooking to figure out and experience helps. The best way to approach the problem is to read the recipes carefully, plan where the down time

— the half-hour you're going to sit while something cooks — is going to fall, so you can be doing something else. Plan ahead. (BD)

DISHES

It pays to wash the dirty dishes as you go. That way, you don't run out of platters and pans and counter space. (BD)

See also *Kitchen Control,* **above.**

TASTELESS FLAVORINGS

Here are three flavorings that are practically worthless: Garlic powder (or garlic salt), dried parsley flakes and reconstituted lemon juice. All three are much better in the form nature gave them. (AR)

TEN GREAT MEAT DISHES

Before you start slapping dead flesh around, pay attention to the cuts of meat available. Even the cheap stuff's expensive, so be sure you get what you want. The higher grade cuts of meat are always preferable.

1. Beefsteak: Go for tenderloin, sirloin, T-bone, Delmonico or porterhouse cuts. If you're busted, try a piece of chuck; stay away from London broil. If you're having company, figure a half-pound per person.

Make it hot: The best way to cook steak is over very hot coals, either outside on a grill or inside on an improvised fireplace rack (use a few bricks and a rack from the oven). Position the grill or rack an inch or two over the coals. Toss the meat on and let it cook for as few as two minutes (for a thin cut) or as long as ten minutes (for very thick cuts), or until a few drops of blood appear on the uncooked side. Then turn the steaks over and cook them for about the same amount of time again. After you've done this a couple of times, you'll get the notion of cooking times down pat. If you want to see how things are progressing, you can cut into a piece of meat *after you've turned it* to see how red it is inside. Have a good time with the salt and pepper after broiling the meat; if you use salt before or during the cooking process, you'll cause the juices to run out of the meat. And that's bad. Also, avoid garlic powder or anything other than salt and pepper.

Pan-fried: The second-best method of cooking steaks is to use an iron skillet on the stove top. This is fun because it makes a lot of mess and generates an impressive amount of smoke, so before starting, open a window or two and turn off the smoke alarms (we're serious). Turn the heat under a dry frying pan to high until the pan is about as hot as you think a pan could be. Then put a little piece of fat in the pan and shove it around to lubricate the pan bottom. The pan should sound very angry — lots of hissing. Boldly toss in the steak and lightly drape some foil over the top to keep the spattering grease under control (don't try to seal the foil or anything; this is just to keep the mess to a minimum). Wait until blood shows on the uncooked side, then carefully turn it over. Give it another few minutes, add salt and pepper and serve. (PKL)

Ground beef also has its own modest virtues. After all, a well-wrought hamburger is a thing of greasy beauty. And, by simply adding a crucial ingredient to the recipe, you can achieve something quite, uh, unhamburgesque. In the case of this one, called *Beefsteak Haché,* the secret is

a quarter cup of sour cream, along with the expected

pound of ground chuck,

a tablespoon of well-chopped onion,

a large egg,

a healthy dash of ground black pepper,

a little less than a teaspoon of salt,

some butter and

a pinch of parsley.

You combine everything except the butter, cream and parsley; shape the beef into three half-inch-thick steaks or four smaller ones. Treat a hot skillet with a little butter (careful: butter burns fast), brown the steaks to taste, then remove them to a warm tray. Prepare the sauce by stirring the sour cream into the butter and fat left in the pan. Add salt and pepper and sprinkle with parsley. Pour the sauce over the steaks and serve. (AW)

2. Veal, the flesh of poor, little, brown-eyed, milk-fed baby cows, is horribly expensive. In this recipe for veal piccata, the meat is called a "scallop" because it's much too small to be called a steak. So, get

six veal scallops ready, along with

a half cup of flour in a paper bag,

six tablespoons of butter (most producers wrap butter in paper with the

tablespoons already marked),

about twelve fresh mushrooms, sliced lengthwise,

a couple of tablespoons of chopped parsley,

six slices of lemon,

the juice from a lemon

and a half cup of white wine or vermouth.

Pound the veal until it's thin and even. You can really have fun with this. Although some people like to use a meat mallet or the flat side of a cleaver, try using your fist and a cutting board. Nothing quite sounds like raw meat when you're working it over. Try slapping it around while you work on your Bogey impersonation. Call it a meatball and ask it who asked it, anyway.

Next, put some salt and pepper on a piece of veal and drop it in the bag of flour. Shake it lightly so the flour coats the meat, then remove it and set it aside. Repeat with the other pieces.

Now heat the skillet (but not as hot as you would for steak) and toss in three tablespoons of butter. As soon as the butter starts to lose its composure, add the sliced mushrooms and maybe a half-teaspoon of lemon juice that you can squeeze out of one of the lemon slices. When this little stew is done (the mushrooms will be darker and wilted), put the whole mess — mushrooms, liquid and all — on a separate plate and give the pan a quick once-over to get it clean, then put it back on the fire and heat it up again.

As soon as the pan has been reheated, add the remaining three tablespoons of butter. Next, add the pieces of veal and cook them quickly until they're beige on both sides, with maybe a hint of brown around the edges. When they've reached that point, take them out of the pan and put them on a serving platter.

Next, with the heat still on the pan, you're going to get some of the gunk off the bottom of the skillet by pouring in the wine (or vermouth) and scraping the bottom. Add the mushroom and lemon juice, let it cook for a minute or two, then pour the whole thing over the meat. Put the lemon slices around so the plate looks nice, and sprinkle some of the parsley around the way they do in restaurants.

This recipe will serve four polite people. (TE)

3. Liver: "Oh boy," you say to your six-year-old nephew, "it's *liver!*" They should call it something else, because if you call it liver it tastes horrible.

In this recipe, it tastes good — good enough to trick a dopey nephew, that's for sure. Follow the instructions carefully, though. For example, it's important that you get

two pounds of *very, very fresh* calf's liver in quarter-inch-thick slices.

Also, get five thick slices of bacon,

a bunch of scallions (chopped in one-inch bits, using only the green part)

and a half cup of flour. Put the flour in a paper bag.

You'll also need salt and pepper.

Now if you can't get truly fresh, right-off-the-cadaver liver, skip this whole thing. What you want is to see the butcher conduct the operation, you want to watch him chainsaw his way through the calf's ribcage and reach deep inside the bloody hulk of the beast and, with his huge butcher's hands, rip the still-quivering organ out of the animal. You want to watch him slice the liver while you wait, and, while his hands are still dripping with blood, you want him to remove the membrane from around the liver slices. Nothing else will do. The liver must be fresh. The membrane must be removed.

Back home, heat up a skillet, add the bacon and cook it slowly until it's crisp. Pull the bacon out of the fat and let it drain on a couple of paper towels; leave the bacon fat in the pan. Now turn up the heat and let the fat get very hot while you shake each piece of liver — one at a time — in the bag of flour. The flour should completely but lightly coat each piece. Next, place each piece of liver in the hot fat and cook it for no more than a minute or two on each side. This is important; cook it too long and you'll be sorry. Place the cooked meat on a serving platter. Turn off the heat.

Next, add the scallions to the pan; stir them for a minute until they're sort of cooked, then pour them over the liver. Crumble the cooked bacon over the platter, add salt and pepper and serve to four people. (PKL)

4. Pork: You have to remember this about pork: cook it forever, make sure it's done through and through, allow nothing pink to survive. Otherwise, the pig gets his revenge.

For this recipe for marinated pork chops, you'll need

> four inch-thick chops,
> six tablespoons of cider vinegar, and
> three tablespoons each of sugar and soy sauce.

Start by trimming off most of the fat from the pork chops. Next, add the vinegar, sugar and soy sauce and stir them together in a flat broiling pan from which you have removed the rack. Put the raw chops in the mixture and let them set for about twenty minutes, turning once after ten minutes.

Put the chops in a broiler and cook them slowly at 300° for thirty to forty minutes. You might want to baste the chops a couple of time with the sauce while they cook. Turn the chops once during cooking so both sides will brown. Serves four. (MYR)

5. Lamb: Here's a recipe for a large group of people (not a Rotarians convention or anything; we're talking maybe eight or ten). It's a weird dish because some people will think they're eating steak, while others will peg it for lamb right away.

You'll need

> a large leg of lamb, boned and butterflied (we'll explain in a sec);
> four cloves of garlic cut into little slices;
> a quarter-cup of olive oil and
> the juice of one lemon.
> For taste, you'll want some rosemary and
> some salt and pepper.

A decent butcher will take the bone out of the leg of lamb and cut it open like the big slab of meat that it is (using what's called a butterfly cut), and trim the membrane and sinew. It should look like a giant steak, except the thickness will range from about three-quarters of an inch to two inches.

Play First-Date-with-Anthony-Perkins and stab the piece of meat repeatedly, inserting a garlic sliver in each puncture. (If Californians had thought of this, it would be a religious ritual.) The garlic — and the stab wounds — should be evenly distributed throughout the piece.

Now for a change of pace. Gently rub the olive oil all over the outside of the meat. Sprinkle with salt, pepper, lemon juice and rosemary.

The lamb should be cooked like a steak — that is, over very hot coals, for about ten minutes on each side. Because of the varying thickness of the meat, there will be some pieces that are rare and others that are well-done. (*Anon.*)

6. Roast duck: This recipe for roasting one of the cutest animals known to man is for ducks of the barnyard persuasion; the preparation of game birds is quite different and too complicated for this selection. Get

a dead duck, of course. Also, you'll need
one apple, cored and quartered but unpeeled, and
an onion, also cut in four pieces. You'll want
water, at least a cup,
and salt and pepper.

Take out the guts and sprinkle salt and pepper all over the duck, inside and out. Place the duck upside down (breast side down) in a large cast-iron skillet; add the water, the apple and the onion. Put the skillet in a 375° oven and, after an hour and a half, drain off all the liquid; there'll be a lot, maybe a coffee can full.

Slide a rack under the duck (or use something else; the object is to get the duck off the bottom of the skillet), turn the duck breast side up and return it to the oven for another ninety minutes. When the cooking time has elapsed, take the duck out of the oven and, using some scissors, cut the duck into four pieces. (TE)

You can get quite fancy here, if you want, by going ahead and making a glaze for the duck. It's easy: all you have to do is mix up a cup of apricot preserves, a cup of honey and one or two tablespoons of brandy. Slowly heat the goo in a small pan for four or five minutes, then pour it over the duck and put it in the oven for another ten minutes. Serves two guys or four girls. (SRW)

7. Shrimp: Bugs of the sea taste mighty fine cooked creole-style. Get

a couple pounds of fresh, uncooked, unshelled shrimp, medium- or large-sized;
a stick (that's eight tablespoons) of butter or, if you must, margarine;
two tablespoons of hot sauce. There are a couple of good Louisiana-style sauces
that will work fine; Durkee, for one, makes a widely
distributed brand of Louisiana hot sauce.
Get a half cup of white wine and
squeeze the juice out of a lemon.

Heat the butter in a skillet over medium heat until it bubbles; do not let it turn brown and burn, though. Add the shrimp, the lemon juice and the hot sauce, and stir while it cooks — maybe four minutes. Next, add the wine and cook for another four minutes.

Pour the shrimp and the liquid onto a big platter. This stuff tastes great served with warm, crusty bread. This is finger-food fun; you have to take the shrimp out of the shell by yourself, and you use the bread for dunking. Serves four really messy people. (PR)

FILLETING A FISH

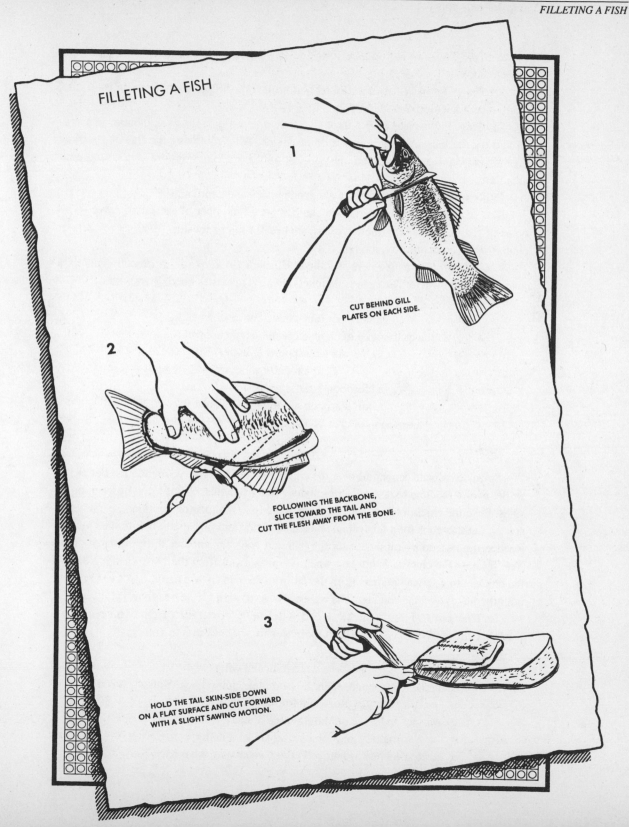

1 CUT BEHIND GILL PLATES ON EACH SIDE.

2 FOLLOWING THE BACKBONE, SLICE TOWARD THE TAIL AND CUT THE FLESH AWAY FROM THE BONE.

3 HOLD THE TAIL SKIN-SIDE DOWN ON A FLAT SURFACE AND CUT FORWARD WITH A SLIGHT SAWING MOTION.

8. Fish: You love it, you hate it. If you love it, here are two really classic, simple ways to cook it:

Broiling: Dot fish fillets with butter and broil for a couple of minutes on each side, then squeeze a lemon over them. That's it.

Sautéing: Pull a piece of fish through a little pile of flour. Heat some butter in a skillet and fry the fish for a few minutes on each side. After removing the fish and turning off the heat, squeeze a lemon into the pan, stir up the fish bits from the bottom and pour the mixture over the fish.

Either way, garnish with freshly chopped parsley and paprika.

Lots of different kinds of seafood can be cooked in either of these two ways — all types of fish, scallops, soft-shelled crabs, shelled shrimp or lobster. Bivalves (oysters or clams) won't cook this way, though. (GR)

9. Chicken: The recipe here is called "Chicken Good Wife" in French. There's a joke there, somewhere. The taste is no joke, though. This tastes good. Start with

a three- or four-pound cut-up chicken,
a quarter cup of chopped scallions or chopped shallots,
six tablespoons of butter,
a cup of white wine, a
tablespoon full of chopped parsley, and
a half teaspoon of tarragon. The rest —
a teaspoon of chervil and some sprigs of watercress —
is optional.

Sprinkle salt and pepper all over the chicken, and, after you've melted the butter in a skillet over a medium heat, cook it for about twenty minutes, or until it's browned on all sides. Push the chicken to one side of the pan, add the shallots (or scallions), parsley and spices. Let this cook for a few minutes, then add wine and mix it all up with the chicken. Reduce the heat to a simmer, cover the pan and cook for another thirty minutes or so. You'll know the chicken is cooked when it comes away from the bone easily. Remove the chicken to a serving platter, skim the fat from the pan (if you can't, don't worry), and pour the juices over the chicken. The watercress is for garnish. Serves four. (SB)

10. Chicken II: From "Chicken Good Wife" to "Chicken from Hell." This recipe for Buffalo Chicken Wings is a taste treat for masochists. Check it out: You get

a couple dozen chicken wings and
a bottle of hot sauce. A bottle. Complete. Jump back. You also need
three tablespoons of butter,
a jar of blue cheese dressing, some
celery and some carrot sticks. Finally, some
cooking oil (peanut, safflower, vegetable, what have you).

Cut each wing in half at the main joint; remove and discard the wing tip. Wash what's left and pat it dry on paper towels.

Heat about four inches of oil in a deep sauce pan (the sides have to extend at least five inches above the level of the oil) over medium heat. Add the chicken in small batches to the oil, cooking each batch until it turns sort of golden. You've got to be careful here. Deep-fat frying is really dangerous (**see** *Kitchen Safety* if you don't think so).

Melt the butter in a large saucepan, turn off the heat, and pour in the whole bottle of hot sauce. Then add the cooked chicken wings, put a lid on it and shake the pan until the wings are coated with the sauce.

You serve this with blue cheese dressing, celery and carrots to ease the pain a little. Also beer helps. A case of beer helps a lot. (PB)

Chicken annex: The ideal bachelor chicken recipe: Buy a Perdue Oven Stuffer Roaster and follow the instructions to the letter. It's fantastic. (FP)

A PERFECTLY ADEQUATE, FUNCTIONAL SAUCE

Chop up a handful of shallots (usually hidden in the corner of the produce section, shallots look like small, dark onions). Fry the shallots with some boneless meat — chicken, veal, scallops, goat, just kidding — until the meat is completely cooked, at which time there should be some brown residue sticking to the bottom of the pan. Take out the meat and set it aside on a plate. Pour a wine glass full of dry, white vermouth into the pan and add a pinch of dried parsley. Stir the mixture until all the brown residue from the bottom of the pan is dissolved in the vermouth. Next, pour a half cup of full cream into the vermouth mixture, reduce the heat to low and stir until the cream thickens. Finally, pour the sauce over the meat.

Note: It always takes longer for the cream to thicken than you think, be patient. (JO)

TEN GREAT VEGETABLE RECIPES

There's a great and unjustified prejudice against vegetables, probably a residue of their long association with gurus from the Asian subcontinent. Modern Men can eat vegetables without shame, and, since these recipes are almost insipidly easy, they can cook them without fear.

1. Asparagus: Cut off the light-colored ends of each stalk by making a long, diagonal cut. That's about all the prep you need for these, one of the most elegant vegetables. Proust used to go to the Ritz in the middle of every night for a side order of asparagus.

There are two reliable ways to cook asparagus (and many other vegetables):

Method One: Boil just enough water to barely cover the asparagus in a skillet over medium heat. Add a teaspoon of salt, the same amount of sugar and about two or three tablespoons of butter. Finally, add the asparagus and cook it for about five minutes. Don't overcook; asparagus shouldn't be all limp. (TE)

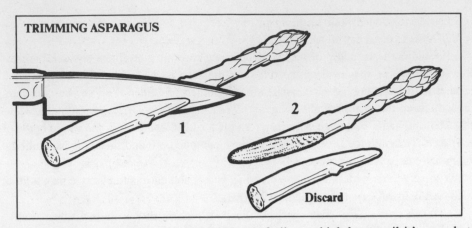

TRIMMING ASPARAGUS

Discard

Method Two: Heat about two tablespoons of oil over high heat until it's very hot; add the asparagus and stir-fry for about forty-five seconds. Then add a third cup of water, cover the pan immediately, and let cook for a few minutes over high heat.

Serve asparagus with something red on the plate — sliced roasted red peppers, maybe, or pimientos. You can also serve asparagus with chopped ham. (GI)

To roast sweet red peppers, cut them in two, lengthwise, and take out the seeds and the white stuff. Slice the halves into long sections. You can rub the sections with olive oil, but it's not essential. Bake, grill, or broil the peppers until the edges start to blacken.

This seems almost like a nonrecipe, but these things make a perfect complement to almost any green vegetable dish. (AR)

2. Broccoli: Cut off the little tree-parts, called "florets," and slice some of the stalks into pieces less than a quarter inch thick.

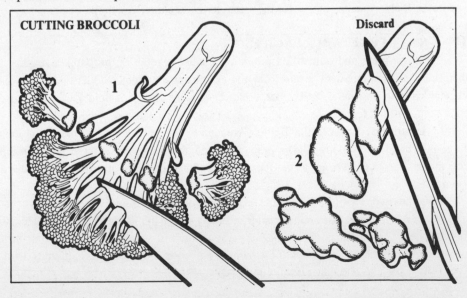

CUTTING BROCCOLI

Discard

To cook, **see under** *Asparagus,* **above.**

If you want to impress somebody, add a Polonaise topping (this stuff is also good with other vegetables). All you need is a finely-chopped hard-boiled egg (**see** *Eggs*), a half cup of dry breadcrumbs (the unseasoned kind), five tablespoons of butter and about a quarter cup of chopped parsley. Heat the breadcrumbs in the butter until they turn golden brown, then add the egg and the parsley, let it cook for another minute, then pour it over the broccoli. Try it; it's pretty good. (TE)

3. Green Beans: You can get by just following the cooking instructions printed **above under** *Asparagus.* Or you can do it right — in which case, you'll need

a pound of green beans. Get them fresh and cut off the ends. Just takes a sec.
You'll also want three tablespoons of olive oil,
two tablespoons of butter,
a couple of garlic cloves all chopped up,
four or five teaspoons of lemon juice and a
teaspoon of finely chopped lemon rind.
Some salt and some sugar. And last but not least,
a quarter cup of grated Parmesan cheese.

Cook the beans by boiling them for ten minutes or so with a teaspoon each of salt and sugar and a couple tablespoons of butter. Drain off all the liquid.

Douse the beans with a little cold water, then set them aside to drain.

Sauté the garlic in the oil for a minute or so, then add the remaining ingredients and the beans. After a second, remove from the fire and give the pan a good shake. Serves four. (JB)

4. Red Cabbage: Sounds like a two-bit comic strip character, right? In fact, it's a damned tasty little vegetable. This recipe, for a sort of red, hot slaw, requires

a half head of red cabbage,
a half an onion, chopped,
a half cup each of red wine and water,
a quarter cup of sugar,
a peeled, cored, thinly sliced apple,
a quarter cup of vinegar (red wine vinegar, if you have it),
a small, grated potato,
a tablespoon of oil,
a half teaspoon of cinnamon and
some salt and pepper.

Sauté the onion and the apple in the oil for a few minutes, then add all the rest of the ingredients, except the potato. Stir well, cover the pan and simmer over a low flame for an hour. Mix it up in there from time to time. Finally, after the hour's up, add the potato, leave the lid off and cook it for another half hour.

This serves four, but red cabbage keeps quite well, so you could easily double the recipe and have lots for leftovers. (TE)

A great salad can be made from cold, cooked red cabbage, cucumber slices, a little corn, a slice of onion, some tomato wedges and some diced cheese. Deep-six the works under some of Kraft's best. (DB)

5. *Zucchini:* This cucumber-looking veg also travels under the alias "Italian" or "summer" squash and tastes great hot or cold.

Cold, you cut it lengthwise into four or more long stalks and dip them into some salad dressing; blue cheese is nice.

Hot, you can boil slices in a teeny bit of water, covered, with a pinch of salt and some Parmesan cheese. Or, if you want to get fancy, take

> three or four medium-sized zucchini (unpeeled),
> a large onion (peeled, sliced or diced),
> three tablespoons of olive oil and
> some salt and pepper.

Grate the zucchini and onion onto a kitchen towel. Make a mound of the stuff in the center of the towel, fold the edges of the towel over the zucchini mixture and twist the ends to wring the water out of it.

Heat the oil in a skillet over medium heat. Add the wrung-out zucchini and the onion and let it cook for about five minutes. Add salt and pepper. Serves four. (NRE)

6. *Greek Rice:* Alpha Epsilon Pilau. So easy a home ec major can do it. You need:

> four tablespoons of butter,
> a cup of uncooked white rice
> and two cups of chicken stock.

In a large skillet, sauté the rice in the butter for about five minutes or until it turns sort of opaque. Then add the chicken stock, reduce the heat to a simmer, put a kitchen towel over the pot, put the cover over the towel, pull the towel tight, press down on the lid and put the corners of the towel on top. Try not to let the towel catch on fire.

Let the rice simmer for twenty minutes. Serves four.

7. *New Potatoes in Burnt Butter:* Boil eight to ten small, unpeeled, new potatoes for about fifteen minutes. Drain off the water and put the potatoes aside. Melt a stick of butter (a quarter pound) in the pan until it turns dark brown. Be careful, though, because if the butter goes all the way to black, you've blown it. Put the potatoes back in the pan, cover and shake so the butter coats the spuds. Add salt and pepper. Serves four. (LD)

Here's *another potato recipe:* In this exciting adventure in Irish delicacies, you boil ten new potatoes for fifteen minutes, drain off the water, then add equal amounts of butter, sour cream and parsley or chives to the pan. Season with salt and pepper. (JYT)

8. Cooked Beets: Pretty and pretty good. And real easy:

Don't peel or damage the skin before cooking. Trim off the greens so that about an inch of stalk is left on the bulb. Simmer the beets in boiling water for about forty-five minutes. You can tell it's done if the skin slips off when touched.

Slice them or dice them, combine them with melted butter, lemon juice and salt and pepper. Or mix them with a little sugar (maybe a half teaspoon), about half a cup of sour cream, some chopped parsley and a dash each of salt and nutmeg. (AR)

9. Artichokes: Cut off the stem and put the vegetable upright in a half inch of boiling water for maybe forty minutes. You can tell when an artichoke is cooked if the leaves pull off easily. Put it on a plate and serve with a little melted butter or a dollop of mayonnaise. (If this is your first date with an artichoke, **see** *Tricky Foods*.) Put a little bowl on the table for discarded leaves. Suggested chatter: "Who was the first person who ever thought of eating these things?" (JO)

10. Sautéed Carrots: All you need are

> six to eight carrots that you've scraped and cut into thin strips,
> a tablespoon of butter for each carrot,
> an optional pinch of marjoram and
> some salt and pepper.

Parboil the carrots strips for about eight minutes, or until they're about two-thirds done. (In this case, parboil means you boil the carrots for a while, but not long enough to completely cook them.) Drain off the water. Heat the butter until it bubbles, then add the carrots. Cook over medium to high heat until the carrots are lightly browned. Season and serve to four to six people. (JB)

TEN GREAT BREAKFASTS

Look, if you're eating breakfast on your own, you might as well eat right. Here are ten truly brilliant breakfasts; after that you're on your own — again.

1. Train Pancakes: These were originally called "New York Central Special Wheat-cakes" and were served aboard the Central's celebrated Flyers. For ten cakes, you need

> two egg yolks (see below),
> one and three-quarters cups milk,
> three tablespoons of maple syrup,
> two cups of flour,
> a couple of teaspoons of baking powder,
> half a teaspoon of salt and
> a half-dozen tablespoons of butter, melted in a large skillet.

To separate an egg: Do this over the sink. Break the egg into two halves, pour the intact yolk into one half and let the white drain away, then pour the yolk back into the other half, and let a little more white drain away. This usually takes about three passes to separate the yolk from the white.

Vigorously beat or stir the egg yolks, then slowly add the milk and then the maple syrup. Next, sift in the dry ingredients, stir, then add the melted butter. Stir the mixture until it has a silken smoothness, then let it stand for about five minutes.

Heat the skillet that had the butter in it over medium heat until it's hot enough to make a drop of water "dance." Add enough batter to make a pancake and let it cook until air holes become visible on the uncooked surface. Then you flip it. Don't turn a cake more than once, and make sure the pan isn't *too* hot. (WCH)

2. Boy Scout French Toast: This is one of those good and greasy dietary catastrophes that tastes as good as a breakfast can. You'll want

four to six slices of bacon,
a half-dozen slices of white bread (preferably thick-sliced),
two eggs,
a quarter cup of milk and
two or three tablespoons of sugar.

Cook the bacon slowly in a skillet, and when it's done, let the bacon drain on a paper towel or something, but don't toss the fat. Leave the heat on low.

While the bacon's cooking, combine the eggs, milk and sugar in a shallow bowl. Stir it all up, but not so much that it begins to act funny. Just mix up the ingredients a little. Then take a piece of bread and dip it in the mixture so that both sides are thoroughly covered. Cook the bread in the bacon fat, turning only once during cooking.

Now. What did you do with the bacon? You ate it, right? Right. (SF)

3. Eggs: They come before chickens, which make better dinners or suppers.

To fry an egg, heat the skillet and melt a little butter in it. Once the butter has liquified, turn the heat up to high for about twenty seconds, add the eggs and cook over high heat for another twenty seconds or so, until the edges get crinkly Then turn the heat down to low and continue cooking slowly for another minute or so. You'll be able to tell by looking how done the egg is. If you want the eggs over, slide the spatula under them in a quick, firm motion, ensuring that the yolk and as much of the rest of the eggs as possible are on the spatula. Turn the spatula with a gentle, graceful flip of the wrist.

To scramble an egg, whip the eggs in a cup or bowl first. Coat the skillet with butter, then pour the eggs in. Stir the eggs as they cook, pushing the run-off from the edges back toward the center of the pan. Bits of ham, Tuscan peppers, cheese, tomato, pepper or onion can be added either before cooking, when the eggs are in the bowl, or during cooking. Do not use a hot pan when scrambling eggs.

To soft-boil an egg, bring a pan of water to the boil first, then add the egg. Three minutes will give you a very soft egg; five minutes will allow the yolk to begin to congeal. Remove from the pan, rinse briefly in cold tap water, then, using a knife, slice off the narrow tip of the egg. Use a spoon to scoop out the rest.

To hard-boil an egg, place the egg in a saucepan, then add cool water. Put the pan over heat, and allow the egg to cook for ten minutes *after* the water has started to boil. Rinse thoroughly under cold tap water before shelling.

To poach an egg, boil about six inches of water in a large saucepan. When the water has reached a rapid boil, stir the water so it rotates in the saucepan like a whirlpool. Quickly turn off the heat, break one or more eggs into the spinning water, then cover. Allow two to four minutes for the eggs to cook. Timing takes experience; one way to gauge it is to put the toast in the toaster just before you put the eggs in the water and see how closely their cooking times coincide.

When the toast is ready, lift the eggs out of the water with a slotted spoon and place on the toast. (TAE)

A savory meal can be made by poaching toast in a stew made of broth, onions and a bit of wine. Place a slice of cheese on the toast, then put the egg on the cheese. (HJG)

To shirr an egg breakfast for two, you'll need

four eggs, a teaspoon of butter,
two teaspoons of cream and one or more of the following:
cooked crumbled bacon,
cooked chopped onion,
cooked sliced mushrooms
cooked chopped ham,
cooked chopped peppers,
chopped parsley, or a dash or chervil or whatever.

You get the idea.

Liberally grease an ovenproof soup dish with butter; add any of the ingredients above. Add the eggs — without breaking the yolks — and spoon the cream over the surface. Some cooks add a little lemon juice (about one-half teaspoon). Season with salt and pepper, and bake in a 300° oven for ten or fifteen minutes.

This seems like a lot of trouble, but shirred eggs can be an elegant breakfast. (AR)

4. Red Flannel Hash: This is an old New England favorite for breakfast or dinner. Make this the night before or you'll be serving breakfast late in the day. You need

two pounds of cooked brisket of corned beef,
three small, cooked beets (**see under** *Beets,* **above,** or use canned),
three cooked carrots (**see under** *Carrots* **above**),
four barely cooked boiled potatoes,
a cup of cooked cabbage (see below), although this is optional, as are

two medium-sized, cooked turnips (**see below**).
A quarter cup of cream is not optional, however, and neither are the
five tablespoons of butter required for the hash. Don't forget the
salt and pepper.

To cook vegetables like cabbage, use as little water as possible in a saucepan. Bring the water to a boil, add a teaspoon of salt and a teaspoon of sugar, and boil the vegetable until it is just tender to a fork's prod.

Make the hash by coarsely chopping and mixing together all the ingredients except the butter, which should be melted in a skillet. Add the hash and sauté slowly, or bake in a 350° oven for forty minutes. Either way, the hash is done when it turns a nice brown. Serves four. (SBBS)

5. *Lox and Bagels:* There's no cooking here, just a trip to the deli and an evacuation of your wallet. The result is an elegant repast. Ask the deli man for

a pound of Nova Scotia lox (belly lox is too salty; Scottish,
Irish or Scandinavian is just as good, but even more costly);
a half-dozen bagels — plain (water), onion, egg, pumpernickel, whatever;
a pound of cream cheese or chive cheese;
a thinly sliced, peeled onion;
a couple of sliced tomatoes and
a couple of lemons cut in wedges.

Toast the bagels, and set them out on platters spread with the other condiments. Do-it-yourself for four. (AR)

6. *Kippers and Onions:* Another deli treat, but this one takes a little kitchen work. For each person, you will want

one smoked kipper (whitefish), although trout can be substituted.
While trout's a lot more expensive, it's twice as good. Add
a peeled and thinly sliced onion,
a boiled, peeled potato, a variety of
toasted rolls, bagels or bread,
and some lemon wedges.

Sauté the onions in a skillet over medium heat until brown. Remove the onions, add a little more butter and heat the kippers on both sides. Serve each fish covered with cooked onions, with the potato on the side. (AW)

7. *Ham with Redeye Gravy:* This one will set you up for the day, especially if served with biscuits or grits. Or both.

Brown some ham in a skillet over medium heat. (The best ham in the world comes from Virginia, North Carolina and Tennessee; the best ham not only makes the best gravy, but obviously the best breakfast, which is why we're here.) Remove the ham, stir in a tablespoon of flour, stir some more and cook until browned. Gradually, stir in up to one cup of hot water. Stir the gravy until thick, then add a tablespoon of brewed coffee.

For perfect biscuits and grits — two great breakfast time staples — become a product loyalist. The instructions on the box of Bisquick are easy to follow and right on the money. Ditto the instructions on boxes of Quaker grits. Serves two. (JSA)

8. Hashed-brown Potatoes: By themselves, of course, hashed-browns don't make much of a breakfast. But follow this recipe, add a fried egg or two, and you'll be close to prenoon culinary greatness. The first thing you need, obviously, will be

three medium-sized, unpeeled, quartered and parboiled (for ten minutes) potatoes;
an onion, peeled and chopped;
five tablespoons of butter or oil or a combo of the two;
some paprika, and some
salt and pepper.

(Parboiling, **as noted under** *Carrots,* **above,** is the partial cooking of a substance — in this case, potatoes.) Coarsely grate or chop the potatoes. Heat a skillet over a high flame until quite hot. Then add the butter (or oil), and finally the potatoes and onion. Sauté over high heat stirring only infrequently so the potatoes will get crispy around the edges. Just before the cooking is completed, sprinkle the potatoes with paprika and season with salt and pepper. Serves three or four. (THR)

9. Baked Grapefruit: Like the *Train Pancakes* **above,** this recipe comes from the golden era of railroad diners — in this case, from the New York Central's great rival, the Pennsylvania Railroad. Combine the two and you can have an Amtrak deluxe breakfast.

You must have two large grapefruit,
and four tablespoons of each of the following:
sugar (or honey), sherry and melted butter.

Cut the grapefruit in halves, loosen the segments and remove the seeds. Sprinkle each half with sugar, sherry and melted butter (in that order) and bake in a hot (400°) oven for about ten minutes. Serves four. (WCH)

10. Wheaties. Sometimes, you just can't beat 'em.

SOUPS, SALADS AND STEWS

Here's where cooking gets a little tricky, although these recipes can all be done by rank amateurs, guys who have never cooked a thing before in their lives. The only thing is, you have to follow the instructions. After you make one of these, then you can wing it.

But start by following the rules.

1. Watercress Soup: Here's a quick and easy Chinese soup to start with. Don't be put off by the long list of ingredients, though, the first of which is

a pound of watercress, very coarsely chopped. Next,
four ounces of chopped pork, followed by
a teaspoon each of cornstarch and salt;
half teaspoons of pepper and grated ginger (preferably fresh);
a quarter teaspoon of sugar; and
one tablespoon each of soy sauce and cooking oil (preferably peanut). Finally,
you need two cans of chicken broth and a couple of eggs.

Mix together the pork, cornstarch, sugar, salt, pepper, ginger and soy sauce; stir it all up. Heat the oil in a large saucepan, then add your mixture and cook it briefly, twenty seconds tops. Next, add the broth and bring to a boil. Reduce the heat, add the watercress and simmer covered for about five minutes. Finally, turn off the heat, crack the two eggs into the soup, recover and wait until the eggs are poached. Serves six to eight. (HWE)

2. Black Bean Soup: Sometimes it's easier to buy the best. For example, if you want really good black bean soup, don't try to make it yourself. Go to the supermarket and get a can of a premium brand black bean soup. Follow the cooking directions on the side of the tin, except you can add a tablespoonful of sherry to the soup as it cooks. Garnish each individual serving with a tablespoon of one of the following:

Finely chopped onion; finely chopped hard-boiled egg; fresh parsley; a thin slice of lemon. (APS)

3. Grand Central Oyster Pan Roast: This quick and easy recipe is from the famous Oyster Bar in New York City's Grand Central Terminal. Although it's rich enough to give you some serious discomfort, it also represents a more civilized way of eating oysters — cooked and in a bowl instead of raw like a sinus problem on the half shell.

For two people, figure eight oysters each, that's sixteen, plus

a stick of butter and
a couple of tablespoons of chili sauce. You can see where this is going.
Add two teaspoons of Worcestershire sauce and
a teaspoon of lemon juice,
a cup of cream,
a dash or two of celery salt and
the same of paprika, and
two pieces of dry toast.

Cook the oysters and their juice in a saucepan over medium heat for a minute. Now add half the butter and everything else except the cream and the toast, stir it and cook it for another minute. Now you can pour in the cream. Heat the whole works until it's almost ready to boil. Then take it off the heat, place the toast in soup dishes and pour the oysters and the sauce over the toast. Add the rest of the butter and sprinkle around a little more paprika. (OB)

4. Kale Soup: Kale is one of those obscure vegetables like chard that everybody forgets about. This recipe, a Portuguese number, will make you want to jump up and shake hands with kale, since it's hearty enough to qualify as a stew and since it's the only way we know that kale can be made edible.

Obviously, you're going to need a lot of kale, say a pound, all washed and
roughly chopped; then
three medium onions, peeled and chopped,
four or five medium-sized potatoes diced into about eight pieces each,
four tablespoons of butter,
two cans of beef broth and
enough water to produce a total of six cups of liquid. Also, try to find
a pound of linguica, which is some kind of Portuguese sausage. If you strike out
there,
substitute a pound of chorizo, the Italian equivalent. Finally,
some hot sauce and
some salt and pepper.

Melt the butter in a large pot or kettle (Do you have a kettle? This is your chance to actually use it, so get all the dried flowers out of it and give it a good rinse) and cook the onions in the butter until they become transparent. Add the broth, the potatoes, the kale and the sausage and put a lid on it. Let this mixture simmer for forty-five minutes or so, then season with salt, pepper and hot sauce and serve. Easy, si? (BJ) It must be noted that eating too much of this stuff will make you damn regular, if you get the meaning.

SALADS

1. Some Salads: You know what salads are — a bunch of raw vegetables with some meat or cheese tossed in. You can make them simple or you can make them fancy. Iceberg lettuce, which is sort of the white bread of the salad world, is easy to use, since, unlike all other lettuces, you don't have to wash it (although you should), and it tastes just fine. We saw in a movie once where the guy slammed down a head of iceberg lettuce stemfirst on the kitchen counter, then reached in and pulled out the heart.

The Basic American Salad consists of iceberg lettuce and tomato wedges, with a dollop of Kraft's Thousand Island on top. You can dress it up with little cubes of American cheese and bits of Spam. If you keep adding stuff to it, like strips of cold turkey, different cheeses, some shredded chicken and hard-boiled eggs, you get a *Chef's Salad*, which is one of the greatest salads devised by man. (**See also** *Salad Dressings* **below.**)

For a *Caesar Salad* you'll need

a large head of romaine lettuce, washed, dried and hand-shredded,
two or three cups of white bread, torn into chunks about an inch square,
a third-cup of olive oil in one container and
two thirds cup of olive oil in another.
Skin and lightly crush three or four cloves of garlic,
drain and wash a tin of anchovies,
a raw egg and get
a tablespoonful of lemon juice, along with
a third cup of Parmesan cheese and
some pepper, and you're set.

Sauté the garlic over a very low heat in the third cup of olive oil. Don't let it over-cook (it turns tan in color). Toss in the bread scraps and get them coated in the oil and garlic mix. Spread the bread on a sheet of aluminum foil and bake it until golden brown in a 350° or 400° oven.

While that's going on, make the dressing: Pulverize the anchovies in a bowl, stir in the egg and mix it all up. Add the other two-thirds cup oil, stirring as you go. Then add the lemon juice to taste.

Put the lettuce into a salad bowl and mix in the Parmesan cheese and the pepper. When the croutons are done, add them and the dressing to the bowl. Toss and serve at once to four people. (JB)

Simple Endive Salad: The Belgian endive is a remarkably handy vegetable resembling a greenish-white cigar. Cut each endive in half lengthwise and remove a V-shaped section from the bottom (the stalk end) about two inches long and separate the leaves. Put the leaves on a plate with some slices of tomato and maybe a few pieces of cucumber. Makes a fancy-looking salad. Tell her the Belgians don't call it an endive at all, but something pronounced like witloaf. (**See** *Italian Dressing*.) (JO)

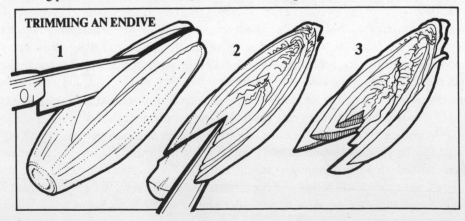

TRIMMING AN ENDIVE

Orange-Endive Salad: No mystery about what you put in this one. Start with

two or three endives,
the juice of half a lemon,
an orange, peeled and cut into sections,
a third cup of heavy cream,
a tablespoon of chopped parsley and
some salt and pepper.

The endives in this recipe require some prep work. You have to slice each one in half lengthwise; cut out the core in the center by making a long "V" cut down the length of the piece. Soak the endives in lukewarm water for half an hour, then drain.

Whip the cream with an egg beater, mix in the lemon juice, add salt and pepper to taste, and finally add the endive and oranges. Mix it all up, then garnish with parsley. Serves four. (TE)

For a *Cucumber-Dill Salad,* you need

a large cucumber,
a quarter to a third cup of sour cream,
some minced dill (fresh, if possible),
about a teaspoon and a half of lemon juice,
one or two tablespoonfuls of finely chopped onion, and
some salt and pepper.

Peel the cucumber, and slice it very thinly. Place the slices in a bowl, sprinkle some salt on them, then leave them alone for an hour or so, at which time you can drain off any liquid from the cucumbers, stir in the sour cream, the dill, the onion, the salt and pepper and the lemon juice. Chill in the fridge until it's time to eat. Serves three or four. (TE)

2. Salad Dressings: All salad dressings are variations on the following theme: three parts oil (olive oil, salad oil or dairy products) to one part acid (vinegar, lemon juice, what have you). With that in mind,

Make *a Basic Vinaigrette Dressing* by putting in a jar three-quarters cup of oil (preferably a good olive oil), a quarter cup vinegar (any kind except cider), a teaspoon of salt and half as much pepper. Shake it up good.

Now that you've got vinaigrette down, you can soup it up with some modifications:

Try adding a teaspoon of English or Dijon mustard instead of the pepper. Or you can thoroughly mash a clove of garlic with the salt before adding it to the mix. If you want, you can add herbs, like parsley and chives, or any of the following (but not in combination): tarragon, basil, dill, chervil. (JB)

Another good, basic dressing is *Egg-Lemon Dressing,* which is nothing more than

an egg,
two-thirds cup of olive oil,
the juice from a lemon and
some salt and pepper.

Beat the egg in a bowl, gradually add the oil while stirring vigorously, then mix in the lemon juice and the salt and pepper. Again, you can modify it by adding something like a tablespoonful of finely chopped onion. (AR)

Finally, a dressing using a cheese: *Roquefort Dressing*. You have to use real Roquefort cheese for this; no other blue cheese will do. So take

a cup of whipping cream,
four to six ounces of crumbled Roquefort,
the juice of a lemon and
some pepper.

Whip the cream with an egg beater, then stir in the crumbled cheese. Add the lemon juice and pepper to taste. (TE)

Now, with all that said, on behalf of lazy bachelors everywhere, we want to congratulate the international salad dressing manufacturers' cartel for supplying some really good bottled salad dressings. Wishbone and Kraft in America, Reddy and Salvé in Europe, whatever they have in China and Africa, we thank you. A bottle of ice-cold Thousand Island dressing is all you need to take a lettuce out to dinner.

STEWS

Stews are man-food. You think of a good stew and you think of all those great food adjectives — hearty, rich, new and improved.

These are recipes for stews, but really, stews are sort of free-form exercises. If you spot something on the shelf that looks like it ought to be killed and cooked, grab it and toss it in a stew pot. It'll all work out. All of these, except the last one, are cheap and easy to make.

1. For a traditional *Lamb Stew,* pick up

three pounds or so of shoulder or leg of lamb, cut into inch-wide squares,
a half cup of flour, which you should empty into a paper bag,
four tablespoons each of butter and cooking oil,
a couple of cups of boiling water,
six medium-sized onions, peeled,
four carrots, scraped and chopped up in inch-long lengths,
three small turnips, peeled and quartered,
one or two cloves of garlic, crushed,

> a tablespoon of salt,
> a teaspoon of thyme,
> three or four potatoes, quartered and boiled,
> a package of frozen peas,
> a quarter cup of chopped parsley and
> some pepper.

Sometimes if you tell the butcher you're a Modern Man, he'll do all the dicing and slicing for you. If you're lucky, he'll even trim the fat off the lamb. No luck, do it yourself. Wash yourself in the blood of the lamb, amen. Heat the butter and oil in a big stew pot. Put the lamb in the paper bag filled with cornstarch and shake it up, baby, until the lamb is coated with the flour. Brown the lamb in the hot oil/butter combo.

Next, add the boiling water to the lamb so the meat is just covered Add the salt and simmer, covered, for about an hour. Next, add the carrots, turnips, garlic, thyme and the onion and continue cooking for at least another hour, or until the meat is very tender. Now remove the stew from the heat and let it stand for half an hour or so; the fat should rise to the surface, and you want to skim as much of it off as possible. Then add the potatoes and slowly return to the boil. Add the frozen peas, cover and turn off the heat. If the liquid at this point isn't thick enough for your taste, mix one or two tablespoons of flour in a quarter cup of water; stir well, mix into the stew and cook for another ten or fifteen minutes. Garnish with parsley and pepper. Serves up to a half-dozen. (JB)

2. Pot Roast: If you've never eaten a decent pot roast, you've missed one of the great treats. Despite the long list of ingredients, it's a snap to make. Get

> five pounds of beef (chuck, brisket, rump or round roast),
> a half cup of flour, which you should put in a paper sack,
> four tablespoons each of butter and cooking oil,
> a peeled and quartered onion,
> two teaspoons of salt,
> a teaspoon each of pepper and thyme,
> a bay leaf,
> two-thirds cup of water,
> a half-dozen scraped and sliced carrots. The carrot pieces should be big;
> allow four pieces per normal-sized carrot. Then
> a couple of peeled and quartered turnips,
> four or five medium-sized, quartered potatoes, and
> ten small, white, peeled, whole onions.

All you do is shake up the piece of meat in the bag of flour, heat the butter and oil over a medium flame in a stew pot and brown the meat on all sides. Then you add the whole onions, the seasonings, and the water, cover the pot and let it stew for three and a half, maybe four hours. Add the vegetables, and arrange the meat so it sits on top of them. Let it go another forty-five minutes or an hour. That's it. Serves six. (WRe)

3. Choucroute is a French term meaning *sauerkraut,* or pigs-in-the-cabbage. They sell it in cans over there, and it's not bad — but it's not nearly as good as this recipe, which calls for

> three or four pounds of sauerkraut, well-rinsed and drained,
> two large apples, peeled, cored and thinly sliced,
> a cup of dry, white wine,
> four strips of bacon, diced,
> four or five pork chops,
> a pound of ham chopped up into big chunks,
> four or five Polish sausages (or garlic franks or veal franks or würsts or any combination) cut into large pieces,
> six peppercorns and
> six juniper berries, which are sometimes hard to find, but definitely make a big difference.

Put the sauerkraut in a large pan, skillet, pot or casserole dish. Mix in the apples, the bacon, the wine, the berries and the peppercorns. Bake covered for a little over two hours in a 300° oven. Then put the chops and the ham on top of the sauerkraut, put the lid back on and cook for another hour. Finally, push the sausage pieces into the sauerkraut and cook for another half an hour or so.

Serve this with mustard, pickles, boiled potatoes and bread. Serves eight. (SB)

4. Lamb (or *Beef* or *Chicken) Curry:* Oh, yes, very good.

You'll need

> two pounds of either beef or lamb with all the fat trimmed off and cut up into half-inch cubes. If you're opting for chicken, get a small fryer already cut up. For the rest, get
> two large, peeled and chopped onions,
> two apples, with the cores removed and sliced thinly,
> four cups of canned chicken stock. Heat this up. Then
> a cup of flour,
> four tablespoons of cooking oil,
> one or two tablespoons of curry powder,
> a half cup of heavy cream, and
> salt and pepper.

Get a skillet hot, and, over a medium flame, brown the meat in two tablespoons of the oil. Add the rest of the oil, and sauté the apple and the onion until they turn light brown. Stir in the flour and mix thoroughly, then add the curry powder and cook for another minute. It's the curry powder that makes the stuff hot; if you really want to sweat it out, add a healthy dash of cayenne pepper. Pour in the hot chicken stock, season with salt and pepper and bring to a boil. Add the meat, then place the skillet in a 350° oven for an hour or ninety minutes. After the baking's done, stir in the cream. Serve with rice, chutney, raisins and toasted, chopped almonds. (TE)

5. Chili: Look, every range rider's got a recipe for chili. This one is probably as good as any, with the added advantage that it's easy to make. If yours is any better, send us a copy of the recipe and we'll run it through our Modern Man Bitchin' Kitchen Testing Program. Get

two or three pounds of ground beef, or
two or three pounds of chuck steak diced into quarter-inch cubes,
four tablespoons of cooking oil, and
four to six medium-sized, peeled, chopped onions. Then some canned goods, like
two 20-ounce cans of peeled tomatoes,
a 10-ounce can of tomato sauce,
a 6-ounce can of tomato paste, and
a 20-ounce can of chili, pinto or kidney beans, your choice.
Some salt, maybe a tablespoonful, and
a teaspoonful of hot sauce, and
four tablespoons of chili powder.

The hot sauce makes this stuff hot, so go wild if you want to play with fire. Heat the oil in a large stew pot, sauté the onions until they turn transparent, then add the beef and continue cooking until the meat turns brown. Add the remaining ingredients and let the whole thing simmer uncovered for at least an hour, longer if possible. Check for taste before serving, then garnish with raw onion and roughly grated cheddar cheese. Serves eight. (AR)

6. Cioppino: This is it, the end of the road for stews. This dish costs a bundle, is complicated to make, makes the kitchen smell like Barnacle Bill's socks and requires an abundance of fresh food. Otherwise, it's a great, one-dish meal that can be prepared in advance and will impress everyone.

Cioppino is an Americanized version of an Italian translation of French bouillabaisse. You can change the ingredients to suit the catch of the day, but try to use fresh stuff — otherwise, you're wasting your time and your money. You need

three pounds of firm, grained fish, like halibut, haddock
or barracuda (the edible sort),
a pound of king crab leg,
a lobster or two,

a pound of peeled shrimp,

twenty or so clams, mussels, oysters or a combo,

three-quarters cup of olive oil,

a cup and a half of chopped onions,

a cup of chopped green pepper,

three or four cloves of crushed garlic,

a number-ten can of peeled Italian tomatoes,

from which the seeds must be removed,

two or three cups each of seafood broth (see below), tomato (or Clamato)

juice and dry white wine,

a pound of mushrooms, sliced lengthwise,

a teaspoon of basil,

half a teaspoon of oregano,

a half cup of chopped parsley and

salt and pepper.

Put a little water in a big pot and steam the clams, oysters and mussels until the shells open. If, after five minutes of steaming, the shells don't open, don't eat them, chuck them out. For the good ones, remove the shell with the meat and discard the empty half. Put aside. In the same pot with the broth from the bivalves, place the lobsters and steam them until they turn red (this takes maybe ten or fifteen minutes); the antennæ should break off when the lobster is lifted by it. Break off the claws and the tail; put the rest of the lobster carcass in the stock and make cuts in the claws with scissors to facilitate eating later. (Be sure to leave the meat in the shell, though.) Cut the tail crosswise in sections, leaving the meat in the shell. Put the lobster aside and do the same thing to the crab leg. Add to this the reserved shellfish; put any fish skin, heads, or other scraps into the stock; add enough water to make two or three cups of broth and let simmer for twenty minutes.

In a big kettle or stewpot, heat the oil and sauté the onions, green peppers and mushrooms. Add the tomatoes, wine, tomato juice, fish stock and spices. Bring to a full boil, add the fish, reduce the heat, cover and let the mixture stew for fifteen or twenty minutes. Five minutes before you're ready to remove the stew from the heat, add the shellfish and the shrimp. Turn off the heat, correct the seasonings and add the parsley.

Serve in warm bowls, shells and all, with warm bread for dunking, dry red wine and lots of napkins. (AR)

BREAD

It takes bread to make bread. The best thing you can do is go to a bakery and buy the stuff, especially if your time is worth more than 50¢ an hour. Not only that, but the bread will taste better.

There is of course a certain charm to baking your own loaf. It's one of those hobby things, and there are books full of dough lore that will tell you all you knead to know. Har. Besides, they say making bread is good for you psychology-wise (it's soothing, they claim), so maybe making bread can save you a bundle you'd otherwise pay some shrink. This book has (in addition to a cornbread recipe) one general all-purpose real bread recipe. Goes something like this:

The *Al Jazzbeau Collins Beer Bread* requires three cups of self-rising flour, two tablespoons of sugar and a can of beer. You mix together the flour, sugar and beer lightly and form it into a ball. Don't overwork it. Put the ball into a well-buttered baking pan, cover it with a towel, and place it in a warm, draftless room for an hour while it does its self-rising trick. Preheat an oven to 350° and bake the loaf until it's done. (AJC)

To determine if bread is done: Insert either a *silver* knife or a straw from a broom into the loaf. If nothing sticks to it, the bread's done. This goes for cornbread, too. (HGF)

Cornbread: This is the real stuff, the food God invented chili for, and all you need is

a cup of sifted flour,
a cup of yellow cornmeal,
three teaspoons of baking powder,
one teaspoon of salt and
another one or two of sugar,
a cup of milk,
a half cup of melted butter, and
three well-beaten eggs.

Combine the ingredients in a bowl, mixing them together thoroughly. Pour the mix into a well-buttered baking pan and bake at 400° for a quarter hour or so.

Cornbread's a little like pizza in that you can choose modifications, like

a half cup of chopped Tuscan peppers,
some strips of crumbled bacon,
chopped ham or onion or
coarsely grated cheese. (AR)

PASTA

To big bachelors everywhere, pasta is more than a food. It's a going-steady dinner companion, a best friend smothered in tomato sauce and cheese. A guy can eat on pasta for a week for well under a fiver.

Something as good as pasta has to be cared for. You don't just grab a mittful and toss it in the coffeepot until it softens up a little.

To determine the proper serving size grab the spaghetti with your thumb and forefinger. The amount of spaghetti you can get between your thumb and forefinger will feed four shy people or two normal ones.

How to cook pasta: Salted water boils faster, so put a teaspoonful of salt in a gallon or so of water and bring it to a rolling boil. At this point, you can add a little olive oil to the water if you want. It seems to prevent the pasta from sticking together. Break the spaghetti in half and let it fall gradually out of your hand and into the water. Try to allow the sticks to fall horizontally, and not in a big, lopsided pile. Give the water a stir and let it boil uncovered until it's cooked.

When's that? When it sticks to the wall it's done, at which time you pour the pasta into a colander, rinse it very briefly with cold water to stop the cooking process and return it to the pot.

Five Good Pasta Dishes: One for every mood and every moment, one for you.

1. *Late-night Bachelor Pasta:* Cook up some number–eight elbow noodles, and just before they're done, add part of a can of peas (but not the pea juice). Drain the pasta, put in a quarter-stick of butter, sprinkle some garlic powder on it and drown the whole thing in Romano cheese. Stir it all up and eat it. Tastes best right out of the pot. (DB)

2. *Spaghetti* or *Noodles Alfredo:* After the pasta's been drained and returned to the pot, add a half stick of butter and a quarter cup of cream, a half cup of grated Parmesan, a dash of pepper and some nutmeg. No salt. Stir and serve four. (JYF)

3. *Pasta Carbonara all'Americana:* You can use spaghetti or noodles with this dish. The way it works is you cook four or five strips of bacon and beat an egg while the pasta's cooking. When the bacon's done, take it out and put it on a paper towel someplace, but leave the fat in the pan. Turn off the heat. After you've cooked and drained the pasta, put it in the pan with the bacon fat and mix it all up. Then you add the bacon, the egg and some Parmesan cheese, maybe a half cup. Put a lot of pepper on it and serve to four. (NLN)

4. *The No-Boil, Never-Fail, Gets-You-Laid Lasagna Recipe:* Not that our contributor makes any promises, mind you. Still, it might pay to get

four or five cups of spaghetti sauce ready, along with
a half pound of lasagna noodles,
a pound of ricotta cheese (or cottage cheese, in a pinch),
eight ounces or so of shredded mozzarella cheese and
a cup of grated Parmesan.

Spread a cup of sauce across the bottom of a baking pan (13" x 9" x 2" or something close) and arrange half the *uncooked* lasagne over the sauce and pour a cup of sauce over the lasagne. Then in consecutive layers, add the ricotta, the Parmesan and the mozzarella, another cup of sauce, then the other half of the lasagne followed by more sauce, then the same trio of cheeses again. The idea is to make layers of sauce on either side of the lasagne. The final order, from bottom to top: sauce, noodles, sauce, ricotta, Parmesan, mozzarella, sauce, noodles, sauce, ricotta, Parmesan, mozzarella. Bake it at 350° for 45 or 50 minutes, then take it out and let it sit for a quarter hour. *Al dente* every time. (NW)

Well, not exactly: When we tested this in the MMBK, we split on the merits of the dish. One of us liked it, one of us didn't hate it and one of us did (he thought the pasta tasted raw). None of us got laid, though.

5. *'Ghetti Oil:* Drop a half-cup of freshly-grated Parmesan cheese and a pinch of paprika into a wooden salad bowl that's been rubbed with garlic. Add hot, boiled spaghetti and cover with a quarter-cup of heated olive oil. Toss for two. (AW)

DESSERTS

The best desserts are purchased in chocolate shops, ice cream stores and bakeries. But if you just have to do it yourself, here're a few for you.

1. Apples, wine and cheese: It's easy — set some cheese (Camembert is good but stinky) on a small board, cut some apples into as many little wedges as you can (after removing the core), and serve yourself.

Add some *vino blanco plonko* or whatever and you've got a dessert that teeters precariously on the very brink of yuppie pretentiousness. Feeds art galleries full of jerks, so watch it.

With this cheese	*Serve this wine*
Bel Paese	Beaujolais, Moselle
Bleu	Chianti, Bordeaux, Red Burgundy
Brie	Dry Sherry, Chianti, Red Burgundy
Camembert	Red Burgundy, Pouilly Fumé, Vouvray
Cheddar	Red Bordeaux, Red Burgundy
Cheshire	Beaujolais, Red Côte D'Beaune
Edam	Medium-dry Sherry, Red Bordeaux, Red Burgundy
Feta	Red Bordeaux, Red Burgundy, Chianti, Bardolino
Fontina	Beaujolais
Gouda	Graves, Beaujolais, Chablis
Gruyere	Red Burgundy
Jarlsberg	Red Burgundy
Monterrey Jack	Red Burgundy, Red Bordeaux, Chablis
Muenster	Red Bordeaux, White Bordeaux
Port du Salût	Chablis, Meursault, Johannesburg Riesling (GWW)

See also *Wine,* **above.**

2. Strawberry Sherbet: You need a blender and a freezer for this one. Easy? You bet.

Take a pint of fresh strawberries and cut every one of the little things in half. You have to remove the green leaf on the top and as much of the white core as possible. To do this, you make a V-shaped incision and extract the offending bits. Drop the berries one by one into the spinning jaw of the Hamilton-Beach. Add sugar and lemon juice to taste (figure something near a half cup of sugar for a pint of strawberries). Put the liquid in the freezer for a few hours. Serves four. (AT)

3. Uncle Rick's Cherry Goo: You probably don't have a couple of cans of prepared cherry pie filling around the house, so go get some, along with some butter and a box of Duncan Hines spice cake mix. When you get home, preheat the oven to 350°, empty the cherry filling into a baking dish; spread half the box of cake mix over the cherry filling and sprinkle a melted stick of butter over the cake mix. Add pineapple if you have to. Bake the stuff for almost an hour, checking from time to time to make sure it's not burning. (FAS)

A NOTE ON CONTRIBUTORS

This book is not an illustration of journalistic ethics; we don't know most of our contributors, we awarded anonymity on request, we didn't verify anybody's names — some of which are clearly inventions — and it wasn't possible to investigate the ultimate source of much of their material. We found our contributors through the serendipitous process described in the Introduction and we felt that since they'd tried their best to write a book for us, the least we could do was leave them alone.

We didn't leave their copy undisturbed, however. All contributions were edited, and most — but not all — were substantially rewritten. When two or more contributions overlapped, we used the best one and credited the contributor (although from time to time we felt it right to list more than one contributor).

ACKNOWLEDGMENTS

We owe a deep debt of gratitude to Mr. Timothy Corfield, the author and compiler of *The Wilderness Guardian,* a book originally written for use by East African park rangers, but of widespread practical application to most Modern Men, including us. We have included quoted material with the permission of Mr. Corfield; other material from his book also appears here in an edited form. Although credited to *The Wilderness Guardian,* any errors that have occurred in the editing process are ours. If you wish to obtain a copy, write to us for details.

In the portions of this book that deal with cooking, we are indebted to Chef Tell Erhardt, from whom we have received serious inspiration. We can recommend his books to any aspiring chefs, without reservation.

In the portion of this book that deals with etiquette, we have expanded on subjects suggested by contributors. In so doing, we have consulted many books of etiquette and we are grateful to their authors for the general guidance we received.

We were, we note happily, assisted by several Modern Women, whose names appear below. And a special thanks to Spence Waugh for the index.

The production of this book was the province of Michael Rose, to whom we are obliged not only for his professional diligence (and some vital editorial contributions), but also for his friendship.

Illustrations were produced by Alan Rose, along with material from various Government publications.

And finally we thank Craig D. Nelson, our editor at Harper & Row, who kept the train on the track. (DB, AR, AW)

The contributors listed below appear alphabetically according to the first initial. We thank them all.

AB	Angus Baxter	BJ	B. Jenkins	DO'R	Don O'Reilly
ABe	Angelo Bennedetto	BK	Bob Kankowski	DR	Danny Robinson
ACT	Allan C. Tarlow	BN	Bill Nichols	DRA	Daniel R. Alleyne
AD	Andy Dunkley	BO	Bruce Odom	DRe	Diane Reese
AEW	A. E. Willet	BP	Bruce Pollock	DRT	Dwight R. Trembly
AHSC	American Historical Supply Catalog 2	BPy	Bernard Pyne	DS	Duke Singer
		BR	Ben Rillers	DSA	D. S. Arnot
AI	Allen Irizarry	BS	Bruce Stein	DSE	D. S. Ehrman
AJ	Andrew Jackson	BSA	Brandon S. Albright	DSF	Darlene S. Farwell
AJC	Al "Jazzbeau" Collins	BT	Brian Thomas	DSH	Dennis S. Hazelton
AL	Aaron Leibman	BV	Brian Vasquez	DSP	Daniel S. Peters
ALo	Anne Lopes	CCP	C. C. Parmenter	DST	Dana S. Thomas
AM	Anthony Mancuso	CD	Chas. Denholtz	DT	Del Torres
AMcA	Al McAvoy	CDr	Chuck Drew	DW	Dean Woodruff
AMP	A. M. Pirie	CFD	Christopher F. Dasatti	DWA	Dorne W. Alkey
AP	Albert Penniman	CGF	Clyde G. Freeman	DY	Daniel Yaeger
APS	Allen P. Spaulding	COP	Charles O. Porrino	EA	Ernest Akin
APT	Arthur P. Tedkin	CP	Conrad Pence	EDM	Edmond D. Margolies
AR	Alan Rose	CR	Craig Reynolds	EDV	E. D. Ventriss
ARa	Arthur Raymond	CS	Cliff Steinbring	EF	Edward Fraser
ARM	Andrew R. Monahan	CSA	Charles S. Anderson	EFO	Edgar F. Owens
AS	Art Schuyler	CV	Chris Vandevander	EFS	Edward F. Smith
ASM	A. S. Michelson	CW	Chuck Widman	EN	Edward Nadelmann
ASw	Alex Swift	CWS	Charles W. Swink	EP	Eric Posner
AT	Albert Townes	DA	Delbert Axelrod	EPL	Edw. P. Lamarsh
ATH	Arnold T. Henry	DAW	D. Albion Weeks	ER	Edward Rothman
ATR	Arthur T. Roemer	DB	Denis Boyles	ES	Ed Smith
AW	Alan Wellikoff	DBr	Dave Brubaker	ESD	Edwin S. Darnolt
AWG	Al W. Grant	DC	Danny Crouch	ESt	Ephraim Stein
AY	Al Yearwood	DD	D. Derderian	EV	Edmund Villiers
AYP	A. Y. Peterson	DE	"Doc" Engle	EWS	Eric W. Sayre
BA	Brian Alexander	DEW	David E. Walsh	FA	Fred Arlanio
BB	Betty Benson	DF	D. Feitelson	FAS	Frederick A. Spaulding
BC	B. Cochrane	DFK	David F. Kantrowitz	FB	Fred Bolten
BD	Benj. Delsey	DFR	D. F. Rowe	FC	Francis Cristo
BDa	Brian Daniel	DG	David Grossman	FCi	Franco Ciaprelli
BDi	Brad Davis	DH	Dorian Hastings	FD	Frances Delaney
BGF	Barbara Gross Feldman	DHe	Dept. of Health, NYC	FDF	F. David Freund
BH	B. Honig	DJ	David Jones	FDS	Frank D. Silva
		DK	Donald Kapshaw	FE	Frank Epley
		DL	Doug Llewelyn	FES	Felix E. Schmidt
		DLe	Daniel Lessa	FF	Falken Forshaw
		DM	Dean Maynard	FFC	F. F. Crenshaw
		DN	Dennis Nieves	FFe	Fred Fenton
		DNO	Dan N. Odey	FGC	Fred G. Conover

FHG	F. H. Gulickson	GVS	Gerhard V. Strauss	JFr	Jimmy Friedman
FJN	Foster J. Newell	GW	Gary Witzenburg	JFP	J. F. Peters
FM	Frank Morton	GWa	Gale Wall	JG	Jerry Gitano
FPW	F. Paul Wilson	GWA	G. W. Alvarez	JGF	John G. Frimer
FR	F. Rainey	GWW	Great Western Winery	JGG	James G. Grey
FS	Fritz Sklar	GY	Gill Yulbride	JGP	James G. Pollack
FT	F. Tompkins	HB	Hollis Bolman	JGR	J. G. Rainey
FTo	Frank Torrino	HC	Harry Carter	JGu	J. Guilfoyle
FW	Franklin Willstatter	HDF	Hamilton D. French	JGW	John G. Wechsler
FWi	Frank Williger	HE	H. Emery	JH	Jim Hickey
FY	Floyd Yerkes	HF	H. Field	JHe	Jack Herrmann
GA	Gloria Anderson	HFD	H. F. Dennis	JHG	Josef H. Gwertzmann
GAD	Gerard A. DuBois	HFr	Howard Frosten	JHK	Jeffrey H. Kelly
GAL	G. A. Lowney	HG	Henry Grabois	JHL	J. Howard Lombardi
GB	Gary Berniss	HGF	Harold G. Frankfurt	JHP	John H. Pines
GBMc	G. B. McGregor	HGK	Harmon G. Kelley	JJ	Joseph Jerome
GBP	G. B. Poorahni	HGO	Herman G. Orel	JJF	John Joseph Farwell
GC	George Comtois	HGU	H. Gabriel Ullmann	JK	John Kocaj
GCC	George C. Coble	HH	Herbert Howell	JKG	John K. George
GD	Gene Dowdell	HJ	Howard Jakes	JKJ	John K. Jephson
GDr	George Drew	HJG	H. James Growick	JKL	Jonas Lund
GE	Gordon Erlich	HK	Howard Kohn	JLH	J. L. Henrici
GF	Gene Faust	HKP	H. K. Penn	JMcD	John McDonald
GFr	Gary Franks	HMG	H. Michael Glazer	JO	John Ouderkirk
GG	Gary Gilmore	HMJ	Harvey M. Jenks	JOP	John Owen Pendunne
GGC	Greg G. Clebinski	HRE	Hugo R. Escobar	JR	John Roger
GGMcD	Gregory G. McDonald	HS	H. Schuyler	JSA	Joseph S. Arnhold
		HTD	Harold T. Donovan	JSR	John S. Rolland
GGo	Geo. Gondlock	HTR	Harold T. Russo	JT	James Turner
GH	Gus Handler	HWE	Howard W. Eng	JTh	Joe Theodore
GHJ	George H. Johnson	JAG	James A. Gillies	JV	Jill Vernette
GI	Geo. Irvin	JAK	Jack A. Kay	JY	Jerry Younge
GJ	George Joyner	JB	James Beard	JYF	James Y. Fyer
GLS	Gregg L. Stebben	JBi	Jonathan Bird	JYG	Julius Y. Guttman
GMcK	Gerald McKennan	JC	John Crossment	KB	Kerry Byrne
GMP	Gale M. Pinnock	JCC	Jack C. Coggins	KCC	K. C. Casey
GP	Grant Prentice	JD	Joe Dickenson	KCH	Kevin C. Heath
GR	Geoffrey Renaud	JDeN	Joe DeNicola	KD	Kurt Dystra
GRE	Geo. R. Eckman	JDO	J. D. Oliver	KDO	Keith D. Olanoff
GRo	Glen Rogers	JDS	John Dale Sergent	KE	Konrad Eggers
GS	Gary Seiffer	JE	John Elmquist	KER	Kerry E. Robbins
GSt	Gene Stone	JEC	Julian E. Cohen	KF	Ken Fountain
GT	Ginny Tinkleman	JEM	Jane E. Mills	KFr	Karl Frost
GTh	Geoffrey Thompson	JF	Joshua Frankel	KG	Kenner Godfrey
GVO	G. V. Overman	JFQ	John F. Quinn	KGG	Karen G. Gould

KGo	Kyle Golney	MDF	M. D. Forbush	PEC	P. E. Collins
KH	Kelly Horn	MG	Mitchell Green	PEP	P. Earl Pinkus
KHR	K. H. Riley	MHG	Milton H. Gooding	PF	Paul Frager
KJ	Ken Johnston	MJF	Mary Jane Fenton	PG	Paul Gregory
KJC	K. Jones Carter	MK	Mark Klein	PJO	P. J. O'Rourke
KJH	Keith J. Heaton	MKa	Maggie Kassner	PJY	P. J. Yarborough
KJO	Konrad J. Oppenheim	ML	Martha Landry	PKG	Pam K. Goldstein
KJP	K. J. Posadas	MM	Mary Metcalfe	PKL	Philip K. Levy
KJT	Ken J. Terrence	MN	Mike Nussbaum	PM	Peter Mann
KK	Kadi Kiiss	MNB	M. N. Brody	PN	Patrick Nash
KLB	Keith L. Bloch	MNR	M. Neal Rubin	PNe	Pedar Ness
KLL	K. Leland Lewis	MP	Matthew Polk	PNW	Peter N. Wilson
KLS	Kestor L. Stevens	MQ	Mack Quill	PP	Paul Peterson
KLT	K. L. Tepper	MR	Michael Rose	PR	Paul Rodrigues
KP	Karen Phillips	MS	Margery Stein	PS	Peter Spaulding
KQ	K. Querella	MYR	M. Y. Rose	PSp	Phil Speck
KR	Kevin Rohlfs	NA	Nick Alexiou	PSW	Peter Weaver
KS	Keri Stern	NB	Nick Bannon	PT	Pat Thompson
KT	K. Thomason	NC	"Nick" Charles	PTK	Peter T. Kohner
KU	Ken Urkowitz	NCM	National Center for	PV	Pat Victor
KUG	Kenneth U. Griggs		Missing and	RB	Richard Bronson
KWO	Keith W. Owens		Exploited Children	RBr	"Rags" Brophy
LA	Larry Appleman	ND	Ned Dunning	RBS	Ronald B. Slidell
LB	Leon Brudner	NF	Nathan Fredrickson	RC	Ralph Cooper
LBW	Louis Black Worley	NG	Neal Gibbons	RCP	Ralph C. Peckham
LC	Larry Crews	NGa	Norman Gatt	RCu	Ron Cullen
LCu	Lance Curtiz	NGF	Norman G. Farrand	RD	Rene Davis
LD	Laurel Douglas	NHG	N. H. Gross	RDa	Randy Darling
LDF	Lawrence Davis Fenton	NLN	Nancy L. Nash	RDK	Roy D. Kinneer
LDL	L. D. Loby	NRE	Norman R. Eicholz	RDo	Randy Dozier
LEW	Lester E. Wright	NS	Ned Smith	RDY	Raul D. Ynez
LGP	Larry G. Pence	NV	Nelson Vaughn	RE	Roger Eason
LH	L. Huynh	NVB	N. V. Brian	REd	Richard Edwards
LHMcG	L. H. McGraw	NW	Neil Wolfson	REJ	R. E. Johnson
LJ	Linda Johnson	OB	Oyster Bar Restaurant,	REP	Roy E. Price
LK	Lucas King		Grand Central	RER	Rick E. Rosenber
LKH	Lee K. Holtz		Terminal, NYC	RES	Richard E. Symonds
LKP	L. K. Perelman	OG	Oscar Garcia	RET	Ronald E. Tarlow
LL	Lou Lewis	OH	Owen Hendricks	REW	Richard E. Wells
LM	Larry Mathews	PA	Peter Aldersohn	RF	Ross Fedrin
LO	Lawrence Orenstein	PAI	Peter A. Ionacci	RG	Ron Gottersman
LP	Lewis Price	PAT	Paul A. Thomas	RHW	Robert H. Waldman
LR	Lauren Rose	PB	Phil Bratty	RJF	Robert J. Friedman
MBe	Mary Bees	PC	Peter Covington	RK	Russ Karaviotis
MBW	Michael B. Wellikoff	PCV	Paul C. Vitale	RMacK	Robert MacKenzie

RP	Rocky Peppard	SMY	Steven M. Younge	TW	Thomas Wilechka
RRa	Robert Rakita	SO	Steve Oldencamp	TY	Todd Yeaton
RSB	Ronald S. Brown	SOP	Simon O. Phillips	TZ	Ted Zimmerman
RSW	Richard S. Wilentz	SP	Sig Pierson	USG	US Government
RT	Roy Tillson	SPC	Steven P. Carlisle	VB	Vernon Burgess
RTT	Rod T. Talley	SR	Stan Riedel	VBC	"Vagabond Bill"
RW	Robert Wilson	SRW	Slade R. Wolfe		Carter
RY	Richard Young	SRy	Steve Ryder	VC	Vernon Conway
SA	Sam Arango	SS	Sandy Singer	VFE	V. Fredrick Englehardt
SAF	S. A. Fredette	SW	Spence Waugh	VNF	V. N. Forrest
SAR	Sherry A. Reese	SWi	Steve Wilson	VP	Van Patrick
SAW	Sherman A. Wyckoff	TAE	Terrence A. Ely	VR	Victoria Raines
SB	Sunset Books	TCF	Tony C. Fino	VS	Vicky Stafford
SBBS	Sara B. B. Stamm	TD	Tod Dinsmore	VT	Virginia Tovic
SBO	S. B. Odum	TDY	T. D. "Touchdown"	VW	Vic Walford
SC	Steward Cashman		Yakes	WAR	William A. Ryan
SD	Sarah Dickerson	TE	Tell Erhardt	WCG	Wm. C. Garrison
SDo	Sam Doherty	TF	Tom Fox	WCH	Will C. Hollister
SDr	Sam Drew	TFG	Tony F. Gamelli	WD	Warren Donner
SEE	S. E. Erikson	TFY	Thom F. Yount	WDo	Will Dobreau
SF	Steven Forman	THR	T. H. Routliffe	WF	Walter Frisch
SFE	Sidney F. Elmore	TKJ	Tim K. Jones	WG	Wilderness Guardian
SFR	Sheldon F. Riemer	TKY	Tommy K. Young	WJ	Wm. Jennings
SGH	S. G. Haines	TM	Tom Mases	WLD	W. Lloyd Douglas
SJ	S. Karajaropolis	TMcK	Tim McKeever	WM	W. Mastroianni
SJH	Sonia Jovena Holland	TN	Tony Nunez	WN	William Nader
SJo	Stu Jobrack	TR	Terry Rankin	WNi	Wayne Nirenberg
SJP	S. Jeromme Pickett	TRD	Theodore R. Davies	WR	Warren Rosenthal
SK	Stan Kurshen	TRF	T. R. Freind	WRa	Wm. Randon
SKL	Scott K. Lardine	TS	Tom Scott	WRe	Wayne Rey
SL	Steve Lemon	TSc	Terry Schell	WRu	Warren Rubenstein
SLa	S. Lapham	TSi	Tad Simon	WS	Ward Spencer
SLT	S. L. Tejada	TT	Thad Telkins	WST	William S. Turner
SM	Sam Mastronardi	TTW	Timothy T. Weilburg	WY	William Young
SMP	Seymour M. Pfeifer	TV	Tom Vernett	YB	"Yank" Borman

WHAT DO YOU KNOW?

If you know something you think other Modern Men ought to know, or if there's some subject you think we forgot, make a note of it here (or on another sheet of paper) and send it to:

The Modern Man
P.O. Box 15565
Springfield, MA 01115

The material you submit will be edited and quite possibly rewritten to conform to style and to length limitations. And all you'll get for it is your name stuck in the back of the next book, if there is one, and a hearty handshake if ever we meet.

But really, it's worth it.

Your name and address are required. (If you want your name withheld, we'll do it. But we have to have something for our records.)

NAME: _____

ADDRESS: _____

_____

May we credit you by name? _____

SUBJECT: _____

_____
_____
_____
_____
_____
_____
_____
_____
_____
_____
_____
_____
_____
_____

INDEX

Page numbers in *italic* type denote illustrations

466

INDEX

Restaurants *(cont.)*
getting a good table in, 375
group dinners in, 376
maitre d's in, 377
making reservations in, 375
paying checks in, 376
recipes from, 344
sommelier, 377
waiters, 377
Revenge, 53
Rice,
cooking tip for, 403
Greek, 434
Rifles,
see firearms
Roses, 126
Rugs, 211–213
see also carpets
Rum, 368

Sailing,
see boating
Salad dressings,
basic vinaigrette, 443
egg-lemon, 443–444
roquefort, 444
Salads,
American, the basic, 441
Caesar, 442
cucumber-dill, 443
endive, 442
orange-endive, 443
Salvation Army, the, 156
Sauces,
basic, 431
sopping up, 422
thickening, 402
Saunas,
Indian sweat hut, 37–38
Sawyer, Diane, 55
Scabies, 321
Scissors, 404
Scotland, greeting protocol in, 356
Screens, repairing, *269*
Screws,
see tools
Scurvy, 309
Sedatives,
see drugs
Seduction, 126–129
Sewing, 192–193
buttons, 193
with dental floss, 194
patches, 193
Sex,
dirty word glossary of, 128
endurance during, 128–129
exercises, 317
foreplay, 128–129
marriage and, 138

Sex *(cont.)*
orgies, 133–134
public, 128
selfishness and, 126
vocal, 127, 128
in the workplace, 46
see also seduction, amusements
Shampoo,
see hair
Shaving, 114–116
Shelf Liner, 405
Sherbet, strawberry, 451
Sherry, 368
Shipping, crate construction for, *217*
Shirts,
folding, *99*
ironing, 194
selecting, 190
Shoes,
alternating, 185
drying, 186
eliminating stains from, 186
moose hock, *18*
parts, *187*
shining, 186
snow, *18*
trees, 185
Shopping,
economizing while, 153–154
food, 153
Showerhead, 117
Showers,
quick, 117
women and, 116
Shrimp Creole, 428
Shriver, Maria, 55
Sidewalks, fixing cracks in, *268*
Skunks, 389
Sleep, 317–318
Sleeping Bags,
air mattresses and, 17
assessing quality of, 16
camp bed rule, the, 6
emergency, 16, *17*
Slingshots, *18*
Smoking,
etiquette of, 344
quitting, 381–382
Snake Bites,
see bites, snake
Snuff, 384
Soap, hand-washing, 192
Socks, 183
insulating, *18*
Sofas,
see furniture
Soldering, 249–251
Soup, 439–440, 441
Spices,
see cooking

Spider Bites,
see bites, spider
Spiders, types of, *280–281*
Splinters,
see first aid
Sport Jackets,
see blazers
Sports,
co-ed, 380
etiquette in, 351–354
on TV, 378–379
participatory, 380
spectator, 378–379
see also baseball, basketball,
etc.
Stain Removal, 284–286
Star Trek, 386
Stationery, 396–399, *396, 399*
Steak, 424–425
Stereos,
see audio equipment
Stimulants,
see drugs
Storms, electrical,
see lightning
Stoves,
see appliances
Styptic Pencils, 116
Suitcases, 96–99, *98*
Suits,
altering, 192–194
assessing quality of, 181
basic wardrobe of, 180–181
cheap, 180
eliminating wrinkles from, 190
proper fitting of, 179–180
styles of, 180
vested, 181
see also blazers, dry cleaners,
formal attire
Sulu, 386
Sunglasses, 177
birchbark, *18*
Sunstroke, 310
Suspenders, 195
Sweaters,
care of, 191
Swimming, 380
Syphilis, 320

Tablecloths, 410
Tables,
see furniture
Tailors,
alterations by, 192
Teeth,
see dental care
Telephones,
computerized dialers for, 395
etiquette on, 44, 349